Asian Place, Filipino Nation

COLUMBIA STUDIES IN INTERNATIONAL AND GLOBAL HISTORY

COLUMBIA STUDIES IN INTERNATIONAL AND GLOBAL HISTORY
Cemil Aydin, Timothy Nunan, and Dominic Sachsenmaier, Series Editors

This series presents some of the finest and most innovative work coming out of the current landscapes of international and global historical scholarship. Grounded in empirical research, these titles transcend the usual area boundaries and address how history can help us understand contemporary problems, including poverty, inequality, power, political violence, and accountability beyond the nation-state. The series covers processes of flows, exchanges, and entanglements—and moments of blockage, friction, and fracture—not only between "the West" and "the Rest" but also among parts of what has variously been dubbed the "Third World" or the "Global South." Scholarship in international and global history remains indispensable for a better sense of current complex regional and global economic transformations. Such approaches are vital in understanding the making of our present world.

ASIAN PLACE, FILIPINO NATION

A Global Intellectual History of the
Philippine Revolution, 1887–1912

NICOLE CUUNJIENG ABOITIZ

COLUMBIA UNIVERSITY PRESS *NEW YORK*

Columbia University Press
Publishers Since 1893
New York   Chichester, West Sussex
cup.columbia.edu
Copyright © 2020 Columbia University Press
All rights reserved

Library of Congress Cataloging-in-Publication Data
Names: CuUnjieng Aboitiz, Nicole, author.
Title: Asian Place, Filipino Nation : A Global Intellectual History of the
Philippine Revolution, 1887-1912 / Nicole CuUnjieng Aboitiz.
Other titles: Global intellectual history of the Philippine Revolution, 1887–1912
Description: New York : Columbia University Press, [2020] | Series: Columbia studies in
international and global history | Includes bibliographical references and index.
Identifiers: LCCN 2019044268 (print) | LCCN 2019044269 (ebook) | ISBN 9780231192149 (cloth) |
ISBN 9780231192156 (paperback) | ISBN 9780231549684 (ebook)
Subjects: LCSH: Philippines—History—Revolution, 1896–1898—Influence. | Anti-imperialist
movements—Philippines. | Transnationalism—Political aspects—Philippines. | National
characteristics, Philippine. | National characteristics, Asian. | Decolonization—Philippines. |
Philippines—Relations—East Asia. | East Asia—Relations—Philippines. | Philippines—
Relations—Southeast Asia. | Southeast Asia—Relations—Philippines.
Classification: LCC DS682 .A138 2020 (print) | LCC DS682 (ebook) | DDC 959.9/027—dc23
LC record available at https://lccn.loc.gov/2019044268
LC ebook record available at https://lccn.loc.gov/2019044269

Columbia University Press books are printed on permanent and durable acid-free paper.
Printed in the United States of America

Cover design: Julia Kushnirsky
Cover art: Tintin Lontoc

For Carlos

Contents

Acknowledgments

As with all things I've attempted, this book was only successfully completed due to the generous, patient aid of many. I would like first to acknowledge Yale University, whose faculty and students showed me the possible heights of discourse and original thought. Ben Kiernan was my advisor and mentor, and his boundless enthusiasm, patience, and dedication to my scholarly development made this book possible; his mark is visible to me on every page. Jenifer Van Vleck helped me to think boldly; Peter Perdue gave me my model of a true scholar; Jim Scott's example kept me critical; Dani Botsman showed me how to teach and ensured that I succeeded in all projects we undertook together; Erik Harms's expansive thought inspired and shepherded me at different points. Additionally, I'd like to thank Valerie Hansen, Fabian Drixler, Hal Conklin, Karuna Mantena, Paul Kennedy, and Adam Tooze, as well as Marcy Kaufman, Kris Mooseker, and Rich Richie. It is with them that I boast of having worked whenever anyone gives me the opportunity.

Outside Yale, I must first thank Caroline Hau, whose celerity, expertise, and power of synthesis benefited this book immeasurably. I'm deeply indebted to Jim Richardson, Motoe Terami-Wada, Natasha Pairaudeau, Haydon Cherry, Caelyn Cobb, and my particularly transformative peer reviewers at Columbia University Press, who provided incisive comments and corrections to early drafts and developed this book significantly. Carol, Jim, and Motoe, in particular, provided me much undeserved care and guidance. I also wish to acknowledge the Weatherhead Center for International Affairs at Harvard University and Clare Hall at the University of Cambridge, my recent and current intellectual homes and the places where I completed this book manuscript. I owe a great intellectual debt to Cemil Aydin, Erez Manela, Sugata Bose, Sunil Amrith, Resil Mojares, Al McCoy, Tim Harper, Uday Singh Mehta, Megan Thomas, and Filomeno V. Aguilar Jr. in particular. I'd also like to thank Michael Laffan, Sarah Igo, Julius Bautista, Oona Paredes, Bernardita R. Churchill, Patricio Abinales, Rogers Smith, Frederick Dickinson, Kevin Fogg, Naoko Shimazu, Ricardo Jose, Marita Concepcion Castro Guevara, Vicente Rafael, David Ibbetson, Vernon R. Totanes, Kathleen Molony, and Amanda Barclay. I could not wish for greater professional examples, inspiration, or company.

I am also deeply indebted to the kindness and aid of the Archivo General de Indias, Archivo General Militar de Madrid, Archivo Histórico Nacional de España, Hemeroteca Municipal de Madrid, Fundación Antonio Núñez Jiménez, Archivo Nacional de la República de Cuba, Centro de Estudios Martianos, British Library, National Archives at Kew, Cambridge University Archives, National Archives at College Park and National Archives and Records Administration in Washington, D.C., Public Records Office of Hong Kong, Macau Historical Archives, National University of Singapore, Ateneo de Manila University Archives, University of the Philippines Manuscripts and Archives, University of the Philippines Special Collections, National Archives of the Philippines, National Library of the Philippines, José P. Laurel Memorial Foundation, and Yale University Manuscripts and Archives. I'd also like to thank the Council on Southeast Asia Studies, MacMillan Center, and International Security Studies at Yale, the Institute of Philippine Culture at Ateneo de Manila University, the Third World Studies Center at the University of the Philippines, and the Whitehead Fund of Clare Hall at the University of Cambridge for their support. I am grateful to Tintin Lontoc, Karina Bolasco, Columbia University Press and my colleagues there, Ginny Perrin, Monique Briones, Marisa Lastres, Zachary Friedman, and Yi Deng, for all their work in bringing this book to life.

I wish to thank Cindy Tan Ewing, Tanya Lawrence, Faizah Zakaria, Tri Phuong, Elliott Prasse-Freeman, Lisandro Claudio, Anthony Medrano, Justin Jackson, Ryan Jones, Georgina Blackett, Stephen Krewson, Maximilian Krahé, Das Konsulat, and the old New York Ph.D. gang (Nicholas Mayer, Jonathan

Liebembuk, Elizabeth Frasco, and Sunita Desai) for teaching me how to think and for showing me what youth and brilliance look like in combination. I wish to thank my parents, Stephen and Maitoni, and my brothers, Miguel and Enrique, for their support. Finally, I wish to thank Carlos—for nearly everything else in between and since: this book is dedicated to him.

Asian Place, Filipino Nation

ONE

A Transnational Turn of the Century in Southeast Asia

FAR FROM THE Philippine imperial center of Manila, in 1883 in Matagui-nao on Samar Island in the Visayas region, rumors spread that there was a new king named Conde Leynes, and that a German steamship would arrive in Catbalogan to declare that Spain did not own the Visayas Islands.[1] In 1887 in Zamboanguita in Negros Oriental, Ponciano Elopre, known as Dios Buhawi (God Waterspout) announced himself as God, freed his followers from obligation to pay tribute to the Spanish government, and organized an upland regime.[2] He was reputed to be able to summon rain and to produce coins from a squash or from leaves floating on a river—these coins were said to come "from America."[3] The presence of international elements—references to the larger geopolitical framework of power that ordered the world—in these local Visayan millenarian imaginings illustrates the trans-nationalized setting in which ideas of social regeneration and, later, anti-colonial revolution evolved in the Philippines.[4] This should come as no sur-prise, as the opening of provincial ports to the world market, such as the one in Iloilo in the Visayas in 1855, created linkages that connected provin-cial ports to the rest of South and East Asia,[5] even bypassing the mediation of capital from Manila, which, for its part, had enjoyed port-based regional trade at least as far back as the ninth century.[6]

The long Philippine Revolution of 1896–1906,[7] which began against Spain and continued against the United States, took place against a backdrop of imperial consolidation and local resistance that was truly region-wide: the

French conquest of Cambodia, Vietnam, and Laos and the creation of French Indochina by 1897; the 1885–88 Cần Vương Movement in Vietnam, a contemporaneous anti-French revolt in Cambodia, and the 1903–1905 activism of the Vietnamese scholar-gentry; the full extension of direct Dutch colonial rule throughout the Netherlands East Indies from 1872 to 1910 against stiff resistance, especially in Aceh; the centralization of British power in the Federated Malay States from the 1890s to the 1910s; the British annexation of Upper Burma following the Third Anglo-Burmese War in 1885, the incorporation of Burma as a province of British India by 1897, and the formation of the Burmese nationalist movement continuing into the 1920s. The issues of violence and legitimacy of rule that arose around the Philippine Revolution also found certain parallels in Tonkin, Annam, and Cambodia in the 1870s–90s, with violence and contestation by multiple parties, including anti-Catholic and anti-French mandarins, Chinese bandit armies, Cambodian rebels, and the French. This era also saw the emergence of Japan as a non-Western modern imperial power after the Meiji Restoration of 1868; the early exertion of its dominance over Korea in 1876, which culminated in the annexation of Korea in 1910; as well as the Japanese annexation and incorporation of Taiwan beginning in 1895. Indeed, the Meiji-era reforms that so quickly transformed Japan's geopolitical position reverberated throughout Asia, making Japan a singular example of successful selective adaptation of Western institutions alongside protection of its native Asian culture. This example and the Japanese victory in the Sino-Japanese War (1894–95) introduced to colonized Asia—then experiencing renewed imperial subjugation and incorporation—novel fantasies, hopes, and strategies of a romanticized Asian solidarity. Yet, this transnational and regional historical setting has barely been incorporated into the localized and Western-oriented historiography of the Philippine Revolution.

The Philippine Revolution proved to be a turning point in Southeast Asia. Rather than simply failing to maintain a traditional state, as in Vietnam and Burma, or largely succeeding in maintaining one, as in Cambodia and Thailand, it was briefly successful in establishing a new state—a secular republic. What impact did the region have on the Philippine Revolution, and it on the region? What intellectual threads connected the Philippine discourse to the corollary anti-imperial and positive political imaginings of its neighbor countries in Asia? What were the perceptions and visions of the political that animated the long Philippine Revolution, and how did they relate to the imperial frameworks of power in Southeast and East Asia? How international was the revolution in action, ideas, and influence? These questions remain alternately understudied and unexplored.

My ongoing focus on the Asian context to Philippine history runs counter to the traditional assumption of the literature that the Filipino self-image is historically non-Asian—seeing itself as belonging, instead, to the Western Hemisphere. Many early postwar/Cold War Southeast Asian studies, such as D. G. E. Hall's seminal work *A History of Southeast Asia* (1955),[8] excluded the Philippines from the Southeast Asian ambit of scholarly consideration. Meanwhile, internationalization of the Philippine Revolution's historiography has generally occurred along imperial lines, analyzing it with/against the former Western imperial powers or the former colonies of Spain and the United States, such as Puerto Rico.

The important global moment of the late nineteenth century—with all the changes in technology, sovereignty, human exchange, and ideology that it wrought—is too often apprehended in Asian historiography through a bilateral framework privileging relations with the West. As other scholars, including Elleke Boehmer, Michael Goebel, and Noor-Aiman I Khan, have noted, anti-imperial and nationalist movements developed not only through interaction between European colonial centers and their peripheries but also, importantly, through interaction between peripheries.[9] This insight builds on the foundational transnational scholarship on anticolonial nationalism by Partha Chatterjee, Erez Manela, Cemil Aydin, Michael Goebel, and others, which focuses on global connections and transnational transmission of ideas in the crumbling of the Eurocentric order and emergence of what would become the Third World.[10] This book refocuses attention to East-East relations in Asia as well as to the periphery within the Asian discourse of Pan-Asianism. It illuminates connections between the discourses of the political that proliferated across the transnational Southeast Asian canvas of hardening empires and quickening political visions at the turn of the twentieth century, focusing particularly on ideas of Asianism, Pan-Asianism, Social Darwinism, and the Malay race. This book situates the long Philippine Revolution in its full regional context and in the imperial contests of the turn of the twentieth century, in which imperial powers and anti-imperialists' constructions of "Asia" were forged.

"Asia" was hardly a stable concept or container at the end of the nineteenth century; it was far closer to a blank canvas upon which those threatened by the West projected both their fantasies and fears. "Asia" had originally designated a small ancient kingdom in the southwest region of what is now Turkey, but the term expanded to encompass all of Anatolia, which then became "Asia Minor" as its application widened further east. Jesuits introduced the concept of Asia to East Asia at the end of the sixteenth and beginning of the seventeenth centuries, with the most important source for the term being Matteo Ricci's 1602 Chinese-language world atlas.[11] Because of its very formlessness at the turn of the twentieth century, "Asia" serves as an index of the prevailing geopolitical and international ideological power structures in the region; at the same time, its analysis has allowed me to inflect such purely international vectors with the vernacular vocabularies of power and politics that co-created them. In so doing, I focus on the region of Southeast Asia at the turn of the twentieth century, although Southeast Asia did not emerge as a coherent regional entity until further along in the twentieth century, in order to foreground the subversive anticolonial Pan-Asianism that emanated from the Southeast Asian "periphery" as distinct from that which emanated from the Sinic East Asian "center" of Pan-Asianism, and to highlight the shared colonial experience and transnational anti-colonial collaboration and discourse that would help form the basis for a more coherent political region of "Southeast Asia" later in the twentieth century.

The conceptualization of Southeast Asia as a coherent region and episteme was born of local anticolonial regional collaboration; World War II military objectives; Japanese imperialism; Chinese and Japanese studies of *nanyang* and *nan'yō* (South Seas), respectively; and the post–World War II U.S. academy that invested heavily in area specialists. Postwar area studies academics later identified persistent shared traits to justify their discipline and the categorization of Southeast Asia as a single region: bilateral kinship, high levels of female autonomy, leadership by "men of prowess," a concept of animating "soul stuff," spirit propitiation, houses resting on poles, and a rice-fish diet.[12] For Southeast Asians themselves, the explicit creation of the region as a self-conscious, coherent entity was also a mid-twentieth-century story.[13] The region's gradual self-conscious creation would come to lean on Third World Consciousness and the multilateral regional organizations, such as SEATO and ASEAN, born of the Cold War and its exigencies.

The nineteenth-century Filipino discourse covered in this book treated and apprehended the Philippines's "Southeast Asian" neighbors through their colonial overlords or as fellow "Asians" or "Malays," but not as "Southeast Asians."[14] Nevertheless, the anti-colonial consciousness and transnational Pan-Asian thinking and engagement described in this book was a historical force in the creation of Southeast Asia as a self-identified region, for which reason I anachronistically attend to it. While this book employs "Southeast Asia" as a heuristic and conceives of it as a political construct, it also acknowledges the region's tangible, natural reality, described as it is by a biotic zone stretching from the Marianas Trench to the Bay of Bengal. Indeed, this natural zone helped facilitate the trade, migration, and exchange activities that would underwrite a self-conscious region, alongside the common experiences of colonial history, geopolitics, religious and cultural spread, and positive world-making that occurred therein. Refocusing historical attention to East-East relations thus allows us to consider the internal and early constitution of what would come to be the region of Southeast Asia, and to see the creation of the region as something other than merely the by-product of imperial war objectives and military divisions.

In the Philippines from 1872 to 1912, one sees an early instance of one of the transitions of power that would take place over the twentieth century—from the Old World, European imperial powers to the emerging New World of American and non-Western global power. The attendant, interrelated Philippine discourses on the Malay race and Pan-Asianism are rich sites for understanding the visions of political possibility that the tumultuous turn of the twentieth century engendered, as this book shows. Distant thinkers, movements, and events influenced the intellectual history of the Philippine Revolution, and the revolution would, in turn, influence other distant thinkers, movements, and events. As the first "modern" nationalist and republican uprising in Southeast Asia and indeed of the twentieth century (preceding as it did the Irish rebellion of 1916), the long Philippine Revolution set a powerful precedent for twentieth-century anti-colonial movements that would reshape the region and the globe, and its transnational intellectual connections and regional reverberations merit deep study. This book reassesses the Philippine Revolution's thought and impact, particularly in relation to the landscape of "Asia" then newly reconceived in anti-imperial thought, to allow us to understand the revolution's full historical role and place; to illuminate an important transitional moment in Southeast Asian, imperial, and global history in the region; and to reconnect Philippine history to that of Southeast and East Asia at this pivotal moment of the birth of the Philippine nation. There were visions of world order alternative to those offered by the West, and the legacies of these visions have lived on beyond this transnational moment of political and discursive experimentation. As I show in the Philippine case, they are embedded in the very foundations of the nation that was then emerging.

This book investigates precisely what ground the Philippine nation built itself upon intellectually, excavating its neglected cosmopolitan and transnational Asian moorings in particular, in order to reconnect Philippine history to that of Southeast Asia. The diverse islands of Filipinas were riven with ethno-linguistic variety, and the contours of what would become the Philippine nation-state were in no way presumed.[15] What were the Filipinos' geographies of political affinity—their ambit of natural political identification, solidarity, and sympathy? What were their geographies of dis-affinity? I explore the international and transnational answers to this question, drawing out the Asian plane upon which the concept of the Filipino nation was drawn and along which Philippine revolutionary organizing occurred.

It is in this context that the concept of "place" becomes important. Many empires premised their conquest and civilizing mission on the enshrinement of a certain *idea* as endowing them with the right to rule—whether the due earthly dominion of Christianity under the Spanish or the technological capacity to till the land and assume true ownership over it under the British. As such, some of the strongest critics of various empires rested their arguments on *place*—on the legitimate, affective ties of place and group, with these affinities providing, in and of themselves, claim to rule. My concept of place figures this political and affective plane as the decidedly *nonuniversal* plane upon which to attach and organize a geography of political affinity, in the manner of Edmund Burke. In this way, place is moveable, serving as a localized counterpoint to the "universal" Enlightenment ideals that so often animated non-Western nationalism and nation-states in this period and yet could seem insufficiently specific on their own. It is thus also a window through which one may see these Asian and Asianist actors' nationalisms as something other than merely a coopting of Western formulations of the nation-state and its foundational ideals, though that work was also underway. These actors grounded their Enlightenment-influenced ideals in a politics and ideology of place that brought historical, cultural, and imagined specificity and logics to bear upon their nationalisms, and argued that such affective rootedness was their political source of legitimacy.

But what place, in this sense, did the early theorists of the Filipino nation invoke and construct? Ultimately, the Filipino revolutionaries did not argue their right to rule in the Philippines on place alone; they sought to convey to the international community that they possessed the reason, learning, and (Enlightenment) principles that qualified them to do so. Rather, as I show, place was important when Filipino *ilustrados* and revolutionaries sought to speak to one another as two *Filipinos*[16]—when they were attempting to ground the very concept of a Filipino nation and identity such that it could carry the local toward the national. Meanwhile, in the hands of the Katipunan, the shorthand name of the Kataas-taasan, Kagalang-galang Katipunan ng mga Anak ng Bayan (The Highest and Most Honorable Society of the Children of the Nation), the secret society that began the Philippine Revolution, this relatively defensive, pluralistic grounding of place would also shade into a more offensive, exclusivist grounding of race, in addition to place, as the source of political legitimacy. This transition shows the ways in which place could not suspend the contentious questions of ethnicity, race, and language embedded in the work of national construction. In these ways, *Asian Place, Filipino Nation* is about the emplotment of place in the proto-national and revolutionary thought of turn-of-the-century Filipino thinkers, and how those thinkers' negotiations with and constructions of the place of the Philippines, the place of "Asia," and the spatial registers of race connected them to their regional neighbors undertaking the same work.

Decentering the Nation-State and the West

Traditional intellectual histories of the Philippine Revolution have sought to explain how it came about and have centered exclusively on the thoughts and actions of the ilustrados, examining their grievances, the intellectual catalysts against Spanish colonialism, and the epistemological underpinnings to their first imaginings of a Filipino nation and of the Filipino.[17] The social science turn and the social history movement of the 1970s changed this, aiming to see communities more fully. The move to write "history from below" refocused the narrative away from its external influences and elite leaders and toward its internal history and folk epistemology. The definitive work in this vein is Reynaldo Ileto's *Pasyon and Revolution* (1979),[18] which seeks to understand popular participation in the revolution on the folk participants' own terms to understand their more localized politics of place. David Sturtevant's *Popular Uprisings in the Philippines, 1840–1940* (1976) highlights the longstanding, variegated "turbulent tradition" in the Philippines, and Reynaldo Ileto's *Filipinos and their Revolution* (1998) decenters the event-based narrative of the Philippine Revolution that traced a single political history leading to the establishment of the independent nation-state.[19] Indeed, the elite-driven account of the revolution naturally tends to privilege its nation-state narrative, for it was the elite who imagined the Filipino nation in terms of a modern nation-state endowed with *soberanía* (sovereignty) and who would go on to lead the fledgling Republic and nation-state. While it is important to recognize Reynaldo Ileto's methodological corrective toward the local and folk epistemology, focusing solely on local circumstances in the active construction and political imagining of a polity's national history risks reducing such constructions to their immediate political utility. As Christopher Hill states, "Local circumstances alone do not explain why national history as a practice of writing appeared in so many different parts of the globe," and this "method of representing the past"—constructing one's "national" history—"is inseparable from the nation-state in general, as the universal political unit of modernity."[20]

This decentering of the nation-state has found additional support in the more recent rise of international and transnational historical writing, from which studies of the turn-of-the-twentieth-century Philippines have proliferated. Historians now focused on the comparative colonialisms of Spain and the United States and on the Philippines's place within them. Julian Go and Anne L. Foster's *The American Colonial State in the Philippines* (2003), Julian Go's *American Empire and the Politics of Meaning: Elite Political Cultures in the Philippines and Puerto Rico* (2008), and the edited volume *Endless Empire: Spain's Retreat, Europe's Eclipse, America's Decline* (2012) are recent hallmark examples of this work.[21] An additional body of scholarship traces the ilustrados' transnational intellectual ties to Western Europe. Resil B. Mojares's *Brains of the Nation* (2006) explores the works of Pedro Paterno, T. H. Pardo de Tavera, and Isabelo de los Reyes as they traveled, engaged Western knowledge, and helped to construct a self-conscious Filipino nation.[22] Megan

Thomas's *Orientalists, Propagandists, and Ilustrados* (2012) examines the ways in which European models proved useful to certain Filipinos who employed Orientalist discourses and racial science's anti-colonial potential to reconsider Filipinos' place in the world, as well as to construct new narratives of home and national identity.[23] Benedict Anderson's *Under Three Flags: Anarchism and the Anti-Colonial Imagination* (2005) positions the intellectual ferment of the lead-up to the Philippine Revolution (embodied in José Rizal, Marcelo H. del Pilar, Mariano Ponce, and Isabelo de los Reyes) against the larger backdrop of the nineteenth-century Spanish Empire and the radical, global, anti-capitalist moment in which members of both the colonial periphery and European metropole participated, particularly through the anarchist movement and associated movements in the arts and literature. However, evidence of European anarchism's impact on anti-colonial Filipino thought is thin, and Anderson himself declares that Rizal had no rapport with anarchists and was "wholly innocent of anarchism."[24]

Any intellectual history of the Philippine Revolution must address the intellectual catalysts that traveled to the Philippines from Europe and that greeted those Filipinos who did travel to Europe. However, corollary comparisons of the Philippine Revolution to other "Asian" movements of its kind and time are much rarer (as are accounts of Filipinos' regional, international, and transnational history within Asia and with other Asians).[25] Among those rare few, Caroline S. Hau and Kasian Tejapira's *Traveling Nation-Makers: Transnational Flows and Movements in the Making of Modern Southeast Asia* (2011) uses the lens of travel to crisscross the region and trace the movements, networks, and actions of transnational actors who operated above and below the nation-state across the nineteenth and twentieth centuries, as do Resil B. Mojares's (2011) and Francis A. Gealogo's (2013) essays on Mariano Ponce.[26] Yet, deeper international and transnational examinations of the Philippine Revolution's intellectual negotiations with "Asia" are still needed. This book builds on the transnational and international intellectual histories of Thomas's *Orientalists*, Anderson's *Under Three Flags*, and Mojares's brilliant scholarly articles and lectures on the figure of Mariano Ponce, the Propagandists' claiming of Malayness, and early Philippine "Asianism."[27] It also benefits greatly from the pioneering work on modern Japanese-Philippine relations and history by Josefa Saniel, Grant K. Goodman, Motoe Terami-Wada, Caroline S. Hau and Takashi Shiraishi, Lydia N.

Yu-Jose, and Takamichi Serizawa, and continues the work of Rebecca E. Karl, Lorraine Marion Paterson, and Christopher E. Goscha, who each explore Chinese and Vietnamese identification and collaboration with other Asian countries suffering similar colonial and geopolitical conditions and chart the emergence of a more politicized version of Asia.[28]

The growing East Asian interest in Western political theories necessitated a translation or formulation of the European notion of "society." Japanese philosophers were the first to undertake this, and provided after 1868 approximately thirty different terms.[29] The philosopher Nishi Amane rehabilitated the Chinese Sung dynasty philosopher Chéng Yí's term for "communal religious meetings" and projected on it the European meaning of "society"; it was this conceptualization that eventually took hold in Vietnam. Nishi's term *shakai* became *she hui* when the Chinese recuperated it from the Japanese, and *xã hội* when the Vietnamese borrowed it from the Chinese.[30] More broadly, Lydia He Liu's scholarship on translingual practice examines the words imported between Japan and China from 1900 to 1937, showing that nearly all major terms having to do with politics, economy, culture, and literature circulated translingually and underwent resemanticization.[31] This method of engaging Western concepts through a cross-cultural process of iterative recuperation within Asian circles illustrates the general way in which the Vietnamese scholar-gentry of this period addressed the problem of lost independence. Alexander Woodside terms it "innovative classicism,"[32] while Mark Bradley describes it as the "appropriation and transformation of the global circulation of civilizational discourse by local, Asian actors."[33] Lorraine Marion Paterson refers to it as part of the "tenacious transmission" of ideas, in which the literary accounts of European revolutionary heroes did not originate from French texts but "passed through China and/or Japan for translation, summarizing or rewriting," and "in the course of their circuitous journey, historical depictions were translated, altered, and rewritten."[34] This work also relates to what Rebecca E. Karl details regarding the development of Chinese nationalism in the same period.[35] The Chinese understanding of what it meant to be modern did not draw primarily from Western models, she argues, but from the global moment of the turn of the twentieth century and its unevenness of material power, as well as from the experience of, negotiation with, and responses to confrontation with coercive Western power and capital taking place in Asia. Similarly, the innovative classicism of the Vietnamese was not a one-way translation and reception of Western ideas but active interpretation and reformulation, as well as learning.

In French Indochina, turn-of-the-twentieth-century Vietnamese scholar-gentry sought answers to their national sovereignty challenges in Social Darwinism, Enlightenment thought, and Pan-Asianism, which were contextualized within a globalized realm of contending civilizational discourses. Within this history, Pan-Asianism was central to much of Vietnam's early anti-colonialism, to the development of Vietnamese nationalism, and to their international framing of their new global context. To fill their desire for Western learning, many nineteenth-century Vietnamese intellectuals turned to Chinese translations of Western works and to Japan's process of Western-style modernization for guidance. This not only demarcates the world in which many inscribed Vietnam's future, but it also demonstrates the ways in which Pan-Asianism was a practice and process, in addition to a discourse.

The Vietnamese scholar-gentry's intellectual globalization in this period was a cumulative, cooperative intellectual inquiry conducted with members of other Asian nations sharing "the same culture and same race"—as Phan Bội Châu described China, Japan, Korea, and Vietnam in *Phan Bội Châu Niên Biểu* (1929).[36] This trans-Asian, cross-cultural process involved both the general practice of orientation toward and cultural exchange with East Asia, largely chosen over the option of European interlocutors, as well as the explicit political ideology of Pan-Asianism adopted by many influential Vietnamese scholar-gentry. Paterson examines the impact of Chinese intellectual discourse on Vietnamese literature and culture and argues that this exchange of ideas on foreign influence and Western political thought were more than merely "brush conversations" among the elite.[37] These conversations were deeply transformative and even radical given the reimagining they effected of the role of women and the meaning of "citizenry" in their new world. Indeed, the legacy of this trans-Asian learning and exchange is visible in the Vietnamese Tự Lực văn đoàn (Self-Strength Literary Movement), which began in 1933 but whose name invokes the 1870s "self-strengthening" movement in Japan. Moreover, the founder of the Vietnamese movement, a young journalist named Trần Huy Liệu, modeled it after the Society for Promoting Learning that Liang Qichao (1873–1949) and Kang Yu-wei (1858–1927) founded in China in 1895 following the Chinese defeat in the Sino-Japanese War.[38]

While Pan-Asianism provides a natural regionalization of Vietnamese intellectual history, my analytical focus on the important Asian context to and Asianist thinking of the Philippine Revolution runs counter to traditional Philippine historiography. This traditional assumption forms the premise of the recent work by Sven Matthiessen, *Japanese Pan-Asianism and the Philippines from the Late Nineteenth Century to the End of World War II: Going to the Philippines Is Like Coming Home?* (2016). He argues that "the long years of Western colonization have left Filipinos with the self-image of an Occidental people, and those revolutionaries who opposed American rule in the archipelago had a strict 'Philippines first' mindset"—by which he means that even those who flirted with Asianism and Pan-Asianism did so superficially, being, ultimately, nationalists at the end of the day.[39] Analytically, Matthiessen begins with the Japanese occupation of Manila in 1942–45 and the cultural and political difficulties the Pan-Asianists encountered in their effort to persuade Filipinos of their idea of "Asia for the Asians" and of the Greater East Asia Co-Prosperity Sphere. He then looks backward from that starting premise to explain the inability of that concept to take hold—describing Asianism's hesitant fits and starts in the late nineteenth century until its failure in World War II. However, if we begin our examination in the early revolutionary period and move forward from there, avoiding teleologically projecting backward, we see a different picture. Before hardened alliances obtained and the ascendance of the United States as one of the world's two strongest powers became clear, there was a moment when things could have gone differently, when thinkers were redrawing their geographies of political affinity and envisioning quite a different potential world order, ordered along lines of Asian solidarity. This book begins analytically in the late nineteenth century to examine early experimentations with the concepts of Asianism, Malayness, and the very construction of "Asia" itself, seeing how such experimentation was embedded in the foundations of early Philippine nationalist and anti-colonial thought. Indeed, Mathiessen's account of earlier versions of Philippine Pan-Asianism from the turn of the twentieth century is incomplete and only lightly sketched, and entirely omits the material dimension to Philippine Pan-Asianism. While Matthiessen charges that Filipino Asianists were merely nationalists who sought to benefit from Asianist aid and who superficially explored Pan-Malay and Pan-Asian possibilities, I argue that, for the colonized, no strategy could afford to be purely transnational, nor could it supersede nationalist priorities, and that this distinction is crucial to understanding the Pan-Asianism of the colonized "periphery" as distinct from that of the "center" of Japan. I draw this distinction in order to pluralize and bring greater nuance to our understanding of what was, indeed, a very multivocal Pan-Asianism. This argument that nationalism and internationalism were existentially entangled in the Asian "periphery" at the turn of the twentieth century should come as no surprise, as Christopher Hill, among other scholars, has interrogated their simultaneous emergence (if not existential entanglement) in the global "centers" of Japan, France, and the United States in the same period.[40]

Though incipient, I argue that the early Filipino Asianism of the turn of the twentieth century was crucial to the Philippine Propaganda Movement's political argumentation against Spain, to the concept of the Filipino nation that the ilustrados were constructing in that movement, and to the political mobilization and organizing of the Katipunan and First Philippine Republic. This is no small matter, as the ilustrados' and Katipuneros' intellectual, imaginative, and political work was the foundation on which the Philippine nation was constructed. The Katipunan (also known as the KKK) began the Philippine Revolution on August 23–24, 1896, with the Cry of Balintawak, when the Katipuneros tore their *cédulas personales* (community tax certificates) to mark their separation from Spain. The First Philippine Republic, which was also known as the Malolos Republic, was the government that the Philippine Revolution erected following the declaration of Philippine independence by General Emilio Aguinaldo on June 12, 1898. The government was formally established with the Malolos Constitution proclamation on January 23, 1899, in Malolos, Bulacan. Emilio Aguinaldo was elected as the first president of the republic, with Apolinario Mabini as the first president of the cabinet (Presidente del Consejo de Gobierno). Both these entities, the Katipunan and the First Philippine Republic, claimed "Asianness" to moor the Philippines in its own civilizational location apart from that of Europe and attempted to construct a unified *place* of the Philippines that grounded their historical, affective claim to political legitimacy and grounded their nation, seeking to bridge ethno-linguistic difference.

Core and Periphery in Pan-Asianism—
Turning Toward the Southeast

A new stage of high imperialism began in the 1870s and extended through the first half of the twentieth century, characterized by protectionism and monopoly capitalism following the 1873–79 economic depression, as well as by direct rule and the violence bound up in the intensified struggle to partition the world and the 1881–1914 "scramble for Africa."[41] This sense of quickening geopolitical competition and increasing material disparities made Asian intellectuals more concerned with the global power of the new European discourses on the Orient, race, and empire.[42] That is not to say that this created for Asian intellectuals, political thinkers, and nationalists a bilateral and unidirectional West-East field of change privileging material superiority and imperialism as the world's historical agents. As Rebecca E. Karl's path-breaking work *Staging the World: Chinese Nationalism at the Turn of the Twentieth Century* (2002) argues, Chinese nationalism was in great part a product of the thinking through of non-Western experiences of imperialism and colonialism—for example, the Philippines, Poland, Egypt, South Africa, Turkey, and Hawai'i—rather than learning from Western models. In particular, the Philippine Revolution provided "conceptual connections" that enabled Chinese intellectuals to conceive of revolution and independence as planks of modernity, which they would go on to direct against the Qing dynasty.[43]

European competition had inaugurated a period of colonization for the sake of colonization beyond the arguments of a "civilizing mission."[44] Pan-Asianism emerged in the mid-nineteenth century as Chinese and Japanese thinkers attempted to reconceive their formerly isolated countries within the new international political order dominated by European imperial powers and to negotiate with the potent, novel ideas of the European Enlightenment.[45] Cemil Aydin's *The Politics of Anti-Westernism in Asia* (2007) argues that Pan-Asianism featured an element of anti-Westernism in its evaluation of modernity, Westernization, and the international order, but that this anti-Westernism was born of Japanese intellectuals' prior acceptance of the universality of Western civilization.[46] This occurred amid their rapid work to equip Japan for the new global intellectual and international political challenges it was facing. Non-Western elites' encounter with European exceptionalist narratives and the racial barriers that circumscribed the West's application and understanding of Enlightenment ideals crucially delegitimized the Eurocentric world order.[47] This impelled Japanese intellectuals to construct a more inclusive concept of global civilization, including an alternative discourse of civilization and race.[48] Japanese reform projects centered on the idea of a universal modernity that confronted Europeans' exclusive identification of progress with the white race and belief in the culture of Christianity as the explanation for Western superiority. From these debates emerged a mirror vision of international order—of Pan-Asian solidarity in opposition to Western imperialism.

For many in the Sinic world, East Asia had become a coherent region through the system of tributary trade with China and the shared culture that those relations had established. Out of a vague, romantic, traditional notion of common Asianness during the Meiji era (1868–1912), Pan-Asianism in Japan developed into a more specific political ideology during the Taishō period (1912–26). The Taishō-period ideology promoted regional integration and required a basis of regional solidarity and identity.[49] To the earliest theorists of Pan-Asianism in Japan and China in the 1870s, the Sinic world explicitly and exclusively delimited their projected "Asia."[50] Across this Sinocentric, mainstream thread of Japanese Pan-Asian thought, the discourse stressed cultural unity, based on the common use of Chinese characters; a purported racial kinship of East Asian peoples and ethnicities; the compact geography and specific historical legacy of the Sinocentric order that forged interstate relations and economic ties across East Asia; and the understanding of a "common destiny" (*unmei kyodotai*) in an Asian struggle against Western imperialism and, at times, against Westernization or even modernization.[51] The latter idea of a common destiny was the intellectual vehicle that Southeast Asian Pan-Asianists would use to challenge the mainstream's Sinic delimitation of East Asia. Anti-colonialists and nationalists across Southeast Asia, South Asia, and the Middle East appropriated and reinterpreted Pan-Asianism for their local contexts, in which they enlarged the heuristic definition of Asia to include, at its greatest extent, all oppressed non-Western nations struggling against Western imperialism. There were therefore several discourses of Pan-Asianism, separated, first of all, into those emanating from its East Asian origin in Japan and China, and those conversing with, but originating outside of, this center.

Many articulations of Pan-Asianism fall outside neat, linear stages and resist clear typologies; nevertheless, categorization remains a necessary shorthand to prevent conflation. Within the "core" of Pan-Asian discourse, three distinct threads of Pan-Asianism emerged: the "Sinic" thread of "same letters, same culture" (*dobun doshu*); the "Teaist" thread, which Okakura Tenshin's "Asia is one" thesis exemplifies; and the "Meishuron" ("Japan as leader") thread, as delineated in Eri Hotta's *Pan-Asianism and Japan's War 1931-1945* (2007) and Caroline S. Hau and Takashi Shiraishi's "Daydreaming about Rizal and Tetchō: On Asianism as Network and Fantasy" (2009).[52] Sinic Pan-Asianism centered on solidarity with China, founded on the common cultural heritage of East Asia.[53] This was the "same letters/script, same culture" conceit represented in the work of Konoe Atsumaro and cultural associations and organizations such as Tōa Dōbun-kai and Tōa Dōbun Shoin. It was concerned with racial struggle and arrayed various Asian nationalisms against the international world order.[54] Teaist Pan-Asianism drew from Okakura Tenshin's (also known as Okakura Kakuzō) *The Book of Tea* (1906), and featured more globalist theorizations of Asia, highlighting shared philosophical or cultural traits over an expanse stretching from South to East Asia.[55] More egalitarian, idealist, anticolonial, and extensive in its fuzzy geographical boundaries to Asia than were the other threads, it asserted Asia's philosophical and cultural equality with the West. Meanwhile, Meishuron Pan-Asianism was the expansionist, geopolitics-based thesis of Ishiwara Kanji (Amur River Society) and Gen'yōsha (Dark Ocean Society) that positioned Japan at the head of the Asian alliance (Ajia no meishu) in the crusade to rescue Asia from Western imperialism.[56] In this stance, the Meishuron thread envisioned a crucial role for Japan to transform other Asian nations in its image.

This book takes seriously the alternative visions of world order that Asianism and Pan-Asianism offered the colonized and oppressed, while attending to their dialectical link with a concept (if not reality) of singular, global modernity. Cemil Aydin insists that anti-Western critiques and ideologies in Middle Eastern, Indian, Chinese, and Japanese histories "can neither be seen simply as derivative of the anticolonial struggles nor explained solely as conservative and religious reactions to global modernity,"[57] and that "it is necessary to examine the changes in the legitimacy and inclusiveness of the Eurocentric international order," for "it was the legitimacy crisis of a single, globalized, international system that produced pan-Islamic and pan-Asian visions of world order."[58] In the Philippines too these discourses and political movements were not simply derivative of the anticolonial and nationalist struggles, even as they were implemented toward (and at times instrumentalized for) anticolonialist and nationalist ends. They were positive imaginings of differing, if not alternative, futures. On this point, Aydin provides a complex but compelling narrative, expertly showing how Pan-Asianism existed separately and differently from other discourses, albeit along much of the same historical landscape; but he leaves the place of Western thought within this anti-Westernism understudied. As was the case in much anti-colonial thought, Pan-Asianism was a reaction, a defense, and it coopted Western disciplines of knowledge and techniques of power toward subversive ends. The new world order offered in Pan-Asianism was offered to Asia specifically, despite its claim of inclusiveness, and in this offering it mobilized Western theories of cosmopolitanism and Social Darwinism, particularly those of the anarchist Peter Kropotkin on intraspecies aid and mutual cooperation.[59] As this book shows, in the Philippine case, Western thought and epistemologies were deeply intertwined with Asianism and frameworks of race and nation.

In their edited volume *Pan-Asianism in Modern Japanese History* (2007), Sven Saaler and J. Victor Koschmann indirectly explore the question of the nature and Asianness of Pan-Asianism's envisioned new world order as they tease out the universality/particularity and anti-imperial/imperial aspects embedded in the discourse. What emerges is not the simple development of a romantic, anti-imperial vision toward a hardened imperial justification, neatly corresponding to increasingly expansive Japanese geopolitical aims leading up to World War II. Saaler reminds us that "as late as 1945, scholars such as Hirano Yoshitarō (1897–1980), strongly influenced by Marxist ideas, claimed an 'East Asian universalism' which, in his opinion, had developed in the East Asian village (*furusato*), where the high moral virtues associated with community (*seimeiteki kyōdōtai*), familism (*kazokushugi*), and the agrarian commune (*nōson kyōdōtai*) had been growing for 'many thousand years.'"[60]

Li Narangoa's chapter on "Universal Values and Pan-Asianism: The Vision of Ōmotokyō" in the same volume highlights the Pan-Asian concepts among religious groups and the ultranationalists and military officers who had strong ties to religious sects. In particular, one of the new religious groups of early twentieth-century Japan, Ōmotokyō (Great Source Sect), espoused a Pan-Asian ideal based on virtue, universal pacifism, and universal moral values that simultaneously impelled the sect to embark on an overseas mission.[61] Founded by Deguchi Nao and Deguchi Onisaburō in the late 1890s, the sect criticized the government's Westernization policy and modern institutions, while advocating on behalf of the lower social classes and for the creation of an ideal human community "based on the morality implicit in the collective consciousness of the Japanese folk."[62] Ōmoto reflected Pan-Asianism's own contradictions regarding universal values and ethnocentric regionalism. The aim of "unifying the world by means of religion" is not particular to this Shinto sect, basically all "universal" religions seek this achievement, but Ōmoto in particular advocated Asian unity based on "universal pacifism (or love) as part of its pan-Asian ideal" as the first step in "creating a world mission."[63] Though Narangoa does not explicitly state why this was the first step, I assume that the inferred conclusion is that as the sect's teachings, ideology, and activities mirrored the contradictions within Japanese society, it also mirrored its scope, realistically calculating an indigenous Japanese religion's potential reach to be coextensive with the Japanese polity's potential reach. In this, according to Narangoa, Ōmoto "initiated its overseas mission with the aim of bringing East and West together and averting a war between the two civilizations."[64] Yet, Narangoa asserts that "Ōmotokyō's doctrine was truly universal and reached far beyond the realist political aims of Japanese military planners." Unlike the interpretation of Pan-Asianism as a doctrine that unites Asia but excludes the West, "the case of Ōmotokyō demonstrates both that Pan-Asianism was more complex than this generalization implies, and that it was part of much more ambitious thinking about the world."[65] The sect was an advocate for change within Japan, as well, in order to evolve the country into a true model for the world.

The Japanese thinker Miki Kiyoshi (1897–1945) re-envisioned Immanuel Kant's idea of "cosmopolitanism" as the basis for Pan-Asianism's theory of "cooperativism,"[66] as John Namjun Kim's "The Temporality of Empire: The Imperial Cosmopolitanism of Miki Kiyoshi and Tanabe Hajime" in *Pan-Asianism in Modern Japanese History* (2007) explores. Miki's theorization of Pan-Asian cooperativism insured cosmopolitan freedom within East Asia through imperial subjugation,[67] while, as William Miles Fletcher III's *The Search for a New Order: Intellectuals and Fascism in Prewar Japan* (1982) shows, in Japan it bound the individual to the state and prioritized the "whole" society or nation over the individual.[68] The cosmopolitan defense of imperialism flowed from the moral ambivalence at the heart of both Pan-Asian cooperativism and Kantian cosmopolitanism, neither of which necessarily precludes political projects such as imperialism. For Kant, the right of hospitality only extended to the "right to visit," which theoretically indicates that the highest ethical commitment is to humanity as a whole, rather than to any community in particular.[69] For his part, Miki's reworking of cosmopolitanism in his theory of cooperativism (developed in the 1930s) similarly transcended particular community interests through a logic of inclusion in his imagined "East Asian Cooperative Body," comprising several nations, which rejected Japanese exceptionalism, while still being for nationalism and against racism in general.[70] Nevertheless, the role of Japan as a nation was still particularized in Miki's thought, rather than subsumed as one alongside all other nations in the East Asian Cooperative Body, because according to Miki "the idea of nationalism contains truth in the sense that any world-historical mobilization is inaugurated by a certain nation. Even the present East Asian Cooperative Body has developed on the initiative of the Japanese nation." Yet, "Japan itself enters into the East Asian Cooperative Body, developed by Japan," he reminds us.[71] Interestingly, such national-universal dualism in Miki's thought mirrors that of the Philippines's Pan-Asian president, José P. Laurel, suggesting the existence of such dualist tension in Pan-Asianism more broadly in both the "core" and "periphery" of the discourse.[72]

The place of ethnicity and ethnocentric nationalism within Pan-Asianism's regionalism would become more prominent in the interwar period, but even as its importance increased, it did not necessarily imply imperialist aims, though it often empowered imperialist ends. Kevin M. Doak's "The Concept of Ethnic Nationality and Its Role in Pan-Asianism in Imperial Japan" studies the Yūzonsha (Society of Those Left Behind) formed in 1923 by Ōkawa Shūmei and Mitsukawa Kametarō, both of whom believed that the new global turn toward ethnic nationality occasioned by World War I was also crucial to understanding the problems confronting Asia.[73] In 1922 Ōkawa published *Various Problems in an Asian Renaissance*, in which he outlined his case for Asian regionalism through the turn toward ethnic nationality, which, as Doak writes, made "the case for Asia as a single regional identity with one defining characteristic: the desire for liberation from the colonial yoke of the White Man" and explicitly connected Asian revival to the anti-imperialist ethnic nationalism of Serbs, Irish, and many others following World War I.[74] In this formulation, however, the binding ethnic trait was a common temporally situated political goal, rather than an innate, timeless ethnic marker. It was the naturalized Social Darwinist racial interpretive framework of world order that served to elide ethnicity and the political goals of anti-Westernism. In the context of 1922, broad ethnic racial groupings and racialized political ends were co-constitutive from a geopolitical standpoint.

The scholarship on Pan-Asianism has advanced and expanded significantly in recent decades.[75] Nevertheless, it has largely remained Northeast Asia-centric in scope. Akira Iriye's "Japan's Drive to Great Power Status" (1989) provides a sophisticated heuristic and historical comparison between European missionaries' foreign-based activity and Japanese Pan-Asianists' "private" efforts and support in China and Korea, which highlights the diverse motives and contexts in both cases so as to resist simple reductions to Western imperialism and Japanese expansionism, respectively.[76] Yumiko Iida's "Fleeing the West, Making Asia Home: Transpositions of Otherness in Japanese Pan-Asianism, 1905–1930" (1997), meanwhile, argues that Japanese appropriation of the Western classificatory scheme of the "Orient" amounted to discursive violence toward the diversity of Asian cultures while allowing Japan to monopolize that disseminated and imbibed discourse in turn.[77] Though still biased toward Northeast Asian articulations, Saaler and Koschmann's previously discussed *Pan-Asianism in Modern Japanese History* (2007) provides a more substantive theoretical examination of the varied, discrepant, multiple voices within Pan-Asian discourse, while underscoring the central question within the historiography as to how seriously to treat Pan-Asianism as an ideology.[78] Was it merely an imperialist instrument or was it a "legitimate" world vision? Should one take a functionalist approach to Pan-Asianism to determine its legitimacy, or can we treat the discourses separately from the official political course? Do the para-state Pan-Asian discourses and political actions that were never sanctioned by the state, and indeed were at times deemed subversive, dent our interpretation of Pan-Asianism, which largely focuses on the discourse that was eventually streamlined to become the official state ideology? In seeking to answer these questions, period and positionality are important. What would analyses look like if these questions were posed from outside Japan? This book takes up this issue of positionality in order to diversify the largely Northeast Asian-centric and discourse-focused existing scholarship on Pan-Asianism.

The Sino-Japanese War (1894–95) was pivotal to the development of Asian-ist fantasies outside the Sinic world, particularly in the Philippines, but it was the Russo-Japanese War (1904–5) that was the greatest turning point for the appeal of the Japanese model and Japanese leadership within a more broadly defined Asia. As the first defeat of a white modern military power by an Asian competitor, the Japanese victory prompted the colonized world to ask: If the Japanese could achieve progress and development without colonialism, couldn't other colonized Asian nations do the same? This cru-cially undercut the premise of the European "civilizing mission," and very soon afterward, Pan-Islamic and Pan-Asian ideas began entering broader, mainstream journalistic and scholarly writings on international affairs.[79] Beginning with the Philippine Revolution in 1896 and its brief creation of a modern, secular, native republic, by 1905 the revolt of Asia was fully brew-ing, with nationalists such as Vietnamese Phan Bội Châu increasingly turn-ing to Japan in the wake of the Russo-Japanese War. Indeed, 1905 was the year that Châu began his Đông Du (Go East) movement, taking Vietnamese youth to study in Japan.

In *The Impact of the Russo-Japanese War*, edited by Rotem Kowner (2007), the contributors discuss the various effects of the war. In Europe, where Germany had previously been restrained by a Franco-Russian alliance, it now reoriented its military posture. The new defensive strategy empha-sized attack on France through Belgium, while downgrading the impor-tance of Germany's eastern border abutting Russia. Tal Tovy and Sharon Halevi trace the growing distrust of Japan by the United States following the war, and Harold Z. Schiffrin notes that from being a potential model for China, Japan increasingly became a major threat, especially for the north-east Chinese territory where the Russo-Japanese War was fought.[80] About the colonial Malay world, Michael Laffan writes of the widespread hope that Japan would convert to Islam. Laffan builds on Barbara Andaya's work in "From Rūm to Tokyo: The Search for Anticolonial Allies by the Rulers of Riau, 1899–1914," (1977), which studied the shift from seeing the Ottoman Empire as Muslim Southeast Asia's potential savior from Dutch colonialism to seeing Japan as that savior.[81] Laffan argues that Japan's success in the Russo-Japanese War "had crucial implications for the globally agreed oppo-sition of East and West to be elided with that of Islam and colonizer, in addi-tion to proving the global applicability of modern methods of education and reform."[82] This was particularly so after the Japannerwet (Japanese law) of 1899 by which the Dutch parliament decreed that Japanese subjects were henceforth to be treated as "equal" to Europeans in status and privileges.[83]

T. R. Sareen argues that the war resulted in increased political unrest and a more assertive nationalism in India, with a softened British stance toward both—"the indications are that the British were now willing to admit the fitness of the oriental people for self-government and to initiate the gradual introduction of reforms to some extent."[84] There was a move to give Indians a larger role in the administration of their government under viceroy Lord Minto in 1905, with a portion of the calculus being not only how to handle the increasingly urgent and strident nationalism of the subject populace but also the fear that, according to the director of criminal intelligence in 1918, "the flowing eulogies of Japan indulged in by the politicians with the object of making blacker by contrasts their tales of British misgovernment in India might lead one to imagine that the substitution of Japanese rule for British would be welcome."[85] "It is argued that the increasing power of Japan is a menace to British rule in India which can only be defeated by the establishment of a contented self-governing India with a strong national army and navy."[86] Even as Indian nationalists grew wary of Japanese imperialist actions in Asia, Sareen argues, "moderate leaders of the [Indian National Congress] were deeply impressed and frequently cited the example of Japan to inspire the people with a sense of patriotism and self-sacrifice—the two secrets to Japanese success."[87]

Yet, Paul A. Rodell argues that in Southeast Asia, the war made a minimal impression outside of the Philippines and Vietnam, the countries where nationalists did seek Japanese aid in their anti-colonial nationalist struggles.[88] Though the mid-nineteenth century to early twentieth century witnessed a multitude of anti-colonial rebellions and resistance movements across Southeast Asia, Rodell asserts that local factors and, particularly, each colony's stage of political development affected the region's response to the Russo-Japanese War. While I would argue against Rodell's recourse to "stages of political development," I agree that the 1902 Anglo-Japanese Alliance and the 1908 Franco-Japanese agreement, which signaled Japan's increasing association with the European (and American) imperialists over its Asian neighbors, tempered many potential Southeast Asian fantasies of Asian solidarity under Japanese leadership. These agreements also alienated many Philippine and Vietnamese nationalists. It should be noted, however, that it was the Sino-Japanese War rather than the Russo-Japanese War that had galvanized the first wave of Pan-Asianist fantasies in the Philippines. More broadly, the Bolshevik Revolution in 1917 and Wilsonian principles promulgated after World War I undercut the international appeal of Pan-Asianism and Pan-Islamism. Nevertheless, by 1924 both Pan-Islamist and Pan-Asian visions had established "distinct modes of critiques and traditions in relation to League of Nations-led liberal internationalism and Soviet backed-social internationalism," as Cemil Aydin argues; these relied on the failures of the League of Nations and a dichotomy of the moral East and materialist West.[89] It is this mode of critique and its differing visions of cosmopolitanism, modernity, and world order that this book seeks to explore in Southeast Asia—in the Asianist discourses and organizing of the Filipino ilustrados and revolutionaries, with an eye to the Đông Du Movement of Phan Bội Châu and his scholar-gentry contemporaries in Vietnam.

Supranational in its politics and discourse, Pan-Asianism nevertheless served as a nationalist tool, and this *national* use was characteristic of Southeast Asian Pan-Asianism and the Pan-Asianism of the colonized more broadly, even as it entangled such national forms with decidedly internationalist or at least dualistic registers. Pan-Asianists of the colonized "periphery" often subscribed to the ideology as much out of a realpolitik assessment of their countries' position against their Western colonizers as from a more romantic, idealistic envisioning of Asian solidarity or distinctiveness; indeed, the two impulses were conceptually intertwined. Positive articulations of specifically Asian or non-Western philosophical and political grounds to various nationalisms in Asia buttressed such nationalisms at a time of existential threat and cultural and intellectual anxiety. Pan-Asianism and the example of Meiji Japan, through their assertion of the unique fruits of Asian culture and proof of successful "Asian" modernization, supported the legitimacy and perceived viability of Asian nationalists' claims of rightful sovereignty over their countries in spite of their countries' relative "failure" in what they perceived to be a Social Darwinist struggle of geopolitical and national survival. The content of the Pan-Asian imaginary and proposition on the part of the periphery, however, did not merely amount to a new strategy within the same Social Darwinist competition. The peripheral Pan-Asianists asserted that the "Asia" within Pan-Asia would embody a rightful moral grounding to geopolitics, which they judged as lacking in the international sphere and which they asserted was the unique offering of Asia. This dichotomy pitted a materialist West against a spiritual East. These peripheral Pan-Asianists often interpreted what was a potentially imperial element embedded within the concept of Pan-Asian alliance as instead effecting a new diplomacy and new transnational political arrangement through a federation of equals, albeit knitted together through self-interest in what was a racially charged and materially unequal, amoral competition.

In the thinking of Phan Bội Châu and much of the Vietnamese scholar-gentry, Social Darwinism and Pan-Asianism operated in tandem. However, in confronting stunning demonstrations of the material power that Western philosophy, science, and political economy had made possible for the European nations, some, such as Phan Châu Trinh (1872–1926), believed that the only means adequate to recover Vietnamese sovereignty were Western-style reforms and a Franco-Vietnamese alliance.[90] Phan Châu Trinh was a member of the scholar-gentry and a Vietnamese nationalist from Quảng Nam province in Annam who attempted to appeal to French democratic and liberal principles. He passed the highest mandarin examinations in 1901 but resigned from the mandarin bureaucracy in 1905, disillusioned with the monarchy. He set out, instead, to learn from the West in order to advance Vietnam. Originally from Nghệ An province, Phan Bội Châu (1867–1940) was descended from a family of poor scholars and was a member of the scholar-gentry and a pioneer of Vietnamese nationalism in the twentieth century. In his youth, he participated in the failed Cần Vương Movement in 1885 and passed the regional mandarin examinations in 1900; he began his career of activism, nationalist agitation, and writing thereafter.[91] An admirer of French civilization and the first advocate of Western democracy in Vietnam, Phan Châu Trinh advocated for "working within the French system for self-rule."[92] While believing that France represented the cultural vanguard, Trinh denounced the emptiness of French civilizing policies and the hypocrisy of maintaining liberal ideals for Frenchmen while imposing a repressive, outmoded monarchy upon Vietnam. He urged France to make good on its civilizing mission and ideals. "To govern a country solely on the basis of the personal opinions of one individual or of an imperial court is to treat the people of that country as if they were a herd of goats," Trinh wrote. He denounced the Asian "government by man," and advocated instead the Western democratic "government of laws,"[93] thereby rejecting the opposition of the material West and the spiritual East for what he interpreted to be the more salient distinction.

Nevertheless, Phan Châu Trinh promoted a harmonious blend of Eastern and Western ethics, by means of which he believed humanity would reach its supreme form of civilization.[94] Trinh was acquainted with the works of Montesquieu, Rousseau, Lafontaine, Pascal, and Voltaire through their Chinese translations and interpretations by Chinese thinkers. Serving as a cultural broker, Trinh wrote an epic poem expounding on the modern revolutionary history of the United States and Europe. Yet, Alexander Woodside argues that this poem "also proved the lingering potency of Japanese thought and fashion in the minds of first generation Vietnamese nationalists, for it was really a poetic adaptation of a Japanese novel written about 1885 by Shiba Shirō."[95] Indeed, the Meiji-era reforms that had transformed Japan's geopolitical position seemed to present an attractive and less radical modernization for the Vietnamese to undertake. Trinh's epic poem additionally demonstrated the persistence of neo-Confucian elitism even in Trinh's decidedly progressive, Western-influenced thinking. Rather than impersonal Social Darwinist or "racial" forces, Trinh's narrative of the American Revolution relied on properly cultivated heroes who exhibited the virtues that Vietnamese elites ascribed to superior Confucian men, such as self-sacrifice, courage, righteousness, and devotion to their country.[96] Phan Châu Trinh's revolutionary thought rested upon a classical East Asian morality and worked toward the realization of that moral framework's utopic vision. Trinh rejected the idea of a nationalist crusade that struggled merely to secure the creation of one powerful, prosperous nation-state. To Trinh, "if such a crusade was to end to everyone's ethical satisfaction," Woodside writes, "it had to do so in a kind of utopian universal tranquility, a 'great peace,' that was beyond the nation-state."[97] Counter to the Western separation of politics and ethics prevalent since Machiavelli, Trinh believed that nationalist revolutions could not hold wealth or power as ends in themselves but, rather, must revolve around acts of social reciprocity that would lead to an ethical, serene world.[98]

Yet the familial racial extension to and moral reliance upon Japan could be an uneasy one. On December 29, 1883, the acting Japanese consul Machida wrote to the British colonial secretary of Hong Kong concerning the occurrence of "natives . . . hawking pictures of the war in Tonquin in the streets of this colony."[99] He explained: "These pictures I observe represent a Japanese army jointly with French fighting against the Black Flags." In his letter, he asked whether "the sale of these pictures could not be stopped," and reminded the British colonial secretary: "needless is it for me to add that of course there are no Japanese troops in Tonquin."[100] While the British colonial secretary expressed to his War and Colonial Department that he could "no more interfere in a trifling matter of this kind than the Home Secretary in England could seize the London *Punch* for a similar caricature," he admitted that "at the same time, it may be observed that this caricature has some significance, as showing the popular Chinese jealousy and suspicion of the Japanese, who have advanced so much more rapidly than themselves in the ways of European progress."[101] While this may specifically show Chinese, rather than Vietnamese, anxieties over Japan's rise, it nevertheless highlights the existence of an undercurrent of suspicion and trepidation regarding Japan's future role in Asia alongside the Western imperial powers.

The Asian Philippine Revolution

The Philippines represents the first case of successful trasnationalization of Pan-Asianism, involving cross-border political practice and revolutionary networking toward the goal of overthrowing two Western imperial powers (as opposed to overthrowing dynastic regimes in China and Korea), and this is the first book to highlight it as such. The Vietnamese case followed shortly after the Philippine one. Though only relatively successful, the Philippine case is the first instance of fellow Pan-Asianists lending material aid toward revolution and harnessing transnational Pan-Asian networks of support, activism, and association toward doing so. This sits in contrast with the failure to transnationalize Pan-Asianism in Korea, which led to Fukuzawa Yukichi's 1885 editorial advocating that Japan "leave Asia" ("Datsu-A Ron"), albeit temporarily. The scholarship on Pan-Asianism tends to be intellectual in focus, discounting the important material and affective dimensions to Pan-Asianism in action as practiced in the Philippines and Vietnam. While the ideological depth of the Katipunan and Filipino Asianist thinkers' Pan-Asianism was often conditional and its substance alloyed and localized, they clearly saw Japan as a potential ally, protector, and Asian power with which to be associated in their anti-colonial struggle. The material power of Japan within the imperial geopolitical framework of the turn of the twentieth century is an important dimension that is too often ignored. That material dimension is crucial to understanding the Pan-Asianism of the colonized "periphery" and to incorporating the periphery into this history. So too is the affective dimension, in which fantasies, imagination, and a certain emotionality, of the kind always involved in human networks, formed much of the periphery's engagement with the model of Meiji-era Japan and with Asian solidarity. Affect was crucial to bridging differences in culture and pluralities of national self-interest. It helped, on an individual level, toward building a cognitive basis to Pan-Asianism sufficiently strong to mobilize action across such difference and plurality. This individual emotion is distinct from the more developed "emotion work" studied and exhibited, for example, in the mass politics of the Chinese Communist Party.[102] Asia, much less Pan-Asia, was a kind of imaginary and fantasy. To remove it from a merely discursive framing and to actively apply it toward the urgent goals of the colonized "periphery" required, as this book shows, affective bridges in Japan, Vietnam, and the Philippines. I particularly focus in this regard on Miyazaki Tōten and Mariano Ponce. Only once we incorporate the periphery and the material and affective dimensions to Pan-Asianism as a network and practice (in addition to a discourse) do we obtain a full understanding of Pan-Asianism.

It is also through attention to these dimensions that this book attempts a global intellectual history of the Philippine Revolution, rather than only through drawing a necessarily global scope, as the history in question has global implications, global considerations, and global roots but often operates within an immediately regional, rather than global, setting—though always with an eye to the perceived distinction between East and West. I share the emergent global intellectual historical field's goal of enlarging the field of intellectual history beyond its canonical figures and texts, who and which have been traditionally located in the West. What separates this global approach from being only a recuperation of non-Western thought into intellectual history, however, is its broader methodological grounding in service of that aim. This is also what distinguishes global intellectual history's work from that of older area studies models and civilizational units of analysis, which have long looked at canonical non-Western philosophers and thinkers, ranging from Confucius to Rabindranath Tagore. I employ global intellectual history as a methodology by acknowledging the need to adapt analytical tools in order to bring other or overlooked actors into the intellectual historical field. In this book I look at affective and material dimensions in order to recover the Pan-Asianism of the periphery while seeking to make it legible to and included alongside our understandings of the Pan-Asianism of the center. In this way, global intellectual historical approaches draw from older subaltern historical fields' methodological experimentation but also depart from those fields in aim, as the emergent field seeks to make more global—and even subaltern—forms of intellectual history legible to the prior, established intellectual historical field.

Pan-Asianism as a network and practice took place largely in Asian cities— particularly Yokohama, Kobe, Tokyo, Hong Kong, and Singapore. Indeed, these place names appear almost as a refrain in the Spanish religious and colonial officials' notes, always incanted with threat. These hubs of regional anti-colonial subversion arose due to Japan's singular position as an Asian model to be followed, but also due to the particular international relations of the region at the time. The context of multiple colonial powers administering separate but neighboring Asian colonial territories set the limits and field for Pan-Asian activism, which danced around instances of imperial rivalry and cooperation. For a Filipino under Spanish colonial repression, colonial British Hong Kong was an unintended site of resistance. Both the colonies of other powers and Europe itself became havens for transnational activism directed at other powers. At the same time, Japan's own ambitions in the international world order made Japan susceptible to French pressure to extradite Vietnamese revolutionaries such as Phan Bội Châu. In the end, Tokyo disavowed any official aid to Asianist revolutionaries, even while certain of its government officials, political parties, and branches of government extended their own unofficial assistance.

The Philippine Revolution created the First Philippine Republic—a short-lived government and political vision that emerged from a larger, longer regional backdrop of quickening anti-colonialism and radical secular nationalism. This backdrop illuminates connections between the discourses of the political that proliferated across Southeast Asia during this global moment. Southeast Asian engagement with discourses on Pan-Asianism represented a transnational, anti-colonial vision of political possibility born of the particular international imperial framework of power of the turn of the twentieth century. It advocated Asian and racial solidarity, including under the guidance of Japan, against the encroachments of Western imperialism, having internalized a loose belief in a vague, evolutionary Social Darwinism, which applied biological concepts of natural selection and survival of the fittest to international politics and relations. Filipino discourses on race, evolution, and Pan-Asianism connected Filipino thought to the parallel anti-imperial and positive political imaginings of neighboring countries, particularly Vietnam—as did the Filipino attempt to conceptualize the greater Malay race and negotiate the Philippine nation's place within "Asia."

In exploring these topics, this book offers an intellectual history of the global moment of the late nineteenth century to the early twentieth century from a "peripheral" Southeast Asian perspective through its study of the Philippine Revolution, but with special attention to its intellectual inspirations beyond both the revolution and the emergent Philippine nation-state. It illuminates the history of the Philippine Revolution by situating it and its repercussions within their full international, transnational, and regional contexts. In this, Vietnam's experience, contemporaneous with the Philippine Revolution (1896–1906), importantly highlights the similarly globalized Asian world of ideas in which both Filipino and Vietnamese anti-colonial and nationalist thinkers were then trafficking. From its initial ambit in the Sinic world, Pan-Asianism's spatial dimensions grew progressively wider until they could encompass all of imperially oppressed non-Western Asia. Vietnam is an especially interesting case to examine in this process of widening, belonging to both the Sinic and colonized Southeast Asian worlds.

Assessing the Philippine Revolution's regional reverberations has required me to focus on the intellectual impact of the elites who thought, for the first time, on a national scale, traveled across national boundaries, and possibly exerted influence in other colonies in the region, unlike the particularistic, localized, religio-political, and often anti-statist communities that voiced discontent only within the Philippines. The majority of the intellectual threads common to anti-imperial Southeast Asian thinkers were mediated and negotiated by practitioners of Western, Chinese, and/or Japanese thought, and it was, admittedly, most often the elite who had the ability to engage directly in multilingual transnational discourse. These well-equipped actors are the prime focus of my transnational intellectual study. Despite this restricted group of actors, I have sought to present intellectual history alongside social and political history, to show the world of ideas not merely as abstract discourse but also as lived experience—indeed, often entangled with emotionality and affective bonds—and as constitutive of the world of possibilities in which historical agents acted.

Among the methodological goals of this book is to provide and employ a framework for interpreting the Philippine Revolution alternative to that of the nation (as it has traditionally been treated in Philippine studies), alongside my historiographical goal of returning the Philippines the region of Southeast Asia. Though any deep analysis of this history cannot avoid the national frame, given the revolution's role as the instantiation of the modern Philippine nation, this book's particular lines of inquiry both exceed and subtend the nation-state and the nation, as is discussed further below. This book de-centers the nation-state by attending to the larger, transnational historical backdrop of radical nationalism and anti-colonialism in the Philippines and elsewhere in Southeast Asia, while also laying out what was a more dualistic concept of state and of inter-nation. It, thus, offers the Philippine Revolution as relevant for wider study, using it as a lens to understand an international picture of anti-colonial, nationalist thought germane to the ongoing study of the rise of the nation-state as a twentieth-century global phenomenon.

This book does not treat anti-colonialism or nationalism as a single or homogeneous discourse. Rather, it aims to tease out anti-colonialism and nationalism's common threads and resonances to see what binds the political thinking and imaginings that this moment of imperialism and crisis engendered across such variegated proto-national planes and to see how those connections are refracted in singular experiences. In its examination, Asian Place, Filipino Nation brings into focus the cosmopolitan moorings of the nation-state and the conceptual groundings of place, and shows the ways in which Filipino nation-making could and often did take place transnationally. Counter to the prevailing historiographical and historical narrative, this book argues that the Filipino nation incorporated into its very foundations a vision and sense of belonging in an imagined Asia.

I turn to Asia not only to bear out the more complex world that existed beyond the bilateral accounts of history, which feature the West in engagement with individual Asian countries and dominate the historiography of Asia in the nineteenth and twentieth centuries. While the modern nation-state was a Western invention, it was often globalized through the work of non-Western activists, thinkers, and revolutionaries. The histories of the

colonized polities to follow in this book show more complex, dualistic internationalist formal experimentation that was born of a period in which
mainstream Social Darwinism seemingly arrayed the world into separate
camps, making forms of global federalism seem both necessary and expe-
dient in Asia, while *also* still articulating the nation-state as the locus of
rightful political sovereignty, which saw Asian thinkers and activists seeking to ground anti-colonial political legitimacy in supposedly inalienable
understandings of place and nation. The history of the rise of the nation-
state as *the* legitimate modern political form falls outside the specific scope
of this book but must nevertheless be acknowledged as the background
to the history under question. The rise of the modern nation-state was
contingent and not at all foreordained, as experimentation with federated
Pan-Asian union here shows,[103] yet while this anti-teleological position of
contingency and lost possibilities works in individual cases, in aggregate the
twentieth century does indeed show a global convergence on the nation-
state, as Samuel Moyn has argued.[104] Perhaps the nascent Philippine (and
Vietnamese) national projects therefore should not be over-interpreted
beyond their exceptional and (Asian) normative import. Yet, what we
have here is a curious in-between state when, due to globally prevailing
Social Darwinist frameworks and material inequality as well as subversive anti-colonial potential embedded within Western Enlightenment rhetoric, both transnational racial solidarity in a federated union *and* national
self-determination were deemed necessary and, indeed, existentially intertwined. Given that the distinct appeal of pan-movements and racialized
mobilizations/politics endured deep into the twentieth century, perhaps
the specific logics of these particular dualistic, internationalist forms in the
"periphery" of Asia will be illuminating for scholars of the nation-state, in
general, as well.

TWO

Constructing Asia and the Malay Race, 1887–1895

Early Attempts to Transnationalize Pan-Asianism

THE END OF the nineteenth century saw a dramatic reduction in the commercial, intellectual, and religious isolation of Filipinas. The opening of the Suez Canal in 1869, the intensification of international commerce to Filipinas, the brief Republic of Spain from 1873 to 1874, the flourishing of Spanish liberalism (and its product, the 1876 Spanish Constitution), and the institution of local educational and municipal reforms, including the wider teaching of the Spanish language and the increased native facility to enter civil service, all played a role.[1] Inspired by the ideals of the French Revolution, Spanish Republican Carlos María de la Torre, gobernador general de Filipinas from 1869 to 1871, also guaranteed freedom of press and of association, and raised greatly the expectations of the emerging Manileño middle class and native clergy.[2] Yet, the *principalia*—the native elites through whom the Spanish colonizers effected governance at the local level—gained the most from the nineteenth-century reforms. In this period, the majority of the class sought full assimilation of the colony of Filipinas with Spain, so as to achieve for itself full Spanish citizenship, rights, and privileges, in addition to a status superior to that of the local Chinese.[3] The nonrevolutionary, nonideological nature of the principalia's political aspirations was apparent. The economic developments of the mid to late nineteenth century caused a new mestizo class to ascend, however, and the Propaganda Movement that would follow represented a transition from the principalia's aristocratic, colonial, and elitist position to the mestizo, ilustrado economic class's more national role. While the ilustrados who led the Propaganda Movement were members of the larger class of educated elite and still held a reformist, assimilationist objective, their political position differed from that associated with the principalia specifically and would construct the foundations upon which the Philippine Revolution later emerged.

The Propaganda Movement, which began in 1875 and ended in 1895, grew out of a loose set of independent critiques of the Philippine colonial condition by various ilustrados, notably the Visayan physician Graciano López Jaena's 1874 *Fray Botod*, a satire of the "frailocracía" on the islands marred by lusty, abusive, indifferent, and avaricious friars.[4] It circulated throughout Iloilo and followed directly on the heels of the Cavite Incident of 1872, an unsuccessful mutiny of soldiers at Fort San Felipe and of the laborers who joined them, resulting in the execution of many of the participants as well as suspected sympathizers. Amid the crackdown, the Spanish found the means to implicate and execute three secular priests, Mariano Gómez, José Burgos, and Jacinto Zamora. It was the shadowy trials of the priests and their executions on February 18, 1872, that the Propaganda Movement leaders uniformly marked as their moment of political disillusionment with Mother Spain. This incident also delineated the end of the brief moment of Spanish liberalism that had visited and influenced the archipelago in the person of Carlos de la Torre. The reactionary regime that succeeded him under Gobernador General Don Rafael Izquierdo, who sought to extirpate the clamor for liberal reform, deeply inflamed and further politicized the ilustrados.[5]

The ilustrados both constructed an emergent, novel Filipino national consciousness and advocated for political reform through their writings and scholarship. Following the publication of *Fray Botod*, Pedro Paterno published *Sampaguitas*, a collection of poetry on love of country, in 1880, and Gregorio Sanciano published *El Progreso de Filipinas* in 1881. Pedro Paterno (1857–1911) was a wealthy Filipino socialite, politician, and lay scholar who lived both in Spain and the Philippines.[6] During 1882–83 a small organization established in Madrid, Círculo Hispano-Filipino, grew to promote the collective action of the Filipino community in Spain, publishing a biweekly newspaper and bringing Filipinos together to discuss domestic affairs.[7] Essays advancing reform, progress, and equality in Cuba, Puerto Rico, and Filipinas increasingly appeared in Spanish publications, while the Filipino ilustrados in Europe sought to demonstrate through their works their intellectual and cultural equality with their colonizers, as well as to critique Spanish colonial rule. A high point to this activity was 1884, when Juan Luna's and Félix Resurrección Hidalgo's paintings earned gold and silver medals in the national Madrid Exposition of Fine Arts. Shortly after, in 1888, Filipino ilustrados in Barcelona headed by Galicano Apacible and Graciano López Jaena founded the association La Solidaridad that, in 1889, with the arrival of their friend Marcelo H. del Pilar, would turn into the mouthpiece of the Propaganda Movement, the fortnightly newspaper *La Solidaridad*.[8] Its proximate political goal was winning Filipino representation in the Spanish Cortes, from which Filipinas had been excluded since 1830. Marcelo H. del Pilar (1850–96), who was also known by his pen name, "Plaridel," was a lawyer, writer, and Freemason who led the Propaganda Movement in Spain. Originally from Bulacan, his strident anti-friar opinion eventually earned him an order of banishment in 1888, at which point he moved to Barcelona where his ideas would develop from promoting reform via writing to considering independence via revolution.

The most important Propaganda Movement publication other than *La Solidaridad* was José Rizal's searing 1887 critique of Spanish colonial rule, *Noli Me Tangere*. The polymath Rizal (1861–96) was of Chinese mestizo descent and an ophthalmologist by profession; he exemplified the late-nineteenth-century rising educated class of Filipinos who were upwardly mobile and had the opportunity to live in Europe, and who thus felt Spanish subjection at home most acutely. He was a central member of the reformist Propaganda Movement, and was eventually executed by the Spanish on December 30, 1896, on the charges of rebellion, sedition, and subversion following the publication of *Noli Me Tangere* and of its sequel, *El Filibusterismo* (1891), and the outbreak in 1896 of the Philippine Revolution that the novels had helped, in part, to inspire.[9]

José Rizal and the other writers of *La Solidaridad* newspaper sought to develop a social consciousness that could build a national community, but found that they lacked sufficient commonality around which to rally. There was no lingua franca on the islands, nor had there ever been. Despite wide, successful Catholicization, the archipelago remained divided ethnolinguistically, with only the provincial elite beginning to travel to Manila and abroad together at the end of the nineteenth century, where they could begin to meet as *Filipinos* and to form national bonds and awareness.

La Solidaridad carved out a national space not through shared cultural practice or shared ideology, but through a grounding in place.

The Changing Grounds of Political Rule in Filipinas

Western imperial ideologies often justified rule of a foreign land by a distant power through the enshrinement of a certain *idea* as the first qualification to rightful sovereignty—the due earthly dominion of one's religion, the civilizing mission, the principles and application of enlightened government, and the technological capacity to till the land and thus assume "true ownership" over it have all variously underwritten imperialism. By contrast, some of imperialism's fiercest refutations rested upon the paramountcy of *place*—indeed, Edmund Burke's internal critique of the British Empire in the late eighteenth century was premised on the legitimate, affective ties of place and group. His understanding of place was both territorial (the significance of a particular physical space, with its history, land, rivers, and monuments) and social (involving origins, distinctions, social position). In his understanding, place gave location to individual and collective identities and related both kinds of identities to one another.[10] In this way, as Uday Singh Mehta argues, for Burke, place was the basis of political society, and formed the ground upon which other political notions, such as duty, freedom, and order, gained meaning.[11] Burke asserted that humans inherit predispositions from their own histories, modulated by time and place, and that that emplotment is what conditions moral action, grounded as it is within the moral, associative landscape in which individual identity, political relations, and political collectivity arise and operate.

Place was the premise to Burke's judgment of the East India Company's rule in India as a perversion of natural forms of political association (for the company had no claim to *place* in India). It also disaggregated political society (individual identification as part of a particular political society) from an exclusive association with individual capacities, such as reason. Now, right to rule could be premised on sentiment, association, and identification, rather than on reason alone. Burke's rhetorical moves sought to reconceive space—employing narrative, description, and familial metaphors—in order to enlarge the ambit of British sympathy. While this framework did also ground the Filipino ilustrados' anti-colonial and nationalist thought, in Burke's hands it did not yet represent a truly sympathetic commiseration with non-European peoples, though it did point to a potential grounding for anti-imperial thought. Burke's critique was a self-critique, further underscored by the complete omission of Indian agency and voices in his appeals. The Indians were replaceable in his thought; indeed, in some ways, empire figured only as a trope in Burke's writings, not as a violent reality.[12] Here, meanwhile, I use "place" to denote a political, affective, nonuniversal, exclusivist plane upon which to ground political affinity. In this usage place is the localized opposite or counterpoint to "universal" Enlightenment ideals, which, while inspiring, often seemed insufficiently specific as foundations for emergent nationalisms. Place provided an entry point for nationalisms constructed in universalist Western grammar to become particularized and specified—even exceptionalized, in certain imaginations.

At the beginning of the nineteenth century, Filipino creoles such as "Conde Filipino" Luis Rodriguez Varela led revolts as part of the transoceanic liberal political convulsions in Spain and Latin America. These self-proclaimed *"hijos del país"* (sons of the nation) laid claim to place as a way of asserting their political difference from the peninsular Spaniards living in and ruling Las Islas Filipinas. Though international in consciousness and led by those self-styled as sons of the nation, these early Creole revolts were ultimately only Manila-based. At the end of the nineteenth century, the Propagandists first highlighted Asia, then specified the Malay race and its historical environment, and finally suggested the particularities of a generalized Philippines that also rested on the prior two geographies. *La Solidaridad* newspaper's poetry eulogized this place's rivers, to which it imputed an automatic knowledge and affinity on the part of the Filipinos, and its theorizations of race attributed unique developments arising from its climate and environment. As subsequent chapters show, the Katipunan in the lead-up to the Philippine Revolution would take this grounding primacy of place a step further, invoking Inang Bayan (Mother Country) in "Pag-ibig sa tinubuang bayan" (Love for one's homeland).[13]

At a speech in honor of Señor Becerra, a liberal Spanish statesman, on December 23, 1890, reprinted in *La Solidaridad*, López Jaena invoked place—geography and the environment—as a language through which to highlight the vulnerability of imported culture. "Remember one thing more, gentlemen," he intoned, "it is now an incontrovertible fact that there was a time when the Philippines formed part of Asia. It was separated to form an Archipelago and therefore will not be reunited again, nor will it disappear, but on its surface great changes frequently occur due to the fact that water, which is filtered across those layers of clay, lime and volcanic soil gets to the spheroidal state and to a temperature higher than that of water vapor." He went on to describe what this heralded: "It acquires tremendous force, seeks the line of least resistance. And destroys and sweeps away everything."[14] This was a warning that without reforms to stabilize foreign civilizational and cultural transformations, a place can and will exert force through its own older natural forms—for that is the "line of least resistance," the one that is natural and foundational. "We Spaniards should therefore remember this. Let us not forget that when people are pressed without giving them a release valve through which they can breathe, if their sentiments acquire great explosive force, then a time may come when, like water seeking the line of least resistance, it will destroy and crush everything completely"—and with this ending he eloquently moved from culture and place to politics and human will, which will seek justice, even by force, if ultimately required.[15] In reprinting this speech, *La Solidaridad*'s writers must have seen hope in López Jaena's recognition that *place* was a natural foundation of political culture.

Unlike the other Filipino newspapers that had preceded it in Europe, *La Solidaridad* was not dominated merely by mestizos but by newly self-identifying *indios* who reclaimed their Malay racial ties. It also billed itself as an international paper, and listed correspondents in Paris, London, Austria, New York, Havana, Hong Kong, Saigon, and Borneo. Among other topics, *La Solidaridad* published works on comparative colonialism and followed the publication of Malay scholarship as deeply salient news for those from Filipinas, drawing an enlarged geography of Filipino identity with the Malays. "The Dutch professor, Mr. Enrique Kern, has just published a very interesting account wherein this reputed Malay linguist, on the basis of a comparative study of 111 Malay dialects, showed that the original home of the Malay race was in the area of Indo-China," the Crónica (News) section from June 15, 1890, reads.[16]

The Philippine archipelago has long been part of the larger Malay world, and it remained so even under the Spanish Crown, as well as a participant in trade with Chinese merchants. From 700 to 1571, the spread of Malayo-Islamic culture across archipelagic Southeast Asia, including the Philippines, was comparable to the contemporaneous expansion of majority ethnicities and dissemination of textual religions among the mainland Burmese, Siamese, and Vietnamese. The establishment of the Spanish colony of Filipinas beginning in 1571 then formed a break, removing the islands from the development pattern of the rest of the region.[17] Yet the lack of sufficient native wealth to lure many Spanish *conquistadores* to live on the islands and to dedicate significant imperial resources to their administration imposed deep limitations on this "hispanization," as John Leddy Phelan's work has shown.[18] An example of this is the fact that at no point over the three centuries of Spanish administration did greater than 5 percent of the local population speak Spanish, in stark contrast to the Spanish colonies in the Americas, which all became fully Spanish-speaking though many were under Spanish administration for far shorter periods than was the Philippines.[19] Meanwhile, though Christianization was widespread and deeply significant, the Filipinos were not merely imprisoned in a hegemonic system of meaning imposed upon them by the Spanish.[20] Rather, as Vicente Rafael's work has noted, the Filipinos had their own understandings of the world and they interpreted and appropriated Christianity through that understanding, giving rise to the uniquely Philippine practice of Catholicism, which incorporated local animist and indigenous practices.

James Francis Warren describes the trading zone of *prahu* (a large native sailing ship) centered in the Sulu Sultanate in Jolo in the Muslim south of the Philippines as part of this larger Malay world until the 1870–1900 Spanish naval campaign decimated all *prahu* shipping in the area.[21] The Sulu sultanate had grown in wealth and power by taking advantage of the European desire to trade with China. Beginning in the late 1870s it provided Britain with Malay sea and jungle products, which the British could trade for Chinese tea. While the "Sulu Zone" expanded and contracted according to the sultan's hold over outlying chiefs, at its peak it included the east coast of Borneo (now parts of Malaysia and Indonesia), as well as the Sulu archipelago and the west and south coasts of Mindanao (in today's Philippines). Yet when did racial consciousness among "Malays" in this area begin, and at what points did this optic operate transnationally?

The Malay term "Melayu" (Malay, or Malaya) appears in the historical record in the fifteenth century during the era of the Sultanate of Melaka (Malacca) from 1400 to 1511, when the sultanate dominated the Straits of Malacca and the Malay language became the trading language of insular

Southeast Asia. Anthony Reid records that the term "Malay" at first referred only to the Malaccan royalty and its subjects (an ethno-political category), but in the seventeenth and eighteenth centuries it gradually came to refer to the many Malay-speaking regions of the Malayan peninsula, Sumatra, and surrounding islands, and thus included various ethnicities, including Chinese.[22] Chinese and European writings mirrored this change. During this period, German pioneer of comparative ethnology Johann Friedrich Blumenbach's 1775 work, *De generis humani varietate*, introduced to the study of man the classification techniques pioneered by Carl Linnaeus and developed by Charles Darwin, paving the way for the development of "race" and "racial science," and featured a division of five races: white Caucasians, yellow Mongoloids, brown Malays, black Ethiopians, and red Americans.[23] Yet, even as the concept of racial divisions began to be developed, the corpus of Western racial thought did not truly acquire a biological sense or hierarchical implications until the nineteenth century, and this timeline is also mirrored outside the West. In the nineteenth century, as thinkers in colonial Malaya interacted with their European counterparts, their vernacular ethnic categories, such as that of "Melayu," began to lose their indigenous meanings, while at the same time acquiring new racial tones.[24] In this period a word for "race" itself also developed. Anthony Milner traces how the word *bangsa*, which once referred to "caste," increasingly began to refer to "race"— moving from usages such as *bangsa syed* (the caste of the Syeds) and *bangsa kechil* (of low birth) to *bangsa India, bangsa Bugis,* and *bangsa Melayu.*[25]

With regard to increasingly expansive imaginings of the Malay community—the transnational imagined community—Islamic reforms in the Malay world during the early twentieth century advocated new forms of global community that were knitted together through religion but that also built open social, political, and commercial networks across the region.[26] Though these early expansive visions lost their compelling force amid the national struggles of colonial Malaya, Joel S. Kahn notes that a transnational Malay world continued to exist in the "diasporic alternatives to Southeast Asian national imaginaries," particularly the re-emergent regional and global Islamic solidarities that have at times destabilized nation-building projects in the Philippines, Indonesia, and Thailand.[27]

As in colonial Malaya, the primary theorizers of national origin in Filipinas—the nineteenth-century ilustrados José Rizal, Pedro Paterno, Trinidad H. Pardo de Tavera, and Isabelo de los Reyes—"'discovered' *Malayness* by way of Europe," as Resil B. Mojares describes.[28] From Ferdinand Magellan's first interaction with the Philippine archipelago in 1521, European explorers conceptualized it as belonging to a larger, though ambiguous, geographic and cultural realm of Malay peoples. Spanish Jesuit missionary Francisco Colin's *Labor Evangélica* (1663) detailed three kinds of people in Las Islas Filipinas: Malayos, Tingues, and Negrillos, listed in order of civilization. The Malayos were "the first class, the civilized peoples" who possessed "command and lordship" in the most coveted areas of the land, while the Negrillos were a "barbarous race" living in the covers of the mountains and forests, and with the Malayos formed the mixed-blood Tingues.[29] In Colin's study, the Malays originated from a district named Malayo in "the mainland of Malacca" in the Malay Peninsula, but had since scattered across the region's archipelagos.[30] Later, Austrian scholar Ferdinand Blumentritt—who was one of Rizal's closest friends and a central member of the ilustrados' Propaganda Movement—would promulgate the "migration waves" theory that so influenced the ilustrados. This theory propounded that the original Negrito settlers of the Philippine archipelago were displaced by two subsequent "Malay" waves of migration. The first wave comprised the ancestors of the Igorots and other "mountain tribes," while the second wave comprised the ancestors of the "civilized Filipinos" such as the Tagalogs and other lowland peoples.[31]

Drawing on such works of European comparativism and the Enlightenment tendency to classify, the ilustrados reclaimed Filipino Malayness at the end of the nineteenth century as part of their process of constructing and imagining the Filipino nation. Trinidad Pardo de Tavera (1857–1925) was a wealthy Filipino physician, scholar, and politician of Spanish and Portuguese descent, and a leading member of Philippine elite society. He and José Rizal both consulted Malay chronicles and Dutch, British, and German linguistic, anthropological, and paleographic studies on the Malays in the British Museum, including the Johore *Makota Radja-radja*. Filipino nationalist writings of the period commonly referred to Filipinos as belonging to the Malay race, and they used evidence found in European scholarship to argue that Filipinos were of "Malay civilization" in their languages, customs, religious beliefs, social institutions, psychology, and cultural practices. Rizal declared himself to be "Malayo-Tagalo,"[32] and his 1890 annotations to *Sucesos de las Islas Filipinas por el Doctor Antonio de Morga* (1609) explored hypotheses of shared racial and civilizational origins for Filipinos with Sumatrans, Polynesians, and even Japanese.[33]

The ilustrados theorizing the Filipino nation apparently thought an association with an older, richer documented civilizational realm (a generalized "Asia") necessary, due to the visible lack of ancient kingdoms and ruins around which Filipinos could assemble their nationalism. T. H. Pardo de Tavera's monograph on the Sanskritic origins of the Tagalog language, *El Sanscrito en la Lengua Tagalog* (1887), aroused great fervor and admiration among the ilustrados, notably Rizal. Asserting Malayness, meanwhile, was a way to counter the argument of Europeans who described the archipelago as overrun by an anarchy of tribes and races. Yet within their reclamation of Malayness, these ilustrados also carved out a very distinct national space on which a more specific enunciation of "place" would rest and through which nationalism could also be put in service of broader Pan-Malay and Pan-Asian goals. During the Philippine Revolution, Baldomero Roxas and Gregorio Aguilera, who were active as part of the revolution in Lipa, Batangas, founded a Republican organ called *Columnas Volantes de la Federación Malaya* (1899–1900) and declared themselves moved by "noble sentiments that cherish the beautiful idea of seeing the Philippines not only independent but progressing at the head and in union with all the peoples of *Malasia*."[34] In this we see the constituent national entities serving the shared goals of the larger transnational collective in the same way that Japanese thinkers had theorized Japan to do for the broader Pan-Asian collective. Yet, how did the ilustrados theorize the Filipinos' connection with the Japanese?

Of "Family" and "Neighbor"—Japanese Futures and Chinese Foils

Writing from Paris on May 30, 1888, four years after he won a gold medal at the Madrid Exposition of the Fine Arts—proving to the world that Filipinos could produce art on par with that of their colonizers—Juan Luna wrote to fellow reformist and member of the Propaganda Movement, José Rizal, "My dear friend Rizal: . . . Tell me what happened to you in our country, for you said nothing about it in the card which I received from Hong Kong. . . . Tell me also about your travel impressions, especially about your stay in Japan whose people is so attractive to me."[35] "I am an enthusiastic admirer of their painting and I think that it is as advanced as that of Greece and Italy," he went on. "We should study more that country whom we resemble so much."[36]

Luna was not alone in his admiration of Japan nor in his desire to see racial resemblance between the Filipinos and Japanese. While in Japan,[37] Rizal noted that he was taken for a Japanese man.[38] Further, in his contribution to *Trubner's Record* in July 1889, Rizal compared the Tagalog and Japanese versions of the fable of the tortoise and the monkey and suggested a possible Malay origin for the Japanese people.[39] Rizal wrote to Blumentritt on March 4, 1888, of his admiration for Japan's order and cleanliness and for the trustworthy and industrious Japanese, among whom crime was rare. He differentiated them from other Asians, notably the Chinese, writing: "What a difference between them and the religious and superstitious Chinese!"[40] While in Japan he formed a romantic relationship with a young woman, Osei-san, who taught him to paint in the Japanese style, took him on tours through the relics in Japan's museums and libraries, and guided him around Tokyo and its surroundings.[41] He lamented to Blumentritt: "If I could stay here a couple of years, I would study all [these aspects of Japanese culture and society] and I could do it with more facility than a European because I look like a Japanese, and here, like in the Philippines, they do not have much trust in the European."[42] Yet, in the pages of *La Solidaridad*, Japan appeared less a kindred "Malay" relative to the Filipinos than an alternative historical possibility—one imagined possible precisely through this resemblance that Luna and Rizal asserted. This resemblance we can assume to be geographical, for the Japanese were largely unlike the Filipinos except through their common location in an Asia beset by Western imperialism and through a geographic construction of an "Asian" race.

This tentative expansion of Filipino affinities of place and belonging to include Japan was a progressive move that stands out when it appears, unlike the common and unproblematic use of the inclusive "we" in *La Solidaridad* when relating the struggles of fellow Spanish colony Cuba and their impact.[43] Meanwhile, in a March 15, 1889, article, the example of Japan appears as a thing apart from the track and history of Filipinas, as well as from much of the rest of the world. Recounting Japan's parliamentary and constitutional "revolutions" achieved "by peaceful and quiet means," the article concluded that, "Such conduct of the Japanese Emperor in relation to his people who are under his power and charge had never been registered in the annals of history of nations. God wants this example of Japan imitated by the old dynasties of this old World for the prosperity and welfare of their peoples."[44] Japan appears here as a counterexample, rather than a relative, and, more hopefully, as a future model, imbued as it is with apparent moral (because divine) right.

The ethnic Chinese commercial minority in Filipinas, on the other hand, was a target of prejudice in the pages of *La Solidaridad*. There are repeated references in the paper to differences between the Malay Filipinos and their Sinic neighbors in Asia—particularly regarding "Sinic vice." For example, a staff article from November 30, 1890, reported on Chinese quackery and sneakiness, while describing the Chinese as a people apart from the Filipino indios.[45] This distancing may have also been leveled at times, however, as a political tool. Alongside descriptions of Chinese foreignness, deception, and depredation in the colony sat the paper's public confirmation that "the Philippines is a Chinese overseas colony with a Spanish flag."[46] Published in the context of an article refuting the anti-Filipino slurs of a Spanish writer,[47] this confirmation seems meant to provoke the Spanish to make good on the assimilative and civilizational promises of their colonialism, rather than merely leaving their subjects to languish amid Sinic vice.

Rizal asserted that the Spanish government itself recognized racial similarity and affinity not only between the Filipinos and other Malays, but also with the Japanese. In his famous article "Sobre la indolencia de los Filipinos," published serially from July to September 1890 in *La Solidaridad*, he wrote: "Fearing to have the Filipinos deal frequently with other individuals of their own race, who were free and independent, as the Borneans, the Siamese, the Cambodians, and the Japanese, people who in their customs and feelings differ greatly from the Chinese, the Government acted toward these others with great mistrust and great severity . . . until they finally ceased to come to the country."[48] In this interpretation, the Chinese stand apart from the rest of Asia, while the Japanese purportedly stand with Southeast Asians and Filipinos racially and culturally (even though the Japanese were integrated members of the Sinic world). The inclusion of the Japanese but not the Chinese on these terms seems a difficult paradox to reconcile, except through the Propagandists' desire to aggrandize their own race by claiming the Japanese as among their own while holding a status superior to the Chinese immigrants in their midst, in the same manner as the Spanish did. Given that many among the rising ilustrado class of the late nineteenth century were *themselves* Chinese mestizos by descent, the active disassociation from newer Chinese immigrants shows the workings of the national construction of place and identity over generations.

The issue of place, apparently, was also important in assessing potential imperial rivals. Spanish writer and Ministro de Ultramar Segismundo Moret y Prendergast warned in the July 31, 1895, article "Japan and the Philippines": "It is good to point out that all Philippine governors general and its most intelligent authorities have always been occupied with Japan," in particular, "they have seen elements in its race of an emigration that, contrary to what is found in the Chinese race, is tied to the soil; that forms families; incorporates itself to the territory; and, in the different combinations that could be foreseen before the revelation that its vitality made Japan an important ally or a powerful enemy."[49] Nevertheless, in this reading, Japan may have posed a menacing threat, because, unlike Edmund Burke's pronouncement against foreign rule, Japanese émigrés were able to acquire attachments of place in a new land, in a manner that might even have been racial. Thus the specter of Japan and of a future "Asia for the Asians" might have seemed insidiously present, even through immigration. This distinction between Japanese and Chinese is ironic, given the ethnic Chinese population's ability to adapt to a territory to the degree that the Chinese-descended mestizo ilustrados were consciously disavowing Chinese identities for their new Filipino ones.

Grounding the Philippine Nation—Constructions of Asia and Civilization

The Propagandists inscribed the new Filipino nation they were seeking to construct within a more ancient Asian landscape, imbued with civilizational importance recognizable even to the Europeans. Doing so worked to confer a separate existence on the Philippines apart from that of Spain. Indeed, it was a political act to locate Filipinas within Asia, because the asserted inalienability of place described the archipelago not only as separate and autonomous from Spain historically, but also currently. The Propagandists sought to recover their Tagalog language, a member of the Malayo-Polynesian linguistic family, as a marker of autonomy and identity.[50] Yet, even the use of written Tagalog as they knew it inscribed Filipinas within—not apart from—the

Spanish Empire, for it was Catholic missionaries who had systematized the Filipino dialects into the Roman alphabet. The Propagandists thus developed a Tagalog orthography. Rizal wrote of it excitedly to Mariano Ponce on August 18, 1888, as "perfectly in accord with the ancient writing and with the Sanskrit origin of many Tagalog words as I have found out through my research in the British Museum."[51] This act of recovery not only effected a symbolic separation from Spain but also restored Tagalog to its precolonial Asian world.

Not all of the ilustrados employed such precolonial Asian influences for decolonizing purposes. Pedro A. Paterno's *La Antigua Civilización Tagalog* (1887) was an inventive, "flamboyant" (as Resil B. Mojares aptly describes it) scholarly project that bid for ancient Philippine grandeur. One of the wealthiest men from Filipinas at the time, Paterno lived between Spain and the archipelago, and was equally comfortable and celebrated in both places. He would go on to intercede voluntarily on the side of the Spanish in the Philippine Revolution, brokering the Pact of Biak-na-Bato with Emilio Aguinaldo on December 14, 1897. Later, under Aguinaldo, he would be elected president of the First Philippine Republic's Malolos Congress in September 1898 and served as its prime minister in the middle of 1899 before the Americans captured him in April 1900. Nevertheless, he would later advocate for incorporation of the Philippines into the United States. This history of identification with the elite, even the foreign colonizing elite, helps contextualize his project to recover what he called the "ancient Tagalog civilization" and to compare it to the world's "high" civilizations using a European cultural scientific methodology, which included comparative taxonomies, evolutionary schema, and copious citations.[52] His explicit aim was to win the recognition of Mother Spain for the Tagalogs (notably not the Filipinos more broadly) as equals.

While the evidence base of his scholarship was specious and its findings dismissible, what is important to note in Paterno's work was his recovery of Tagalog civilization within a narrative of *historia universal*—in a unified evolutionary arc that placed an ancient Tagalog civilization next to the Hindu, Muslim, and Euro-Christian civilizations.[53] Ultimately, as Mojares rightly concludes, "While he pointed to the persistence of elements of this ancient civilization, . . . he effectively relegated it to the status of the exotic and forgotten, representing it in the static form of an ethnological treatise instead of the dynamic form of a historical narrative."[54] This stands in distinction to Isabelo de los Reyes's and *La Solidaridad*'s respective projects, which were confrontational toward Eurocentric scholarly methodologies even as they appropriated them, as the rest of this chapter shows. Paterno was more interested in historical world order than in the continuing power of place.

In comparison, Vietnamese scholar-gentry leader and Pan-Asianist Phan Bội Châu subscribed to a linear evolution of civilization, citing Western ethnologists' theories of human societies first progressing from animals to barbarians through a civilizing process.[55] This represented a departure from the Confucian assertion of a golden age set in the past, which society should strive to recreate. Châu asserted that Vietnam had entered this linear civilizing process only a few years before and might reach a "great epoch" in several decades, just as Japan had reached a zenith of civilization forty years after the Meiji Restoration.[56] This is a far simpler theorization of historicized civilization than that proposed by Filipino thinkers and revolutionaries, perhaps due to the greater theoretical "burden" that would fall on the Filipinos in order to argue for their inclusion in the history of civilization and progress, as this chapter will show.

Despite their disparate motivating priorities, however, all the Propagandists who sought to recover Filipinas's origins and to awaken the Filipinos' national and historical consciousness located the Filipino nation, firstly, within Asia. "A plant I am, that scarcely grown, / Was torn from out its Eastern bed, / Where all around perfume is shed, / And life but as a dream is known"—these are the opening lines of Rizal's poem "Me Piden Versos," written in Madrid for his mother in 1882. Though Filipinas had barely known its own surroundings and taken root, having "scarcely grown," it was located firmly within the cradle of the East—its "Eastern bed." Moreover, there was something seemingly destined and easy to the image of natural development rooted at home in Asia. As with the line of least resistance, the work to uproot Filipinas from its Eastern bed was unnatural. The bed of perfume and dreams presented itself as not only more natural, but also Edenic. In Marcelo H. del Pilar's interpretation in his 1888 *La Soberanía Monacal en Filipinas*, Asia, like the global-historical world writ large, appeared as constructed through the interactions of sovereign-national powers. To wit, Filipinas emerges and registers within that landscape through the geopolitical and historical desires of the great powers that made that world.[57] Meanwhile, in *La Solidaridad*, Asia largely appeared as constructed through the history of civilization, and was noted for its heights of achievement—albeit in a defensive tone perhaps related to del Pilar's interpretation of the global-historical world, drawn by the dominant hands of power and geopolitics. This construction of Asia is similar to that which appeared in the pages of the Japanese Pan-Asian society Kōakai's publication *Kōakai hōkoku*, except that in Kaneko Yahei's "General Discourse on Asia," the Japanese interpretation was more daring in its depreciation of Europe's early benighted state and the historical role of Asia in civilizing Europe.[58]

An important feature in the Propagandists' construction of Asia through the history of civilization was the premise that there is something like universal civilization, and that it merely passed from one incarnation to another, from East to West and back again. This ephemeral, unitary concept of civilization formed the mechanism by which the civilizational construction of Asia reconciled itself with the history of the rise and fall of great powers and the current state of material inequality between East and West. Rizal discussed this civilizational tenet in his May 15, 1889 article in *La Solidaridad*, writing: "Religion, civilization, science, laws, and customs came therefore from Egypt, but in travelling along the pleasant shores of the Elaides, they were shorn of their mystic robes and they put on the simple and charming clothes of the sons of Greece." "Science and civilization had been until then the patrimony of the Orient," he underscored, "but following the natural course of the stars, it directed its step to the Occident, and when it got to the heart of the world, it tarried as if to draw all nations and races together."[59] From here he spoke explicitly of the uses of travel and of learning from others, while implicitly working to reassert the East's place in the history of high civilization. These are precisely the theoretical premises and moves that would later characterize Japanese-sponsored World War II president José P. Laurel's historical and political thinking, and that grounded his Pan-Asianism.[60]

From this starting point of universal civilization then flowed *La Solidaridad*'s political work of presenting the historical achievements of the Filipinos as on par with that of other Asian civilizations. The poem "Las mujeres de Oriente" by Rafael Ginard de la Rosa, published in *La Solidaridad* on August 15, 1893, traversed the landscapes of Egypt, Arabian deserts, temples of Iran, and the "blue cataracts of the Nile," saw the "maidens of the Ganges," the women of Borneo with their "sparkling heat of passion," and Turkish concubines, but concluded that "of all these foreign roses . . . in none of them can I find more beauty than in the roses of the Philippines, women on whose lips the word of others is a song."[61] In one deft move, the poem thereby succeeded in associating the Philippines with all these evocative scenes and histories of the Orient, claiming them for itself through association, while besting them in natural endowment. Another article chided that the well-known vases of antiquity, which had so impressed sixteenth-century Spanish colonial officers, were made by the natives, and not by the Chinese or Japanese, as had been assumed.[62] Meanwhile, an article on August 31, 1891, celebrated the formal technique displayed in Filipino artist Vicente Francisco's sculpture entitled *Hauling Water*, and boasted of his scholastic triumphs in the Academy of San Fernando and of his prizes in drawing and sculpture won in Europe.[63] While in the former artistic example the sixteenth-century Filipinos' artistic production passed for Chinese and Japanese, in the nineteenth century it passed for European.

The future (and present) Filipino project, however, was not only to master civilization's achievements, but to craft a Filipino aesthetic on par with and yet distinct from that of the others—something native that they could claim, as the Chinese and Japanese could, in the face of the Europeans who lorded over them culturally. *La Solidaridad* advanced this task on Francisco, "a futuristic artist, one who feels and understands what is native," and who "could, by forgetting the old formulas of exaggerated classicism, form a Filipino art distinct like those of the Chinese and the Japanese which are well-known in Europe."[64] "The key" to this, the article concluded, "is the study of the natural," with which we return again to the primacy of place.[65] Indeed, it was only through the line of least resistance that something uniquely Filipino—something true and distinguishing—could issue.

Grounding the Philippine Nation—Constructions
of Place and Indio History

Place is a social construction in the sense of its use to root identity. In this construction it organizes what otherwise could be collectively incoherent registers of cultural practices and histories, refracting (and eventually attracting) them around single sites and allowing the site itself to form the skeleton that lends narrative or collective coherence, even if only imagined. It thus requires active participation in its continual making and remaking, as well as acceptance, which in its process then doubly works to construct collectivities—both formally and substantively. In this sense, it is not only the decidedly nonuniversal plane upon which to ground political identity and from which to derive political legitimacy, but also the constructed space able both to house and to generate an atemporal, generalized, and unified narrative of national history. The poem "Los cantos del Pasig" by Rafael Ginard de la Rosa, published in *La Solidaridad* on October 15, 1893, uses the river of the Pasig in a Tagalog-speaking region to help ground Filipino place—stirring Filipino feeling and indeed constructing it through a shared reference seemingly bereft of class and division, upon which could rest the kind of collective, leveling premise required for an emergent nationalism. "Son of the Pasig, your brown face / dreams peacefully of this shady woods / in the simple house of your love."[66] Filipino nationalism here, which is related to place and to the natural, subtly introduces race ("your brown face"), which the ilustrados understood as related to adaptive evolution and attuned to one's particular environment and climate. Such a particularized evolution only makes place that much more natural and important, embedded as it is in one's historical racial development. By the Pasig, "the anxieties of real life pass away and / before me opens the smiling world / of the floating spirits in the crowns / of the tropical forest." Within this scene of belonging, the simplicity and effortlessness of connection to one's home, to one's place, to "the waves of this river / to which you belong and are equal with" is fully manifest.[67] Yet, despite *La Solidaridad*'s best efforts, the Pasig River was not yet metonymic and unable to substitute for the nationalism or nation it was meant to symbolize, particularly at this point when regional and ethnolinguistic divisions would have painted the reference as decidedly Tagalog and urban, rather than Filipino.

Such conflicts of ethnicity and language that remained unresolved in the Propagandists' attempts to construct generalized, unified enunciations of place highlight nationalism's temporal strategies, more generally, for national unity. Constructing an atemporal nation that could be anachronistically read back in time also involved an orientation toward the future, which allowed for the elision of ethnic, racial, linguistic, socioeconomic, and other conflicts in the present. Christopher Hill has identified atemporality, futurism, and a "national" calamity mentality as among the characteristic traits (and problems) of the narrativization of the nation. Within this framework, anti-colonial nationalism's crisis of sovereignty and its need for revolution can be seen as an exemplar of calamity. Combining an exigent national sovereignty crisis with an atemporal construction of the nation (which can idealize a lost imagined past) allows that nation to stay the conflicts of the present in favor of an orientation to the future through the assertion that national problems will be fully resolved at some later point, provided proper action (often involving unity and submission to elite direction or vision) is taken in the present.[68]

Isabelo de los Reyes's scholarship highlights the ways in which the "Filipino" nation, in de los Reyes's use of the word, was not yet coherent, whole, or in any way held in common among its purported members. De los Reyes's *El Folk-Lore Filipino* (1887) attempted to locate the nation, to tie it to its place(s), and to give it content and form. Originally from Ilocos, de los Reyes is the founder of Philippine folkloric studies. He was a Filipino scholar who would go on to become a politician, labor activist, and original founder of the independent Filipino Protestant church, the Aglipayan Church.[69] There were multiple scales to the politics of place then underway, and while de los Reyes sought to foreground "Filipino," he was simultaneously charged as overly attending to Ilocano customs. His methodology of place-making was the opposite of Rizal's. While Rizal began with place as his premise and then cast around for histories, traits, ties, and common sentiment to root that place, de los Reyes began with custom and culture, and used its manifold forms as his instrument to then see something like place that was created in its process. Drawing inspiration from the Enlightenment's scholarly projects to classify and describe, de los Reyes sought to record the varied customs of the Filipinos in all their superstitions and habits—the "primitiveness" of which embarrassed his fellow ilustrados at *La Solidaridad*, who felt he was only exposing their people to European ridicule. De los Reyes was one of the first to declare what he was, and to ask why others should be ashamed of what they were—"Indios think it is shocking and shameful to write *El Folklore Filipino* because, they say, this is to publicize our own simplicity. I am an indio and an Ilocano—why should I not say it?"[70] To buttress his argument he drew on the long history of folklore and local tradition in Europe. For its part, *El Folk-lore Filipino* won the silver medal in the 1887 Philippine Exposition in Madrid.[71]

Despite the oft written-about influence that the French Revolution and Spanish liberalism had on him, Rizal also felt he had to resurrect native traditions and bind racial ancestry in order to construct the Filipino nation.[72] Rizal sought to make indios aware of their historical and racial ties so that they could surmount individual, sectarian, class, and ethnic interests to develop a community coherent and distinct from others—a nation. Rizal annotated *Sucesos de las Islas Filipinas* (1609), a history by Antonio de Morga, teniente gobernador de Filipinas from 1595 to 1603, in order to issue rebuttals, commentary, and clarification to Morga's presentation of Filipino history.[73] Ultimately, Rizal instrumentalized and discarded Morga's work to further his own thesis that Spanish colonization slowed, rather than introduced, Philippine civilization. This was his avowed aim despite writing in Spanish and working with a Spanish text, which the majority of his countrymen would not be able to read. This underscores how conditioned Rizal's nationalism was by European methodologies—how his own practice relied on appropriation and "subversion" of European methodology and ideology. Unlike *La Solidaridad*, however, Rizal's annotations did not seek to answer the racist anti-indio tracts of European writers such as Quioquiap, the pseudonym of Pablo Feced, who was a prolific journalist and brother of the ex-governor José Feced y Temprado. "I do not write for the Spaniards in Manila," Rizal explained to Blumentritt, "I write for my countrymen and we all detest Quioquiap."[74] His objective, rather, was to advance a Filipinized interpretation of the archipelago's history with explicitly nationalist objectives, the language in which he was working—and the class dimension it involved—notwithstanding. Rizal's annotations to Morga's history, then, represent a progression from *La Solidaridad*, which sought to lift the Filipino in the eyes of the *Spanish* from whom they sought reforms as well as in the eyes of the Filipino whom they sought to form.

Published in 1890, Rizal's annotations argued that Philippine civilization three hundred years into Spanish colonization was no better off than it had been prior, and could have developed independently into something far greater. Rizal chided in one annotation, "This [point refers to] an Indio who already would know how to smelt cannons even before the arrival of the Spanish. . . . in this difficult branch of metallurgy, as in others, the current Filipino or the new Indios have fallen behind."[75] He argued that the islands had their own culture before 1521 and did not require salvation from barbarism or a new religion. He emphasized the precolonial existence of advanced metallurgy (with fire cannons made by an indio called Panday Pira in Pampanga), ship building, Chinese trade, indigenous literature, and a system of writing—all of which were purportedly ruined by the Spanish and, in the case of literature, apprehended as the works of the devil.[76] This form of patriotism drew criticism from fellow Propagandist de los Reyes, who argued in his *Historia de Ilocos* (1890) that this purportedly "lost" civilization Rizal discussed remained present in its true character, preserved in the people's present customs.[77] This contrast underscores the implicit ranking of civilizations and belief in Enlightenment-era understandings of progress that guided Rizal's work, and what was either a need for ancient, buried achievements in order to justify his vision of the Filipino nation or in order to mobilize adherents to his style of nationalism.

While Rizal's historical reading in *Sucesos* is questionable and somewhat exaggerated, it is important that, as John N. Schumacher also notes, Rizal "wrote as a Filipino and an Asian, and he worked intensely to read once more through Asian eyes the accounts that had come from European pens."[78] Indeed, this is precisely how twentieth-century nationalists would "read against the grain" of the colonizers' archives and form their respective nationalisms; what differentiates this early Philippine case from that of the twentieth century's decolonized nations is that Rizal sought proof of a "long history" for the Tagalogs. He claimed that Ibn Battuta's *Tawalisi* and Chao-Ju-kua's *Mayi* refer to Filipinas, and that Ptolemy's *Geographia* indicates the Philippine islands of Mindanao, Leyte, and Cebu as well as of those of Celebes, Java, and Borneo. Rizal imagined locations in sixteenth-century Mercator maps and ambiguous references in the writings of Marco Polo, among others, as references to Filipinas.[79] In this long history, Rizal also excavated Filipinas's older regional ties, bringing to the fore commonalities in the region. In his annotations to chapter 5 of *Sucesos*, Rizal asks his readers to observe that China, Japan, and Cambodia maintained relations with Filipinas, and points out a certain sea vessel used by a mandarin in Cambodia that the Philippines was still using then.[80] Aside from the Malayan racial origins of the Filipinos and the shared ancient Sumatran traditions, Asian piracy and trade within the region feature in his annotations to chapters 7 and 8, and join Filipinas to a larger, regional history of interaction.

The contrast between the differing nationalist tools of Rizal's reclamation of a long indio history of cultural achievement and de los Reyes's study of autochthonous culture echoes certain Enlightenment-era debates on the significance of culture. Within these debates in Europe, the acknowledgment of "culture" as a marker of human agency provided one foundation for the emergence of anti-imperial thought. Sankar Muthu argues that the question of support for European imperialism as an instrument of progress or of oppression turned on an interpretation of cultural agency.[81] He explains that the noble savage characterized by Jean-Jacques Rousseau and Michel de Montaigne during the high Renaissance period usefully served to critique the excesses and artificiality of Europe, but it dehumanized the Amerindians in their extreme exoticism and deprived them of what would have made them recognizably human to Europeans—culture. Without cultural agency these noble savages become anonymized and undifferentiated. In Montaigne's interpretation, the motivating agent in their societies was instinct and a seemingly automatic observance of natural law, which ultimately denied these savages rationality and choice. Muthu argues that the rise of anti-imperialism in Enlightenment thought required a rejection of noble savagery and insistence that all humans were cultural beings, the establishment of which opened the possibility for true empathic commiseration with non-Europeans.

It was upon recognition of peoples' adaptation of this agency to their environments that Enlightenment thought could begin to acknowledge all peoples' humanity and all peoples' cultures—rather than merely denigrate their failure to "reach" up to Europe's culture along a unilinear path of progress. This was decidedly de los Reyes's position, counter to Rizal's tacit fixation on civilizational hierarchy and cultural achievement. But del Pilar took the idea of humanity further, and, in a sense, turned back on the idea of culture as the marker of humanity. The Enlightenment's theoretical move away from enshrining noble savagery (or those without culture) toward recognizing all people's human agency through culture was reversed in his October 31, 1891, *La Solidaridad* article "Cultura?," which sought to shift the discussion from culture to rights. The article responded to the centralist position of the Republican Party—"the only one among those of democracy (monarchist and republican) who has continued to evade the rights of the Philippines"— to finally accede to the Philippines's right to representation, but to limit it to "areas whose culture allows it."[82] The Republican Party's interpretation of culture implied a capacity not only to implicitly rank various cultures but also judge them for fitness to combine with other higher cultures along this ranking. Culture therefore was not just bare human agency but, after conceding agency and humanity to all peoples, was also the marker of human capacity along the history of progress—exactly what the *imperial* Enlightenment thinking propounded. In his response, del Pilar sought to separate culture (which now had inherent rank attached to it) from humanity, thereby undoing the work that the anti-imperial Enlightenment thinking had done. Basing his argument on the application of universal suffrage in Spain—even to Catalans who did not speak Spanish and to the 81 percent of Spaniards who could not read and write—del Pilar wrote: "We see no reason whatsoever to tie up the cultural state of a people to the rights inherent to their personality."[83] For, "wherever a person exists, his right to life exists, wherever a legitimate organized people exists, the law exists. With or without culture entering into the consideration of the nation to which it belongs."[84] If culture is not required as a qualification to pay tax or to die in defense of the flag, he wrote, "culture should not be made a requisite to carry on social life to which they have a right."[85] In his argument, it was neither culture nor place that accorded political rights. Instead, his understanding reflected the subject position and grievances of the colonized: that wherever a state or an organization of peoples into a society exists, the law of that state or organized society must apply universally. The law must be agnostic to individualized judgments of culture or fitness, if one is to speak of rights. If a man exists, he has a right to life, and if an organized society is present, all men are part of it (just as they are subject to it) in equal measure.

For del Pilar, this was not only an argument leveled at the Spanish but also at his fellow ilustrados, who were themselves guilty of such implicit cultural ranking and denial of rights. This was the basis for del Pilar's defense of the "Igorots of Bontoc" and other non-Christian tribal groups in Filipinas, who received at best inconsistent support from the ilustrados. "Culture is incidental to the right of representation, just as it is incidental to the personality of a society," he declared.[86] He based this argument not just on humanity but also on the danger inherent in enshrining excessive vagueness into the application of such an important right. This was a procedural defense. The judgment of culture "offers a wide field for crooked applications," he warned; and del Pilar sought to guard against the dangers of foreign or despotic rule through an even, guaranteed application of rule—through procedure.[87] Indeed, Rizal did not refer in his annotated *Sucesos* to non-Christians in Filipinas as "Filipinos" in the same collective manner that he did the Hispanicized peoples of Luzon and the Visayas. He claimed to desire to awaken racial pride among "their" (the Filipinos') race, but failed to include the indigenous animists, non-Christian Chinese, and Muslims in this grouping.

Of Hierarchies, Race, and Malayness

The question of hierarchy is bound up with the question of race, for the concept of race was thought to imply an immutability or biological/genetic basis to a human hierarchy.[88] *La Solidaridad* published several articles that worked to expose the subjectivity of hierarchy, demonstrating examples in which one's perspective dictated the criteria employed to rank. If one began with the idea of the Western white male as the most civilized, then one would array the criteria to judge all races such that the Western white male a priori ranked as the most civilized. The paper also sought to show the way in which rigid ranking and categories of race obscured actual diversity of behavior. The article in *La Solidaridad*, "Tattooing and the Superior Race," for example, traced the various European traditions in Serbia, Bosnia, Herzegovina, Croatia, Slavonia, and Dalmatia, where Serbian Catholics and Greek Orthodox Christians were among those who employed tattoo traditions with religious meanings.[89] This meant to show those who denigrated the Filipinos' civilization that "the Europeans, the anthropoid gods, superior beings with boundless intelligence, include a nation with a general custom (favored by the Franciscan friars of Bosnia and Herzegovina) that is found only among savage tribes in the Philippines."[90]

The ilustrados believed that race had crucially shaped the hierarchical colonial model to which they were subjected and, in turn, race also shaped their interpretation of their history under Spanish colonialism. In their reading, the Spanish treatment of the indios (the prohibition of native expression, development, and flourishing) is what worked to condition and produce the indios' behavior, which behavior was then deemed to mark the Filipinos as racially inferior in the eyes of the Spanish. "You cannot blame the native—the Filipino—for what you yourselves have done. Do not Javanese people belong to the same race as the Filipinos?" *La Solidaridad* asked, referring to the comparatively greater achievement of the Javanese peoples under their Protestant Dutch colonizers. Then, "Do Catholicism and Spanish civilization cause degeneration of the Filipinos?" the paper challenged.[91] In this way, while arguing against rigid, biological hierarchy, the ilustrados ostensibly believed in ephemeral but objective manifestations of superiority and inferiority, as seen in the cultural difference between Dutch and Spanish and what this difference was able to achieve in their respective colonies. Similarly, in terms of anthropological racial superiority, the ilustrados proclaimed the question beyond need of further debunking, citing the examples of manifestations of superiority in races previously deemed inferior, and vice versa.[92] While del Pilar claimed this to be grounds to excuse the entire theory of racial ranking, which was no more than "biased accusations of indolence," it actually further underscored his belief in objective differences of superiority and inferiority and in an ostensible hierarchy.[93]

The ilustrados employed race as a category and treated races as real, but they argued for an understanding of race through multilinear evolutionism rather than deterministic, orthogenetic Darwinism. (Orthogenesis is the obsolete hypothesis that organisms have an innate tendency to evolve in a unilinear fashion due to an internal mechanism/"driving force.") This despite the fact that their use of racial categories had its own hierarchizing logic and involved responses to Western practices of ranking that only served to legitimize the framework of that hierarchizing. The Propagandists employed the semiotics and findings of science to draw explicit contrast to the subjectivity of the purportedly politicized, self-interested, unscientific position of the Spanish friars who asserted the indios' racial inferiority. This was an appropriation of the methodology of the racial supremacists who equally arrayed the semiotics of science to legitimize their position. In this work, however, the Propagandists (and later the revolutionaries) understood the instability of the racial categories they applied, and their discussions of race in their political projects ranged from the expansive to the exclusive.

Rizal described the way in which Spanish colonialism consciously worked to turn the Filipino into a beast of burden, a "race without mind or heart," in his most famous article in *La Solidaridad*, "Filipinas dentro de cien años," published serially from September 1889 to January 1890. For this reason, Rizal undertook to reawaken the Filipinos, who "forgot their writings, their songs, their poetry, their laws, in order to learn by heart other doctrines, which they did not understand, other ethics, other tastes, different from those inspired in their race by their climate and their way of thinking."[94] His mention of climate and consonant ways of thinking carve into race a certain natural and concrete reality—race was not merely a social construction; it was also inalienable from location and place.

This understanding reaffirmed the ilustrados' multilinear evolutionism, which imagined each race and peoples developing separately in ways consonant with their particular environment. As the Malays evolved in response to their climate, multilinear evolutionism had transformed what would otherwise be a leveling effect (one would expect the workings of heat upon all people, of all races, living in Filipinas to be the same) into a racial attribute. In his "Seamos Justos" published in *La Solidaridad*, Rizal writes that "in the Philippines the effects of the climate create havoc on passions and a state of anemia, owing to the heat producing a disequilibrium manifested in a nervous irritability"; this is what has caused the "common characteristic observed in the Malay race, sometimes provoked by hunger, heat, etc.," of "the *amok* or blind passion of the moment."[95] Rizal's scientistic explanation here is notable. Trained as a doctor, Rizal couched his arguments in the language of science to appropriate its semiotics, thereby hopefully removing his understanding of race from the merely subjective, political realm.

The ilustrados, and the Propagandists with a particular fervor, categorized the Filipinos as definitively Malay in terms of race. Yet, what was the content of their construction of the Malay race? How did they define and conceive it as apart from other races? "In the anthropological sense, [what] we mean by the term 'Malay,'" Blumentritt wrote in his article "Notes on the Meaning of the Word 'Malay'" in *La Solidaridad*, is "the population of the large part of the African island of Madagascar, the Malaccan Peninsula, the Dutch East Indies, the Philippine Islands, the eastern part of Formosa, and the thousands of islands and islets which are designated as Micronesia, Polynesia, and New Zealand."[96] This anthropological and linguistic definition covers what European and ilustrado scholars understood as the larger "Malayo-Polynesian race," but scholars also then further distinguished between the eastern and western Malays. Eastern Malays were Polynesians, including the Micronesians and Maoris in New Zealand. Western Malays lived east of the Palaus and Carolinas, and were the group with whom the Propaganda Movement identified.[97] In the ethnographic and ethnological definitions, the tribes of the western branch of the Malayo-Polynesian race, who were understood to include the "Javans, Sudanes, etc., including Tagalogs, Pampangos, Bicolanos, Ilocanos, Visayans, Cagayanes, Tagbanuas and Zambals of the Philippines (perhaps also including the Tinguians)," are termed "Malay" to distinguish them from "the tall tribes of Indonesians, etc., including the majority of the non-Christian Filipinos."[98] The article went on to cite "modern studies" that purportedly hypothesized not only a religious distinction from non-Christian Filipinos but a codified racial separation as well. Nevertheless, exactly what it meant to be Malay is only suggested (through broad historical interaction, shared language family and attributes, and adaptation to particular climate), rather than positively classified.

La Solidaridad reinforced the Filipino connection to the larger Malay world throughout its issues, casually reporting new "Malay" publications and studies as part of Filipinas's assumed sphere of interest and concern. As mentioned earlier, the "Crónica" of June 15, 1890, reported on the findings of a Dutch professor regarding 111 Malay dialects and alerted readers to its forthcoming translation into Spanish. The eulogy piece for "G. A. Wilken" upon the death of the Dutch scholar similarly brought this connection home.[99] *La Solidaridad*, and in particular Mariano Ponce, also hotly challenged the charge that the inhabitants of Filipinas were not Malay. Ponce (1863–1918) was a Filipino physician, writer, Propagandist, and founding member of *La Solidaridad*. He would go on to serve as the Philippine Revolution's emissary to Japan and was the revolution's leading Asianist voice. He is discussed in detail in chapter 4 of this book. He would go on to represent Bulacan in the Philippine National Assembly during the American colonial period. Ponce dedicated an article, "Pag-diwata Barrantes" (To God-like Barrantes) to the Spanish writer Vicente Barrantes, writing: "His excellency has the nerve to say that the Malay element is not exclusive, not even preponderant in the Philippines. To what race then do the Filipinos belong?"[100] Writing indignantly, Ponce continued, "All ethnographers of the world will be grateful to His Excellency if he were to surprise us with the news that the natives (with the exception of the Negritoes) do not belong to the Malay race. And not only the scholars would be grateful, but even the children of the primary schools of Austria and Germany because they know from their teachers."[101] This fiery article and the deep offense taken at Barrantes's assertion reveal just how much the ilustrados' civilizational and racial pride depended upon their identification with the Malays. This underscores not only the instability of these racial constructions but also their perceived importance to the sense of nationalism that the ilustrados were constructing, in which global hierarchies and international perceptions of civilizational achievement were deeply implicated. The easy disavowal here of the "Negritoes," which was the blanket term of the time for the tribal, animist, indigenous peoples of Filipinas, also evidences the implicit workings of an internalized sense of hierarchy. The Negritoes were either a liability to the ilustrados' quest to win political and civilizational recognition for the Filipinos or an easy instrument by which to shore up their own racial superiority and to step up from the lowliness of their current state—a way to say to Europe: nuance your denigration of Filipinos, for your stereotypes may fit "them" but not "us."

Facing Spanish persecution, Rizal spent a week in 1892 traveling through Sandakan, Borneo (in Malaya), to seek a land grant from the British government to establish a Filipino colony there at home among racial brothers.[102] Prior to that, while still in Europe, Rizal's Paris-based organization Indios Bravos agreed on a secret agenda of liberating first the Philippines, then Borneo, Indonesia, and Malaya.[103] From 1889 to 1890 Rizal published a history of the "Malayan Filipinos" and their encounter with the Spanish explorer Miguel López de Legazpi in "Filipinas dentro de cien años." "The Philippine races, like all the Malays, do not succumb before the foreigner, like the Australians, the Polynesians and the Indians of the New World," Rizal wrote, drawing the Philippines into a global geography of the colonized and their survival in the face of extermination.[104] "In spite of the numerous wars the Filipinos have had to carry on, in spite of the epidemics that have periodically visited them, their number has trebled, as has that of the Malays of Java and the Moluccas," he recorded.[105] According to Rizal, part of the advantage of being among the colonized was that "the Filipino embraces civilization and lives and thrives in every clime, in contact with every people."[106] Adapting to a different race's civilization, acknowledging the word of God in Christianity, and now traveling abroad to establish and publish papers such as *La Solidaridad*, Rizal saw in the Filipinos' subject position the ability to recognize civilization and to negotiate with and thrive in the world of the foreign. To the ilustrados, this adaptive ability strengthened the Filipinos' potential within an interpretive frame of multilinear evolutionism, an evolutionary trait that the white Europeans supposedly did not have in the same store.

Similarly, rather than a determinism of climate, one sees in Rizal's article "Sobre la indolencia de los Filipinos" a primacy placed on human adaptation. "A man can live in any climate, if he will only adapt himself to its requirements and conditions," he wrote. "What kills the European in hot countries is the abuse of liquors, the attempt to live according to the nature of his own country under another sky and another sun."[107] As with race, there was nothing inherent to the tropics that produced a certain kind of laborer or a certain kind of indolence. Rather, the key lay in the human constructions built within and adapted to a certain history and environment, and, at least to Rizal, in a manner of thinking unique to one's race that was the sum of all such constructions and environmental factors. Following the ilustrados' reading of Darwin, there were no stable, fixed disadvantages. Indeed, Rizal wrote: "Before the arrival of the Europeans, the Malayan Filipinos carried on an active trade, not only among themselves but also with all the neighboring countries," and he noted a thirteenth-century Chinese manuscript's mention of the Filipinos' activity and honesty in this commercial trade.[108] These "Malayan Filipinos" then, who had also participated in political contests with Siam and Sumatra, were not inherently marked by indolence, as their Spanish critics charged, but in the right political arrangements were given to commercial activity, and were fair and honest.

These acts to claim Malayness hierarchized the peoples in the same ways that the European sources (from which the ilustrados derived their genealogical, anthropological, and historical evidence) did.[109] In claiming Malayness, the Malayo-Tagalogs doubly distanced themselves from the pagan tribal peoples in their midst by emphasizing associations with both Malayan civilization and with Christianity. Among the notable exceptions to this was de los Reyes, who attacked such divisions using the lines of argumentation leveled against the Spanish by his fellow Propagandists. De los Reyes asserted that differences between peoples resulted from history and environment and that they were not innate; he polemically posed that just as there were Tagalogs recognized as equal intellectually to Europeans, so there were tribal Aetas surpassing Tagalogs in intelligence.[110] This was an act of dehierarchizing and rejection of global rank that most of the ilustrados could not yet stomach, given the implicit hierarchical logic underpinning their political project in *La Solidaridad*: to show they were equal to Spaniards intellectually and had the basis for a nation that could stand its ground racially, civilizationally, and historically as part of Asia, while also bearing the fruits of Spanish Catholicism and of mastery of European learning and arts. Indeed, how could they prove these qualifications without recourse to European systems of ranking and without reinforcing existing structures of hierarchy, for instance, against the Negritoes?

The secret of nationalism, as Ernest Gellner theorizes in *Nations and Nationalism*, is that one of the elite, high cultures pervades and defines the whole of society.[111] According to Victor Lieberman's description in *Strange Parallels*, this elite culture spreads horizontally—marking its borders—and intensifies vertically, deepening its penetration across class and group within those borders.[112] The ruling clerisy and members of literate high culture use their textual cultural technology to codify, to disseminate, and then to police the culture and nationalism they establish. Leaving aside the necessary relationship between industrialization and nationalism that Gellner asserts and his staged, self-contained understanding of economic development, this is the process one sees here consciously taking place in the publication of *La Solidaridad* and in the collaboration of Filipinas's native educated elite in their shared project, the Propaganda Movement. As the Spanish missionaries had done, the ilustrados began to take into their hands the enunciation and definition of their nation, largely blotting out the folk "little traditions" and the non-Christian and tribal minorities from their official nation-making. Separately, their emplotment of place within their constructions of the Filipino nation served an anti-imperial purpose. Emphasizing *place* rejected the imperial primacy of *idea* as first qualification to rule. In so doing, it successfully embedded "Asia" and the ideas that could be mobilized around "Asia"—the Malay race, unitary human civilization, and even the power of an ascendant Japan—into the very foundations of what was then becoming Filipino nationalism.

Courting Pan-Asianism

An 1894 *La Solidaridad* article on the diplomatic negotiations between Spain and Japan argued for the benefits of allowing Japanese immigration to Filipinas; yet it also warned that, counter to the Spanish fear of Japanese invasion of the archipelago, "what Spain should fear"—and "it is important to take very good note of this" the article counseled—"is the redemptorist policy of that Asian empire."[113] For "if it were possible to live a free life in the Philippines as it is lived in Hongkong, Singapore, Japan and other countries surrounding it," and Filipinos had direct contact with such models, the article asked, why wouldn't they seek to implement them?[114] In face of these dangers of the supposed Japanese redemptorist policy and annexation threat, *La Solidaridad* urged the Spanish government instead to "renew the relationship between the Philippines and the Spanish Parliament."[115] Indeed, this was *La Solidaridad*'s proximate, primary goal—to secure Philippine representation in the Spanish Cortes.

Coverage of the Sino-Japanese War (1894–1895) and the advance of the Japanese nation constituted nearly the entirety of *La Solidaridad*'s 1894–1895 issues. This was an instance of a non-Western, inter-imperial rivalry, yet it had a galvanizing effect that refigured Japan in the anti-colonial imagination, as chapter 3 of this book shows. Granted, at this point *La Solidaridad* had found itself perpetually short of funding and staff, which undoubtedly affected its ability to treat a wide range of topics; nevertheless, how deeply the war consumed the paper is significant. Over 1893–95, *La Solidaridad*'s articles consistently goaded the Spanish about having fallen behind Japan and Turkey militarily, while at the same time admiringly reporting on topics such as Yamato, Japanese ancient and modern history, Japanese contemporary politics, and the constitution and management of Japanese councils of ministers, memories of the Japanese empire, and the performance of Japanese colonial ministers in Korea.[116]

The Sino-Japanese War had stirred the Filipino nationalists' imagination. The dream of acquiring Japanese aid, imitating the successful Japanese model, and entering into the Pan-Asian orbit, which was then gaining traction among intellectuals, greatly expanded their perceived political possibilities. An article by del Pilar titled "Human Interest and Patriotic Interest," published on December 31, 1894, illustrated the great virility of the nation of Japan, which he said was ready to burst forward at any point, and meticulously cataloged its achievements and historical progress.[117] Echoing the observations of a particular Spaniard, Mr. Moret, del Pilar concluded: "Filipino Malays are opening their eyes before a spectacle that is edifying for them"—that "their racial brothers in Japan are becoming a great power capable of presiding over the destinies of the Far East."[118] Though this perhaps only continued *La Solidaridad*'s established tactic of using race and the specter of Japan to scare Spain into ceding Filipinas its desired reforms, there were already at that time Filipinos soliciting Japan to preside over Filipinas's destiny.

José Ramos was a member of the Philippine organization La Propaganda and its later incarnation, the Junta de Compromisarios, which worked to fund the Propaganda Movement, and through these networks he had been working to secure Japanese aid for the movement even prior to the conclusion of the Sino-Japanese War. After receiving a tip that the Spanish authorities were preparing to seize him as a leader of the Propaganda Movement, he fled to Japan, arriving there in August 1895.[119] He sought refuge in Yokohama in the house of Ishikawa Yasu, whom he later married and whose surname he eventually adopted upon becoming a naturalized Japanese citizen.[120] From there, Ramos endeavored to secure Japanese aid for his compatriots and dreamt of one day leading a group of Japanese immigrants to march on Manila. Ramos attempted to buy Japan's surplus rifles at the end of the Sino-Japanese War, which, for Ramos, would have been a particularly symbolic purchase, signifying as it did a rising, awakening power in Asia.

Greater numbers of Propagandists fled to neighboring Asian cities as the Spanish authorities cracked down on the Propaganda Movement, seeking to arrest its members operating in the archipelago.[121] Doroteo Cortés, a member of the Junta de Compromisarios, arrived in Kobe with twenty-three family members and a retinue of domestic help. The chiefs of police of every prefecture that the Cortés party visited watched, recorded, and reported all of the family's movements.[122] The Japanese police reported that Cortés was in contact with a former Japanese soldier, Yamada Kōtarō, who had visited Manila claiming to be a lieutenant colonel on "a secret mission to reform Manila," and that Cortés saw Ôi Kentarô, a leader in Japan's Freedom and People's Rights Movement (Jiyū Minken Undō), whom he had met in Singapore.[123] Cortés reportedly solicited Ôi Kentarô's assistance delivering to the Japanese authorities a request to turn Manila into a Japanese protectorate.[124]

The Propagandists did not believe that Japan necessarily had to threaten or to alienate Europe in order to achieve its due hegemony in Asia. "Given the practical aspect that seems to shine forth in both its internal and external policies that its own prosperity, which redounds to its own benefit, depends on good relations and harmony, the idea of *America for the Americans* has no place in Japan's policies to transform it into *Asia for the Asians*," del Pilar explained.[125] "In the same way that European hegemony does not need to position itself against the rest of the world to maintain its dominance in Europe, the Asian hegemony of Japan can sustain itself without alienating *all* the European powers."[126] There seems here to be a statement of fact, of naturalness, of the inability to alienate the Asian from Asia in such a way that made the dominance of Japan, now that the nation had modernized, into an inevitability. It was the line of least resistance for Asia to accommodate an Asian dominance, which even the presence of other superior foreign powers could not displace. There was seemingly something natural to place, to race, and, thus, to Asianness that would leave room for native leadership. Indeed, the Spanish, too, often noted the "inevitable sympathy" between Japan and Filipinas on these grounds.[127]

"The Japanese are Malay and the Filipino inhabitants are Malay," *La Solidaridad* proudly, if inexplicably, declared; and "Those who have closely studied the Malay race and its ancient civilization cannot cast aside the qualities of nobility and virility that characterize the Malay."[128] This racial connection also raised the question of the natural solidarity—and perhaps alliance—that would obtain between countries. Discussing the Spanish Mr. Moret's speech, the same article reported that he "did not dare propose the problem of the possibility of a Malay league between the Japanese and the Filipinos. However, he did indicate the probability that Japan would take over and since Formosa is just a step away from the Philippines, the problem was presented in other ways."[129] What of this potential for a Malay league? Indeed, the Propagandists were deeply eager to claim the rise of Japan as their own, within their particularly racialized worldview. "The Malays are representative of the new power whose appearance in [the Asian] hemisphere is compared by Mr. Moret to the appearance of a new sun capable of awakening the vitality and energy of the Malay race," the paper claimed.[130] This was, *La Solidaridad* took pains to note, "the same Malay race that constitutes the nucleus of the population in the Philippine islands."[131]

What was the reaction and perspective of the Japanese with whom the Filipinos sought association? The 1868 Meiji Restoration and concomitant period of reforms had dismantled the Tokugawa shogunate and much of the country's prevailing political-economic system—abolishing the *han* system of "feudal" domains for a centralized, unitary, bureaucratic state; reforming the tax system to stabilize the national budget; promulgating a constitution and creating a modern bureaucracy; and leveling old forms of official class privileges toward creating a modern citizenry—alongside other social and industrializing changes. Japan was a rapidly rising country and had reopened full channels of foreign commerce, thereby ending the *sakoku* (locked country) policy restrictions on Japanese travel, foreign trade, and foreign relations that had lasted from shogun Tokugawa Iemitsu's edicts in 1633–1639 to American Commodore Matthew Perry's forced opening of Japan to Western trade in 1853–1854. Yet, in the 1880s Japan was still testing itself upon the world stage. It would not be until 1899 that Japan was in a position to begin revising the terms of the unequal foreign treaties it had signed with the Western imperial powers, which had symbolically designated Japan as a second-class state in the international order.

Spain and Japan's Nineteenth-Century
Relations in the Pacific

It took twenty years to regularize relations between Spain and Japan following the Meiji Restoration, with negotiations and exploratory activities leading to the opening of a Japanese Consulate in Manila in 1888; the establishment of reciprocal direct (though irregular) shipping lines between Japan and Manila;[132] the opening of a branch of the Imperial Insurance Company in Manila; and an overall increase in the low-level trade between Filipinas and Japan. This trade was small, however, and on November 26, 1893, the Japanese closed the Manila Consulate and transferred its duties to the Hong Kong Consulate for three years.[133] Nevertheless, 1889–1898 saw a significant increase in Japan-Philippines trade, due to Japanese purchase of Philippine products. As Josefa Saniel records, "the total trade between the two countries increased at a rapid pace from 251,114 yen in 1889 to 3,409,616 yen in 1898. The yearly imports from the Philippines advanced from 227,486 yen in 1889 to 3,294,183 yen in 1898." Yet, despite the increase, "from 1889 to 1898, Japan's trade with the Philippines, except in 1894, remained less than 1% of Japan's total trade for each of the calendar years included."[134]

As early as the 1880s and 1890s, some Japanese nationalists advocated territorial expansion to the Philippines as a solution to their country's geopolitical and domestic problems. Those whose gaze fixed so far south were outliers, however, even among those advocating an "all Asian consciousness," most of whom largely worked in Korea and China. By 1891 Japan had successfully laid claim to various island groups with the consent of the Western Treaty Powers, including the Bonin Islands (Ogasawarajima), the Ryūkyūs, the Kurile Islands (Chishima), and the Volcano Islands (Iwojima). While these islands were annexed under the domestic administration of Japan, without inaugurating a colonial framework of governance, this territorial expansion brought Japan physically and politically closer to the prospect of overseas colonial acquisition.[135] Indeed, the 1891 annexation of the Volcano Islands caused a momentary stir in Madrid, followed in February 1892 by the arrival of Japanese warships in Manila.[136]

Japanese activities in the early 1890s in the Spanish Pacific island holdings of the Marianas and Carolinas caused similar anxiety, and Japan's occupation of Formosa (Taiwan) following victory in the Sino-Japanese War appeared threatening to the Spanish. This was particularly perceived due to the publication of Japanese opinions in favor of expansion to Filipinas as well as Japanese attention to the challenges Spanish rule was then encountering in its Pacific colonies.[137] Fukumoto Makoto (writing under the name Fukumoto Nichinan) published articles in *Nippon* on the 1890 uprisings in the Carolinas and the retaliatory Spanish military expeditions, and on native uprisings unreported in the *Official Gazette* and other Manila newspapers, such as those in Jolo in 1890 and in Morong, Manila, and Bulacan, as well as an attack on a Franciscan church by the Pasig River in 1891.[138] A Spanish translation of Fukumoto Nichinan's article on Japan and the Southern Seas ("Nihon to nanyō") reached the Spanish Legation in Japan in May 1890; it urged the Japanese government to prevent Filipinas from falling under the possession of a powerful empire such as Germany, to the danger of Japan's southern border, and it assumed Spanish military weakness as a fact.[139] There is a growing body of scholarship on Japanese writings on the Philippines in this period,[140] often highlighting the dimension of fantasy and imagination involved in Japanese territorial expansion as well as in Pan-Asianism, which resonates more broadly with the literature on the role of ideology, particularly Pan-Asianism, in Japanese empire building.[141] Political novelist, Pan-Asianist, and later a member of the first House of Representatives of the Japanese Diet, Suehiro Tetchō, who famously met José Rizal aboard the SS *Belgic* in 1888 but had never been to the Philippines, wrote a work that has been studied extensively, *Nanyō no Daiharan* (Storm over the South Seas). It was written in 1891, before the Philippine Revolution and before the Sino-Japanese War, and actively constructed concepts of independence and revolution alongside three other works of his that drew a picture of oppressed islands in revolt against the West.[142] Bimyō Yamada translated portions of Rizal's *Noli Me Tangere* into Japanese, published as *Chino no Namida* (Bloody tears) in 1903, and published *Aguinaldo*, a novel on the Philippine Revolution, in 1902. Shunrō Oshikawa published *Bukyō no Nihon* (Japanese chivalry) and *Shin Nihontō* (New Japanese islands) in 1902 and 1906, respectively, which were adventure stories aimed at young Japanese boys, imagining a courageous Japanese samurai named Kentōji Danbara fighting alongside General Emilio Aguinaldo against Spain and the United States.[143] Hiromu

Shimizu analyzes the ways in which discourses on Japanese expansion to the South Seas drew on phenomena such as Japanese migration to the Philippines and Filipino-Japanese intermarriage to "solve contradictions between the Filipinos' and Japanese's interests" by imaginatively bridging imperial territorial expansion and independence through fictive kinship ties.[144]

Asian solidarity mobilized affect, in addition to fantasy, toward the creation of networks willing to lend material aid toward revolution and reform, overcoming cultural distance and sometimes even traditional class gulfs to subsume such divides affectively within a larger racial romance. The Japanese Pan-Asianist activist Miyazaki Tōten,[145] who dedicated his life to advancing China's revolutionary, republican movement as a means of reviving all of Asia and to embodying and realizing the ideal of Pan-Asianism, described meeting several hundred Chinese laborers in 1895 soon after the conclusion of the Sino-Japanese War. They were "so-called coolies, people who are despised as though they were birds or animals," he explained, who "seemed so filthy even the farmers of our party didn't want to get very close to them," and yet he could "not help loving them." "I regarded them as Chinese people on whom I was basing my life. . . . Since I felt no hostility toward them, were they not my friends?" he asked. Moreover, he commented, "How quickly they took to me! How honest their speech!"[146] Once the Chinese laborers discovered that Miyazaki was Japanese, one man "explained about the treaty of peace" ending the recent war between their countries "and quietly urged the [other] coolies not to take offense," he recounted. "And this was spoken by a coolie who some would despise as a bird or animal." "Thanks to them," Miyazaki concluded, "I felt no hardships during the long eight-days' journey that took us to Siam."[147] In this way, affect was pivotal to the humanization of Pan-Asia and personal extension of geographies of political affinity. This was true in the center of the discourse in Japan and China, among men such as Miyazaki, Sun Yat-sen, and disgruntled former samurai in need of a purpose, as well as in the periphery, where engagement with the center fell outside historical Sinic world interactions and easily facilitated language crossings, instead resting on fantasy.

Japan's victory in the Sino-Japanese War drew the West's attention to the balance of power in Asia. The Spanish press played up the "Japanese phantom," with dramatic editorial comments predicting "a beautiful future of simultaneous war in Cuba, [and] the Philippines" to the effect that "the government of the restoration may write on the ruins of the Spanish nation the historic epitaph, *Finis Hispanae.*"[148] In the wake of the Sino-Japanese War, Spain took precaution to conclude a treaty locating the territorial boundaries between the Japanese and Spanish territories in the Pacific, construct naval facilities in Subic Bay in Zambales, and increase the military forces and number of Spanish cruisers in the colony.[149] In the late nineteenth century, the perceptions formed in the West were what mattered for Japan's international stature and goals. "Progress for Japan required distancing Japan from Asia," Marius B. Jansen argues in *China in the Tokugawa World.*[150] Yet, there were Japanese activists and thinkers who advocated cooperation and solidarity with the country's Asian neighbors, especially focusing on Korea in the 1880s.

Ôi Kentarô, of the Jiyū Minken Undō, organized an abortive expedition to Korea in 1885 to stir up activism for reforms there, hoping that success would advance the progress of democracy in Japan.[151] Feminist educator and author Fukuda Hideko was among the roughly 130 radical leftists who participated and were arrested on their way to incite rebellion in Korea in what came to be known as the Osaka Incident. This was not the only effort; Tarui Tôkichi, also of the Jiyū Minken Undō, actively collaborated with Korean and Hong Kong revolutionaries to "revive" Asia. Meanwhile, Ôi wrote *Nikkan gappo ron* (Argument on the unification of Korea and Japan), advocating union with Korea as the best measure to stabilize East Asia and to resist Western imperial encroachments.[152] Together Ôi and Tarui formed the Toyo Jiyu-to (East Asian Liberal Party) in 1892. For their part, Korean reformists quickly picked up Pan-Asianism in the early 1880s, and it became a popular mode of thought there.[153] Kim Ok-kyun (1851–1894) was a leader in Korea's radical reformism and is known to have submitted to King Kojong a tract in 1882 entitled "A Proposal of Raising Asia" ("Hŭngach'aek"), written following a trip to Japan during which he met with Japanese and Chinese Pan-Asianists.[154] However, tensions surrounding the role of Japan within a supposedly horizontal Pan-Asia as well as more tactical Japanese organizing failures clouded Pan-Asianism's chances in Korea. Even still, idealistic Pan-Asianism would last in pockets of Korea even beyond Japanese imperialism and would transcend it, with thinkers as late as Ch'oe Won-shik, a Korean literary critic born in 1949 and known for his opposition to South Korea's historical authoritarianism, believing that only true Asian solidarity (not the Japanese-led, imperial kind) based in "symmetric" reaction to Western

"Orientalism" could save a divided Korea from subjection to a Western-dominated international system.[155]

The Japanese Pan-Asianist activities of Ôi, Tarui, Fukuda, and their colleagues, however, were considered the province of idealists and the political fringe, and often united radical liberals with ultranationalist conservatives (such as the Gen'yōsha group) in a complex logic that served transnational messianism and muscular Japanist expansionism at once.[156] "They lived on the borderline of political and social respectability," Jansen writes of the Japanese Pan-Asianists who aided the causes of men such as Sun Yat-sen and the Filipino revolutionaries, and this is what allowed their activities to pass fairly unnoticed, even as they called upon more established Japanese politicians, such as Inukai Tsuyoshi, for financial support for their activities.[157] There was a personal, emotional element to this, as well. Jansen recorded: "Their intrigue, at home and abroad, provided an ideal emotional outlet for former samurai disturbed by the rapidity of the transition from the self-importance of Tokugawa days to the restless boredom of industrialization and westernization."[158]

The program of humanitarian social and economic reforms alongside tutelage that Ôi Kentarô and his "radical liberal" followers advocated in Korea provided the blueprint for later, similar programs focused on the Philippines and Sun Yat-sen's China.[159] They also pushed in Korea radical reforms that had been blocked in Japan, reasoning that success in Korea would have political implications for Japan, as progress elsewhere in Asia would discredit Japan's claim to leadership, thereby forcing the Tokyo government's hand.[160] These included labor reforms, limitations on wealth, which was deemed deleterious to national unity, and a widening of the franchise to create larger constituencies including share croppers, city artisans, and the unemployed—all aimed toward building stronger national unity and privileging equality over individual rights and private property.[161] Ôi sought to anticipate and solve the problems of Western modernity by avoiding the ills inextricable from unfettered capitalism.[162] Unable to find wide bases of support within Japanese society, however, the radical liberal groups became prone to adventurism, which, as Jansen has diagnosed, both discredited them and brought them closer to the ultranationalists on the other side of the spectrum, which in turn had consequences for the evolution of Ôi and Miyazaki's strain of liberalism.[163] Both the ultranationalists and radical liberals had a troubling preoccupation with national unity, and depreciated individual rights to this end. Nevertheless, Ôi's discussion of freeing the rest of Asia from "bureaucratic feudalism" and spreading Japanese-style modernization toward social and national emancipation aligned with the reasoning and goals of Korean, Filipino, Vietnamese, and Chinese revolutionaries. However, even Fukuzawa Yukichi, the famous advocate of Western learning who tried to influence reforms in Korea and supported Korean reformers, eventually gave up. "After pro-Japanese groups failed in their attempt to take over the direction of government policy in Seoul in 1884, and as the French victory in Indo-China pointed to the further increase of European power in Asia, Fukuzawa turned his back on the idea of providing aid and comfort to reform forces in Asia," Jansen records.[164] Fukuzawa wrote in March 1885 that Japan should "leave Asia" ("Datsu-A Ron")—though only temporarily.[165]

Yet, the failure to widely transnationalize Pan-Asianism to Korea is a more complex matter, given the fraught and multivalent relationship between the two countries. While earlier adventurism and war plans in Korea around the 1870s were self-centered instruments among the Japanese samurai class to humiliate the new Meiji government, which disgruntled, regional former samurai in places such as Fukuoka opposed, as well as to restore the samurai class's martial values, class purpose, and government share, the later 1880s Pan-Asianist idealism very easily shaded into more dictatorial, aggressive forms. The Kokkentō (National Power Group), for example, held that Korean decadence and corruption was so advanced in Korea and China that *compulsory* "guidance" rather than Ôi's more benign tutelage was necessary.[166] Ultimately, ideological confusion as well as the government's withdrawal of official financial assistance in the form of loans doomed both the liberals' programs as well as larger Japanese Pan-Asianist prospects in Korea.

Tokyo's hopes for inclusion in the Euro-American world order from the Meiji reform period onward may have helped reaffirm mainstream Sinic Pan-Asianists' adherence to a more limited, Sinocentric mapping of Asia, which conveniently skirted the colonized territories of the European powers to focus only on the traditional Sinic sphere of interest in which Japan had been historically embedded. This held among the mainstream until Japanese commercial and imperial interests progressively extended southward in the lead up to World War II and forced a revision of the definition of Asia in all of Japanese politics more broadly. Before that expansion, however, outside the more radical Meishuron and Teaist strands of Pan-Asianism, there had been relatively little pressure from or collaboration with Southeast Asian Pan-Asianists to force a meaningful interrogation of the operative definition of Asia.

The more inclusive vision of Pan-Asianism ran counter to official Japanese policy throughout the first quarter of the twentieth century, and during this period politicians carefully steered clear from evincing grand, Pan-Asian aspirations before their watchful European counterparts. Nevertheless, various Japanese Pan-Asian associations over 1900–1914 promoted a Greater Asianism (Dai Ajiashugi), regional cooperation, and the forging of direct links with fellow Asians outside East Asia.[167] During this period, the right-wing group Gen'yōsha supported Asian revolutionaries, including Mariano Ponce from the Philippines, Phan Bội Châu from Vietnam, Rash Behari Bose from India, and Abdürreşid İbrahim from Central Asia. In April 1907 Indian students in Tokyo gathered to commemorate a seventeenth-century rebel, Shivaji, who had initiated an uprising against the Mughal emperor, and several Chinese attended the meeting. When in October these Chinese and Indian activists established the Ashū Washinkai (the Asian Friendship Association) in Tokyo, Châu was a founding member. The society intended to draw not only Indians, Chinese, and Japanese as members, but also Vietnamese, Koreans, Siamese, Filipinos, Burmese, and Malaysians.[168] Ashū Washinkai's constitution, written by Chinese scholar and reformist Zhang Binglin, declared that the object of this organization of Asian nations suffering from "the same sickness" was to "oppose imperialism and recover the independence of Asian nations which have lost sovereignty."[169] Yet, the constitution also implicitly recognized the unreliability of the Japanese in this goal, and explicitly barred Asians "in favor of expansionism" from membership "no matter what principle they hold."[170]

Thus, even prior to the Taishō period, certain Japanese and Southeast Asian intellectuals and activists were moving to enlarge the Pan-Asian map. Following his late-nineteenth-century travels across Europe and the United States, Suehiro Tetchō, a celebrated writer and political activist in the Jiyū Minken Undō, was deeply anxious about Japan's prospects in the international world order that the West so powerfully dominated. It was this anxiety that created in him, as in many of his Philippine and Vietnamese nationalist counterparts, fantasies of Asian solidarity. "As early as 1881, he was already calling for a Sino-Japanese alliance as a geopolitical counterweight to Europe," write Caroline S. Hau and Takashi Shiraishi.[171] Importantly, "this alliance—which would not be based on the assumption of a Sinocentric (nor Japan-centric) Asian civilization—was expected to expand in the near future to include such countries as Korea, Annam, Siam, India, and Persia."[172] The East Asian delimitation of "common culture" that had undergirded Japanese Pan-Asianism continued to break down internally in the 1910s as Japan's economic and commercial interests in Southeast Asia advanced.[173] In 1915 Japanese Pan-Asianists established the Association of the Southern Sea (Nanyo Kyokai), which laid the groundwork for the New Greater East Asian Order (Tōa Shinchitsujo) of 1938, which would expand to include Southeast Asia from the Japanese occupation of Indochina in 1940 onward.

Hau and Shiraishi warn against treating Pan-Asianism as merely a set of ideas articulated by certain intellectuals or officials, an approach that renders it as a predominantly Japan- or China-centered phenomenon.[174] Instead, their use of network science methodology interprets Pan-Asianism as a "network formed through intellectual, physical, emotional, virtual, institutional, and even sexual contacts, or some combination thereof," and highlights the role of traveling nationalists, transnational associations, and fantasy.[175] This framing allows for the inclusion of Southeast Asia in the history of a broader Pan-Asianism before the latter became official policy in 1938. Indeed, Pan-Asianism was an interaction between state and society that transcended and yet also mobilized individual states; it responded to, but often also wistfully exceeded, the realpolitik of the region.

A decade following the failure to transnationalize Pan-Asianism to Korea, much had changed. Now Southeast Asian nationalists directly sought Japanese support for their domestic causes and the inclusion of Southeast Asia in a Japanese project of "Asian regeneration." The Philippines represents the first case of successful trasnationalization of Pan-Asianism as an actual movement, and directly compares to the failure in Korea that led to Fukuzawa Yukichi's 1885 editorial advocating that Japan leave Asia. The Asianist politicians, activists, and thinkers that the Filipinos and Vietnamese encountered in Japan differed from their predecessors, even if certain Japanese figures or networks formed a continuous thread from the planned insurrection in Korea in 1885 through to the end of the Philippine Revolution and the Japanese Pan-Asianist support for Sun Yat-sen's revolutionary organizing work in China.[176] The Meiji state had fully established and stabilized itself by the late 1890s and Japan began to experience its first successes in the international sphere, but the Asianist support that the Filipinos and Vietnamese found in Japan came from a loose-knit group of liberally inclined Japanese realists, most often from the political right.[177] Though they talked of oriental morality, common culture, and common cause, these Japanese Asianists still had little to offer their Southeast Asian friends beyond their personal commitment and contacts with other groups.[178] It is these networks that this book now explores.

THREE

The Philippine Revolution Mobilizes Asia, 1892–1898

Spanish Imperial Anxieties, the Vietnamese Đông Du
Movement, and a Coming Race War

"WHO IS NOT reminded of the Philippines in reading these lines?" asked a *La Solidaridad* article after detailing the realities of colonial rule in nearby British Malaya; "solamen est in miseris tenere socios" (it is comforting to have partners in misery), the paper concluded.[1] At the close of the nineteenth century, Filipinos were redrawing their geographies of political affinity along lines of colonial repression. Such shared understanding of colonial suffering worked to amplify the role of Southeast Asia in the Filipinos' geography of political affinity.[2] Conversely, it also enshrined Asian cities where they could enjoy greater political freedom, such as Hong Kong, into their geography of political revolution. Abutting empires in the region created inadvertent safe havens for the colonized of one empire to operate outside the regime of repression found at home, yet remain just next door. Pan-Asianism as a network operated mainly by means of meeting in and movement through major cities. "Just as Trinidad was the asylum of those persecuted by the suspicions of the Spanish regime in continental America," Marcelo H. del Pilar recorded, "Hong Kong has become the haven for the sons of the Philippines."[3] Boasting "freer atmosphere," greater "liberty" and "respect," and "inviolability of the home," "it is only there that [the sons of the Philippines] [found] the peace, tranquility, and respect" they lacked in their country.[4]

From Madrid, José Rizal wrote to José Basa on January 21, 1891, of his new grand plan for himself in Hong Kong—a move that Basa had long been encouraging Rizal to make. "As the Propaganda did not want me to go home" to the Philippines, Rizal explained, "we have conceived here the idea of establishing a school or college in Hong Kong, directed by me, to teach languages, science, and arts, in the style of Jesuit colleges."[5] Mariano Kunanan, a wealthy businessman from Pampanga, had promised to provide the seed money for the school, for which Rizal drew up the regulations and mission. Hong Kong seemed to the Propagandists to be a place of relative freedom— where acquiring education, advancing, and speaking in the languages of the colonizers were not considered inherently suspicious and were done freely. It was this struggle in Filipinas for educational opportunities, particularly for an institute to teach the indios the Spanish language, that Rizal's second novel, *El Filibusterismo* (1891), treated at length. José Rizal was determined to join José Basa in Hong Kong, and repeatedly begged for passage money to join him there following Rizal's ideological split with the Propagandists in Spain.[6] This request would be repeated in his letters several times, with increasing urgency over April and May of 1891[7]—"I am longing to join you now or return soon to Manila. So that I insist on the passage-money."[8]

Rizal had come to believe it useless to agitate for reforms from Europe, for which reason he parted with *La Solidaridad* and the Propaganda Movement. "I believe my retirement is necessary," he wrote to Propagandist Deodato Arellano on May 1, 1891; "My chosen place is either the Philippines, Hong Kong, or Japan, because Europe seems to me a place of exile and I am hereby notifying the Propaganda of my intention so that it may make its decision."[9] Graciano López Jaena agreed that Hong Kong was the best site for Rizal's labors, writing him from Barcelona on October 15, 1891: "In Hong Kong you will find a handful of enthusiastic young men, not yet contaminated by the mean passions that divide us in Europe. I founded for them the *Asociación Filipina*, which is working well. Develop their enthusiasm, guide their ideals along the right path. With your exquisite tact you will get out of them much good for the Philippines."[10] He warned Rizal, though, to "above all prevent Kastilas [Spaniards] and foreigners from joining the Association as members. The members should be pure and genuine Filipinos, so that our lofty purposes may be realized."[11] There was, it therefore seems, a racial assumption to "genuineness," upon which hung the success of their mission to build a Filipino nation. This new phase of Filipino nationalism and anti-colonial agitation would indeed traffic more heavily and explicitly in race, as this chapter shows, though it remained an ambiguous, unstable category in the minds of the ilustrados and revolutionaries who employed it.

When Rizal gave up on the Propaganda Movement and returned to Asia—having decided that the appropriate battlefield was at home—it marked the beginning of a new phase to the anti-colonial struggle. The Propaganda Movement that began in 1875 was ultimately abandoned, and, giving up on the slow work of publishing arguments for reform, Filipinos instead turned to secret societies (José Rizal's short-lived Liga Filipina and its resurrected successor as well as Andrés Bonifacio's Katipunan) and later to violence in the form of the Philippine Revolution. The gobernador general had agents following Rizal for some time, before eventually deporting him to Dapitan in Zamboanga province on the island of Mindanao in July 1892 after finding anti-friar leaflets in his sister's luggage upon their arrival from Hong Kong. Andrés Bonifacio formed the Katipunan that same year.[12]

From Rebellion to Revolution

The resurrected Manila-based 1893 organization La Liga Filipina launched the political career of Apolinario Mabini, and the Katipunan launched the political career of Andrés Bonifacio. Andrés Bonifacio (1863–1897), from Manila, belonged to the urban middle class of the city and was self-taught after the age of fourteen, when he left school to support his siblings. Working in crafts, trade, and business positions, he and his brothers earned a decent living. Bonifacio was a Freemason and would come to be known as the "Father of the Philippine Revolution." Meanwhile, upon the 1896 outbreak of hostilities, the Spanish authorities arrested Apolinario Mabini (1864–1903),[13] a self-taught writer, lawyer, and politician of humble origins (he was the son of an unlettered farmer), but as he was already paralytic due to polio, they considered him harmless. To the contrary, Mabini would go on to become the "brains of the First Philippine Republic," as he would later be known, and, at Emilio Aguinaldo's insistence, eventually joined the government in 1898 as the chief private advisor to the president of the Republic.

La Liga Filipina had guaranteed funds for the continued publication of *La Solidaridad* in Spain by imposing a monthly quota of five pesos on each member, but it wasn't long before collections dwindled.[14] Mabini continued to support the Propaganda Movement and *La Solidaridad* and would set up the Junta de Compromisarios for this purpose when La Liga was dissolved. The Katipunan, a secret society founded by Andrés Bonifacio, first organized in the urban heart of Manila beginning in 1892. The Katipunan then spread to the surrounding eight provinces of Central Luzon,[15] with Cavite province (home of the future First Philippine Republic president, Emilio Aguinaldo) as a stronghold. Emilio Aguinaldo (1869–1964)[16] was a Filipino revolutionary, military leader, and member of the provincial governing elite. After taking over the leadership of the Philippine Revolution, he would go on to lead the Filipino resistance against the Spanish and then the American forces.

Mabini wrote Marcelo H. del Pilar from Manila on August 19, 1895, to inform him that *La Solidaridad* must cease publication and that the theater of relevant action had shifted. Funds from Manila were no longer flowing, because many had come to believe that "the newspaper is useless, since the authorities refused to listen to our clamors for help," Mabini lamented.[17] At this moment of crisis, when reformism had seemingly lost out and violence was rising in Luzon, Mabini consoled his "friend Pilar and Mr. Ponce," writing: "We shall try our best to send you the amount we can collect, just in case you would wish to leave that place [Spain]."[18] "Everyone wants you to go to Japan, where some from here already are," he advised.[19] The Filipino focus had decidedly pivoted back home to Asia, and away from Europe.

At home, revolution had already hovered near the horizon as early as 1893. Despite his nonparticipation, Rizal was an explicit part of the Katipunan's imagined future Philippines and their plan for revolution. The Katipunan revered Rizal and, unbeknownst to him, had even appointed him their honorary president. Not only Rizal but Japan too figured centrally in the Katipunan's plans. An undated letter signed "Primer Relámpago" described the society's plan to charter a boat, sail to Dapitan, free Rizal, and then leave in disguise with Rizal to Japan where he would act as the Katipunan's representative.[20] The letter also declared that "the first thing" the Katipunan must do was to send eight individuals to Japan to study arms and artillery without interruption for a month, so that they could eventually return to the Philippines with their knowledge—and, better yet, bring back with them small arms to be hidden in the mountain of San Mateo.[21] Failing that, they should pay Japanese artillery experts to aid the Philippines in this effort.[22] Then, "When we already have a representative in Japan, with or without Tagalog or Japanese gunboats, we can proceed to choose a commanding general and those who will be the members of our government."[23] Thus it appears that these were the priorities for the Katipunan: acquiring arms, placing a representative in Japan after which they could form their government, securing Japanese aid, and freeing Rizal—seemingly in that order. So what distinguished this new plan from Rizal's own plan for the Philippines?

The difference between rebellion and revolution, as historian Huỳnh Kim Khánh has noted, may be summarized through Albert Camus's statement in *The Rebel* (1961) that a rebel is "a man who says no, but whose refusal does not imply a renunciation."[24] Drawing upon a different example, in Vietnam, prior to Hồ Chí Minh's (or Nguyễn Ái Quốc's) writings and theorization, *cách mệnh* (revolution) meant "to take away the mandate," referring to the *thiên mệnh* concept of the "mandate of heaven." However, Hồ Chí Minh's anti-colonial writings in *Thanh Niên*, the clandestine four-page weekly paper first published in 1925, redefined cách mệnh to mean the Copernican understanding of a transformation of the total political, economic, and social order, involving the destruction of the old regime and construction of something new in its place.[25] Hồ's redefinition therefore revoked the appellation of cách mệnh from such early opposition to the French as the Tax Protest Movement of 1907, the attempt to poison French troops in Hanoi, and the mutiny in Thái Nguyên. These early acts, to Hồ, had been rebellions, but not revolutions. "Reforms are more or less numerous changes brought about in the institutions of a country, changes which may or may not be accompanied by violence," he wrote; however, "Even after the reforms, there would always remain something of the original form." By contrast, "Revolution entirely replaces the old regime with a new one."[26] This distinction that Hồ made between his work and that of the earlier scholar-gentry also bears certain parallels to the mind-set shift that Bonifacio effected in redirecting his efforts from the Propaganda Movement to the Katipunan. The advent of the Philippine Revolution changed the mainstream Filipino vision of politics and political possibility, while redefining the historical acts of defiance and rebellion that had come before it. The Philippine Revolution did not merely look backward to restore the past and redress its wrongs in the present. Indeed, with the assumption of violence, any room for accommodation or hope of inserting the indio into the existing political framework died. Rather, the Philippine Revolution imagined, and briefly built, a new premise for the future. Yet, what then was the relationship between the reform movement and the revolution that followed? Reynaldo Ileto asserts that while the Katipunan did have some ancestry in the Propaganda Movement and its Enlightenment/modernist intellectual foundations, such connections have been overrepresented and overemphasized in the literature.[27] He argues, instead, that the Katipunan's philosophy issued from Philippine society and culture, and drew heavily from the folk millenarian tradition. While recognizing that Ileto's interpretation has served as a needed corrective and has provided a stronger multidimensional understanding to the revolution's history, this book reaffirms the intellectual relationship between the reform movement and the revolution, even as it distinguishes between the two.

This relationship was explicit in many aspects of the Katipunan's rites and intellectual history. According to an 1894 Katipunan document attributed to Bonifacio,[28] during the ritual for the initiation of a Bayani, which elevated a Katipunan member with the rank of soldier (Kawal) to the rank of patriot (Bayani), the "Most Respected President" would ceremonially reflect on the martyrdom of priests Mariano Gómez, José Burgos, and Jacinto Zamora and then trace the political lineage of the Katipunan to the reform movement that preceded it, specifically naming the newspaper *El Eco Filipino*, founded in Madrid in 1871.[29] Additionally, many of the Katipunan's nativist tendencies had also been present in the Propaganda Movement as well as in Rizal and other ilustrados' writings. A prime example was the importance of the new Tagalog orthography, which resurrected precolonial linkages. Rizal and Mariano Ponce were great advocates of this new orthography, just as Emilio Jacinto and Bonifacio were in their own newspaper, *Kalayaan*.[30] Only a few years after the ilustrados began excitedly developing and employing it in 1888, the Katipuneros adopted it, with the new orthography appearing in documents from as early as the Katipunan's founding year in 1892.[31] This question of the Philippine Revolution's nativism and the relationship to the Propaganda Movement, however, is not the primary historiographical corrective of this book.

This book argues that the Philippine Revolution's intellectual history was importantly international in its framework and global in that framework's implications and considerations. Its internationalism obtained, not merely through its intellectual connection to European liberalism but also through its Asianist political thinking and organizing. The globalism of the revolution's framework issued from the regional colonial condition in which it consciously situated itself as well as from the global history and future it theorized. The revolution was fully attuned to the modern colonized world and to "Asia," and, in its attention to this dimension, this book agrees with Jim Richardson, who argues that the Katipuneros perceived their own battle as "part of a wider, transnational war. They cheered the rebels in Cuba, wanted to establish a presence in Hong Kong, and sought aid from Japan."[32] Indeed, Emilio Jacinto, in his April 1896 poem, "Sa Bayang tinubuan," called upon his enslaved compatriots to emulate their brothers in Cuba.[33] An article in the Katipunan organ, Kalayaan, reportedly saluted the Japanese victory in the Sino-Japanese War, and held up Japan to be admired and emulated.[34] While the Katipunan looked back to the Filipinos' precolonial civilization and history, much as the Propagandists had also done, it did not seek to resurrect the native past or indigenous customs. As Richardson points out, in the Katipunan's 1896 code of conduct, the Kartilla, "The Tagalog words that resound loudest beyond doubt, are . . . Liberty (Kalayaan), Equality (lahat ng tao'y magkakapantay), Fraternity (kayong lahat ay magkakapatid), Reason (Katuiran), Progress (Kagalingan), and Enlightenment . . . (Kaliwanagan)."[35] These were hardly the watchwords of a nativist past or folk tradition. Rather, the Katipunan formed an understanding of what a modern, rationalist, and secular government should look like, just as the Propagandists had, and with this vision they looked toward a Philippine future.

The Changing Bases of Revolution—from Foundations of Asia and of Place to Mobilizations of Race and Articulations of the Nation

The Katipunan was forced to launch its revolution prematurely on August 23, 1896, after the Spanish government uncovered its existence.[36] The Philippine Revolution began on this date with the Cry of Balintawak—when the Katipuneros tore up their cédulas personales in defiance of allegiance to Spain. Despite the revolution's premature launch, the Katipunan's organization in Cavite under Emilio Aguinaldo was at that point sufficiently strong that the Katipunan lodges of each town in Cavite easily seized their respective local governments with little opposition.[37] Greater military success, strategy, training, and technique under Aguinaldo quickly won for him a growing leadership position in the revolution. He soon overshadowed Bonifacio, and was elected president of the Revolutionary Government—which was to replace the Katipunan—at the Tejeros Convention held on March 22, 1897. Bonifacio and his brother Procopio were brought to trial on charges of sedition and treason against Aguinaldo's government. Bonifacio was executed in the mountains of Maragondon on May 10, 1897.

The revolution continued under Aguinaldo but began to flounder, until on December 14, 1897, he signed the Pact of Biak-na-Bato with Spain, effecting a truce between the two parties and securing amnesty, indemnity, and exile to Hong Kong for the revolutionaries. Aguinaldo had planned to use the indemnity payment to purchase arms and continue the revolution, and immediately set about doing so while in Hong Kong.[38] There he also became acquainted with the American consuls Rounsenville Wildman and E. Spencer Pratt of Hong Kong and Singapore, respectively; they connected him to Commodore George Dewey, who assured Aguinaldo of American support for Philippine independence. Dewey, Wildman, and Pratt helped arrange Aguinaldo's return to the Philippines on May 19, 1898. He arrived after being sidelined by the United States at the Battle of Manila Bay on May 1, 1898, when the U.S. Navy decisively defeated the Spanish navy. Despite this, Aguinaldo declared Philippine independence under the (hopeful) aegis of the United States on June 12, 1898, and then organized the First Philippine Republic (or the Malolos Government). With the outbreak of the Philippine-American War on February 4, 1899, and the formal declaration of war by the First Philippine Republic against the United States on June 2, 1899, the long Philippine Revolution continued, and entered its final, anti-American phase. Ultimately, as Remigio E. Agpalo describes, "The Philippine Revolution [was] . . . a socio-politico-cultural process," that "underwent three stages—the beginnings in the Bonifacio Phase (1896–1897); its full flowering and fruition in the Aguinaldo Period (1897–1901); and its decline, starting with the capture of Aguinaldo in 1901 and its end with the death of Macario Sakay in 1907."[39] Of this socio-politico-cultural process, this chapter specifically studies the Katipunan's Asianist orientation and strategy, following a brief exploration of Bonifacio and Aguinaldo's differing visions for the revolution with regard to concepts of race and place.

The end of the Propaganda Movement and the radicalization of the Filipino political agenda toward violent struggle for independence came with a discursive move away from the persuasive, theoretical plea of place to the mobilizing stance of race, though the two continued to coexist and inform each other. As Emilio Jacinto (1875–99), a close ally and advisor to Bonifacio, wrote in the undated text "Sa mga kababayan" (To the compatriots): "For seven years *La Solidaridad* worked incessantly and exhausted its whole strength in order that we might achieve some modest right to a human existence." "Now," he went on, "we are weary of raising our hands aloft in constant supplication . . . the phrase Mother Spain is only a distraction and deceit . . . there is no mother and no child," he concluded.[40] This in itself was a denunciation of reformism through a disavowal of the existence of Spain as a mother. Omitting possibilities for wider inclusion or accommodation, Jacinto moved directly from this denunciation to an interpretation founded on race: "There is nothing else than a race that oppresses and a race that is oppressed."[41] But a strategic tempering and widening of inclusion would eventually follow this radicalizing, exclusive rhetoric. Later, Bonifacio's rhetoric of race and mobilization of the Tagalogs (with "Tagalogs" and "Filipinos" elided such that the former was conceived as encompassing and speaking for the latter) would be replaced by Aguinaldo's more diplomatic, international language of the "Filipino nation."

Aguinaldo's language recalled that used by the Propaganda Movement, which had sought to conceptualize and articulate a Filipino nation in such a way that would not only awaken the Filipino but also win international (particularly European) recognition. This is not to say simplistically, however, that the transition from Bonifacio to Aguinaldo was a transition from the local back to the international or from the proletarian to the bourgeois, with the latter being a stereotype too often glibly imposed. Both the Katipunan and the Malolos Government consciously sought to embody modern, rational, secular governance, as they interpreted and defined it, and both drew from the Propaganda Movement that had nourished and preceded them. Rather, the distinction is situational and, perhaps, progressive. Bonifacio had to start the revolution, while Aguinaldo had to finish it, and the particularly internationalized framework in which it was situated operationally and discursively demanded different defensive and offensive strategies at different stages of its advance.

Bonifacio and the Katipunan understood Philippine history as Asian history, and they located Filipinas's precolonial condition of independence and autonomy as occurring within the temporal and spatial ambit of Asia. The importance that this originary autonomy held gave Asia a corollary importance in the Katipunan's political imaginary. The Katipunan's initiation rites

included a formulaic, performative recitation of the Katipunan's promulgated interpretation of Tagalog history. "What was the condition of Kataga-
lugan [the Tagalog people] in early times?" the initiator asked. To this, the
initiate had been coached to respond that the Filipinos had had their own
civilization, alphabet, and religion before the Spaniards arrived; they enjoyed
political liberty, used artillery, wore clothes of silk, and maintained diplomatic and commercial relations with their Asian neighbors.[42] Meanwhile, a
piece published in *Kalayaan* and attributed to Jacinto, entitled "Pahayag,"
read: "The peoples under my protection witness progress, betterment, and
abundance in everything, as are due to me in Japan, America, and other
places. . . . My name is Liberty."[43] In this way, Jacinto interpreted the return
of liberty as linking Filipinas to Japan (and America) once again. These were
also acts of reading the nation back temporally—a narrative epistemological
strategy, per Christopher Hill's analysis, to construct a unifying national
history.[44]

Bonifacio employed not only Asia generally but Japan specifically as a
powerful symbol of Asian achievement and freedom from the West, in much
the same way that the Propaganda Movement had. The famous revolutionary rallying call attributed to Bonifacio, "Ang dapat mabatid ng mga Tagalog"
(What the Tagalogs should know), begins with the primary assertion: "In
the early days, when the Spaniards had not yet set foot on our soil, this Katag-
alugan was governed by our compatriots, and enjoyed a life of great abundance, prosperity, and peace. She maintained good relations with her neighbors, especially with the Japanese, and traded with them in goods of all
kinds. As a result, everyone had wealth and behaved with honor."[45] As in
Jacinto's "Pahayag" piece, Japan is singled out from among all the Asian
neighbors to be historically or potentially linked with the Philippines, even
above the archipelago's longstanding Malay and Chinese trading partners.
The Propagandists employed Japan as a symbol of current power to heighten
by association the Filipinos' sense of their Asian civilization and Asian history as well as to awaken racial pride; Bonifacio and Jacinto did the same for
the Tagalogs, puffing up Tagalog pride through specifically Japanese Asian
association.

In addition to the Philippines's general location in Asia and the symbolic
use of Japan, the more particular and national rhetoric of place also figured
prominently in Bonifacio's thinking. The ritual for the initiation of Bayani
detailed the persecution that reformists and suspected *filibusteros* were

suffering, and listed separation and exile as the cruelest forms.[46] The ritual dwelt on the very great pain that such unnatural dislocation from one's place and breaking of bonds caused. "There came imprisonments and deportations to foreign lands," the ritual text read, described as "bitter" and as "treachery." The text importuned those present to "witness the good parents who became demented in a sea of suffering, struck down by misery," and to note the "poor unfortunates, stranded far from the land of their birth and their loved ones in life, deported and cast away on pitiless, malodorous shores where they weep tears of blood, and at times rage that they were not put to death."[47] Indeed, the Katipunan initiation rites cited such separation from the place of one's race and identity as among the deep dangers and punishments that could potentially befall a Katipunero, and asked the initiate to prove his deepest commitment to the cause by swearing to face even such punishment.[48] One of the best-known Katipunan texts is a paean to patriotism and to place, "Pagibig sa tinubuang Bayan" (Love of country), a poem attributed to Bonifacio and published in *Kalayaan* in March 1896.

> Ah! The land it is that gave us birth,
> Like a mother, and from her alone
> Came the pleasant rays like the sun's
> That warmed the benumbed body . . .
> And every tree and branchlet
> Of its woods and its laughing meadows,
> Bring back to the mind the memory
> Of the mother and past days of gladness.[49]

More than a paean, however, this poem also advocated for reorientation toward place, not only as the source of affiliation and political will but also as the director of that will. "Misfortune and death seem lighter / When we suffer them for our country, / And the more that for it we suffer, / The more our love grows—oh, marvel!"[50] Herein, place showed a transformative, beautifying capacity that could turn past and present suffering into love. Still further, it suggested that reorientation and dedication to place would form a nation, because it is sharing a common mother that makes men brothers—"Strike a blow to save your country, / Since she is our common mother."[51]

The works of Jacinto—particularly *Kartilla* and *Liwanag at Dilim*, both written in 1896—were central to the Katipunan and the Philippine Revolution's early intellectual and discursive underpinnings. Bonifacio drew significant inspiration from *Liwanag at Dilim*, quoting it at length and patterning his vision for the Philippine self-government after it. Agpalo describes *Liwanag at Dilim* as "a political philosophy of a *pangulo*-led democracy based on civility,[52] the rule of law, social justice, and the nature of man who is gifted with liberty, ennobled by work, and endowed by reason that originates from and lives in the greatness, goodness, and divinity of God."[53] Bonifacio adopted the *Kartilla*, in place of his own *Decalogue*, to serve as the code of conduct for the Katipunan. Written in Tagalog, unlike the Propaganda Movement's Spanish, the *Kartilla* consisted of thirteen normative propositions dwelling on self-actualization, morality, honor, and purpose, but embedded within it was also a defensive position against racialized colonial hierarchies. The *Kartilla* defended innate humanity and leveled racial distinction—"All men are equal whether the color of their skin be white or black. One man may surpass another in wisdom, wealth, or beauty, but not in that which makes him a man."[54] While the *Kartilla* thus recognized material differences and individual advantages, it ascribed basic humanity to all and posited this equality as the basis for human relations. It was a rejection of the colonial condition of ranking and being ranked. The Spanish figured in the *Kartilla* both racially and colonially (by virtue of their power in religion and government), but they did not appear positively—they appeared only in negation. Thus the last, thirteenth, position stated: "Man is not worth more because he is a king, because his nose is aquiline, and his color white, not because he is a priest, a servant of God, nor because of the high prerogative that he enjoys upon earth."[55] This is relevant for the way in which race inflected the ultimate vision of a redeemed Philippines that the *Kartilla* offered. It was a vision in which the Spanish were not physically, materially present except as absorbed within historical experience. Unlike other texts, such as those in the Katipunan's organ, *Kalayaan*, that sought to awaken the Tagalogs to their history of oppression and injustice, the *Kartilla* sought to shape the conduct of the Katipunan and to give life to a united, noble, empowered race. It was therefore a positive imagining of the nation it sought to effect, and the Spanish were not part of this imagining, were not directly mentioned at all. According to Pío Valenzuela, the final act of the Katipunan initiation featured the blindfolded initiate receiving a dagger, being led to a seated "enemy" or "traitor" whom he located by touch, and being ordered to stab him to death.[56] In this way, the Katipuneros were challenged to identify and to eliminate from this future nation those from among them (Spanish or not) who were to have no place in it. The *Kartilla* concluded that, when the longed-for sun of liberty would rise at last and its rays diffuse everlasting joy among the "united race of brethren" (*nangagkaisang magkalahi't magkakapatid*), the suffering and lives of those who came before would not have been in vain.[57]

Bonifacio's printed Tagalog-language broadside to the Katipunan, "Mararahas na Manga Anak ng Bayan" (To the brave sons of the nation) of February 1897, made this racial history explicit. "You must realize that the reason why we give our life and all that we have, is for us to be able to hold and to cherish the much desired Independence of our nation which will bring forth comfort and avenge our desecrated honor crushed by slavery and buried in the abyss of subhuman treatment."[58] He concluded his address by reinforcing the division between races as both a historical actor and a motivating goal in this war: "On our side is the right. Ours are noble deeds. The Spaniards, that contemptible race that found its way here, are fighting for the wrong. They are annihilating and raping an alien nation."[59] This mention of alienness returns the concept of place as relevant to this racialized vision of political morality and national grounding. "To preserve the sanctity and glory of our race so that the world may recognize our nobility, let us not imitate our Spanish enemies in debasing the conduct of war. Let us not fight and kill merely for the sheer desire of killing. Rather, let us do so in defense of the Liberty of our country."[60]

Race was inextricable from the way in which the Katipunan understood its grievances against Spain. Further, the Katipunan interpreted race as an active agent in the Philippines's history of suffering (which occurred along racial lines), as an organizing component to realizing its future (when we are united as a race we will overcome the racial suffering we've endured), and as an essential element to its ultimate purpose and vision. What remained unexpressed in this, however, was the still particularly *Tagalog* scope in which Bonifacio was working. Each member of the Katipunan signed in his own blood the Katipunan Oath, the Tagalog language of which foregrounded race (*lahi*), while eliding "Tagalog" and "Filipino," assuming that the former could encompass the latter. The oath began: "I ___, hereby swear in the name of God, that I will give my life, my strength and the little that I have, and that I will sacrifice my love for my wife, my children, parents, brethren, for the sake of defending our mother land, and for the sake of the Tagalog race and of the Society of the Sons of the People."[61] The preamble of the *Kartilla*, meanwhile, included the clarifying footnote: "The word 'Tagalog' means all those born in this Archipelago, even a person who is a Visayan, Ilocano, or Kapampangan, etc., is therefore a Tagalog, too."[62] This was a nod to the need for a national vision, but not yet an enunciation of it. It would ultimately be Aguinaldo and Mabini who challenged and enlarged this field of vision in an attempt to make the revolution truly national.

Aguinaldo originally regarded the revolution much as Bonifacio did— as a revolution of the Tagalog nation—but, by the end, he arrived at a view of the revolution as a national vision, part of international history and universal civilization, based on rights and self-government won through struggle.[63] Aguinaldo's early Manifesto to the Municipal Captains of Cavite, issued in Tagalog on August 31, 1896, read: "Dear Municipal Captains and Countrymen . . . As an answer to this declaration of war, we started to rebel against this tyrannical race, and I am very glad to inform you that the towns of Cavite el Viejo, Noveleta, and San Francisco de Malabon are already free and the government is now in the hands of [Tagalogs]."[64] The use of "Tagalog" by both Aguinaldo and Bonifacio, even when attempting to unify through concepts of lahi/race, speaks to the divided nature of Fili-pinas. These Tagalog leaders, and many from the Propaganda Movement (with the notable exception of those such as Ilocano folklorist Isabelo de los Reyes), attempted to use Tagalog "civilization," customs, and language as a placeholder for the national—to mobilize national sentiment and unity around the only sense of culture and place that they personally knew of in what was a deeply local, differentiated archipelago. This was particularly so for the nonelite classes who did not have the supra-language of Spanish nor the means to travel across the archipelago or to meet with other "Filipinos" of different provinces in Manila or abroad in Europe and Asia.

The rhetoric of Aguinaldo's Spanish-language Manifesto of July 1897, in contrast, marked a different idealism (and perhaps strategic pragmatism) for the revolution. After the defeat of the first phase of the revolution in 1896–97, when the Spanish reconquered the entire province of Cavite, the second phase began on the run, as Aguinaldo referenced in the title of his manifesto, "Desde Estas Montañas."[65] "We raise our voices to all those in whose breasts beat noble hearts; to all those who have courage, honor, dignity and patriotism. We make no racial discrimination; we call upon all who possess honor and a sense of personal dignity; the Filipino, the Asiatic, the American and the Europeans all alike suffer; and we invite all those who suffer to aid in lifting up a fallen and tortured people; a country destroyed and sunken in the mire of debasement."[66] This rhetorical move was similar to the strategy of the ilustrado-led Propaganda Movement that sought to persuade by including the Spaniards in the morality of its argument. Aguinaldo, facing recent defeat on the battlefield, removed the rhetoric of race to rest on a more inclusive concept—humanity. "We reject no one, not even the Spaniards, for we have gallant Spaniards in our ranks; free from prejudice and solely through love of justice, they defend our demand for the recognition of ourselves and our dignity."[67] From his foothold in the *montañas*, Aguinaldo called on all residents of the Philippines, thereby returning to the comparatively defensive strategy of place rather than the more offensive strategy of race, to join the land's shared struggle for independence. In both Bonifacio's and Aguinaldo's addresses, however, nobility or righteousness rested on the same grounding: the rightful liberation of the nation—the purpose that endowed their violence with honor.

Aguinaldo's October 31, 1896, proclamation, "Al Pueblo Filipino: Libertad, Igualdad, y Fraternidad," was addressed to the "Ciudadanos Filipinos" and enjoined them to heroism in the struggle for independence under a republican government.[68] It also outlined the vision for the revolutionary government, whose national administrative structure would persist in Aguinaldo's June 1898 independence decrees and even in key provisions of the eventual Malolos Constitution.[69] The revolutionary government featured the following: (1) a Central Committee to act as the directing authority for the revolution, overseeing prosecution of war and organization of an army of 30,000 men with arms; (2) elected municipal committees administering the government of the towns completely independently from the central committee, except only in their support of the revolution through provision of men, food, and money to maintain the army; and (3) a revolutionary congress, comprised of a delegate body from each municipal committee working in union with the Central Committee.[70]

Beyond the immediate domestic ambit, however, there were many who also saw the Katipunan's assumption of arms as enacting a vision for a liberated Asia. It is this Asian field—and how much connection to it the revolution was able to effect—that the remainder of this book examines.

Spanish Imperial Anxieties and the Geography of Asian Imperial Subversion

By October 2, 1896, the liberal Spanish daily newspaper *El Imparcial*'s front page would feature the article "Filipinas—Cuestión Palpitante: Lo Urgentísimo," darkly warning the Spanish public of a petition supposedly delivered to the foreign relations minister of the Japanese Empire and signed by "more than twenty thousand Filipinos" requesting Japan's annexation of Filipinas.[71] There were also rumors that a few Japanese were implicated in the outbreak of the Philippine Revolution in Manila.[72] Consul Shimizu, chargé d'affaires in Hong Kong, was sent to Manila to verify these rumors and to consult with the German consul in Manila, Lieutenant Spetz, whom the Japanese government had requested to protect the Japanese and their interests in Manila.[73] Shimizu established, over a two-week Philippine trip from September 26 to October 7, 1896, that the Japanese in Manila, who were "all peaceful merchants," as he recorded in his report to Vice-Minister of Foreign Affairs Komura Jutarō, were in no way involved in the Philippine Revolution, though he noted the native people's admiration for Imperial Japan.[74] The rumors of Japanese involvement in the revolution betray the peculiar power that the specter of Japan then held, particularly given that, according to Shimizu's report, only nine Japanese were actually in Manila at the time.[75]

In 1896 the Catholic religious orders in the Philippines furnished the new Spanish gobernador general del archipielago, Camilo de Polavieja, with their notes from the lead up to the Philippine Revolution, which broke in late August 1896. Reports of Japan's looming and actual threat recur repeatedly throughout the pages. A report from July 24, 1896, described how the indios rejoiced at the sight of the wrappers of a tobacco company, La Batalla, which was adorned with pictures of Japanese soldiers and Japanese battleships.[76] The orders considered this a form of propaganda that strengthened Spain's enemies in the islands and the ignorant indio masses' respect for military power—dangerously, that of Japan.[77] The head of the Guardia Civil Veterana, the urban gendarmerie force of Manila, in his October 28, 1896, notes to the Spanish representatives in Singapore, meanwhile, described the empire of Japan grasping the "laurels of such easy victory" against China and now attempting to "exert its dominance in the West."[78] He relayed that Andrés Bonifacio intended to contact the Japanese government and that the Filipinos followed the Spanish setbacks in Cuba with great interest and satisfaction, hoping Japan would play in the archipelago the role that the United States was then playing in the Antilles.[79] The reports of the Franciscan Order to Polavieja echoed these same observations, adding that many of the best-known Filipino separatists moved to Yokohama after the Japanese victory in the Sino-Japanese War in 1895, while still more made frequent trips there.[80]

Though the writer Carlos Recur had remarked in 1879 that "from the commercial point of view the Philippines is an Anglo-Chinese colony flying a Spanish flag,"[81] toward the close of the nineteenth century, Spain reimposed protectionist duties such that, "before the final eclipse of Spanish power, the Iberian rulers ... wrested from the formidable foreign capitalists a measure of economic self-respect," as Filomenio V. Aguilar writes in *Clash of Spirits*.[82] Indeed, in the 1880s, Spain had imagined itself humiliated and dismissed by foreigners observing its inability to direct its subject population and exert full rule over the islands. It was this that led to the renewed colonization program, *reducción de infieles*, which sought to subdue the Philippine interior, highlands, and marginal elements subverting Spanish sovereignty. The reducción and Spain's renewed protectionism had multiple audiences. There was a steady flow of foreigners into the "international colony," who seemingly needed to be reminded of Spanish sovereignty. Not only foreigners needed reminding—Josefa Saniel records that during the late 1860s to early 1870s Chancellor Otto von Bismarck entertained but ultimately refused the sultan of Sulu's request for German protectorate status over the southern region of Filipinas as well as a second similar overture from an Austrian national, Baron von Overbeck, who owned interests in northern Borneo.[83] The prelude to the revolution therefore featured a double confrontation within the international colony, as Spain attempted to rearticulate its sovereignty to meet foreign capitalists' symbolic and material challenges to Spanish power,[84] and as Filipino ilustrados, millenarians, and southern Muslims increasingly turned toward and pinned their political protests on foreign intercession and liberal international rhetoric.

The reports of the religious orders and the colonial Spanish government based in Filipinas betray a long preoccupation with Japan, particularly its allure as a model and potential ally. The Guardia Civil, the Spanish colonial civil guard, reported in 1895 that such Japan-centered Asianist thinking was fashionable in the archipelago and that its inhabitants, "dreaming of [Japan's] protection and support" and as a "model of culture, wealth, liberty, and strength," "directed their efforts uselessly to Japan," such that "Doroteo

Cortes, with that Ramos, Basa, Español, and others" emigrated to Yokohama and established a separatist commission there in correspondence with Manila.[85] This commission was the Hong Kong Committee. The religious orders' and colonial government's notes were preoccupied with Japan and Hong Kong's roles as central Asian sites enabling the safe haven and growth of anti-colonial subversion in Filipinas.

The reports incanted the place names regularly, almost as a refrain, keeping up a beat of suspicion and perceived threat. "It is known that [Alcantara who was thought to be in Japan but actually resides in Hong Kong] fled to Hong Kong with Langay in the ship 'Sum Kiang' with the money and protection of the [Free] Masons," read one typical report from the religious orders on May 7, 1896. "In Hong Kong he sees Doroteo Cortes daily and confers with him."[86] Another from April 17, 1896, enjoined the colonial government to intercept the correspondence and verify the registry papers of known subversives; it read: "Villareal is a furious Mason, he is actually in Japan. Ramos, owner of the old shop 'La Gran Bretaña' is actually in Japan."[87] The Guardia Civil asserted in an 1896 report that in Manila, Filipinos frequently embarked for Japan under "the pretexts of recreational, instructional, or artistic trips, but that are in reality for them to conspire."[88] Hong Kong and Japan recurred repeatedly in the reports as regular destinations of the Filipino Propagandists, Masons, and *laborantes* in their political travels, and an official 1897 report to the Ministerio de Ultramar urged its consideration of the appointment of more police agents "in the neighboring colonies and particularly in Hong Kong, whose consulate it may be viewed as appropriate to elevate to the level of Consulate General."[89] Later, on January 3, 1898, a further report expounded the importance of the foreign police and foreign intelligence: "It should be necessary in certain points, Singapore, (?), Yokohama, and Hong Kong, but in the latter it is essential, I am considering this of capital importance."[90]

Japanese cities (particularly Yokohama, but also Kobe) and Hong Kong were crucial nodes in the region's geographies of revolution—a geography whose insidious effect was imagined as covering "the neighboring colonies and Japan" in the religious orders' and the Spanish government's suspicions.[91] The Guardia Civil reported that La Liga had an important delegation in Hong Kong headed by Yldefonso Laurel.[92] A May 2, 1896, report from the religious orders to Gobernador General Polavieja recommended arranging with Spain's representative in Japan to monitor the movements of the

Filipinos residing in that country and making the same recommendation to the consuls in Hong Kong, Singapore, Saigon, and Shanghai, the transit points and organizing grounds where local authorities should stay abreast of the potential Filipino agitators' actions.[93] A member of the Propaganda Movement was reported in the religious orders' notes from July 6, 1896, as changing his name three times and boarding the ship the *Eleano* for Singapore and from there sailing to Saigon and Hong Kong, under the last name Lapati.[94] The notes recorded that "while living in Hong Kong," Lapati, who reportedly sought to reproduce in the Philippines the bloody separatist war of Cuba, "came to know all the Filipinos there."[95] This tone and broad generalization demonstrate the particular suspicion reserved for Hong Kong and what it meant for Filipinos to reside there. The same presumption of suspicion applied to Japan. "One should not forget," warned a report from the religious orders on May 2, 1896, "that given the way in which the aforementioned Señor [repeatedly] leaves the Archipelago for abroad, it is certain that he is going to Japan to conspire against Spain."[96] The religious orders' notes from June 1, 1896, recorded the rumors that the Propagandists—"Cortes, Ramos, Luna, Zamora, del Pilar, Villarroel, Agoncillo, Lecaroz (?) and other Filipinos who are in Japan"—had delivered a memorandum to the Government of Mikado requesting protection for the revolutionaries.[97] Further, it cited that the Central Junta of the Propagandists not only had established itself in Japan but had also purchased a merchant ship to sail from Japan to Manila and Iloilo to bring the separatist cause home.[98]

The cities of Hong Kong and Yokohama were safety valves—cosmopolitan cities in which Asian subversives could act with greater political freedom as well as cities in which they imagined richer alternative lives counter to their colonial conditions. It was for this latter reason that Rizal desired to set up a school for Filipinos in Hong Kong or Japan, just as Phan Bội Châu did for Vietnamese. To the Spanish, Hong Kong was a site outside their effective surveillance and the nearest locus of subversive thought and activity for their Southeast Asian colony, which sat within a crisscrossed network of Asian revolutionary activity that also crucially included Singapore, Saigon, and Yokohama. The subsecretario del Ministerio de Ultramar forwarded a letter from Hong Kong to the Ministerio de Estado on November 21, 1892, about the disturbing and vicious attacks in that colony's press (appearing in the *Hong Kong Telegraph* since July 1892) against the gobernador general de Filipinas and the Catholic religious orders, as well as a piece in *Truth* on

October 20, 1892, arguing in favor of José Rizal following his arrest (deemed "a disgrace to the Spanish and clerical authorities concerned").[99] Yet, on this, the Spanish consul in Hong Kong could only lament that, alas "the press is free here."[100] Beyond Hong Kong, Gobernador General Blanco also diligently sent full accounts of the revolutionary proceedings in Cavite to the Spanish representative in Singapore. Additionally, notices and copies of the *Straits Times* articles of June 30 and July 4, 1857, on the uprising in British India, along with a detailed handwritten list of the regiments involved therein, were included in the Spanish imperial military's files on the Philippine Revolution. It seems that the field of relevant instances of anti-imperial subversion and its models had a long memory and was interpreted very widely indeed.

The religious orders' notes from June 30, 1896, alerted the Spanish government to a further twist to the purported Japanese connection, and underscored Spanish paranoia regarding the Japanese threat. This was based on a lengthy interview conducted with an indio purportedly well acquainted with the prevailing rumors and discussions in (unspecified) Masonic lodges. The leaders of the lodges were reportedly telling their members that Spain would soon have a war with Japan, and that the Japanese were already said to be building up arms to be able to attack Filipinas by land and sea.[101] Whether or not these pronouncements were actually made in the lodges, the orders' repetition of these rumors revealed Spanish fears. The religious orders also noted that the Katipunan periodical, *Kalayaan*, was published in Yokohama and smuggled from there to Manila. This was not in fact true and was a calculated ruse on the part of the Katipunan, whose revolution and society had a strong international consciousness. The place name of "Yokohama" conjured the specter of transnational activism and subversion, and was strategically used to encourage membership growth through its symbolic power, as the Katipunan itself admitted. The religious orders' notes also dutifully listed indios who were discovered to own books from El Bazar Japonés, a fact noted with due suspicion, because, as the April 30, 1896, note recorded, El Bazar Japonés, situated in the Plaza del P. Moraga, seemed "to be merely a pretext," for "in reality they say that it is the subversive center where a great number of disaffected come to change impressions, sustain the propaganda, and receive letters, papers, and instructions that come from Japan and other places."[102] The possession of literature from Hong Kong could similarly conjure conspiracies in the eyes of the Spanish state, as in the case of the April 1889 arrest of certain indios from Tondo against whom suspicion of rebellion had been "reinforced by the seizure of printed matter from Hong Kong."[103] The Guardia Civil additionally reported that a Japanese corvette warship, the *Kongo*, had arrived in Manila Bay in May 1895 without any explanation for its sudden appearance, and was "mysteriously visited and entertained by a commission of Filipinos in El Bazar Japonés, where they stayed."[104] The Guardia Civil report then qualified this notation, writing later, in a reflection on the precursors to the revolution: "Coincidences, perhaps, but alert!"[105]

Japan held the same mix of allure and subversion for the Vietnamese scholar-gentry. Several associations encouraging studies abroad, known as the Khuyến Du Học Hội, existed in the Mekong Delta area, many of which were influenced by Phan Bội Châu.[106] Phan Bội Châu's own Đông Du (Go East) Movement successfully brought Vietnamese youth to study in Japan from 1905 to 1909. Similar associations also appeared in China, following the Sino-Japanese War, sending Chinese youth to study in Japan.[107] Philippine national hero José Rizal had also envisioned such a school in Hong Kong or Japan for Filipino youth. With regard to the Vietnamese movement, at first Châu had had a difficult time securing funding and as such found few applicants to his study program in Japan; he returned to Japan in October 1905 to consult with his friend Liang Qichao for strategic advice.[108] Liang advised him to write a pamphlet; Châu penned "Khuyến Quốc Dân Tư Trợ Du Học Văn" (Encouragement to citizens to contribute for overseas study), and Liang published 3,000 copies for him for free.[109] "In Japan we can be educated as free men," the pamphlet declared. "Five hundred families should put their money together and send one student."[110] Interestingly, another pamphlet written by a Catholic priest living in Tokyo, Mai Lão Bạng, targeted Catholics in southern Vietnam. The pamphlet, "Facitie in Dei Gloriam" (Do it for the glory of God) enjoined them to go to Japan to imitate the example of Joan of Arc, blending the symbolic power of both Japan and France in a single appeal.[111]

Through complicated routes on merchants' junks via Guangzhou or disguised as Chinese on liners boarding at Saigon, students began to arrive in Japan. They were mostly scions of rich families in Nam Kỳ (Cochinchina) from Mỹ Tho, Gò Công, Cần Thơ, and Long Xuyên who saw the possibility for social advancement or desired to be associated with Prince Cường Để

(1882–1951), the surviving member of the Nguyễn dynasty who Châu had helped to escape to Japan and who was working with him there as part of the movement.[112] Most of Châu's colleagues and participants in the Đông Du Movement were degree holders or men who had studied for the Confucian court examinations. In his autobiography, Châu described the logistical operations and setting of his movement in Japan: "In the second decade of the Third Month we moved to Binh-Ngo-Hien (Year-of-the-Horse House) in Yokohama. Binh-Ngo-Hien was a small center, the first to be established by our Dong-Do (Sail East) [sic] movement." With regard to money, he recalls that: "By that time, Tang-Bat-Ho had made his way back into our country and forwarded to us several hundred piasters; in addition, the Marquis had also brought with him quite a substantial sum of money. We made use of this to rent a two-story [sic] Japanese house with ample space and to hire a Japanese to teach our youth spoken and written Japanese."[113] Upon seeing the first wave of Đông Du Movement students in Japan in late May/early June 1906, Phan Bội Châu records that fellow Vietnamese nationalist Phan Châu Trinh said to him: "That some [Vietnamese] students now can enter Japanese schools has been your greatest achievement."[114] Trinh, however, urged Châu not to "make appeals for combat against the French." He advised: "You should only call for 'popular rights and popular enlightenment.'" "Once popular rights have been achieved, then we can think about other things," he explained.[115] Châu disagreed.

Throughout his life, Châu was committed to violent political action, and in this sense we should not unduly privilege the role of education in his thinking. He subscribed to the Italian radical thinker Giuseppe Mazzini's belief that "education and insurrection should go hand in hand," with which Châu became familiar through reading Liang Qichao's *I-ta-li Chien-kuo San-chieh Chuan* (Biographies of the three heroes of the building of Italy).[116] The school curriculum of Châu's Đông Du Movement reflected both his physical force strategy and his Pan-Asianism. Châu reported that the Đông Du students, in addition to learning the Japanese language, studied general subjects in the first half of the day, "such as mathematics, geography, history, chemistry, physics, ethics, and so on."[117] Then, "in the second half of the day military studies were taught, with particular attention paid to military drill."[118] These studies "were to be entrusted to the Common East Asian Culture Society, and the schooling was to take place in the Tōa Dōbun Shoin (Common

East Asian Culture Institute)."[119] The instruction to emulate the "heroes of antiquity" ran throughout the lessons, according to the students' recollections.[120]

Ultimately, the French intervened and made it impossible for the Đông Du Movement to continue. In August 1908, the Sûreté, the criminal investigation branch of the French police, sent an intelligence agent to Hong Kong. Certain student accounts report that the agent found incriminating documents from students, while other accounts indicate that one of the last students to participate, Nguyen Van Hoi, had informed the Sûreté in Saigon about the location of one of the colleges in Tokyo, leading to the movement's end.[121] With the signing of the Franco-Japanese treaty in June 1907 and consistent pressure from the French Consul in Tokyo, the movement could not have lasted long. The Japanese government issued a "Banishment Ordinance" expelling the Vietnamese students from their institutions, and Japanese police officers went to the Dōbun Shoin in January 1907 to enforce this.[122] "The Institute in an instant became a scene of panic," Châu related.[123] Soon only ten Vietnamese remained in Japan, abandoned to their own devices and without resources or a supporting organization. Châu's writings were confiscated and burned at the French Embassy, and Châu himself was forced to leave Japan on March 8, 1909. "My pain is acute," he wrote in his memoirs. "I feel as if I have been skinned and slashed."[124] He declared that he would farm in Thailand until he could exact revenge.[125]

In total it is estimated that around five hundred Vietnamese students participated in the movement, with more than two hundred from Cochinchina—no small number.[126] Moreover, the Đông Du Movement represented a departure from prior revolutionary and nationalist initiatives against the French. The Cần Vương Movement was local in practice and national in orientation, and the Đông Du Movement was international in practice and Pan-Asianist in orientation, though of course there were continuities and a shared trans-Asianist practice of translation and learning between the two. Furuta Motoo writes, "In pre-modern times the Vietnamese developed an explicit national self-consciousness within the East Asian world order. This was their 'Nam Quoc' (Southern Country) consciousness, suggesting that Vietnam shared the same civilization with China, but had its own well-defined territory, culture, dynasties, and history."[127] The Đông Du Movement is significant for its abandonment of a distinct but limited Nam Quốc consciousness and its participation in the larger Sinic world that Vietnam inhabited. In this, the Đông Du Movement succeeded its predecessor. Though some of the Cần Vương insurrectionists had sought refuge in China after their movement failed, the Đông Du Movement was, as Nguyen Van Khanh and Nguyen Van Suu note, Vietnam's first patriotic movement to cross national borders and develop internationally linked activities, and it applied exiled former Cần Vương insurrectionist networks abroad to this effort.[128]

Bringing Asia into the Philippine Revolution

"[Spain] says (always the same thing) that the insurrection in the Philippines is due to racial hatred, that we are still beardless to think of independence, that, in the last analysis, we would get out of Herod to fall into the hands of Pilate (the Japanese)," Francisco Villa-Abrille, a wealthy Filipino from Davao, wrote to Rizal, then in Hong Kong, on September 27, 1896, from Argentina.[129] Counter to what the Propagandists had been doing—deploying the specter of Japan to win reforms from Spain—Villa-Abrille believed that Spain itself was playing up Japanese desire to acquire the archipelago as "a weapon or stratagem to frighten us" into abandoning the revolution; but "I cannot believe that Japan aspires to acquire the Pearl of Oceania," Villa-Abrille concluded.[130] Moreover, "I firmly believe," he declared, "that the role that Japan is called upon to play will be that of liberating Oceania and the West Coast of the Pacific from European domination." "What an honor it would be for us if we could, once we are independent . . . cooperate with that nation to carry the flag of freedom to all the islands of the Pacific Ocean!"[131] Villa-Abrille considered this to be the true goal of the Philippine Revolution: to spread freedom from Western domination from the Philippines outward to its fellow peoples in Sumatra, Java, and Borneo, with whom he believed the Filipinos shared a heritage.

As with all the peripheral Pan-Asianists of this period, Villa-Abrille's transnational solidarity was at once a genuine political goal, defensive international strategy within racialized geopolitics, and a nationalist tool. "If this revolution fails, we must work to bring about the uprising of Java and other islands I have mentioned to you, for these islands have nearly forty million inhabitants who are a good nursery to found a nationality," he explained.[132] What he meant was that, while it would be an "honor" to work alongside Japan in this transnational Asian mission to bring freedom to the Pacific, he also acknowledged the Philippines's weakness and, thus, its need to be part of something larger, preferably a united, strong nation of its own brethren, even at the cost of falling under temporary Dutch rule. He counseled that the Philippines should "endeavor to bring into Dutch rule the Philippine Archipelago so that in this manner Java, Sumatra, the Philippines, etc. will be only one nationality," for "to fight afterwards Dutch rule, the Dutch being scarcely four million souls, the Filipinos alone would be enough"—with "Filipinos" used here to signify a now amalgamated mass of "Malays."[133] "Once this union is formed and our independence attained, we have nothing to fear from the Japanese."[134] For the colonized, no strategy could afford to be purely transnational, nor could it supersede nationalist priorities. While scholars on this topic such as Sven Matthiessen contend that this nationalist priority discounts these early Filipino Asianists as genuine "Pan-Asianists,"[135] I argue that one must distinguish the Pan-Asianism flowing from within the uncolonized world, centered on Japan, from that flowing from the still-colonized world, such as the Philippines under Spanish rule and the Vietnamese in French Indochina. Peripheral Pan-Asianism's networks, political organizing, and fantasies challenged the so-called "pure" Pan-Asianism that flowed from the center of uncolonized Japan, by featuring the nationalist priorities of the colonized world as central both to Pan-Asianism and to its larger political strategies.

Social Darwinism was introduced to Vietnamese intellectuals around 1900 through Chinese writings, particularly on Herbert Spencer. For many scholar-gentry, Social Darwinism served to diagnose Vietnam's existing weaknesses and to articulate a path to national restoration and independence. Phan Bội Châu's bodily, racial understanding of colonial conquest and of Vietnam's history was evident in his 1905 "The History of the Loss of the Country," in which he invoked the metaphor of the food chain in an ecosystem: "Every day (the French) proceeded to carve us up like fish and meat. Alas! Soon will it not end with no survivors of our own kind in Vietnam?" He went on to make clear the hierarchy within this: "France is a strong and vigorous country, but it picks on and insults small and weak Vietnam. What kind of country does that? The French are supposed to be civilized, and yet they treat the stupid, blind Vietnamese as if they were fish or meat."[136] Further, in the later 1929 work *Phan Bội Châu Niên Biểu*, he declared that he learned from Charles Darwin "the struggle for survival in the world, the sad state of our country, and the decline of our race."[137] In this he seems to understand supposedly Darwinistic concepts of competition and natural selection as applying to nations as a whole within a global struggle. Phan Châu Trinh, meanwhile, was moved to write the poem "Độc Giai Nhân Kỳ Ngộ" (On reading chance encounters with beautiful women)[138] after reading Liang Qichao's translation of the poem "Kajin no Kigū" (Chance encounters with beautiful women) by Tōkai Sanshi, in which one sees again the same understanding of a global sphere of struggle, as it opens with the lines: "The race for survival is jolting the whole world / Hearts broken, heroes and heroines gather at the Liberty Bell."[139]

Chinese and Japanese thinkers had reformulated traditional Chinese concepts of "common civilization" (tongjiao/dōkyō; tongwen/dōbun) over the last quarter of the nineteenth century; then, under the influence of Social Darwinism, they created the neologism tongzhong/dōshu, or "common race."[140] The French colonizers too had a hand in the scholar-gentry's acceptance of race as a real, discernible agent in the workings of history and civilization, reinforcing the existence of a transnational "yellow race" to which the Vietnamese belonged.[141] Through this engagement with Western racial thinking abstractly and directly, in the form of colonialism, Châu decided that, in the global politics of survival, ái quốc (love of country) was stronger than the Confucian trung quân (loyalty to the king). Châu noted in his pamphlet "A Letter from Abroad Written in Blood" that the Vietnamese destruction of the Cham countries of Lâm Ấp and Chiêm Thành demonstrated that "it is not rare that a nation disappears completely."[142] This invoked both Social Darwinism and the theme of mất nước. Châu described the French government's systematic attempts to "stamp out the Vietnamese" through "a cunning method of aggravating the Vietnamese 'stupidity and weakness.'"[143] The Vietnamese would ultimately be blamed if they continued to "look on idly," he charged—for "only those who strengthen themselves can save themselves."[144]

Châu did not believe in a racial hierarchy. He saw in Social Darwinism not an essentialist trap but a positive theory that explained a nation's strength as the result of its historical development, thereby opening to any nation the opportunity to advance by developing itself. In his 1907 "A Letter from Abroad Written in Blood," he charged: "Thinking about our race, we are most definitely not a kind of ignorant, squirming, weak animal. The waves of the Bach Dang River brought forth the Tran king, and from he mists of Lam Son valley suddenly arose the first emperor of the Le." "Moreover," he wrote, "there was glory and heroic valor in our ancestor the Quang Trung emperor, who once flourished in the region of and beyond the Hai Van gate and Mount Hoanh." This was not merely a distant Vietnamese past, however, but a recalling of their current opportunity and challenge: "Now heaven has reopened the divine gate, so it is time."[145] To Châu, a nation's survival depended upon its struggle. This struggle needed not be borne alone. Kōtoku Shūsui and other Japanese thinkers as well as Liu Shipei—a Chinese intellectual with whom Châu was in contact—all drew upon Peter Kropotkin's Social Darwinist theories of intra-species behavior. Kropotkin emphasized "mutual help" among members of a species and argued for it as crucial to the species' survival in nature's harsh living conditions.[146] For the Filipinos, Chinese, Japanese, and Vietnamese intellectuals who had internalized Social Darwinism as an explanation of the difference among nations (rather than as inequality existing within a single nation, as it was originally theorized in Europe), Kropotkin's argument served to bridge Social Darwinism and Pan-Asianism. Phan Bội Châu wrote further in "A Letter from Abroad Written in Blood": "In this age when strong powers are competing against each other and the world is engaged in a struggle for survival, we would be a loser unless we absorb civilization from abroad, acquire sympathy from a strong neighbour, and pit our small nation against a big enemy."[147]

How, though, did the Pan-Asianists in East Asia's uncolonized center of Japan relate to their comrades-in-sentiment in the colonized Southeast Asian periphery? Pan-Asianist organizations such as the Tōa Dōbun-kai (the Society for Asian Solidarity) developed from within the Sinic thread of Pan-Asianism, which emphasized the importance of Chinese-Japanese cooperation in establishing peace in Asia and worked toward preserving Chinese integrity from the rapacious West. This discursive East Asian strain did not concern itself with the Filipino cause, which was taking place outside the Sinic world. Rather, it was the more inclusive Teaist and the muscular imperial Meishuron strains of Pan-Asianism that lent themselves to appropriation by and cooptation of Filipinos. The Kokuryūkai (the Black Dragon Society)[148] was among the organizations that stressed the Meishuron perspective that Japan should not worry about potential Western reaction, and should instead work to establish its position as the leader (*meishu*) of East Asia.[149] Both the Sinic and Meishuron strains, however, "had in common the assumption that there was something special about Japan's relations with China, and that the East should hold its own against the West," as Akira Iriye notes.[150] They rejected the need to accommodate the Western policies and precepts then dominating the international community. In Japan, this Asianist reaction was a response to the Meiji period's effort to harmonize East and West. In the colonized world, however, Asianism drew upon a much deeper sense of oppression and cultural loss. The Teaist thread of Pan-Asianism was capacious enough to welcome the Filipino Asianists' more expansive, if ambiguous and general, fantasies of Asian solidarity.[151] This thread was defined by Okakura Tenshin's declaration in 1902 that "Asia is one" and his belief that "an expansive force of love which seeks something ultimate and universal" set Asian civilization apart from that of Europe.[152] This position appealed readily to Southeast Asians, who felt victimized by the West and sought to declare their historical importance, to reawaken their sense of common, civilizational "beauty," and to contribute "once again" to "world civilization," having regained through solidarity their cultural sovereignty and political agency.

The Katipunan under Andrés Bonifacio repeatedly approached the Japanese government and sought to collaborate with individual Japanese sympathizers to their cause. Though ultimately official Japanese state aid never came, individual Japanese sympathizers were always to be found and did render unofficial aid, including an early pre-revolution agreement with a group of Japanese naval officers to purchase arms, which was never fulfilled due to the Katipunan's inability to pay the advance.[153] The Katipunan had three main concerns as it prepared to launch its revolution prematurely. A notice to members of the Supreme Assembly of the Katipunan on May 27, 1896, summoned them to a meeting to take place on May 30, 1896, on two *bangka* (native boats) along the Pasig River, where under the cover of darkness they would discuss not only their plan for a final conflict but the organization of a banquet to thank Japanese residents of Manila who had helped the Katipunan.[154] The notes from that meeting, meanwhile, show that the Katipunan had realized that the secret police were on high alert and that the society must act quickly to maintain an advantage. The main worry, however, was financial, for the Katipunan believed it first needed funds to (1) send a messenger to Dapitan to find out from Rizal his views on how to proceed; (2) send a delegation to Japan; and (3) prepare for the uprising itself.[155]

Pío Valenzuela's memoirs allege that resolutions approved in the town of Pasig in May 1896 were made known to Rizal, and that he approved them. These resolutions were reportedly fourfold: "1) attract to the Katipunan the educated and rich Filipinos; 2) collect funds for the purpose of buying arms and everything necessary for the revolution; 3) send a commission of educated Filipinos to Japan, which will take charge of buying arms and munitions and soliciting the help and protection of the Japanese government on behalf of the Filipino revolutionists; 4) effect the separation of the Philippines from Spain by force of arms, the only way to secure the independence of the Philippines under the protection and help of Japan."[156] Valenzuela affirmed this in his testimony on September 2, 1896, to Court Colonel Francisco Olive y Garcia, who was acting as judge of the cases against Valenzuela on charges of rebellion and illegal association, but they remain otherwise unverified. His memoirs allege Rizal to have said at this juncture: "So the seed grows. The resolutions of the association are very just, patriotic, and above all, timely because now Spain is weakened by the revolution."[157] It was at this point that Rizal supposedly warned Valenzuela that he did not believe the revolution should be allowed to begin prematurely, before the Katipunan had acquired sufficient arms. "The Philippines does not reckon yet with the help of Japan," Rizal purportedly said; "I hope she helps us, because it will be difficult to stage a second revolution after the first fails." Rizal then reportedly related a story from his time in Japan, when a Japanese minister put three merchant ships at his disposal to transport arms to the Philippines. After his failure to secure a loan from Francisco Roxas toward this purchase, he explained, "I returned to my native land so that I could unite myself with my brother Filipinos. Being united, we could manage to procure all that is necessary for our emancipation. I see that all of this is now being done by the Katipunan."[158] According to Valenzuela's memoirs, then, while Rizal did not approve of a premature revolution, he approved in general of a Philippine Revolution and had himself set about moving the country in that direction. However, the veracity of Valenzuela's account is disputed, and Rizal's trial records do not mention his provided specifics. Regardless of the truth or fabrication of Valenzuela's account, it is important to note the Asianist fantasy present.

After discussing the plans for his escape to Japan—or to Hong Kong, which Rizal suggested as an alternative if the ship provided were too small or lacked sufficient coal to reach the preferred destination—Rizal reportedly communicated to Valenzuela another desire. "Tell our countrymen that, at the same time that we are preparing for a war against Spain, I desire to see a college established in Japan which will be converted later into a university for Filipino youths. I shall be greatly pleased to be the director of said col-lege."[159] This not only reprised his earlier idea of a school in Hong Kong but set an intellectual precedent for Phan Bội Châu, who later also envisioned an education abroad in Japan for his countrymen in the throes of emergent nationalism. Both men, too, became aware of Japan's potentially expansive imperial ambitions. Rizal warned that if the Filipinos did not do anything for their own independence, Japan would seize the country within a quar-ter century at the latest.[160] For their part, the Filipinos seem to have placed their hopes in an imagined deus ex machina role that Japan could play in their fortunes. A letter sent urgently to Mariano and Santiago Alvarez on October 29–30, 1896, bore witness to the extreme personal danger that Bon-ifacio (and possibly Jacinto) risked in returning to Manila from the country-side in an effort to get a message to Filipino nationalists living in Japan imploring them to send back weapons.[161] Bonifacio hoped that José Moritaro Tagawa, the owner of the Japanese bazaar in Binondo who had previously hosted and interpreted for the Katipunan with the officials from the *Kongo*, would transmit this message.[162] In July 1896 Bonifacio had approached Tagawa asking him to help arrange purchase of Murata rifles from Japan, but Tagawa grew frightened, declined, and never sent the message.[163]

Following this failure, José Alejandrino was later sent to Hong Kong and Japan to procure arms for the Katipunan. This marked a moment of change both at home and abroad. As Bonifacio's leadership was already being eclipsed by that of Aguinaldo at home, under Aguinaldo, the Philippine emissaries in Japan would begin to see success in securing material aid from the Japa-nese in a way that they had not under Bonifacio. Seeing the strict British surveillance under which the Filipinos were operating in Hong Kong, Ale-jandrino decided to leave for Japan in February 1897. His letters from Yoko-hama to the Committee in Hong Kong detail his various efforts to rent ships and buy artillery.[164] "The Hong Kong Committee functioned not only as a listening post of the Revolutionary Government," Teodoro A. Agoncillo summarizes, "but also as a procurement office and propaganda agency."[165] Alejandrino's letters urged his compatriots to convince the Revolutionary Government to prioritize sending him the money to complete such pur-chases as the only way to achieve their goals.[166] He experimented, investi-gating a variety of possible arrangements, ranging from fishing boats trav-eling to the Carolinas Islands to Japanese commercial ships sailing to the Philippines. According to Alejandrino, the Japanese government had assured the Spanish government that it would not permit Filipino revolutionary actions in and expeditions from Japan, and gave secret instructions to its police to impede all expeditions bound for the Philippines.[167] Nevertheless, even under these conditions Alejandrino was able to find people such as one "Mr. Norman," who, according to a letter sent on March 6, 1897, reportedly sought to help him purchase arms without condition—solely desiring that the Philippines be free—and who offered to serve as an instructor to the Philippine revolutionary army, or in any other similar capacity in which he could be of service.[168] Mr. Norman's disinterested enthusiasm was not necessarily representative, however, as many of the Japanese who rendered the Filipinos aid were at one point connected to the military and/or sought to establish Japanese influence over the archipelago for power and geopolitical purposes. This is unsurprising, given the contradictions at the heart of the Pan-Asian discourse regarding questions of empire, which were never fully bracketed by the workings of affect, philosophical bases of cooperativism, or genuine political sympathy or solidarity.

Ignoring the Act of Declaration of Philippine Independence issued by Emilio Aguinaldo on June 12, 1898, the U.S. Army and the Spanish forces jointly arranged the sham Battle of Manila so that on August 13, 1898, the Spanish could honorably surrender to the Americans while avoiding acknowledging their Filipino adversaries or risking the city falling into their possession. Through the Treaty of Paris signed on December 10, 1898, the Spanish Empire relinquished Cuba and ceded Puerto Rico, Guam, and portions of the Spanish West Indies to the United States, in addition to accepting the purchase of the Philippines by the United States for a sum of $20 million. Despite the formal imperial transition, the long Filipino Revolution continued, with the Philippine-American War phase to the struggle formally beginning on February 4, 1899.

Fighting a Race War

The proximate goal of Japan's modernization had been to shake off the unequal treaties imposed on the country by the Western powers over 1854–68 as well as the second-class global status that those treaties had signified for the country. While, starting in 1894 (and especially after its victory in the Sino-Japanese War in 1895), Japan began successfully revising these treaties, these revisions would remain unenforceable until 1899. As such, the Japanese government did not involve itself officially in the Philippine Revolution; however, Japanese individuals were officially sent to visit the Philippines to observe the revolution's progress, and did unofficially lend their support to the cause, often stressing a racial bond between Filipinos and Japanese.[169]

Josefa Saniel's research shows that Sakamoto Shirō, a nationalist *shishi* (man of spirit), traveled to the Philippines as a civilian and from there wrote extensively to Japan's Taiwan General Staff, reporting on Philippine conditions.[170] He went to the Philippines in March 1897 with the blessings of the governor general of Taiwan, General Nogi, and served as a special correspondent for the newspapers *Jiji shimpō*, *Chugai shimpō*, and *Tokyo shimpō*, as well as an agent of the Manila Osaka Kaigi Bōeki Kaisha, a trade company, reporting on the events then unfolding and meeting the Japanese residents of Manila. He lived in Tondo, and his house became a gathering place for the Japanese in the city; he was elected president of Manila's Japanese Association.[171] His reports to the Taiwan General Staff recorded that he interviewed various consuls in Manila, and that Filipino revolutionaries visited his house to provide him with reports on their activities.[172] According to his biography, written by Ozaki Takuya, Sakamoto was invited to and participated in various Katipunan meetings and was nearly caught by the Spanish authorities when they raided a Katipunan meeting house on March 25, 1898.[173] Sakamoto wished Japan to aid the Philippines, and he felt that the revolutionaries were particularly deserving of aid, given the kinship between the Japanese and Filipinos.

Among the official military *shishi* observers was Captain Tokizawa. Through Minister Hoshi in Washington, Foreign Minister Okuma successfully obtained permission from the American government on July 27, 1898, for Captain Tokizawa, then in Hong Kong, to accompany U.S. troops as an observer. While there, Tokizawa renewed his prior contacts with Filipino revolutionaries, and even met with Emilio Aguinaldo in mid-July, 1898—a meeting arranged through Teodoro Sandiko, who was assigned by Aguinaldo to negotiate with the Japanese Consulate in Manila and to seek Japan's aid.[174] Aguinaldo reportedly assured Tokizawa that when his forces attacked Manila they would respect any house flying the Japanese Imperial flag.[175] Saniel's research also shows that in Cavite, Tokizawa was informed by Aguinaldo's officers of a gift they had received from Japan of two cannons, information that apparently took the captain by surprise.[176] A letter from Sandiko to

Aguinaldo on August 9, 1898, shows the depth of information that Tokizawa was freely passing back to the Filipino revolutionaries—including that he was told the Americans would attack Manila three days hence, that the Americans' opinion had turned against the Filipinos, and that the Japanese would be the first to recognize Philippine independence if the United States retained part of the Philippine archipelago but left a portion to the Spanish.[177] Advocating Pan-Asian unity and mutual aid, Tokizawa told Sandiko that he was planning to return to Japan on a secret mission, and would ask his government to provide secret assistance, if it could not for the moment provide it openly.[178] This return mission to Japan never took place, however. At a well-attended dinner party at the Japanese Consulate in late October 1898, Tokizawa advocated for an alliance between the Philippines and Japan, to thunderous applause, and the Japanese audience reportedly intimated to Sandiko, also present, that should the Filipino government send young men to Japan to study, they would be well received by the Japanese Crown.[179]

It was not only the Japanese who saw racial kinship as a relevant factor in the Philippine Revolution. "We are dealing therefore, with a race war; a rebellion of the natives against the Spaniard," wrote the gobernador civil de Manila, Manuel Luengo, to the Spanish ministro de Ultramar, who handled the colonies, on October 1, 1896. "It is more than a war for independence, because the rebels preach the extermination of a noble and worthy race— the Spaniards. Thousands of people who are awaiting sentence at the hands of the courts have so declared."[180] Indeed, there was a racialized aspect to both the Filipino and Spanish interpretive frameworks. For example, Luengo counseled against granting the rebels amnesty, as the gobernador general had previously done, "because the evil is very deeply rooted" in this "infamous and impoverished race" of Filipinos, who traffic in hypocrisy and use it as a tool.[181] "But there is more, something more horrible," he intoned, "that demonstrates in a very evident and unqualifiable manner that fanaticism has penetrated into their souls and has converted them into wild beasts."[182] In this way, the Filipinos were at certain turns indeed fighting a race war, facing their wholesale racial dehumanization into irrational animals.

Just as race had inflected the interpretation of Filipino history and the vision for the Filipino nation in the Propagandists' *La Solidaridad* and in the Katipunan's *Kartilla*, race continued to frame the intellectual history of the latter American half of the long Philippine Revolution. Apolinario Mabini was Aguinaldo's closest advisor; he reorganized the provinces and munici-palities to replace the Spanish administrative system overthrown by the revolution and impose order upon impending anarchy. The form that the First Philippine Republic eventually took was in great part a result of Mabi-ni's vision. Mabini's May 1898 text "El Verdadero Decálogo" (The true deca-logue) described the ideals to which he believed the Philippine Revolution should ascribe. Aguinaldo authorized its continued publication alongside Mabini's proposed constitution for the first Philippine government. Its third ideal—following only the first two ideals of due love and worship of God—centered squarely on developing the Filipino race through individual achieve-ments. "Develop the special talents that God has given you, working and studying according to your capabilities," Mabini counseled, perhaps also echoing the Propagandists' attunement to the Filipino race's purportedly particular endowments and historical and environmental evolution.[183] Through this path "you will achieve your own perfection," he advised.[184] He believed that through this individual and racial achievement, the Filipino would also ultimately contribute to the progress of the larger ambit of human-ity. "While the borders of the nations established and preserved by the ego-ism of race and of family remain standing," he concluded, "you must remain united to your country in perfect solidarity of views and interest in order to gain strength, not only to combat the common enemy, but also to achieve all the objectives of human life."[185] In this, Mabini seemingly understood the geopolitics and the international framework of nation-states to be oper-ating along vertices of race and family, the latter of which I interpret him to mean class and subnational personal self-interests. What he envisioned was for a united nation and a strong race to emerge, and he judged this to be the only way for the Philippines to survive internationally. "Look on your countryman as more than a neighbor," he exhorted. "You will find in him a friend, a brother, and at least the companion to whom you are tied by only one destiny, by the same happiness and sorrows, and by the same aspira-tions and interests."[186]

Yet the explicit presence of race in the thinking and rhetoric of the Spanish government and the international community, in addition to that of the Filipino revolutionaries, also made it necessary for the First Philippine Republic to deflate and to deny it, as the fledgling republic sought to achieve international recognition and national viability—a goal that required a strategy different from that used to mobilize the revolution. At the opening of the Revolutionary Congress at Barasoain Church on September 15, 1898, inaugurating the First Philippine Republic's governance of the Philippines, President Emilio Aguinaldo proclaimed in his speech, "We shall open the country's gates to all men of good will, without race distinction, who wish to find in our fertile soil a well-being not contrary to our laws or public order, thus inaugurating a new era of fraternity and harmony adjustable to the multiple necessities of modern life and principles of international law."[187] Again, during the parliamentary discussions at the Malolos Congress, the international element was present not with reference to Asia, but rather to the Hispanic decolonized and Western worlds. The long debates on religious liberty and separation of church and state invoked by the Malolos Constitutional Commission featured argumentation such as the following, recorded in the minutes of the November 23, 1898, session of the Malolos Congress:

> To prove the first part of his contention, Mr. Calderon requests permission from the table to read concordant articles of different constitutions, such as those of Serbia, Greece, Prussia, Russia, Guatemala, Denmark, England, Italy, Peru, Chile, Ecuador, Costa Rica, the Swiss region of Geneva, Friburgo, Vaud Valais and others. He infers as a result the title under discussion is not anachronic, as had been affirmed, since all modern constitutions were like that, and it should be noted all these have their precedents in the Spirit of the Laws of Montesquieu, in the North American Constitution and in the French Revolution. Those were the ones the Commission took as pattern in writing the proposed constitution.[188]

Instead, China and Japan appear in the minutes as examples of "continuous horrors" committed against Christian missionaries due to "opposition to Occidental policies."[189] As Bonifacio's mobilizing rhetoric on race gave way to Aguinaldo's more inclusive rhetoric of nation, the Katipunan's Asian networks of anticolonial subversion and racial solidarity gave way to the First Philippine Republic's affirmation of its universalism through Westernism or, alternatively, its relative conservatism. It would stand for a kind of secular liberalism legible to the Western powers with and from whom it sought peace and recognition, while denouncing oppositional Asian attacks upon the Christian religion that the "civilized," legible Filipino nation shared with the West.

Despite this public deflation and denial of the salience of race on the part of the First Philippine Republic, race remained deeply salient to the ongoing Philippine Revolution. A soldier under General Aguinaldo and a member of the First Philippine Republic's constitutional convention, Clemente Zulueta, published in 1898 during the throes of revolution an illustrated magazine called *La Malasia* that covered topics relating to the Malay race.[190] Gregorio Aguilera, a friend of Rizal who studied in Spain with him, edited *Columnas Volantes de la Federación Malaya*, a bilingual newspaper published in Lipa, Batangas in 1899.[191] Several noted Propagandists, ilustrados, and revolutionaries were on the editorial staff, including Baldomero Roxas, José P. Katigbak, Pedro Laygo, and Luis Luna, as well as the Tagalog scholar and preeminent vernacular writer of the time, Albino Dimayuga Custodio, who edited the Tagalog section. The weekly paper grew to circulate in several provinces and aimed to serve as an organ of the Filipino people marching ahead and together with the Malayan people as a federation.[192] Apolinario Mabini himself published an article on September 6, 1899, entitled "Debemos Aprovecharnos De Las Lecciones Que La Historia Guarda Para Nosotros," in which he declared that the revolution had as "its sole objective and final goal" the aspiration "to maintain alive and bright in Oceania the torch of liberty and civilization, so that, illuminating the gloomy night in which today the Malay race lies debased and degraded, the Revolution will show the road to its social emancipation."[193] Written by Aguinaldo's closest advisor and the First Philippine Republic's minister of Foreign Affairs, this is the strongest statement we have of the deeply racial interpretive framework and Pan-Malay vision operative in the Philippine Revolution.

Mabini's writings echoed the thinking on race, Asia, and universal civilization that the Propagandists had articulated in *La Solidaridad*. "Please pardon me," Mabini wrote to a friend on November 3, 1899, "if I cannot agree with you that the cradle of mankind was in the neighborhood of the equator."[194] After citing his reasons, based on the history of the passing ice ages and development of animal life, he clarified: "I think we find in the town near the equator not the cradle but the future of the human race."[195] Mabini reasoned that God allowed for the existence of avarice because it gave him a tool through which to "extend civilization" and to eventually "humiliate the proud and exult the humble."[196] This statement explained the existence of unequal progress across civilizations at different points in time, but unified them as existing within a single universal narrative. He argued that it was the law of nature that the "route of civilization" leave wide tracks in the "vast field of history" passing from "Babylon and Phoenicia, now Syria, in Asia, Egypt and Carthage in Africa, Greece and Rome, in Europe; the United States, in America" on to the "Philippines, in Oceania."[197] Universal civilization was thus carried continuously and housed by many, he believed, indifferent to whether it landed East or West, above or below the equator. This was not only civilizational, but in Mabini's argumentation, racial. "It is true," he wrote, "that the colored race, compared to the white race, is inferior up to the present in culture and civilization."[198] But Mabini did not believe this state to be innate or fixed. Slipping from race to culture, Mabini argued: "History teaches us that culture takes root, not to perpetuate itself in a certain locality, but to flower and bear fruit, in order that the wind may spread its seeds to all distant regions." "Besides," he warned, "in the same manner that the earth turns sterile with continuous civilization, to the point where the artificial fertilizer is no longer capable of giving life and substance to new plants by such a superior process, a society with a rich life and corrupted customs, which brings always abuse to refined culture and towards which man is always inclined, weakens and degenerates until it lacks the necessary vigor to continue advancing up the road of civilization."[199] It is at this point, he asserted, that the youthful vigor of a new nation takes up the mantle of civilization. "Present and future wars will serve for the aggrandizement of the races that now groan under the weight of ignominy and slavery," he foretold.[200]

Mabini theorized a role for inequality of progress across cultures—this inequality ultimately prevented the inevitable process of creeping decadence and decay from stifling universal civilization. At the point of decay, a youthful, adapted, different nation would necessarily take up the mantle of universal civilization and breathe into it new life, through which role he reinserted the Philippines into the march of progress.[201] In this way, Mabini's thinking on universal civilization advanced that of the Propagandists. The Propagandists' theorization of universal civilization had turned to history in order to diminish the importance of the Philippines's perceived cultural and racial inferiority (which they now theorized as a temporary, historicized state) as well as to tie the Philippines to a history of past and universal greatness. Mabini then took their theorization of universal civilization, which was oriented toward the past, and built into it a causal process that predicted the Philippines's future greatness. This intellectual move mirrored the one that took place more broadly in the transition from the Propaganda Movement to the Philippine Revolution. The Propaganda Movement had established a foundation for a Filipino nation built upon "reclaimed" Asian history and a "reawakened" racial Malay consciousness, thereby drawing from the past to buttress the grounds, the *place*, upon which a Filipino nation could stand. The Philippine Revolution took this intellectual armature, which was oriented toward the past, and prescribed a future for it, theorizing and mobilizing the action that would achieve it.

FOUR

The First Philippine Republic's Pan-Asian Emissary, 1898–1912

Transnational Cooperation, Affective Relations, and the Pacific Empires

[P]ues nuestro Gobierno y nuestro pueblo no abondonarán jamás la política de aproximación al Japón convencidos cada día de su importancia, y de que uno y otro país, en union de los otros del Extremo Oriente, tienen communes intereses que defender en el porvenir, como misión especialísima.

—MARIANO PONCE TO GALICANO APACIBLE, JANUARY 11, 1899

"THE CITY OF Victoria, which is what the city of Hong Kong is called, impressed me greatly," Mariano Ponce wrote, long after the conclusion of the Philippine Revolution.[1] "Nothing in the world afterward made such a grand impression on me, because this was the first city with movement, animation, life—anyway that my eyes had seen."[2] Ponce had initially escaped arrest in Barcelona upon the outbreak of the Philippine Revolution in 1896, but he was later apprehended and spent a night in jail.[3] Upon his release, Ponce fled Barcelona to Hong Kong by way of Marseilles, leaving on November 1, 1896, and beginning what would become his itinerary as the revolution's foreign emissary, seeking the support of Asian co-revolutionaries, politicians, and thinkers. Along the way, his rhetoric and thinking would enlarge as it appropriated, negotiated with, and developed alongside the Pan-Asian discourse he encountered abroad. This chapter studies Ponce's Asianist thought and his work to promote an Asianist alliance between the Japanese and the Filipinos.

Ponce handled the "international desk" of *La Solidaridad*, which as early as 1893 had covered Japanese expansionism and then in 1895 devoted itself almost entirely to fastidious coverage of the Sino-Japanese War. In that period,

Ponce's writings, like Marcelo H. del Pilar's, had used Japan's rise as a foil—as a tool by which to argue for reforms from the Spanish government. Their writings in La Solidaridad warned that Spain should fear the grassroots "redemptorist policy" of "Asia for the Asians," rather than the military threat Japan posed, for the "identity or equality of races between Japanese and Filipinos" would radicalize Filipinos against Spain to make the survival of the Spanish flag in the Far East impossible.[4] Hence, they reasoned, Spain should grant Filipinas its requested political reforms, in order to keep the islands united with Spain.

Ponce's interest in Japan, Asia, and the Malays ran deeper, however, than a mere reformist instrument, as his lifelong scholarship shows. His 1890 folklorist article "El Folk-lore Bulaqueño," studying his native province, Bulacan, compared local Bulaqueño customs with Malay and Polynesian ones.[5] He saw them as existing within a shared historical and cultural frame, unlike "others that seem foreign,"[6] as Isabelo de los Reyes had put it in his introduction to Ponce's work.[7] Ponce's numerous historical articles on comparative colonialism across Southeast Asia "imagined a global space in which colonies had a simultaneous, interconnected existence but differed in degrees of progress and assimilation into a 'modern' world order," as Resil Mojares analyzes.[8] Even after the end of the Philippine Revolution he would publish and lecture on Indochina, China, and Japan. Indeed, his admiration for the rise of Japan and frustration with Spain were main factors in Ponce's move from reform to revolution. Ponce believed that enlightened colonialism had a tutelary function, aiding others along what he interpreted to be a path of universal (somewhat unilinear) progress; but he also believed that function to be temporary, as each evolutionary phase/level of colonial development demands its adequate regime.[9] Japan's rise as an imperial and global power following the Sino-Japanese War, however, showed Ponce a new tutelary possibility and political path separate from Mother Spain and, at least to a far greater degree, from Europe, and helped him to remap the Philippines's geography of political affinity.

Arriving in Hong Kong in November 1896, Ponce joined the Filipinos resident there to form a revolutionary committee, known as the Comité Central Filipino, which sought to win international aid for the revolution. Ponce served as the committee's secretary general, distributing leaflets on Rizal's execution and the progress of the revolution, corresponding with an international network of sympathizers and potential contributors, and closely monitoring the foreign press for its coverage of the struggle.[10] Meanwhile, the Spanish consul and minister's envoy were hotly pursuing the Filipinos in Yokohama.[11] In June 1898 the Hong Kong Junta led by Emilio Aguinaldo named Ponce as the Philippine representative to Japan; he was charged with discovering Japan's policy toward the revolution and its various parties, enlisting its aid, and, most crucially, securing and shipping arms and ammunition from Japan. Ponce's mission was given prime importance, ranking fourth out of twenty-eight budget items of the Aguinaldo government from May 1898 to February 1899, with the representative in Japan receiving PhP 20,524.70 out of the total PhP 678,610.42 spent over the period.[12]

Operating principally from Yokohama, Ponce lived in Japan from June 1898 to March 1901 and used English as his language of communication. He met Japanese officials and persons of all levels and joined meetings of various Asianist societies, including the Shokumin Kyōkai (Colonization Society); the Toho Kyōkai (Oriental Cooperation Society), founded in 1890 by Japanese intellectuals to study the East Asian political landscape and opportunities for the spread of Pan-Asianism; and the Oriental Young Men's Society.[13] The latter, Ponce recorded, "included Koreans, Chinese, Japanese, Indians, Siamese, and Filipinos, and came to count with a respectable number of members and to gain the patronage of prominent Japanese politicians," for whom the problems of Korea and the Philippines were reportedly active topics of discussion.[14] Though there is no evidence that Vietnamese nationalist Phan Bội Châu and Ponce ever met, they certainly both knew people in the same Pan-Asian network. Japan, and Yokohama in particular, was home to various Asian political revolutionaries and exiles. Resil Mojares's research shows that in Japan Ponce met the Chinese Confucian scholar Kang Yu-wei, who led the "Hundred Days of Reform"; the exiled leaders of the Korean reform movement Prince Park Yeong-hyo, War Minister An Kyong-su, and Home Minister Yu Kil-chun; and the Chinese revolutionary and future president of the Republic of China, Sun Yat-sen.[15] Among the Japanese Pan-Asianists, Ponce formed connections to the ultranationalists Hirata Hyobei and Fukushima Yasumasa. Fukushima was a colonel, and later general, in the Imperial Army. Hirata had reportedly been in contact with Filipino revolutionary agents as early as 1895 and was rumored to be the intermediary for Prince Konoe Atsumaro. Ponce, in his letter to "William Jones, Esq." (who was actually Felipe Agoncillo),[16] on July 7, 1898, asserted that the Japanese were the allies who the Filipinos desired "more than anyone else"—as the two countries were "related in race and geography," and "have one, shared destiny."[17] Indeed, he believed Japan was the only country that the Philippines could ask for assistance.

Such a purported shared destiny and relationship were not merely the fantasies of Pan-Asianists in the colonized countries outside the Sinic world who asserted a "racial" relationship for symbolic, instrumental, and strategic purposes. Western domination, colonialism, and rising nationalism were redrawing understandings of what and who constituted Asia. Indeed, the famous Japanese activist Miyazaki Tōten, who assisted Sun Yat-sen and Kang Yu-wei and maintained a lifelong devotion to China's revolutionary movement, would discover through his interactions with the Philippine Revolution the ways in which the definition of Asia extended outward. Miyazaki recounted being "able to meet some men of high purpose, from the Philippines," and how "although my aspirations centered on China," "I couldn't help" but be drawn in, even if "when I think about it, it seems fickle of me." "Not only did I fail to exercise discipline over myself; I succumbed to this new enthusiasm."[18] The non-Sinic world was taking up the mantle of Asia, and its Pan-Asianists were traveling directly to its new power center in Japan. Apart from Ponce and visitors from India, Sun met with Phan Bội Châu, to whom he reportedly said: "When the Chinese Revolutionary Party succeeds, it will pour all of its efforts into helping Asian protégé countries become independent. We will start first with Vietnam."[19] This trend did not, nevertheless, herald a new, flat sense of Asia within Pan-Asianism. Miyazaki declared that his brother, Yazō, shared all of his views on religion and society—Miyazaki even credited him as providing "the compass whereby I could steer my life's course"[20]—and he recorded Yazō as explaining to him: "Talk and discussion won't do any good. What we should do is to devote our lives to a project of getting into the Chinese interior." From there, he concluded, "Let China once revive and base itself upon its true morality, then India will rise, Siam and Annam too will revive, and the Philippines and Egypt can be saved."[21] Thus, in the view of many Pan-Asianists in the center of the discourse in Japan, while the borders of Asia within Pan-Asianism were extending outward, the moral and existential fate of the periphery, such as that of the Philippines, necessarily depended on the strength of the center.

In his "Letters Written in Prison," Phan Bội Châu wrote of Japan's victory in the Russo-Japanese War as "also a great advance for us," enlarging Japan's victory to a broader racial victory for Asia.[22] "Our minds may now contemplate a new, exquisite world. . . . It is impossible to deny that thanks to the Russo-Japanese war our consciousness has been raised."[23] Châu moved his resistance movement directly to Japan, traveling there from 1905 to 1908. When Châu met with the modernizing Japanese politicians Count Ōkuma Shigenobu and Viscount Inukai Tsuyoshi and the Chinese nationalist Liang Qichao, these men evinced a similarly racialized understanding of their historical moment. Châu reported that they spoke to him of "the problem of rivalry between Europe and Asia"—a problem that had placed them on the precipice of a race war.[24] "If Japan wished to assist your country, then she would have to open hostilities with France," they told him.[25] "Once hostilities were opened between Japan and France, then it is likely that conflict would be ignited worldwide. At present, Japan does not have enough power to stand against the whole of Europe. Could you possibly be patient and await your opportunity?"[26] It is significant that the men Châu met perceived their real enemy to be "the whole of Europe," and their real struggle as racial—or at least cultural/civilizational—and that they positioned Japan as unquestionably standing at the helm of the Asian race, which should patiently await Japan's moment. Châu betrayed this same understanding in his "Letters Written in Prison" when he wrote: "During the Russian and Japanese struggle the fierce competition between the White and the Asian made us wake up."[27] To them, there was indeed a race war—whether it was brewing under the surface and liable to erupt, definitively coming, or already tacitly underway.

Phan Bội Châu, like fellow Vietnamese scholar-gentry nationalist Phan Châu Trinh, was clear-eyed about Japanese expansionism. Both denounced Japanese aggression toward Korea, particularly in Châu's essay "Yunnan." Further, Châu employed the analogy of Japanese annexation of the Ryūkyū Islands to discuss the Vietnamese nation's destruction by the French in his essay "New Letter with Blood and Tears on Ryukyus." Nevertheless, he rejected Chinese thinkers' Social Darwinist conception of revolution, Tóng-ménghuì, in which ethnic Hans struggled against Manchus for self-rule.[28] It seems that Châu excused the behavior of the strong, thus absolving Japan in the Ryūkyū Islands, but admonished lack of unity among the weak, thus denouncing unproductive ethnic in-fighting in China. Indeed, Châu, Trinh, and other compatriots praised Vietnam's former glory as exhibited in its past conquest of Vietnam's southern neighbors.[29] Trinh wrote in his "A New Vietnam Following the Franco-Vietnamese Alliance": "By exerting our inner power (nội lực), our people were able to expand and spread out along the Southern coast. In the process, Cambodia and Laos came under our sphere of influence. That our country now occupies a place on the map of the world is thanks to that foreign policy."[30] Similarly, Châu was not an idealist—his ultimate goal was a strong, independent Vietnam. Châu's Pan-Asianism functioned above all in the service of this self-interested existential political-economic end, not in service of what were secondary goals of Asian or worldwide harmony. This was not all solidarity, unity, and brotherhood. Pan-Asianism was a romantic fantasy and trafficked in emotionality and bonds of friendship, but it was grounded in power calculations and instrumentalized by those in colonized Southeast Asia for nationalist purposes first and foremost. In the racialized geopolitical and intellectual framework, the colonized believed such racial solidarity necessary to their existential political projects.

Transnational Cooperation and Affective Relations

The Japanese government, which greatly feared provoking the United States, was still deciding "the Philippine question" in 1898. At this tense moment of potential U.S. intervention, Colonel Fukushima drew up a list of questions regarding the ongoing Philippine Revolution, which Don Faustino Lichauco, an ilustrado member of the revolutionary junta, answered on behalf of Aguinaldo's government and returned to him on July 17, 1898. Lichauco expressed to Fukushima that the European powers had the desire and ambition "to be the sole directors of the affairs of mankind," and that "thus they desire to interfere with the advance of America and Japan. They are not satisfied with maintaining relations of friendship and commerce."[31] He continued, drawing on the U.S. Monroe Doctrine as a blueprint for Japan's future actions in Asia, "America, taking a wise position of defence, desires to keep them out of the New World: this plan shows the [Far] East what it should do."[32] A distinctly Pan-Asianist solidarity, premised on common interests, is the ostensible rationale for the suggestion that "the union of the people of this part of the world by the bond of common interests is a duty which confronts us so that that [sic] we can turn aside this current from the West which moves to overwhelm us." Indeed, he continues, "We cannot permit any foreigner to govern our own house, since they will do it always for their own selfish interests."[33] Lichauco's appeal to Colonel Fukushima redrew racial lines such that the Japanese and Filipinos could be understood as inhabiting the same "house."

Lichauco also introduced the Philippine Revolution as following Japan's path and sharing Japan's aims, such that Japan could recognize in the revolution the birth of its brother in the south. "These are the ideas which predominate in the Filipino Revolutionary party and carrying out this programme we desire to obtain the Independence of this country, organizing its government according to the best procedure among the civilized and cultivated nations of the world; so that it will be able to offer its assistance to the other nations of the [Far] East for this purpose and for the attainment of this ideal."[34] Further still, Lichauco attempted to draw in Japan by emphasizing moral responsibility in a shared burden. "Japan should see then that when the Filipinos implore her aid at this moment they are working for a larger purpose than the mere attainment of their independence," he highlighted.[35] This idea of a shared destiny and shared burden in Asia, stated in a July 26, 1898, letter to Felipe Agoncillo, would form the heart of Ponce's appeals for Japanese sympathy and aid, even despite the fact that he knew from his friend "Mr. Hirata" that the new Japanese government was not yet in a position to occupy itself with the Filipinos' cause.[36] Ponce was told that the Japanese worried that the Filipinos would ultimately "employ against the Yankees one day whatever aid the Japanese would grant them now."[37]

Despite this desire to avoid provocation, in August 1898 Ponce began receiving private offers of support from Japanese individuals. In August, Ponce secured an offer in Yokohama of 20,000 Maüser rifles at a price of $10 each,[38] according to Ponce's letters. As he wrote in a letter to D. W. Jones on August 23, 1898, the same seller proposed bayonets for $1.50, artillery belts for $0.80, cartridges for $30 per thousand units.[39] Then in November Ponce began receiving more encouraging signs from Japanese politicians. "Conde Katsu [sic],"[40] whom Ponce described in a November 10, 1898, letter to Galicano Apacible as "one of the oldest and most influential politicians in the court," assured Ponce of the Japanese desire to aid the Filipinos, "promising favorable results with regard to the attitude that the new Government would take," which was "dominated by the military faction, sympathizer to our cause."[41] That month, Ponce also began fielding offers from individual Japanese supporters to train the Philippine Revolutionary Army. "The Japanese Government finds it worthwhile to give us one of the most expert chiefs of the Army Staff, if our Government wishes to request it," Ponce counseled Galicano Apacible,[42] chairman of the Hong Kong Committee, on November 28, 1898.[43] That Japanese chief was "the same Tokishawa [sic] who knows many of our friends and speaks Spanish" and is "very enthusiastic about our Cause and our Government."[44] Ponce repeated that "the Japanese Government wants nothing more than our independence," and urged Apacible that "all they require is that our Government write a letter to the Japanese government asking chief Tokishawa [sic] to be assigned to our army and that the letter arrive here before December ends."[45] He assured Apacible that upon compliance with these requests, Colonel Fukushima would be able to assign Tokizawa to the Philippine Revolutionary Army and have him set off for his post by January 1899. As Tokizawa was slated for a few operations in north Japan in January, Ponce explained that it was necessary that the Philippine government request his assignment to the Philippines by December. All this information Ponce repeated to Apolinario Mabini as well on November 30, 1898, stressing the opportunity it presented and the urgency required for the Philippine government to seize it.[46]

It seems that Tokizawa did not make it to the Philippines, for by January 2, 1899, Ponce was writing Apacible that "we are searching now for retired soldiers or reserves that wish to go," with the constant condition that "they are of good conduct, speak English or French, and aren't very demanding, without prejudice to the officers that the Government gives us."[47] Meanwhile, the minister of war had asked Ponce to try to provide the Philippines with at least fifty Japanese men.[48] Ponce responded that it would be difficult for the Japanese government to commit that many officers. The Philippines did wish to seize upon the opportunity to receive Japanese training and was in need of men, generally. "Convinced each day of its importance," a few days later, on January 11, 1899, Ponce declared and reaffirmed to Apacible that "our Government and our people will never abandon the policy of closeness to Japan." He believed that "both countries, in union with the others of the Far East, have shared interests to defend in the future as our special mission."[49]

By January 31, 1899, Ponce informed Apacible that he had secured another Japanese Army officer to send to Malolos to train the Philippine Revolutionary Army—Nagano Yoshitora, "who was highly recommended by Colonel Fukushima and the Commander Akashi."[50] He requested $200 a month, with lodging and an attendant, but was happy to accept whatever the Philippine government wished to give him so long as he was able to live on it. Ponce reported that he had spent significant time in Formosa, where his superiors said he conducted himself irreproachably. Though he didn't speak any other language but Japanese, Ponce requested that the consulate in Manila provide interpreters for him, an expense justified because Nagano Yoshitora came with high recommendations. "We should indicate to our Government," Ponce additionally counseled, "the usefulness of giving him a core of people to organize in the Japanese style, in order for us to better appreciate the system."[51] Further, Ponce relayed that not only was Nagano very enthusiastic about the Philippine cause and people but also apparently had already "thought of residing there all his life, searching for a means to live in the event that our Government no longer needs him."[52] In fact, by June 8, 1899, Ponce was able to write to Apacible that "the carriers are Mrs. Hara, Inatomi, Nishiuchi, Nakamori, Miyai and Hirayama," and they "are going to join our army."[53] "I hope that you will give them the instructions necessary for them to reach our Government and put themselves at your service," Ponce emphasized.[54] According to Aguinaldo's letters, meanwhile, one of the first confirmed Japanese military officers to join the Philippine Republic's army was indeed "Mageno Yoshitora"—likely Nagano Yoshitora—who embarked for the Philippines on February 11, 1899.[55] Another volunteer arrived on February 20 bearing a letter of credence from Apacible to Aguinaldo.[56] This volunteering and organizing was person-to-person Pan-Asianism in action—with the colonized moving from the periphery in Southeast Asia to join those in the center of Japan and vice versa—under the noses of the Western colonizers dotting the region. It was also the reverse flow, and this particular plane—revolutionary war that brought former Japanese military men directly to the Philippines for inter-Asian training and transmission of Japanese leadership out to the periphery—that highlights both the ambivalence surrounding Asian imperialism that was embedded within Asianism as well as the expanding understanding of race and racial geopolitics within the Social Darwinist framework of the period.

Pivotal to this Pan-Asianism in action was emotion and affinity. "One cold winter night of 1899, in Tokyo," Ponce wrote, "I was invited to dine at the house of a prominent Japanese politician, the Hon. Inukai Ki [Inukai Tsuyoshi], member of the Imperial Diet, descendant of a samurai, ex-minister of public education, and leader of the Shimpotō [Progressive Party] in Parliament. . . . Among the guests was Sun Yat-sen."[57] The subtle drama of the prose—with the dramatic gravitas to the introduction of the character of Sun Yat-sen and the descriptive scene that preceded it—suggests the internal emotion and pride that Ponce felt. Soon after, Sun Yat-sen asked his Japanese friends and former samurais Miyazaki Tōten and Hirayama Shu to help arrange a purchase of arms for the Philippine Revolution. Miyazaki recorded Sun as asking him in Yokohama in 1899:

> Is there any way you can get guns and ammunition to the Philippines? . . . There is a representative of the independence army in Yokohama. Since I have planned to go to the Philippines with you, I visited this man and revealed my secret support for him. He was overjoyed, and promptly entrusted me with a great matter: the import of guns. It was our very first meeting, and see how he trusted me! I must do everything within my power for this cause. Moreover, this man's spirit is exactly the same as ours. I want to ask you to use all your strength for these valorous Filipinos.[58]

Here one sees how emotion—"see how he trusted me!"—formed the bonds that underpinned the political ideology of Asian solidarity through affection. According to Miyazaki's recollection, when Ponce first met Miyazaki, Ponce "pounded the table, as if unable to control his indignation" when Ponce declared of the recent U.S. declaration of war against the Philippines, "There's nothing worse than to be betrayed by those you have trusted. . . . We believed what they said, we risked our lives, and we fought because we wanted that independence."[59] It is interesting to note, whether in Ponce's speech or only in Miyazaki's recollection, the emphasis placed on emotions of trust and betrayal, rather than arguments of rightful sovereignty or law. "Oh, my friend from a chivalrous Asian country," Ponce asked Miyazaki, "will you not take pity on our spirit?" "I was full of sympathy," Miyazaki recounted. "We got along well together, and the more we talked the more passionate our talk became."[60] From there, Ponce related that President Aguinaldo had plans to go to Japan; Miyazaki "waited for Aguinaldo with Ponce, but he didn't come, so I headed for the city of Canton alone."[61] Miyazaki wrote of his response to Sun regarding Ponce's mission, "My heart was instantly aflame. Sun, Hirayama, and I made secret plans, and I resolved to reveal these to Inukai and to tap his wisdom."[62] Indeed, Miyazaki saw himself as "romantically" working for the region of East Asia, which he understood in racial terms. He wrote of himself as "romantically as always, a chivalrous hero working for the colored races of mankind, and not as the servant of his country nor his emperor."[63] The roles of community and affinity, seen here, are among the dimensions of Pan-Asianism that the scholarship tends to miss, as Caroline S. Hau and Takashi Shiraishi have argued.[64]

The other element stitching together these people who embodied and enacted this Pan-Asianism in action was fantasy.[65] Upon Miyazaki's first introduction to Sun Yat-sen, Sun told Miyazaki that their meeting must be "heaven's will," and Miyazaki reflected: "He spoke as if he trusted me completely. You can imagine how happy I was. On the other hand though," he paused, "I was troubled by the fact that the man did not seem to have very much sense of dignity and presence," owing to the casual manner in which Sun received him, even prior to having washed and changed out of his bed clothes.[66] Even after Sun had done so, Miyazaki maintained, "His hair was combed, his clothes were neat, and as he took his chair his appearance was certainly that of a very proper gentleman. Nevertheless the Sun Yat-sen I had imagined was not like this. I missed something in him; I thought he should have more dignity."[67] While Miyazaki ultimately attributed this mismatch in expectations to his continued "slavery" to traditional "expectations of Oriental physiognomy and bearing," one may also see in it the ways in which fantasy worked both at a larger idealistic level—the fantasy of belonging, of traits and missions held in common, of unity and solidarity—as well as on a more personal level. Miyazaki narrativized his life imagining himself as a romantic hero working selflessly for a higher purpose. The cast of "characters" he wished to associate himself with was another motivation alongside such higher purpose, and whether it was the valorous, trusting Filipino revolutionary or the noble, charismatic, modern leader figure of Sun Yat-sen, this involved a measure of fantasy. Indeed, when Sun told Miyazaki during this first meeting that he believed "heaven will help our cause . . . for the sake of the yellow races of Asia, and for the sake of humanity throughout the world," and that "I am buoyed in this conviction by the fact that you have come to me to participate in our work. You are an omen," he closed his impassioned speech with the assertion that "now it is up to us to exert ourselves in order not to fall short of your expectations."[68] Such reciprocal bonds and mutual estimation helped to structure and reinforce community. Miyazaki reflected on Sun's speech and recalled it thus, "through all this flow of discourse his true nature sparkled, and it seemed a nature full of the music of the spheres and the rhythm of revolution. No one could have failed to be persuaded by it," and in this one sees again the fantasy and romance—"the music of the spheres and the rhythm of revolution"—that imbued Miyazaki's Pan-Asianism.[69] "At this point I committed myself to him," wrote Miyazaki.[70]

Sun himself was increasingly drawn into the logics of shared Pan-Asian purpose and of mutual help. Miyazaki wrote that in 1899, "it became Sun's plan that some of his followers should go to the Philippines in secret, join Aguinaldo's army to speed its victory, and then turn to direct their new power to the Chinese interior, establishing a revolutionary army there."[71] Meanwhile, politician Inukai Tsuyoshi, who had introduced Ponce to Sun, advised that they entrust the Filipino mission to obtain arms to Nakamura Haizan, a member of the Imperial Diet and Inukai's fellow Progressive Party member.[72] Nakamura, too, professed to be moved by a certain element of personal fantasy and of high purpose, and he played upon the bonds of community and affect involved in this partnership. Inukai reported that Nakamura "has recently come down with diabetes, and he knows that he hasn't got very long to live. Yet he's very anxious to make a name for himself. The other day he talked to me for some time about the Philippines. I think he would like to join the Filipino army, but doesn't seem to have any way of doing it."[73] When Inukai and Miyazaki proposed that Nakamura lead the mission to purchase arms for the First Philippine Republic, Miyazaki recalled that Nakamura answered: "I know my life cannot be very long. How fortunate for me, that I can follow you gentlemen and be entrusted with such a noble task!" and Miyazaki noted that "his sincerity and fervor seemed to match his words, and we were overjoyed to have found such comradeship."[74] Given the eventual end to which this mission would come, one may see how affect and community bonds could equally blind the Pan-Asianists' character judgments, to the detriment of their work.

Through a German middleman, Nakamura arranged the purchase of surplus Japanese army munitions from the Okura Trading Company (Okura Gumi Shokai), while through a different broker he also arranged the purchase of an old Mitsui tugboat, *Nunobiki Maru*.[75] On July 19, 1899, the *Nunobiki Maru* was reported to have sailed with 10,000 Murata rifles, 6 million cartridges, 10 machine guns, and assorted military equipment from Moji, bound for the Philippines via Formosa; however, the ship sank in a typhoon near the Saddle Islands two days later.[76] Three Japanese volunteers had been on board, heading south to provide military training to the Filipinos and bearing Inukai's gift to Aguinaldo of a Japanese sword. His accompanying letter, dated June 7, 1899, read: "Inukai Ki, desirous of showing his sympathy and admiration for President Aguinaldo, herewith sends this Japanese sword. He hopes that the President will accept this sword. All those concerned for the security of East Asia will praise the strength with which the President pursues this war and the valor with which he plans its strategy. For this reason, I wish you every success."[77]

Indeed, security was a motivating factor for both the Japanese and for Sun Yat-sen, as they predicted that a friendly staging ground in the Philippines would be pivotal to the success of their own causes in Japan and China. Six other Japanese volunteers, among them Hirayama Shu, had departed for Luzon earlier, and though they landed safely and after difficulties eluding the American guards did eventually reach Aguinaldo and deliver to him Inukai's sword and letter of congratulations, the loss of the arms and boat greatly discouraged them. Save for their sporadic talks with Aguinaldo through an interpreter, Hirayama relays that the "adventurer-shishi" ("men of high purpose" who were Japanese political activists) found their trip useless and wretched.[78] Of their impressions of Aguinaldo, they found him, according to Marius Jansen's research, "bitter and determined to fight to the end. He saw no difference between Spain and America, and he predicted that in the future the affairs of the East would be settled by China, Japan, and the Philippines."[79] "The world of white men," Aguinaldo had reportedly concluded, "could no longer be honored."[80] The Japanese volunteers ultimately abandoned their mission, were narrowly able to flee the Philippines disguised as Filipino fishermen, and left with a sense of the uselessness of their activity there.[81] However, Jansen concluded that the incident had two effects: first, it strengthened solidarity among the Chinese, Japanese, and Filipinos involved—the Filipino generals deeply appreciated the singular display of bravery and help that the Japanese had showed them, at their personal risk; and second, it caused disunity in Japan—after American soldiers captured one of the Japanese in Manila, the Japanese government curtailed all further activity of this sort.[82] Nakamura would later face accusations of corruption from Inukai's colleagues.[83] He had embezzled most of the funds to ease the suffering of his remaining years, both preventing the money that had been raised from being repurposed toward revolution in China and shamefully staining the idea of Japanese chivalry and samurai honesty.[84] For his part, Miyazaki recorded great tears, shame, and distress among the fellow Pan-Asianists working in Hong Kong and Japan about this incident.[85]

Ponce was deeply disheartened and offered his resignation as envoy to Japan, but Sun Yat-sen consoled him that this was merely part of the process of revolution. By October 16, 1899, Ponce was again back to work, writing Sun from Hong Kong, imploring him to help the Filipinos acquire arms—"My Dear Friend . . . How is the state of our affairs? . . . All the excess of money, after buying the vessel, I beg you to employ it in rifles belonging to the same cartridges, never mind whether a hundred, or more or less . . . if this will not delay the departure."[86] However, by November 3, 1899, he had to write "S. Foujita [sic]" in Tokyo that, despite how deeply invigorated the First Philippine Republic was to see its "brothers in race such as Japanese" fighting for its cause, it had become impossible to send soldiers and men to the Philippines from Japan.[87] For this Ponce apologized while thanking Fujita for his help. The Americans were very closely surveilling (and catching) the Japanese. Indeed, the Americans had just taken several Japanese in Manila prisoner. "To send people [to the Philippines] now, would be to hand them over to the Americans," Ponce lamented, "and this is the reason, dear friend, why this Committee cannot openly accept such generous offers."[88] The records of the American Consular Post in Hong Kong from 1898 to 1899 bear witness to this fact. The entreaties of the First Philippine Republic and the efforts of their Japanese allies were closely recorded through intelligence networks out of Hong Kong.[89] On July 20, 1899, shortly after the ship with the arms that Ponce had secured set sail from Japan, the American Consul General in Hong Kong also received a telegram from Military Governor General Otis that read: "Belgian Steamer 'Ejuatoria' cleared Singapore for Hong Kong July 4th. Represented to have arms and ammunition destined for the Philippines."[90]

In January 1900 Ponce attempted to dispatch a second arms shipment through the same intermediaries but found himself caught in the transnational logic of the Pan-Asian movement in which he was working. While Nakamura Haizan again successfully acquired the munitions, strict government surveillance prevented their movement from the Okura Trading Company storehouse.[91] Aguinaldo was then on the run in the mountains, fleeing the U.S. forces that were hunting him. Meanwhile, Sun Yat-sen's uprising successfully broke out on October 8, 1900, in Huichow. Sun argued for the Hong Kong Junta and Ponce to loan the guns to China "since the Philippine effort had failed [and] the weapons were of no further use there." He argued this through horizontal, transnational Pan-Asianism—Miyazaki quotes Sun as saying: "There is neither first nor last in a single cause of great virtue. If our party seizes the opportunity to launch a revolutionary army, it can realize its longstanding goals. And if we succeed it should also lead to independence for the Philippines."[92] Under this framework, nationalist Filipino aims had to concede not only to the realities of the revolution's progress but to the logic of the Pan-Asianist network through which they had acquired Japanese and Chinese aid.

How fully committed all parties were to that network is questionable, however, as rumors later surfaced of possible scams involving both the *Nunobiki Maru* and the second shipment. The Hong Kong Junta had reportedly been suspicious all along, and it was even said that the first boat had sunk with only scrap iron aboard, though the Japanese volunteers did land in Luzon ready to aid the Filipino cause. Sun Yat-sen's forces certainly never received the second shipment, as Nakamura had apparently pocketed a portion of the payment and forged bills, and the arms could not be released to China due to this conflict over payment. Upon learning of this deceit, many Japanese sympathizers were outraged and blamed the revolutionaries' defeat in both China and the Philippines on this betrayal.[93] The Hong Kong Committee, meanwhile, was successful in procuring other arms for the First Philippine Republic, and the American government worked tirelessly through its military attaché in Peking to disrupt the committee's activities.[94] The records of the American Consular Post in Hong Kong also document that the consul received intelligence from "Dorito Cortes"—most likely Doroteo Cortés—that a member of the Japanese Secret Service, Tamioka, was even then "attached to the Suite of Aguinaldo."[95]

In the end, Ponce's stay in Japan was a success mostly in terms of delivering intelligence to the Hong Kong Junta and in shaping foreign Asian opinion on the rightness of the Philippine Revolution. His work *Cuestión Filipina: Una exposición histórico-crítica de hechos relativos a la guerra de la independencia* was serialized in *Keikora Nippo*, published as a book in Tokyo in February 1901, and translated into Chinese and published under the title *Feilubin duli zhanshi* in Shanghai in 1902 and reissued in 1913.[96] Rebecca Karl argues that for Chinese intellectuals it was this piece by Ponce that "first persuasively cast colonialism as a global discursive problem, a characterization that not only facilitated the universalization of the Philippine national experience well beyond its particularities, but one that endured well beyond the duration of the Philippine situation itself."[97] Ponce rendered the history of the Philippine Revolution in a way that was congenial to Chinese intellectuals, who also drew from the narrative a contrast between what they saw to be Filipino unity and Chinese disunity.[98] Karl writes, "Clearly aware of prior biases against the Filipinos held by both the Japanese and Chinese," Ponce crafted "a narrative strategy that aimed at capturing and reinforcing social elitism, by creatively inserting Filipinos into global elite status while rearticulating the social role of that elite."[99] Indeed, Chinese intellectual Tang Tiaoding published an article, "Feilubin zhanshi duduan" (Fragments on the history of war in the Philippines), in the Shanghai journal *Xinshijie xuebo* (New World scholarly journal) on April 12, 1903. Of Ponce's work, he wrote: "I have read this *History* and have shed many a tear; I have grieved for the Philippine people; I have stopped eating. I have . . . sighed over the Spaniards' calculating ambitions. . . . Alas! White people are indeed vicious."[100] Tang Tiaoding's racialized response cast Asia's geopolitical reality as produced and exploited by Euro-Americans, while simultaneously including the Filipinos on the Chinese side of a global racial divide—and of a vanguard intellectual elite engaging with the latest scientific approaches to exigent, global political problems.

For his part, Phan Bội Châu's understanding of common Asian civilization originally centered on the Sinic world, but in Japan, according to Furuta Motoo, "he widened his view through contacts with many Asian revolutionaries," and began to think in trans-racial terms—to believe "that it was necessary for the oppressed peoples (whom he called 'fellows suffering from the same sickness') to unite together."[101] Châu recorded in his autobiography that he joined the Tōa Dōmei Kai (Society for East Asian Alliance) in Tokyo.[102] The league included Indian, Korean, and Filipino activists as well as Chinese revolutionaries and Japanese socialists. Furuta saw in this a precedent for Vietnamese revolutionaries' later associations with other Southeast Asianists struggling against imperialism, particularly highlighting the eventual use of Thailand as an important base for Vietnamese communists to create Indochinese solidarity.[103] William J. Duiker also recorded that, disillusioned with Japanese foreign policy, in October 1908 Châu and his Chinese revolutionary contacts formed a multinational, anti-imperialist organization, Dong-A Dong-minh-hoi (All-Asia Alliance).[104] Boasting membership of revolutionaries from India, Korea, the Philippines, China, Vietnam, and Japan, according to Duiker, the organization "aimed [for] world revolution by all oppressed peoples, but was soon hounded out of existence."[105]

Phan Bội Châu's Asianist orientation was not anomalous among his scholar-gentry contemporaries. The same Asianist orientation was visible even in the Đông Kinh Nghĩa Thục (Tonkin Free School) that Phan Châu Trinh and other contemporaries founded in 1907 in Hanoi and that lasted only nine months before the French shut it down. Though the explicit objectives of the school were to promote Western learning and commercial skills among the Vietnamese masses, the school was actually modeled after Keiō Gijuku Daigaku, the university founded by the famous Japanese modernizer Fukuzawa Yukichi. The widely circulated and influential text "A Civilization of New Learning" (1904) that laid out the school's program of "new learning" reforms also began from the premise that "in ancient times, Asia was the source of civilization."[106] My-Van Tran noted that school members produced poems and leaflets praising Japanese technological advancement and patriotism, and circulated them to "awaken" the Vietnamese.[107] One pamphlet also introduced concepts of Social Darwinism to a wider Vietnamese audience, instructing: "One cannot buy civilization with a price, one must acquire it with sufferings. What is the price? It is thinking. What are the sufferings? They are competition. The more people think, the more they compete. And the more they compete, the more they think."[108] Such a landscape of endless competition and struggle was the scholar-gentry's general interpretive framework for their internationalized historical moment (with international encounter being what was bringing competition to bear on the domestic context) as well as the causal process they attributed to uneven material achievement. In this vision, however, not only are civilizational achievement and national security achieved through thinking and competition, but such achievement and security are thus necessarily suffering, as the pamphlet termed it. It was this bleak understanding of survival through competitive achievement that Trinh tempered with illusions toward the achievement of peace through such suffering, which I reason he envisioned as acquired levels of material, civilizational, and security "equality," providing the basis upon which his imagined "ethical, serene world," built on "acts of social reciprocity," could rest.

A poem written by the principal of the Đông Kinh Nghĩa Thục inscribes racial and familial grounds to Asia:

> Our soul has long derived from Lac Long
> We are children of the Nam-Viet house, people of the yellow race
> China belongs to this extended family
> So do Siam and Japan, within the same village of Asia.[109]

The song "A te A" (Asia), meanwhile, which, Tran My-Van records, "everybody reportedly knew by heart," diagnosed the Vietnamese predicament racially and prescribed its concomitant racialized solution.[110] The song declared:

> See the example of Japan, an Asian land
> Our own race. Why can't we all follow it then?
> A path to knowledge will soon open [to us]
> To take away [our] respect for France one day.
> When comes the West versus East struggle
> We'll change our fate from slaves to civilised beings.[111]

Here, paradoxically, the coming race war is imagined as the historical process that will awaken people to the racial grounds of their lot and potential and at the same time emancipate them from slavelike submission to another, seemingly superior race. The role of Japan is crucial in this, without which the paradox remains unresolved. "Are you familiar with Japan?" the text "A Civilization of New Learning" asked, "For the last thirty years or so, Japan has incorporated European thought and civilization and has achieved its goals."[112] Indeed, even while it lamented the lack in Vietnam of "talented persons like Watt and Edison who continually invent things," the text "A Civilization of New Learning" strongly asserted its contention that "Yellow-skinned people are just as able as white people."[113] These statements both admit an internalized acceptance of civilizational hierarchy while rejecting any fixed, ahistorical, biological explanation. Phan Bội Châu exhorted his countrymen at the end of "A Letter from Abroad Written in Blood": "Struggle my countrymen! Be like Rousseau and Fukuzawa Yukichi and struggle on!"[114]

To these Vietnamese anti-colonial nationalists, Pan-Asianism was a political strategy, geo-political understanding, and cultural practice. This was a result of Vietnam's historical integration in the Sinic world, but it was also an instrumental ideology. In response to the "gripping fear" of Western imperialism and with regard to the powerful influence of Western political and social theories, David G. Marr argues, "new ideas [were] extremely important, but they could never have been received so eagerly and have taken root without the emotional humiliation, the self-doubt that preceded them."[115] Here the role of affect reappears not only as constructing Pan-Asian networks and mobilizing aid but also as creating the originary entry point for open reception of novel ideologies. "Out of disgust and self-denigration arose in these Vietnamese a mood of critical inquiry and hopefulness."[116] This humiliation and an understanding of national weakness made seemingly imperative a Pan-Asian alliance of solidarity and aid; however, it also represented, as did Social Darwinism, a hopefulness for a new future for Vietnam and a new world order envisioned along Asian lines. It was a positive imagining and reclaiming of a future.

A Personal Pan-Asianism

Japan was not merely a stopover or the site of a failed mission to Ponce. In 1898 he married a Japanese woman, Udagawa Okiyo, in whose parents' Yokohama house he had been living. They had their first child in Yokohama, another in Hong Kong, and, toward the end of their lives, two more in the Philippines. Ponce died in 1918, while on his way to China to visit his old friend Sun Yat-sen. He declared that through the decade he lived in Europe, he had never felt the same sense of happiness and solidarity with his fellow men as he did upon returning to Asia. He wrote to Sugimura, K., editor of *The Orient*, on February 25, 1899: "I also love very much this region of the world where I was born; I lived in Europe for ten years, but never have I been happy till I came back here."[117] From Japan, he reported with delight that the former Japanese ambassador to Washington, Mr. Hoshi, protested against American plans to annex the Philippines, that the Japanese newspapers defended Cuban independence and characterized colonization as a sure means to never-ending conflict in the Philippines and Cuba, and that Japanese public opinion was unfavorable toward the Spanish as they were the only European power to denounce Japan's colonization of Formosa.[118] He was similarly delighted when Mr. Hirata published in *The Sun* on August 20, 1898, a photograph of President Aguinaldo.[119]

Ponce had long held Japan as a model for Philippine development—a modern nation that had judiciously discarded customs and habits no longer suited to the age while maintaining its traditional identity, history, and national core. From Yokohama, he wrote Miura, A., on October 7, 1898, of his deep admiration for Japan and told him of how he was then dedicated to studying its guiding concepts. Ponce wished the Philippines to learn from Japan how to harmonize new and old institutions and foreign and local influences. He was, at that point, in the middle of translating Inagaki Man-jiro's "Japan and the Pacific and a Japanese View of the Eastern Question" into Spanish, and lamented that the ancient books, news, and poetry remained inaccessible to him due to his inability to read Japanese.[120] He professed desire to "popularize the knowledge of Japan in my country"—its "demo-cratic spirit"—to give a model for the rising institutions and "to extend the growing tie of sympathy between Japan and the Philippines."[121] This desire to study and learn from Japanese institutions was the official directive of the First Philippine Republic that he was representing abroad, as well as the result of his personal, particular conviction.[122]

Regarding ties of Asian sympathy, Ponce saw no danger in the threat of Japanese expansionism, given the problems Japan was already experienc-ing as a colonial power in Formosa.[123] He told his Japanese friend Miura on October 7, 1898, that "there is no doubt between your country and mine, and mine has an important mission to fulfill in the near future"—for this the two countries should work together, he believed, and he asked Miura to help him to achieve his mission.[124] Similarly, he did not imagine a disadvan-tageously hierarchical relationship between the two countries as they worked together. Ponce wrote proudly to Apacible on November 28, 1898, that the Japanese army chief Tokizawa had affirmed to him that "of all the races in the Far East, the Filipino is first in terms of desire for and aspira-tions of civilization and progress, understanding the importance of one and the other in elevating the country to the heights enjoyed by the most advanced nations of the world."[125] It seems that not only did Ponce unprob-lematically rank Japan as one of those most advanced nations of the world, but he also acceded to and reified such hierarchical understandings of the international community of nation-states. Within such ranking, Ponce considered the emergent Philippine nation to be rising through its active efforts toward self-realization and advancement.

Ponce idealized Asian solidarity, adhering to the romantic Teaist view that the Japanese and the Filipinos were bound by racial and geographical affinities and shared interests vis-à-vis the West, with both nations undertaking shared "civilizational" work in which Japan did not dominate but merely led. Nevertheless, Ponce was a Pan-Asianist of the colonized and Southeast Asian mold, by which he subsumed even his idealized vision of Asian solidarity to particular, national Philippine interests. Sven Matthiessen argues that "neither [Jose] Ramos nor Ponce had a vision of the Philippine role in a possible Greater Asia under Japanese leadership. As a fellow Asian country, Japan simply seemed to them to be the natural ally to overcome Western colonization. Nonetheless, it would be far-fetched to refer to such activists as 'Pan-Asianists.'"[126] Yet, I would argue that, for the colonized, an unmitigated idealism in the negotiation of fields of power was simply impractical and unrealistic. As such, there was basically no "true" Pan-Asianism among the colonized or in Southeast Asia as Matthiessen's framework would categorize it, because during this colonial era in Southeast Asia essentially no activist political thinker was untouched by priorities of self-determination and geopolitical realism. It is important, however, to recover the Pan-Asianism of the "periphery" and to understand the ways in which it interacted with that of the center, rather than merely dismissing or occluding its existence for failure to conform to the center. Further, Matthiessen has failed entirely to appreciate the earlier Asian theorizing that was a crucial ballast of the intellectual and imaginative construction of the Filipino nation in the Propaganda Movement and for the Katipunan. As for future plans for the Philippine role in a Greater Asia, it is true that no concrete plans were hatched, given that the archipelago was not yet a sovereign nation-state, but it is also true that Filipino Asianists held a vision for the Philippines to be part of an Asian movement to spread independence to their neighbors and Malay brothers. On the other hand, it is unlikely that any of them imagined Japanese military conquest and political domination of the entire Southeast Asian region, as Tokyo planned and briefly accomplished during World War II.

In terms of his Pan-Asianism, one of the most important moments in Ponce's Japan-based correspondence was his request to Apacible on November 10, 1898, that the Filipino and Chinese revolutionaries work together and help each other's causes, with Japanese support. Ponce had recently met Lung Tai-Kwang, "the secretary of the leader of the Chinese reformist party, [and] Mr. Kwang Yu-wei [sic]," who had emigrated the month before to Tokyo. "The view of the Japanese in putting us in contact, Chinese reformists and Filipino revolutionaries, is that we help each other mutually," Ponce explained.[127] Kang Yu-wei wished to establish a working agreement with the Philippine Revolutionary government, as the Japanese government had suggested.[128] "If, for example, we prepare some of our isolated ports to be deposits of weapons, ammunition, and supplies of the Chinese revolutionaries, from which points their military can arm itself, in exchange for this service, it would be easy for us to secure first use of these weapons in our deposit, " Ponce pointed out.[129] Additionally, this partnership could also eventually provide the Filipino government with a new source of loan money, once the relationship between the two groups had been established and strengthened. Ponce noted that the Chinese reformist party possessed great resources. "Moreover," Ponce argued, "it is a just cause, legitimate," and the Filipinos should support it. "Its triumph would be of great importance for the future of the Far East," and is "another reason why we should not look upon this reformist movement with indifference."[130] Given Ponce's longstanding relationship with Sun Yat-sen, this was indeed something that Ponce believed and stood for—that the Philippine nation and Philippine Revolution were a part of a larger Asian community and central actors in an *Asian* anti-imperial, anti-Western history that Filipinos, Chinese, and Japanese were all conducting. Ponce wrote to Sun Yat-sen from Hong Kong on January 13, 1900: "I hope that in the near future you will at last succeed for the welfare of our cause, which is the cause of humanity and of the whole Far East too. For this reason we are confident that you will not abandon our business until a prosperous end."[131] Ponce saw the Philippine Revolution as having a hand in the rise of Asia, by which the Asian nations would come to relate to one another and the world as Asian, and not as colonized peoples, and would emulate the Philippines to resist foreign occupation.[132] Ponce also launched a campaign to mobilize Asian protest against American annexation of the Philippines.[133]

The importance of geography and race in his thinking is what makes Ponce an Asianist in particular, rather than merely anti-imperial or a predecessor to what would become known as Third Worldist in general. "They need us, in the same manner that we need them, now and perhaps always,"

Ponce wrote in that same letter to Mabini from November 30, 1898. He argued this mutual need in terms of destiny, hence the lack of temporal bounds—"now and perhaps always." He argued this as being evident and natural, "Because it is not for nothing that we are located in the same hemisphere and are nearly of the same race, with identical customs and habits."[134] This concept of destiny was the framework of Ponce's fantasies of Pan-Asianism, and geography and race were central to his understanding of Asia's shared destiny, which was, on account of those two factors, a decidedly Asian, if not explicitly non-Western, destiny. Ponce was particularly convincing in his mission as emissary of the Philippine cause in Japan, not only because of his history as a Propagandist and his belief in the Philippine Revolution but also because of this sincere belief in the ideal of Pan-Asianism. In a letter he congratulated Sugimura for transforming the magazine *Hansei Hasshi* into *The Orient*, declaring as its aim "the promotion of friendly intercourse—with a view to mutual assistance—between the nations of Asia, the Far East in particular, on the basis of common interests, common faith, and common customs."[135] "My country, the Philippines, aspires to be one of the nations of the Far East," Ponce affirmed to the editor. "She desires to share in this community of interests advocated by your magazine."[136] By this token, he argued, "She, therefore, deserves that 'The Orient' defend her cause."[137] It was in this manner that Ponce was able to use effectively his Asianist sincerity toward achieving his particular nationalist goals. *The Orient*, alongside other magazines and papers, published Ponce's discussion of the "Philippine Question" in 1899, and supported his Philippine Asianist objectives.[138]

The most famous Asianist friendship of Ponce's career was his relationship with Sun Yat-sen. Sun deeply influenced Ponce.[139] To Sun, as Ponce described it, "the problems posed by the various countries of the Far East were so interwoven that they had to be studied as a unit in general for the appreciation of each in particular."[140] Sun was gradually moving toward this position. Further, Ponce wrote, "these countries need to know each other more; among countries that know and understand one another, any desirable relationship is easy to establish."[141] Ponce noted with admiration Sun's enthusiastic sponsorship of the Association of Oriental Youth, which students from different Asian countries had formed in Tokyo and included Filipinos, Siamese, and Indians, as well as Korean, Chinese, and Japanese as members.[142] He wrote, warmly, that he on many occasions heard Sun say to fellow Asians: "Let us get to know one another and we will love each other more."[143]

According to Ponce, such different societies in Asia were bound together through parallel historical experience and current geopolitical realities, and were to come to know and recognize one another through appreciation of their common cultures, norms, and symbols. He noted, for example, the use of the sun in the First Philippine Republic's flag to symbolize progress in much the way Korea and Japan had used the rising sun in their own flags.[144] Ponce set out to have the Malolos Constitution translated into Japanese alongside other works of Philippine history, ethnology, and culture.[145] In his book *Sun Yat-sen: The Founder of the Republic of China*, originally published in Spanish in 1912, Ponce related the fate that befell his acquaintance Korean general An Kien-su, an ex-minister of war and president of the Independent Party, in his struggle against Russian influence in Korea as an explicit parallel to what befell Rizal in his struggle against Spanish domination in the Philippines. Further, "By a mysterious coincidence, Rizal and the Korean general both gave almost the same reply and demonstrated the same stubbornness."[146] But ultimately Ponce concluded that it was not coincidence, for "it could not be otherwise: the same patriotic ideals and the same generous impulses moved each of them to act . . . and it is hardly strange that Rizal and An Kien-su gave the same reasons for their conduct and determination."[147] In this sense, oppressed Asia was bound to yield similar figures, because they faced the same historical moment, with the same aim and purpose—"one thought dominated both," as Ponce put it.[148]

On the state of his fellow Asians, Ponce's prose could at times wax poetic, brimming with affect, for a lost era. In *Sun Yat-sen*, Ponce describes his acquaintance with the Korean crown prince, who fled to Japan to escape persecution instigated by the Russians. "Poor Prince Pak who was then only 35, roamed the Land of the Rising Sun in the company of his daughter— and of his nostalgia for his tragic land, of his grief over the ruin of his noble house, and his mourning for his dead wife. A poor little princess was his daughter—so pretty, so white, so sweet, with her naughty slanting eyes."[149] Ponce continues, "They lived in a little Japanese house in Kanagawa, they who had been born in a regal palace, amid the luxury that abounds in

Oriental palaces." Moved by their turn of fortune, he relates, "I could never enter that humble laborer's dwelling without being touched to see the little Princess Pak, that descendant of kings, that royal bud just opening, in a modest kimono, her attractive aristocratic figure contrasting with the vulgar background."[150] He seems to be drawing a parallel to the oppressed state of the various historic Asian civilizations and nations, who have been reduced to vulgar conditions under Western persecution—indeed it is telling that Ponce does not mention Japanese encroachments upon Korea, only Russian meddling. Yet, despite such oppression, the noble Asian figure humbly submits and touchingly adapts, as represented in Princess Pak's "pleasant and enchanting" prattle, "half in Japanese, which she spoke very well, and half in English, which she already jabbered fast enough."[151] Here Ponce betrays a sense of dynamic Social Darwinist hope—evident in her multilingualism—in addition to an emotionalized response to what he perceives to be the Asian condition.

The Hong Kong Junta recalled Ponce from Japan in 1901, having given up on any expectation of Japanese aid. After Aguinaldo's capture on March 23, 1901, and the surrender of his successor, Miguel Malvar, on April 16, the Philippine Revolution all but ended. The Hong Kong Junta disbanded on July 31, 1903, and its remaining funds, properties, archives, and library were entrusted to Ponce's care. Macario Sakay, Bonifacio's staunch ally, continued open resistance to the Americans, but with his surrender on July 20, 1906, and hanging by the American colonial power on September 13, 1907, the Philippine Revolution died. Hakusei Hiraki (1876–1915) published a poem entitled "Aguinaldo" in 1903, detailing the president's surrender. Dripping in solidarity and sympathy, he writes:

Ware Kono Uta Kono Namida
Kono Ai Ikade Hakumei no
Kishi wo Nagusame Ezaranya
Tamatama Kitare Kyokutō no
Asahi Shiworini Aginarudo.

How can I address this song
This tear and this love
To compensate the brilliant hero who died young
Rise, Aguinaldo, as the morning sun from the Far East.[152]

The cracks in the fantasies and hopes of Pan-Asianism, however, had already long begun to show, even theoretically. By November 3, 1899, a tired Apolinario Mabini had written to his friend Mr. Remontado, "If we have to believe in history, Alexander, Caesar and Napoleon tried the fusion of nations into one to establish a universal empire through conquest."[153] Mabini then went on to cite the despotic attempts of Roman kings in the Middle Ages and the Catholic conquests after Pope Alexander VI in 1493 offered these kings the whole globe. "Today, the great thinkers point out a universal federation as the most reasonable means of fusion," he wrote, "but it seems that the great powers have a different opinion, as it is more advantageous to exploit the weak nations than to protect them with their alliance and friendship."[154] Therein lay the problem not only of imperialism and the kind of cosmopolitanism that Kant and other Enlightenment thinkers advocated, but also of Pan-Asianism. Mabini highlighted in this letter both the dream and the impossibility inherent in any kind of universalistic solidarity. "Undoubtedly, universal solidarity is the most efficient means to realize the highest aim of humanity. Philosophers consider it the essence of infinite progress or of the rising perfection of the rational being to the highest grade possible, but how can we accomplish it?"[155] Mabini believed that, as long as certain nations accept domination while others agree to dominate or to allow others to do so, there can never be "solidarity" or "possible equilibrium."[156]

Miyazaki Tōten, while promoting Japanese immigration to Siam as a means to "awaken" Asia toward liberation, did not see the condescension embedded in that strategy, but instead flattened such asymmetries of power and history, while remaining blind to the privileged position he nevertheless maintained for Japan within this flattening. He embarked upon establishing "a pilot farm for one harvest as a base for settlers" in Siam, thereby "setting up a model community" through the generosity of Thai Chao Phraya Surasakmontri's donation of land and farm tools.[157] With this donation, Miyazaki recounted: "Our vigor was renewed; we took off our Western clothes and shoes and wore undershirts and straw sandals; some of us led the water buffalo and the others guided the plows. We looked like farmers in an old Chinese painting."[158] Despite the "high" purpose, flattening of power, and erasure of historical difference effected in Miyazaki's image of an old Chinese painting, this idealization remained naïve to its own power logic (and patronizing tone). Miyazaki's collaborator, Suenaga Setsu,[159] wrote a poem in Chinese from the same estate where they were building their model farm community, which began: "A thatched hut near the outer city wall, / Tilling and plowing, our purpose is high." From here, he swiftly moved to describing the imperial framework of global mastery and violence that was conjoined to such high purpose: "Spirit of gallantry based on righteousness. / Vigorous men out to rescue the world, Deep into the night, we look at the entire universe, / The light of the Big Dipper shows the glitter of a sword."[160]

Japanese and American Empires Primed for Competition in the Pacific

The *Japan Times*, an English-language newspaper founded in 1897 for the purpose of allowing the Japanese populace to participate more fully in the issues of the international community, steadily tracked the progress of the "Philippine rebellion" and "the Philippine question," which it declared "the most important diplomatic question of the day."[161] In its issue on December 4, 1897, the paper reprinted a piece by Charles H. Cramp from the *North American Review* called "The Coming Sea Power," which described the Japanese "phenomenon" in naval activity and progress. Listing with precision the types and numbers of ships constituting "the spectacle" of Japan's naval increase, "second only to England in naval activity, being ahead of France, much in advance of Germany, and vastly in the lead of Russia and the United States," the article declared that "it must also be borne in mind that the new Japanese fleet comprises throughout the very latest and highest types of naval architecture in every respect of force, economy, and efficiency."[162] Cramp deemed the stunning Japanese naval preparations "miraculous" in their speed and success, and clearly not undertaken "without a purpose," but he nevertheless did not interpret them to be aimed primarily at the United States. He dismissed the "pending Hawaiian affair" (the U.S. potential annexation of Hawai'i and its possible threat to Japanese interests there and in the surrounding ocean) as systematically exaggerated by the English press and fated to never rise beyond the stage of diplomatic exchanges even if the United States were to annex the islands. Cramp wrote that it must be assumed "that Japan's purpose is the general one of predominant sea power in the Orient."[163] "Japan may, and probably does, meditate a renewal of her efforts to establish a footing on the Asiatic mainland," and possibly, he added, "she may have in view the ultimate acquisition of the Philippine Islands."[164] To Cramp, at least, the unproblematic Japanese projection of power in the Asian Pacific was both expected and utterly natural. Yet, there were already those such as Mr. Ariga in the *Revue Diplomatique* who advocated that, as the *Japan Times* summarized, "Japan must adopt an attitude towards the Philippines as America did towards Cuba prior to 1840, and must not allow the Sovereignty over the group to pass to any power but Japan," should it devolve from Spain.[165] Thus the comparisons between the two growing Pacific powers were already commonplace and the ground increasingly primed for some imagined future standoff—and the Japanese press was tracking these opinions for its readership. For the moment, however, the most pressing and immediate foreign affairs issue for Japan remained how to deal with the West in China, as the articles in *Gaikō jihō*, launched in 1898, attested to.[166]

The Japanese victory shortly thereafter in the Russo-Japanese War (1904–5) was the first defeat of a European power employing all the resources of modern warfare and the first time an Asian power had defeated a European one in centuries. Though the American government was, according to Ricardo T. Jose, quite sympathetic to the Japanese in this war at the time, it also recognized the destabilizing potential this held for the Filipinos. "Filipinos keenly read about the progress of the war, recognizing its significance in Asia and its potential influence on the Filipino quest for independence," Jose writes, "and the closeness of war was brought home when three Russian cruisers, which had survived the Battle of Tsushima, arrived in Manila Bay in June 1905," making strikingly visible for all Japan's great victory and entry into the ranks of the great powers.[167] With pacification campaigns still underway in certain areas of southern Luzon, the American colonizers attentively monitored the Philippine independence movement, and reported all possible links with Japan, even developing a war plan against a resurgent Filipino insurrection.[168]

The staff writers of the newspaper *El Renacimiento* devoured news cables on the progress of the war and reported it thoroughly, while a Filipino law student recalled that, "moved by racial affinity, most of the students in Manila, particularly the students in our school who were in spirit the leaders of the new enthusiasm, turned thoroughly pro-Japanese."[169] A group of law students in Manila wrote and presented a congratulatory memorial to Consul Narita Goro. One of the signatories, Antonio Horrileno, later remembered that for Asia before the Russo-Japanese War, "It seemed as if there was no morning; that the sun which rose in the East was a sun not for Orientals but for peoples of other countries." He said that "college students especially" rejoiced at the Russian defeat.[170] Thus even as deepening U.S. global power would remap Filipino affective political geography pragmatically back toward the West, the particular racial perspective through which Filipinos could interpret Japan's own expansion as a wider racial success posed a continued threat to the Americans.

With the shift in the balance of power in Asia after the Russo-Japanese War, President Theodore Roosevelt commissioned the Joint Army-Navy Board to reexamine American defense plans; charged Secretary of War William Howard Taft to recommend defense projects for Hawai'i, Panama, and the Philippines (these would include fortifying islands in the approach to Subic Bay and Manila Bay); and sent Secretary Taft to meet with the Japanese prime minister, Katsura Taro, at the end of July in 1904, even before the Treaty of Portsmouth concluding the Russo-Japanese War was signed on September 5, 1905. Taft sought assurance that the Japanese Empire would recognize American sovereignty in the Philippines.[171] Yet, Roosevelt felt the American hold on the archipelago to be so threatened by the Japanese that, following the 1906 San Francisco School Crisis, in which that city's Board of Education recommended teaching Japanese students in racially segregated schools, and the subsequent diplomatic crisis and war scare that the crisis precipitated, he reversed his prior position on the Philippines. He was now inclined to support a firm, accelerated timeline for increasing Philippine self-determination. He was helped along by the results of the July 1907 Philippine elections in which the Nacionalista Party, which made independence its principal platform, won a resounding victory. "The Philippines form our heel of Achilles," President William H. Taft would later write to his secretary of war. "They are all that makes the present situation with Japan dangerous. I think that in some way and with some phraseology that you think wise you should state to them that if they handle themselves wisely in their legislative assembly we shall at the earliest possible moment give them a nearly complete independence."[172] During the war scare of 1907 that followed the San Francisco School Crisis, the Philippine Constabulary reported Filipinos from varied walks of life as leaning toward Japan.[173] On November 19, 1909, the newspaper *Muling Pagsilang* published an editorial warning the United States that it was the "Russia of the Orient" and would suffer a similar end, while urging Filipinos to champion national independence.[174] In fact, it was Japan and the United States that were more similar in the Pacific, both required to perform new kinds of ideological dances around the changing international rhetoric of rightful sovereignty and the evolving global political landscape in which empires were increasingly situated.

The powers that emerged as new empires in this moment, including the United States, faced new problems of justification of their overseas rule and ideological mission, particularly following World War I and alongside the rise of ethnic nationalisms and anti-colonialism throughout the colonized world in the first half of the twentieth century. Niall Ferguson recounts in *Colossus* (2005) the ways in which the United States engaged in the "imperialism of anti-imperialism," pledging war against empire while its own empire grew apace. Meanwhile, Tomiyama Ichirō's "Colonialism and the Sciences of the Tropical Zone: The Academic Analysis of Difference in 'the Island Peoples'" highlights the concept of "cooperativism," which was propounded by Japanese scholars active in the Pacific Association established in 1938 to conduct research on the South Sea Islands. Cooperativism attempted to "bring about [the colonized's] development in accordance with their unique direction, these policies, being individualistic and particularistic, oppose the uniformity of assimilation policies."[175] Cooperativism's respect of unique traditions and promotion of *national* prosperity within an umbrella of Japanese-led modernity (with modernity envisioned singularly and with Japan as holding a monopoly over it in Asia) is what also formed the premise of even later-stage imperial Pan-Asianism, which would ultimately transform into the Greater East Asia Co-Prosperity Sphere. Though often reluctantly imperial, as Ferguson argues, and avoiding outlaying the resources (particularly human resources) required of its herculean overseas objectives, the United States increasingly sought to remake the world in its image.[176] This desire to remake other regions also finds an echo in the Meishuron strain of Japanese Pan-Asianism that sought to modernize Asia, with Japan as the explicit embodiment of such mastery of global forms of modernity. This strain, which grew particularly under the Taishō period (1912–26), was increasingly exclusionary and later tended toward the idea of "destroying the white tribes," to quote a journalist and historian of the time, Tokutomi Sohō.[177]

The ever more racialized climate of international relations fed Japanese distrust and suspicion of the Western powers, particularly actions such as American restrictions on Japanese immigration to the United States,[178] the

Wilson administration's criticism of Japanese policy in China,[179] and the publication of anxious, racist American books such as Madison Grant's *The Passing of the Great Race* (1916) and Lothrop Stoddard's *The Rising Tide of Color* (1920). There was a sense in both Asia and the West that there was a coming race war, and this sense began to justify Japan's expansion into Asia, as it styled (and genuinely considered) itself as the only potential savior of Asia. Katō Kanji, of the Japanese navy, argued that, "the Yamato race is destined to emerge as the savior of East Asia," and in 1916 a public gathering on Japan's China policy adopted a resolution that asserted, "In these days, when the world is in chaos, peace in the East can only be safeguarded by the Japanese empire."[180] When, after the conclusion of the World War I and the bloody loss of life, the League of Nations failed to include Japan's proposed racial equality clause in its covenant, the last hope of the Japanese for the West's recognition of their modernization and acquisition of the trappings of modernity on Western terms was lost.[181] The actual racial underpinning to the West's purported "universal" humanism and civilization seemed now to have been at last exposed. Japan would never be welcomed as equal, and East and West were intractably opposed to one another, as so many had long suspected but had worked to disprove.

Continued Asian Orientation Beyond the Revolution

The revolution was over, and deep, sustained Pan-Asian aid had eluded the First Philippine Republic. Nevertheless, Asianist orientation lived on well into the American colonial period in the Philippines as well as in Ponce's work, network, and friendships. Ponce stayed on in Hong Kong following his release from duty to the First Philippine Republic, then traveled to Shanghai and Indochina, before returning home to the Philippines with his Japanese wife in 1907. He was an editor of the leading Philippine newspaper, *El Renacimiento*, from 1908 to 1909, and helped establish the Nacionalista Party's organ, *El Ideal*, beginning in 1910. From 1910 to 1912, he served as a representative of the second district of Bulacan in the Philippine Assembly. He died of tuberculosis in Hong Kong on May 23, 1918.

Ponce had admired China's glorious history. In his biography *Sun Yat-sen*, Ponce wrote: "Of the ancient empires that flourished in olden times, China alone persisted." By contrast, "Only melancholy scraps remain of the Egyptian empire, and we know of the Assyrian, Mede and Babylonian empires only through history."[182] Yet he believed that for China to endure it would have to transform—"It will have to open itself to the winds of modern progress."[183] In this task he initially looked upon his friend Sun Yat-sen as "a visionary, a utopian," though he later came to realize that he was actually a "practical observer, highly realistic, and with a clear-sightedness that came from his talent and his great love for the land of his birth."[184] In 1906 Sun was still forbidden by the British government to enter its Hong Kong colony, but Ponce had the chance to see him en route to Saigon. Sun was planning to enter Kwangsi through the frontiers of Indochina, and notified Ponce of his trip so that Ponce could board the French ship as it passed through Hong Kong. A few months later, Ponce recalled, "I, too, went to Indo-China and stayed in Cochinchina and Annam."[185]

Ponce traveled by steamer to Saigon in December 1906 and toured Indochina for several months. His travels resulted in a study of the colony that he presented in the Centro Escolar de Señoritas on October 3, 1914, and published in 1915. Indochina is a country "that has many points of contact with ours," Ponce reminded his audience, and study of this country "should not be dismissed or derided."[186] He also recalled Rizal's note on Champa in his annotations of Antonio de Morga's *Sucesos*.[187] Ponce believed that Filipino interest in the history of Indochina should arise not only from "the memories of the splendor of its past civilization," or "the annals that conserve the history of its ancient princes and greatest events," but also because, "according to the wise Malayists, such as Dr. Kern of Holland, one finds the cradle, the origin of our race in the Indochinese country—deducing this argument from the comparative linguistic study of the languages that we speak here [in the Philippines] and that they speak in Indochina."[188] Ponce referred here to the same study on the Malay language that *La Solidaridad* had also referred to its readers two decades before.

Ponce related the participation of around 260 Filipinos on behalf of the Spanish in the French military conquest of Cochinchina in 1859.[189] While no details are provided of those Filipinos' experiences and reflections, Ponce recorded that the Filipinos "distinguished themselves for their bravery, tenacity, and resistance."[190] Despite this initial pitting of Filipino and Annamite, Ponce stressed their shared experiences under colonialism, such as the failure of the colonizers to teach their subjects the French and Spanish languages—teaching only Latin grammar, instead.[191] Indeed, Mojares reports that Ponce later noted that a Filipino soldier in the revolution remarked to him of the "great error and absurdity" of the Filipinos helping the French fight the Vietnamese.[192] Ponce also noted the policy of cultural and intellectual stultification that the French imposed "so that the Annamites would acquire habits of servitude and would not seek social advancement."[193] "The Annamites are prohibited to travel overseas, to Europe and even to Japan, without his/her corresponding passport, which they can only attain with great sacrifice and influence."[194] Seeking to block all possible civilizing influence from abroad, the French, according to Ponce, had great suspicion of everything foreign, "especially the Japanese."[195] This French suspicion of Japanese influence echoed the Spanish one, though Spain did not restrict travel so heavily, and it would have been natural for Ponce in particular to draw such comparisons.

"The Annamites are an intelligent race, devoted to their traditions and history, and open in the right time to the change of progress of each era," Ponce concluded.[196] His discussion of the Annamite race echoed the Propagandists' discussion of the Filipino race, with both being suited to "adaptation"—which was their races' "great power"—and absorption of other cultures.[197] He admired the Cambodian and Vietnamese ability to maintain their social autonomy, traditions, customs, and religions in a "force of ethnic resistance" amid loss of political autonomy. He predicted that just as the Vietnamese assimilated Chinese civilization, they would also assimilate the best of Western civilization, without undermining their natural and traditional ways of knowing. After the dissolution of the Philippine Revolution, this Social Darwinist vision of creative adaptation and survival—maintaining one's natural customs while assimilating the best of others' customs—became the Asianists' vision for the Philippine future under continued colonization.

With regard to Vietnamese Pan-Asianism, it was crucially inscribed not only in Phan Bội Châu and the scholar-gentry's intellectual and political history, but so too in the early development of modern nationalism in Vietnam. Its legacy of a transnational geography of political affinity would live on in Vietnam even after Pan-Asianism itself had waned. In the 1920s, as Shawn McHale notes, "far from subscribing to a bounded notion of identity defined by the territorial limits of today's Vietnam, Vietnamese participated in public and clandestine realms of discourse that transcended such frontiers."[198] This transnational political affinity would also eventually find an altogether new form in the international communism of the Vietnamese Revolution and the subnational Southeast Asian alliances it engendered.[199]

Asianism continued to inspire certain pockets of the Filipino discourse and world of ideas, but it remained on the sidelines, as did truer sympathy and solidarity with "fellow Asians." In July 1912 Teodoro M. Kalaw, a noted scholar and nationalist legislator during the American colonial period, wrote in his introduction to Mariano Ponce's *Sun Yat-sen:* "It must be noted that for sometime now, there has been a tendency to look with interest upon the political successes of Oriental peoples. I refer to a still timid sentiment for an alliance with, and sympathy for, the members of the ethnic Oriental groups."[200] He qualified this even further, circumscribing the potential geography of Asian political affinity: "Our approaches of moral sympathy refer more principally, for the present, to our neighboring countries, China and Japan."[201] Nevertheless, a fellow-feeling did exist within Asia, he declared. "This sympathy between Orientals was manifested more clearly on the occasion of the Japanese victory over the Russians in the last war, and manifests itself now with the victory of the Chinese Revolution against the traditional institutions of their Empire."[202] Kalaw's own admiration of Japan rested, curiously, on the country's performative Westernization, which he saw as deftly playing to the demands of the international community and allowing the country to compete geopolitically, without disturbing its domestic context through what could have been a far more wrenching, penetrating Westernization. "Japan has followed Western theories, Japanizing them," he explained. "Better still, she has pretended to follow them in order to fortify her own national institutions, preserving their traditional characteristics."[203] He continued, "Clearly, the objective was to reconcile the conservative doctrine, which still had strong and valued supporters, with certain ideas of reform that have already influenced Japanese youth, especially those who had studied in foreign lands and had acquired Western standards of living."[204] This followed the Social Darwinist vision of creative adaptation and survival.

In 1915 Ponce founded the Sociedad Orientalista de Filipinas and acted as its secretary general, with José Alejandrino, another Hong Kong Junta veteran who had worked to procure arms from Japan for the revolution, acting as president. The society and its journal, *Boletín de la Sociedad Orientalista de Filipinas*, advocated for Asianism. The inaugural issue of the *Boletín* ran Alejandrino's article "The Emancipation of the Far East" as its cover story.[205] "For the first time in its history, Japan is in a position to emancipate the Orient," he declared, "to remove it from the sphere of commercial exploitation and in so doing transform China from a distrustful neighbor to a genuine friend."[206] He said this not because he was blind to Japan's imperial advances, but in the hope of urging Japan back to its original purpose. He wanted Asians to keep alive the original, emancipatory spirit of Pan-Asianism.

The Americans, for their part, kept up their paranoia about and vigilance against this spirit.[207] A confidential report of the Philippine Constabulary on August 11, 1917, recorded: "For several days the rumor has been current and commented upon that by the end of next October there will not be an American in these Islands, because they say, the Washington government has transferred the Philippine Islands to the Japanese government in exchange for the Samoan Islands and because of this all the arms and munitions stored in the Ordinance Depot and Fort Santiago are being transported to America."[208] The source of these rumors was the Americans themselves, continuing the Spanish tradition of fear of the Japanese threat. The report continued: "These stories are spread by some American soldiers and they even discuss it on the street-cars; only yesterday I heard a conversation between a soldier and a Filipino, who were talking in English, but the American disembarked at Plaza Goiti and the Filipino told it to another Filipino and to the motorman of the car."[209] "These same rumors I have been hearing now for some time," the report warned, "and every time I hear them they have grown."[210] Further, the Philippine Constabulary Report from August 14, 1917, took note of "a curious suggestion from a Japanese Delegate," Viscount Motono, who "wants to exchange the Philippines for other islands"—and included an English translation of the article originally published on June 30, 1917, in the Manila-based daily newspaper, *La Vanguardia*, on this topic.[211]

Yet, many of the Filipino Asianists themselves no longer looked upon Japan idealistically. An article by Alejandrino in *La Nacion* published on September 7, 1917, a copy of which was included in the files containing the Philippine Constabulary's confidential 1917 reports, observed that with World War I, "the peoples of the colored races have no reason to hope for more just and equitative [sic] treatment from the so-called superior races," and, meanwhile, "the Japanese fear the Occidental nations and despreciate [sic] the Oriental ones."[212] Alejandrino closed the article by asking: "How can the Japanese pretend to play the part of the directors of Asia and who would admit that Japan is really the champion of Pan-Asianism and the defender of the interests of the Orient? . . . Japan's fear of the Occidentals is the origin of inhuman humiliations and its disdain toward the weak nations has produced vanity and indolence."[213]

For the Americans, this continued hope for a *real* champion of Pan-Asianism and continued belief in the emancipatory Asianist spirit (as it was originally conceived) justified a watchful eye over potential solidarity and collaboration among colonized or non-imperial countries. A 1917 Philippine Constabulary report translated an article from the Manila newspaper *La Nación* in its issue of September 4, 1917, "An Unforeseen Contingency," on the danger in sending Filipino militiamen to fight in Mexico.[214] The article posed a flaw in U.S. thinking: Why send Filipino militiamen to Mexico instead of to Germany? Mexicans complain of American interference, and there would be various parallels for the Filipinos to draw between their conditions; whereas in Germany, the United States was fighting for a lofty, unimpeachable ideal. The article referred to Mexico as the Philippines's "sister by education and culture."[215] Indeed, in the decades to follow, Third Worldist solidarity, nonalignment, and even a resurgent Pan-Malay vision in the short-lived Maphilindo experiment were the natural intellectual outgrowths of the Philippines's earlier Asianism, updating Asianism's emancipatory spirit of transnational solidarity among the oppressed peoples to a world vastly changed by Japanese occupation, World War II destruction, and global decolonization.

FIVE

The Afterlife of the Philippine Revolution

Reverberations from China to India to
Third Worldist Futures

What were the Philippines like after 450 years of separation from South Indonesia? This is the obvious question to arise in the heart of a lover of history who confronts the history of the whole of Indonesia.

—TAN MALAKA, *FROM JAIL TO JAIL*

You are building your conception of an Asia which would be raised on a tower of skulls. I have, as you rightly point out, believed in the message of Asia, but I never dreamt that this message could be identified with deeds which brought exaltation to the heart of Tamer Lane at this terrible efficiency in manslaughter. When I protested against "Westernisation" in my lectures in Japan, I contrasted the rapacious Imperialism which some of the Nations of Europe were cultivating with the ideal of perfection preached by Buddha and Christ, with the great heritages of culture and good neighbourliness that went [in]to the making of Asiatic and other civilisations. I felt it my duty to warn the land of Bushido, of great Art and traditions of noble heroism, that this phase of scientific savagery which victimised Western humanity and led their helpless masses to a moral cannibalism was never to be imitated by a virile people who had entered upon a glorious renascence and had every promise of a creative future before them. The doctrine of "Asia for Asia" which you enunciate in your letter, as an instrument of political blackmail, has all the virtues of the lesser Europe which I repudiate and nothing of the larger humanity that makes us one across the barriers of political labels and divisions.

—RABINDRANATH TAGORE TO NOGUCHI YONE, SEPTEMBER 1, 1938

THE END OF the nineteenth century (and beyond) in Asia is too often apprehended through a bilateral framework that privileges relations with the

West at the expense of the broader historical regional context. Despite the treaty arrangements that France imposed upon Vietnam at the close of the century, for example, the courts of Siam and Vietnam remained deeply entrenched in their traditional interstate relations, the meanings and symbolism of which were no less vital to their conceptions and enactments of sovereignty with the presence of the West in their territory and worldviews.[1] The global imaginary that informed various Asian nationalisms at the turn of the twentieth century, meanwhile, created various visions of Asia that were themselves central and grounding to those nationalisms.

"Asia" was the framework in which many nationalisms consciously situated themselves in defense against a hegemonic (whether in aspiration or reality) Western worldview and totalizing, hierarchical European understandings of race and civilization. Rebecca Karl in *Staging the World* examines the ways in which Chinese identification with what would become known as the Third World produced key planks of the Chinese nationalist discourse and made legible the international modern world in which Chinese nationalism was situated.[2] Meanwhile, in the Third World itself, in the Philippines, this book has shown that broad "Asian" identification with Chinese civilization and its ancient glory (but not the Chinese immigrants then present in the colony) as well as with rising Japan and its modern achievements was foundational to emerging Filipino national consciousness, as was identification with a broader Malay race. Nevertheless, I do not wish to argue for a binary reorientation from the "West" to the "rest" as the intellectual source of anticolonial nationalism. Neither has my argument, while providing a revisionist corrective to the Western-oriented (whether colonial or transnational) historiography of the Philippine Revolution, sought to erase the folk consciousness and local depth that the social history and social science turns have gained for the historiography. Per Partha Chatterjee, Christopher L. Hill, and Michael Goebel, I locate the origins of the international, modern anticolonial nationalism discussed in this book, which has been a more elite-driven intellectual history, at the interstices of the colonizer and colonized's intellectual and social histories to illuminate their mutual entanglement within a global field of power and discourse. This entanglement oftentimes resulted in the colonized's rejection of post-Enlightenment claims to European superiority while nevertheless integrating the epistemologies that supported such claims.[3] In this, I have particularly attended to Megan Thomas's insight regarding the ilustrados' use of Orientalist and Western genres, methods, and semiotics for "subversive" anti-colonial ends,[4] and see that European Orientalism's statements of difference between East and West obtained not only as intellectual planks supporting Western imperialism but also then positively *and* defensively as the foundations for Asia's unique role within a shared, universal history of civilization and as the foundations for narrower existential Asian solidarity strategies within a Social Darwinist framework. While I have not directly engaged with the role of global capitalism in the emergence of modern anticolonial nationalism, it is not to discount its organizing effect within this history nor to ignore Hill, Benedict Anderson, and Ernest Gellner's findings regarding a converging modernity and that modernity's role in underwriting the global phenomenon of nationalism—whether modular, "derivative," industrialized, or otherwise in terms of model.[5] Rather, the role of global capitalism and its modernity has been subsumed within my analysis into the reality of and attention to the material inequality that underpinned Social Darwinism. It also led my recognition of the material dimension as deeply constitutive to the periphery's Pan-Asianism in particular.

Reverberations of the Philippine Revolution in China and Indonesia

The Propaganda Movement used its constructed "Asia," to which the ilustrados attached the Filipino nation historically and racially, as a political tool in their claims against Spain, and as a component of their national consciousness and racial awakening. Further, it was a ground for their future sovereignty. Filipinas was not just a province of Spain—it was a place altogether apart, and indeed it was the importance of "place" that grounded their anti-colonial critique and nationalist imaginings. This differs slightly from the process Karl describes among the reformist Chinese, who from 1898 to 1911 carefully watched the Philippine independence struggle, the Boer struggle against Britain, and the Vietnamese struggle against France, among other international struggles taking place in the Third World, as emblematic of China's own problem and opportunity. Karl defines this problem and opportunity to be "how a diachronically Darwinian staged world could be constituted as an active site of global reimaginings within the context of overwhelming Euro-American-Japanese power" and "how this world could be transformed into an immanent stage upon which the Chinese, and others along with them, could act against the very global unevenness that was constitutive of their shared moment."[6]

While the "international" and "global" were deeply present in modern Chinese and Filipino nationalisms and were constitutive of the large part of those nationalisms' semantic frameworks, their respective positionality toward global imperial power differed. The ilustrados (with the exception of Isabelo de los Reyes) were constructing "Asia" in order for the Filipinos to have a place in this diachronic Darwinian staged world, as well as to level its stagedness by asserting a unitary civilization—in whose history they were included by virtue of race. Therefore, the ilustrados' position toward global imperial power, conceptually, was more nonchalant than that of the Chinese reformists. While the Chinese reformists were viewing Japan's rise with alarm, the ilustrados were trying to ride on its coattails, to link themselves to it, and to argue for their own civilizedness and racial rank. China's national problematic differed from but also drew on this anti-colonial practice; specifically, "the conceptual connections Chinese intellectuals made to the Philippine events from 1899 to 1903 helped Chinese intellectuals recognize revolution as a modern mode of being in the contemporary world."[7] In this practice, Karl argues, the Chinese found themselves startlingly "behind" not only advanced global powers including Japan but now also behind actively united (and previously ignored) peoples such as the Boers and Filipinos. As Ou Jujia asked in his 1902 pamphlet "New Guangdong" (Xin Guangdong): "Gentleman! Gentleman! Take a look at the relationship between our government and our people: can it come close to what the Boers did to England or what Cuba [and the Philippines] did to Spain?"[8] Here, the Third World was teaching China the meaning and viability of revolution as a solution to its national problems.

Just as the Vietnamese scholar-gentry in their writings and in Phan Bội Châu's Đông Du Movement enjoined the Vietnamese to emulate heroic figures of antiquity, Mai Menghua, a Chinese reformist and colleague of Liang Qichao, wrote an essay in 1897 praising the abstract values of the literary trope of the knight errant. Mai believed this spirit of the knight errant was essential to the nation. By 1900, however, Mai had linked this trope to the Philippine Revolution. Mai urged the Chinese people to recognize that the global knight errant figure was not merely an abstract trope but rather was actively exemplified by peoples, such as the Filipinos, who had risen up, and was not exemplified by those who had failed to revolt, such as the Indians and potentially the Chinese.[9] This reinterpretation is fascinating for its blending of the Japanese *shishi* and the Filipino revolutionary figures with the literary trope of the knight errant, creating from this an altogether new, modern, national role out of the formerly merely heroic individual, as Lorraine Marion Paterson's research has shown.[10] No longer an abstract trope, this figure was historicized and particularized, drawing upon specific examples from within the Asian geography of political affinity, and was also generalized as a "type" to be embodied transnationally.

In this process of fashioning a new national, revolutionary, heroic type, the Filipino created new modes of sociopolitical practice for the colonized in the modern world.[11] The *Hubei Student World* essay (1903) entitled "Feilubin wangguo canzhuang jilue" (Brief outline of the tragic loss of the Philippines) distinguished "yellow" politics along lines of power, with "the betrayed politics of alliance with Japan . . . replaced by the more promising politics of 'genuine' racial and Asian solidarity offered by the Philippines."[12] Similarly, Ou Jujia had linked the Philippines to China via a common historical and geographically spatial Asianness, while also demarcating the Philippines, not Japan, as the Asian pioneer, being the first to actively defend independence for "Asia" in this era.[13] In this interpretation, it is interesting that the Filipinos rising up for the Philippines is elided with rising up for Asia more generally, assuming a broader Asian geography of political affinity and *action.*

The example of the Philippine Revolution reverberated beyond China too, with its impact particularly visible in the wider Southeast Asian "Malay" world, especially in Indonesia. Famous colonial Dutch writer Multatuli's grandnephew, E. F. E. Douwes Dekker, in April 1913 prepared to tour the Philippines "to study the fast-developing political situation in the American colony,"[14] and went on to write an essay titled "Rizal" in the May 15, 1913, issue of a scholarly journal he founded, *Het Tijdschrift* (The magazine).[15] Dekker described Rizal as a hero—"Half-blood and native began to see him as the savior, the regenerator of the Fatherland."[16] The famous Indonesian Marxist revolutionary Tan Malaka's 1948 autobiography *Dari Pendjara ke Pendjara* featured a chapter on the Philippines that situated the country as part of an expansive historical greater Indonesia and described Bonifacio as "an indigenous Indonesian from Tondo on the outskirts of Manila."[17] Working off the premise that the Malay or Indonesian archipelago was whole and only fell into disunion with the advent of European colonization in the six-teenth century, Malaka asks: "What were the Philippines like after 450 years of separation from South Indonesia? . . . This is the obvious question to arise in the heart of a lover of history who confronts the history of the whole of Indonesia."[18] Indeed, Malaka's chapter evinced throughout a feeling of fel-lowship with the Filipino revolutionaries—he goes so far as to describe "the father of the Philippines" Rizal, the purportedly working-class hero Bonifa-cio, the "famous minister of foreign affairs" Mabini, and Aguinaldo as "all indigenous Indonesians who had little if any mixed blood."[19]

Indonesian nationalist leader Sukarno first mentioned "Jose Rizal y Mer-cado" in a speech on October 10, 1942; he would reference him many times, especially during his first term as president. John Nery also chronicles that, under Japanese occupation, the vernacular newspaper *Asia Raya* published a front-page profile of Rizal on December 30, 1943, as well as an Indonesian translation of Rizal's last poem, "Mi Ultimo Adiós," on December 30, 1944, by journalist Rosihan Anwar (who described Rizal as "a Malay genius" in his preface to the poem). When the United States granted independence to the Philippines in July 1946, a small magazine, *Bakti*, published in Mojokerto, forty miles southwest of Surabaya, ran the following headline on its cover: "Philippine Independence, the Hope of Millions in Asia" ("Kemerdekaan Pilipina harapan berdjoeta-djoeta bangsa Asia.").[20] "Aguinaldo and Rizal roused the Philippines in the early 1900s," Sukarno wrote in his 1965 auto-biography. "All Asia was growing up and in the glorious twentieth century, in which isolation could never occur again, even meek, timid Indonesia caught the feeling."[21] During his youth, Sukarno came into conflict with the Dutch colonial administration and spent thirteen years in prison and exile; according to the Sukarno-era diplomat Ganis Harsono, Sukarno "claimed that during that time he had lived in a spiritual world where he met a host of famous world personalities, like China's Sun Yat-sen, the Phil-ippines's José Rizal, India's Gandhi, Turkey's Kemal Ataturk, Germany's Karl Marx, England's Gladstone, and America's Jefferson."[22] For their part, the Asian revolutionaries in the Philippines, as in Indonesia and other parts of Southeast Asia, saw their struggle as part of a larger, ongoing Asian history and even destiny. Indeed, Shaharuddin bin Maaruf held up Rizal's "great struggle" for emulation in his *Concept of a Hero in Malay Society* (1984). This practice has held until even more recent times. Over October 2–3, 1995, Malaysia hosted the International Conference on José Rizal and the Asian

Renaissance, with then deputy prime minister Anwar Ibrahim as convenor and keynote speaker. On this occasion Ibrahim stated: "We associate Rizal and his like, such as Muhammad Iqbal and Rabindranath Tagore, with the Asian Renaissance because they are transmitters *par excellence* of the humanistic tradition."[23]

While this book has focused on elite anti-colonial, proto-national, and national discourse in order to capture the global, international, Asianist lens to this Filipino intellectual history, there are also other deeper bases for comparison that knit together anti-colonial and proto-national protest in Southeast Asia. A regional tradition of millenarian rebellion and protest is a shared pillar in the epistemological construction of Southeast Asian culture, as Maitrii Aung-Thwin has shown.[24] Very similar modes and articulations of protest obtained throughout Southeast Asia, and the pairing of religion and resistance has proved an important framework for understanding how many peoples across Southeast Asia have conceptualized the historical processes attendant with colonialism and how autonomous vocabularies have continued to serve rural communities in times of crisis, even if the anti-friar sentiment blunted more mainstream religious forces from directing the long Philippine Revolution.[25] The introduction to this book began with reference to the millenarian movements in the Visayas region of the Philippines that were reactions to daily suffering under the Spanish and to the ways in which the potent symbolism of the "international" was appropriated and deployed as a figure of external, almost mystical, power. This desire to appropriate symbolic external power took place among the ilustrados too, who conjured the power of the specter of Japan as a tool in arguing with the Spanish as well as to aggrandize their own racial belonging, even at times hypothesizing the Malay racial origin of the Japanese people.

Growing up with Japan—The Experiences of Southeast Asian Nationalist Leaders

The desire to appropriate the rising Asian power represented in the example of Japan was not limited to the Philippines.[26] Given their colonization under various Western imperialisms across Southeast Asia, it should be no surprise that Indonesian, Indian, Thai, and Filipino intellectuals alike were voyaging to Japan to observe firsthand the seeming miracle of Asian modernization.[27] When Phan Bội Châu met with the modernizing Japanese politicians Count Ōkuma Shigenobu and Viscount Inukai Tsuyoshi and the Chinese nationalist Liang Qichao in Japan, these men evinced a racialized understanding of their historical moment similar to that of the Vietnamese revolutionaries. Châu reported that these Japanese politicians spoke to him of "the problem of rivalry between Europe and Asia"—a problem that had placed them on the precipice of a race war. They told him, "If Japan wished to assist your country, then she would have to open hostilities with France. . . . Once hostilities were opened between Japan and France, then it is likely that conflict would be ignited worldwide. At present, Japan does not have enough power to stand against the whole of Europe. Could you possibly be patient and await your opportunity?"[28] This argument that priority be given to Japan for the good of Asia, and that "all of Europe" was the Asians' actual adversary, prefigured the position in which the pro-Japanese Cambodian nationalist Son Ngoc Thanh would later find himself during World War II.

Son Ngoc Thanh was the first Khmer to speak out for Cambodian independence in the 1930s. He was anti-colonialist, anti-Communist, anti-French, and anti-monarchist. He was living in exile in Japan in the beginning of the 1940s, and collaborated with the Japanese, who invaded Cambodia in 1941, to oust the French. Though he played a role in the *révolte des ombrelles* of 1942, he was himself unable to build a large-scale movement rallying the Cambodian people.[29] Thanh wrote to a Japanese official in Saigon on October 1, 1942: "All of us . . . are quite attached to Japan in the cause of Cambodia's independence, knowing that we can form with all the other states of yellow Asia a compact bloc around Japan, the Liberator and Defender of the Yellow World."[30] In January 1943, after his hopes of swift Japanese aid had diminished, he would write to his Khmer supporters from Tokyo: "We must wait. Only Japan's complete victory in Asia will resolve all the Asian problems to which the lot of our Cambodia is linked."[31] However, after the 1954 Geneva Accords partitioned Vietnam, it was Thailand (and the United States) rather than Japan that supported and trained Son Ngoc Thanh's anti-monarchist, anti-Communist guerrilla Khmer Serei (Free Khmer) movement.

Ultimately, during World War II, the Japanese Empire formed five "independent" Southeast Asian states under its occupation and sponsorship. Burma and the Philippines received formal Japanese-sponsored independence in

1943, while Vietnam, Cambodia, and Laos received it belatedly in early 1945, and preparations for the same in Indonesia were interrupted and never realized. Some Vietnamese political thinkers had long been attracted to Japan, and many of the political groups to emerge in the 1930s and 1940s, following Phan Bội Châu, admired Japan and wished to follow its example.[32] In particular, the Đại Việt organizations formed the Đại Việt alliance and tried to play a role in the formation of an independent Japanese-sponsored government in Vietnam, following Japan's 1940 invasion of French Indochina. These included the Greater Vietnamese Nationalist Party (Đại Việt Quốc dân đảng, or DVQCC) founded by Trương Tử Anh and publicly active beginning in 1939; the Greater Vietnamese National-Socialist Party (Đại Việt Quốc xã, or DVQX) formed in 1936 and active after the Japanese coup in 1945; the Greater Vietnamese Humanism Party (Đại Việt Duy Dân, or DVDD) founded in 1937 by Lý Đông A; and the Greater Vietnamese Authentic People's Party (Đại Việt Dân chính, or DVDC) founded in 1938.[33] However, even after fully expelling the French colonial forces, the Japanese authorities maintained the status quo to the detriment of the Đại Việt organizations that had been organized to receive power from them.[34] By marginalizing these groups, or simply denying them the advantages they had hoped for, the Japanese ultimately allowed the more radical groups, such as the Indochinese Communist Party (ICP), to compete with them on more equal terms. Following Japan's surrender in August 1945, the ICP under Hồ Chí Minh's leadership took control of most provincial cities in northern, central, and southern Vietnam. Japanese deserters and dissidents then leaned toward helping this new Vietnamese government, the Democratic Republic of Vietnam, instead of its nationalist opposition.

In Indonesia, meanwhile, though the occupying Japanese forces did not sponsor independence, they did impact the nationalist political landscape in other ways. In his memoir, Ganis Harsono, an Indonesian diplomat during the Sukarno era (1945–67), recalled how he came of age during the Japanese occupation, despite the various creeping humiliations he would later become aware of, such as the unwritten prohibition against Japanese-Indonesian fraternization.[35] The Japanese sponsored the first daily newspaper written in the vernacular Bahasa Indonesia language, *Asia Raya*, which was a significant innovation for the development of local nationalism, and Harsono was one of its paper boys. He returned to his life as a student under Japanese tutelage at the Bandung Kogyo Daigaku in 1943, which he described as a privileged and protected existence. With "all expenses paid and with enough money at our disposal" and "shielded from the realities of life in Bandung," he recalled that "we were supposed to hear no evil, see no evil, and speak no evil," and that "strict regulations and regimentation were imposed upon us in the fashion of Japanese army life." He explained, "in point of fact, student life in those days was a long round of military drill, Japanese indoctrination, and night vigils, while the lectures on the technical subjects we were supposed to learn took second place."[36] There, "The Japanese taught us the reading and writing of Japanese characters, the spirit of the Samurai, and the qualities of Japanese nationalism," he recorded.[37] This was no insignificant footnote, as the four Indonesian professors in charge of the technical subjects at the school—Professors Rooseno, Juanda, Gunarso, and Suwandi—would all become ministers, at one time or another, after Indonesia proclaimed its independence.

Harsono recalled that by the time Sukarno and Mohammad Hatta declared Indonesian independence in Jakarta on August 17, 1945, the revolutionary spirit had "caught fire, feeding on the incendiary emotions of youth in particular, many of whom were just beginning to feel the hardships of the Japanese occupation."[38] As for the students at 104 Dago Street, "We realized only then that the Japanese regime had been successful in separating us from the political mainstream in Bandung, so that we did not know at the beginning to whom we had to turn for guidance, leadership."[39] Meanwhile, "There was no strong leadership among the students themselves; this had in the past more or less handicapped them in their desire to dedicate body and soul for the defence of their country."[40]

Sukarno ardently supported Pan-Asianism, or "Inter-Asianism" as he called it, and this flowed directly from his nationalism. In this book I have argued that the Pan-Asian thought of the uncolonized world, centering on Japan, was distinct from the Pan-Asian thought produced in the still colonized world at the turn of the twentieth century, with its embedding of national priorities within Pan-Asianism and use of Pan-Asianism as a nationalist tool. Half a century later, Sukarno's Pan-Asianism flowed from his nationalism and its specific Asianist character, as well as from his more generally racialized geopolitical framework, even as he related his nationalism to more universalist principles of humanity. "True nationalists," he explained, had a nationalism that "is not merely a copy or imitation of Western nationalism but is based on a feeling of love of man and humanity."[41]

There was an anti-Western element to his understanding of Asian nationalism, because, as he wrote in his 1928 article "Indonesianisme dan Panasiatisme," he saw the "greater and more important problem" to be that of "Asia against Europe."[42] There was thus also an internationalism to Sukarno's understanding of appropriate Asian nationalism that made a policy of Pan-Asianism both natural and necessary. He called for full inter-Asian cooperation and, according to Bernhard Dahm's research, employed innumerable times his parable of the "Asian circus," in which he explained that if the Indonesian Banteng (wild buffalo) worked together with the Nandi (sacred cow) of India, the Liong Barongsai (dragon) of China, the Sphinx of Egypt, the white elephant of Thailand, and so on, Western imperialism could not last.[43] Under Japanese occupation he revised this parable to be the "Greater East Asian circus," with the teamwork of the animals "bathed in the rays of the rising sun" of Dai Nippon, as he explained in an article published in *Asia Raya* on December 7, 2602 (1942).[44]

Sukarno had founded the Partai Nasional Indonesia (PNI), or Indonesian Nationalist Party, in 1928 and was imprisoned by the Dutch authorities for subversive activity in 1931. The Japanese occupying forces released Sukarno after they invaded Indonesia in 1942, and they gave him a role in working to win Indonesian acceptance of and cooperation with the Japanese authorities. Sukarno tread carefully under Japanese occupation, balancing the wishes of his Japanese political sponsors and the Indonesians he sought to lead, most of whom were suffering under Japanese occupation. "In public speeches he extolled the Japanese nation and promised Indonesian support in the struggle against Western imperialism," J. D. Legge writes. "At the same time he sought to keep alive a vision of an Indonesian future. 'Long live Japan' became a familiar conclusion to his speeches but he added also 'Long live the Land and the People of Indonesia.'"[45] After the war, Sukarno became disillusioned with Japan, calling the idea of imperialist Japan as the savior of Asia "an empty dream," and while he did not explicitly exclude the state from his Inter-Asianism, he affirmed, instead, that Inter-Asianism was for all peoples striving for freedom.[46]

In Burma, Aung San, the nationalist leader who went on to win Burmese independence from the British, began his political career leading students' groups in the University of Rangoon under the All Burma Students' Union. In 1938 he joined the Dobama Asiayone (We Burmans) and went on to become its secretary general. After being arrested (but not prosecuted) in 1939 for conspiring to overthrow the British government by force, and escaping another arrest attempt the following year, Aung San left to travel around India. He later secretly returned to Burma to continue his political organizing, then left again to China hoping to make contact with the Chinese Communist Party. Instead, Japanese agents intercepted his group and took them all to Japan, where they were brought into the schemes of Colonel Suzuki Keiji of the Japanese Army, who sought to overthrow British rule in Burma.[47] Aung San returned again to Burma in 1941 and recruited others to undergo military training with the Japanese. Successfully enlisting the overseas Burmese living in Thailand, these young Burman revolutionaries together formed the Burma Independence Army, which joined the Japanese as an invading force when they ousted the British. While Aung San became a major general in the Japanese Army and later minister of defense in Dr. Ba Maw's government, created under Japanese sponsorship in August 1943, Aung San never committed himself to the defense of Japan's interests in Burma. Indeed, in mid-1943 he worked with others to begin planning an underground movement against the Japanese, and he led his army against the Japanese on March 27, 1945, joining the Allies to expel the Japanese from Burma entirely.[48]

Politically, Aung San was an internationalist and a regionalist, and he advocated Burma joining an Asian regional grouping dedicated to developing Asian unity, cooperation, and freedom, as well as the reintegration of Asian culture.[49] His essay "Defence of Burma" from 1944 suggested a defensive and political alliance with Indochina, Thailand, Malaya, Yunnan, the Philippines, the East Indies, and India east of the Brahmaputra River. While a year later he limited the group, envisioning instead a United States of Indochina that would include French Indochina, Thailand, Malaya, Indonesia, and Burma, he argued for this alliance on the basis of nationalism. "This sort of scientific internationalism, the internationalism of creative mutuality, is indeed in accord with the highest interests of nationalism," he declared in his address to the East and West Association on August 29, 1945, at the Rangoon city hall.[50] This Asianist regionalism predicated on the priorities of nationalism recalls Sukarno's own position, as well as that of the wide range of Southeast Asian Pan-Asianists from the colonized world at the turn of the twentieth century.

Pan-Asianism in the Philippines in the Afterlife of the Philippine Revolution

In the Philippines, too, the Asianist intellectual and political inheritance of the Propaganda Movement and the Philippine Revolution, respectively, lived on deep into the period of American colonization.[51] Indeed, the winner of the American-sponsored 1938 Commonwealth Biography Contest was Carlos Quirino's *The Great Malayan*, a sweeping tribute to José Rizal, whose title alone pointed to the active Asianist potential that endured in the examples of the Propaganda Movement and generalized history of the Philippine Revolution. Similarly, Léon Maria Guerrero III (1915–82), the Filipino writer and diplomat, was one of the most celebrated biographers of José Rizal and the most important translator of Rizal's *Noli Me Tangere* and *El Filibusterismo*,[52] and served as undersecretary of foreign affairs under President Ramon Magsaysay's administration (1953–57), during which post and beyond he advocated for "Asia for the Asians."

Artemio Ricarte, Benigno Ramos, Pio Duran, Ahmed Ibn Parfahn, President José P. Laurel,[53] and even President Diosdado Macapagal embody this Filipino turn-of-the-twentieth-century Asianist inheritance. With regard to this group of notable twentieth-century Filipino Pan-Asianists, Artemio Ricarte forms the strongest link between the Philippine-Revolution and World War II phases of Filipino Pan-Asianism. He was chief of operations for the Filipino forces in the second zone around Manila in 1899 when fighting between the Filipinos and Americans began in earnest. Attempting to infiltrate American lines, Ricarte was captured and imprisoned in Bilibid Prison by the American forces.[54] He refused to swear allegiance to the United States, as did others such as Apolinario Mabini; both Mabini and Ricarte were sent to Guam in exile for two years. While Mabini, in ailing health, finally capitulated in 1903, Ricarte still refused to swear allegiance, and so was sent to Hong Kong in exile again. There he plotted launching his own revolutionary movement against the United States. In December 1903, he successfully returned undetected to the Philippines aboard the *Wenshang*, and once home regrouped a scattered rebel force, preparing them to attack. The Americans discovered his plot and presence, and eventually captured him through the work of Filipino informant Luis Baltazar. Ricarte was tried and convicted for subversion and sentenced to six years solitary confinement. When upon his release on June 26, 1910, he again refused to swear allegiance to the United States, he was banished to Hong Kong once more.

In Hong Kong he published the paper *El Grito del Presente*, keeping alive the racialized interpretation of the Philippines's colonial condition. "Our race is in slavery," he wrote in 1913. "To the interminable series of punishments that accumulate on our existence, only cries and lamentations are heard. . . . On one side the silhouette of hunger appears and on the other side the horrors of the past are seen again."[55] From Hong Kong he also crafted in 1914 a "Constitution of the Revolutionary Government in the Rizaline Islands which are to be erected into a nation with the name of Rizaline Republic," which was his vision of political independence and sovereignty for the Philippines. He moved to Yokohama in 1915 in permanent exile with his family. He would remain there until the Japanese occupation of the Philippines during World War II, when he, now an old man, was finally brought home by the Japanese to aid their Pan-Asianist and occupying efforts there.[56]

During that occupation, his 1943 publication *Nippon at Busido* clarified his understanding of the aspects of the Japanese model and Japanese history that offered salient lessons for the Philippines, as well as his vision for the Philippines's potential role within Japan's Greater East Asia Co-Prosperity Sphere. "If Anglo-Americans look at a tree, they only look at its utility and value," he analogized, "but if the Japanese look at it, they will look at the deeper value it has and wonder at its meaningful roots, branches, and leaves."[57] He cited Japanese poetry—"the highest form of poetry on earth"—as his example of this.[58] *Nippon at Busido*, with its peculiar question-and-answer format, allowed Ricarte to pose the question of which historical story shaped the minds of Japanese children and embedded within them the Japanese spirit. His answer was telling for its demonstration of what he believed to be Japan's true purpose. "There are a lot," he answered. "But I am inclined to choose the book of *The Travels of Momotaro Against the Ogre*."[59] He explained it as follows:

One day, Momotaro heard the news that there lived a red demon and a blue demon in a far off land that terrorize the people who live there. He made it a point to remove them from that island no matter what. He asked permission from his parents to go on his important quest. He was granted permission, so, afterwards, he prepared his things and left for the island. After a long journey, he finally arrived at the demons' island. He brought with him one servant.[60] Once, he and his servant fought with the red demon and blue demon, and finally made them surrender. The legend ended with his prideful return after finishing his responsibility.[61]

"This is not a legend for the entertainment of children, but one story of the War of the Greater East Asia," Ricarte explained. "Momotaro is no one else but Nippon, while his companion is the other Asian nations that are allied with Japan. The demons are the Americans, British, and Dutch."[62] In this the Philippines could be Momotaro's companion. "Look at the flaming sword of righteousness that slays the red and blue demons. The Japanese children are guided by the legend."[63] To Ricarte, this was the meaning of the Greater East Asia Co-Prosperity Sphere that Japan's growing empire was building— and the Japanese government used this same story in its propaganda in this period. To Ricarte, the Philippines would be saved by Japan's leadership, and would be on the right side if it fought alongside its Asian brethren against the "Americans, British, and Dutch."

Pio Duran, an outspoken Pan-Asianist, was associate professor of law at the University of the Philippines during the period of American colonization. In his work and writing, he asserted the West's moral double standard; the Philippines's sisterhood with the East; Japan's ambitions to reconfigure the geopolitical divisions of world order for the good of Asia; and the racialized reality of the international sphere, geopolitics, and oppression.[64] For these reasons, he advocated for Pan-Asianism as the official Philippine foreign policy and political ideology. He related the Philippines's colonial subjection to the racial oppression then dominating the United States domestically. "The same racial prejudice which denies the Negro citizen of the United States the right to take the same street-car or the same hotel which his white brother does . . . is the same racial prejudice which underlies the humiliating and inhuman persecution of Filipino laborers along the Western coast of the United States," he argued.[65] He understood the Philippines to be part of what was a global racial assault. This developing association with non-Asian oppressed peoples, grounded in an original Pan-Asianist sympathy, exemplifies the intellectual transition that was then afoot, as disillusioned Asianists would update and expand their affective political geography to take a more Third World position. This transition away from Pan-Asia and toward the Third World became more necessary after the heavy suffering that many Southeast Asian countries endured under Japanese occupation in World War II.[66]

Benigno Ramos, meanwhile, was a Filipino writer, political organizer, and advocate of Philippine independence and Pan-Asianism under Japanese leadership.[67] Originally from Bulacan and hailing from a relatively poor family, he was a talented student and writer and was highly politicized even from youth. He began his career as a revolutionary poet-writer and also wrote for the weekly *Renacimiento Filipino* beginning in 1911. His writings sought to keep alive the memory of the Philippine Revolution and its heroes, to criticize U.S. rule, and to enjoin others to oppose continued American oppression. In emulation of Jacinto, Bonifacio, Rizal, and the Propaganda Movement before him, Ramos urged poets to use their writing for the betterment of society.[68] He began the Sakdalista protest movement, which between 1930 and 1934 drew more than 68,000 members, and in May 1935 attempted an uprising with roughly 20,000 participants that was quickly crushed. Ramos was a powerful orator, and his Sakdalista followers perceived him as incorruptible, as a modern-day Rizal, the Mahatma Gandhi of the Philippines, even the messiah for a new life.[69]

Ramos left the Philippines in November 1934 ostensibly to advocate for Philippine independence in the United States, but instead he disembarked in Yokohama, the old Asianist site of Filipino anti-colonial and nationalist subversion, and stayed in Japan until 1938. There, radical, politically peripheral Japanese Pan-Asianists welcomed and supported him, including the Diet member Matsumoto Kumpei, even though the Japanese government avoided direct contact with him and spied on his every move and association while in Japan.[70] Ashizu Uzuhiko was one of these peripheral Japanese radicals who took an interest in Ramos. Under the pseudonym Nansen Hokuba, Ashizu published beginning in 1935 a series of writings under the collective title *Pacific Pamphlets* that sought to introduce the Sakdalistas and Ramos's ideas and ideals to the Japanese public.[71] Ramos returned to the Philippines in 1938, but was arrested upon his arrival; his supporters immediately posted his bail and he was released. He joined another political party, the pro-Japanese Ganap, to continue to fight for independence, until he was again arrested in May 1939.

In April 1942, during World War II, the Japanese occupying forces released Ramos from prison, after which he served as one of the officials of the

Japanese-sponsored mass-mobilization organization Kapisanan sa Paglil-ingkod sa Bagong Pilipinas (Kalibapi), and he was a founding member of the pro-Japanese Makabayan Katipunan ng Pilipino, or Kalipunang Makabayan ng mga Pilipino (Makapili).[72] At the end of the war, Ramos retreated to the mountains of northern Luzon with the Japanese Army and a few cabinet members of the Japanese-sponsored republic under President José P. Laurel.[73] An eyewitness claimed Ramos died aboard a Japanese plane that crashed as it took off for Japan; his remains were never recovered.[74]

The Japanese forces invaded the Philippines on December 8, 1941, as part of their confrontation with the United States and in pursuit of widening Japan's Greater East Asia Co-Prosperity Sphere from East to Southeast Asia. Bombing American military bases in the Philippines, landing at three points in Luzon, and approaching Manila, the Japanese took the capital on January 2, 1942, then Bataan and Corregidor over April–May. The Commonwealth government-in-exile under President Manuel L. Quezon and Vice President Sergio Osmeña arrived in San Francisco on May 8, 1942, and installed itself in the United States.[75] The Japanese Military Administration established the Philippine Executive Commission on January 23, 1942. After holding a series of posts in this transitory government, Laurel became president of the Second Republic of the Philippines when Japan granted Philippine "independence" on October 14, 1943. As president, Laurel presented his desired total reform as "comprehensive," "far-reaching," and implying "a complete renovation of the individual and collective life of the Filipinos."[76] In his war memoirs, which were completed in prison in Japan in 1945 while awaiting trial, Laurel similarly described how, during his tenure as president, he never renounced the thought and logic that underpinned the program he pursued.[77] In this light we may treat Laurel's program as a "collaborator" president as an expression of his political philosophy, which he had developed over the preceding two decades, not only of circumstantial opportunity and the logic of collaboration.

In his thought, José P. Laurel defined the Orient not merely negatively as oppressed by Western imperialism, but also positively as the cradle of civilization. For Laurel, the Orient and Occident emerged as real, historical entities in their dialectical history with each other and with a third entity, which was what he imagined as universal civilization. He referred to "Mother Asia" as what "[nursed] the human race and [endowed] it with the most ancient civilization and the most profound religions that the world has ever known" and discussed the Orient and Occident's ostensible passing between and co-creation of "civilization."[78] In a December 1927 speech at the University of the Philippines College of Law, he particularized the West by describing it as one of many cultures, so as not to privilege and deem prominent a single "Western Civilization." Rather, he argued that civilization was propagated at different times by different cultures, and recounted that the West originally learned certain values, spirit, and traditions of thought from the East.[79] Thus he declared on October 14, 1944, in a message to Greater East Asia delivered over station PIAM, "East is East and West is West, it is true, but there is absolutely no valid reason why when they meet they should not meet as equals. There is no reason why as heretofore they should meet as superior and inferior, master and slave, oppressor and oppressed. If they stand equal before God, so must they stand before man."[80] Therefore, despite the real existence in Laurel's thinking of an opposed Orient and Occident, or a differentiated East and West, Laurel's understanding of civilization served to flatten the historical bases upon which something like the European chauvinism that Hannah Arendt described could emerge, and it opened a premise from which to assert his bedrock "universalism."[81]

East and Southeast Asian observers of the late nineteenth and early twentieth centuries believed that international geopolitics and the advance of Western imperialism was leading to an inevitable race war between the Orient and the Occident. In his 1927 speech at the University of the Philippines, Laurel stated that he "would not want to see a mighty world conflict staged. But as Asians, the Filipinos cannot remain indifferent . . . geographically and racially, we belong to Asia."[82] On Greater East Asia Day, December 8, 1943, he linked all "Occidental penetration" into the Orient as a common history, again making real and historical the existence of an Orient and Occident. "No nation in Asia, worthy of the heritage of her past, her sacred traditions, and the right to live under the sun, can henceforth countenance the return of Western rule or influence," he charged. "The Asians can no longer be satisfied with being mere 'hewers of wood' and 'drawers of water' for Occidentals."[83] Here Laurel described a geopolitical, historical landscape that, while built on a depoliticized, naturalized conception of universal civilization (however vaguely defined) to which all men had equal right, had come to represent a very real competition for dominance and a foreseeable race war.

The task then, according to Laurel, was for the Orient not only to awaken and reclaim its inherited bond to the civilization that the Occident had claimed for itself, but also to unmask the corruption of world religion as represented in Western imperialism, which universal civilization was made to serve and legitimize in the hands of the Occident. In the aforementioned 1927 speech he declared that "the Orient should unmask the true nature of Western imperialism and understand its real spirit and designs," which he associated with moral corruption by excessive pursuit of material gain and the establishment of structures of racial and cultural inequality in violation of the essential equality of men under natural law.[84] In his *Moral and Political Orientation* Laurel asserted that "every man is man's brother and equal. There shall not be any discrimination on account of race, creed or color," and that "freedom is a divine endowment and is not a matter of grace from the earthly powers that be."[85] Due to his personal understanding of natural law, Laurel interpreted this task as a divinely sanctioned mission for the Orient. He asserted: "God in His infinite wisdom will not abandon Japan and will not abandon the peoples of Greater East Asia."[86] Similarly, in his November 22, 1943, address in Manila to Subhas Chandra Bose, president of the Provincial Government of Free India, Laurel referred to Bose as the "leader of 350 million Indians in their effort, which is legitimate and divine, to free themselves from the British rule."[87] This remark pierces Theodore Friend's claim that Japan's "Holy War for Asian Liberation" rang as alien and difficult to understand for educated Christian Filipinos for whom "the term 'just war' evokes argumentative principles that rationalized the Crusades."[88] God appears undifferentiated in Laurel's view of natural law through his understanding of "universal civilization," allowing Laurel's statement to Bose to be made from a member of one world religion to that of another. Laurel nevertheless declared that "there is One Eternal God, Creator and Sustainer of the universe."[89] Indeed, he also wrote that "until unity of religion is achieved, the Church and the State must remain completely apart and separate."[90] While he stated that "this separation implies equality of all religions," he nevertheless envisioned this separation as necessary only due to the particular historical moment during which the "millennium of religious union is not yet."[91] Here we see that even within his universalism and championed equality lay a bedrock particularism and inequality, and therefore he could not deny his belief in his own One Eternal God above others. This elision of universalism and particularism, of the universe and *La República Cristiana* (the Christian Republic), obtains elsewhere in his thought.

Laurel's universalism conflicted with his particularism, and his shifts between the two revealed the ways in which his contingent, particularist, historically constructed understanding was deeply embedded in his universalist vision and actually worked to produce that "universalism." In his 1927 speech he affirmed that "at the behest of the Christian religion, Western nations have invaded the East, conquered its territories, ruled its people against their will" and "have forced upon every weak people in the Orient the administration of their own laws and usurped local sovereignty on the pretext of spreading Christian civilization."[92] Yet, "their benighted Christianity . . . has led them at the same time to adopt stringent laws of exclusion against the Orientals in defense of the very sovereignty which they have trampled upon."[93] He stated in an address before the Assembly of the Greater East Asia Conference in Tokyo on November 5, 1943, that "the East is the cradle of human civilization. It has given to the West its religion and its culture, and yet the West has used the same civilization to exploit the peoples and countries when that civilization came."[94] Laurel thus imagined a universalist, divine foundation to world religion and to human civilization, while also positing intractable differences between the systems of law emanating from the West and East, such that the enforcement of one's system over that of the other was unjust and unnatural, though they might stem in part from the same sources. This intractability perhaps resulted from what he interpreted to be the historical perversion of civilization and religion in the hands of the West, which produced exclusionary laws and a benighted version of Christianity.

Thus, for Laurel, this dialectical history and the contingent, historical products that resulted from it, necessarily revealed to the Orient its connection to the Occident, and inextricably returned the Orient to the Occident in its divine mission of "unmasking" the particularist corruption to which the Occident had subjected the originally Eastern "universalist" civilization. Laurel asserted that world religion and human civilization originated in the East—"World Civilization saw its first light at the northern base of the snow-capped Himalayas, and then, crossing Central Asia, it entered Greece and developed into the grandeur which Rome spread over Europe."[95] Further, in Laurel's thought, the East was able to differentiate which particular historical products adhered acceptably to human civilization's universal principles (the grand Roman Empire) from those that did not (modern Western imperialism). This interpretation privileged the

East's current judgment of the West's caretaking of purported human civilization in a way that delegitimized the West's ability to correctly or morally assess the validity of its goals or that accused the West of failing to adhere to the putatively operational, desirable objectives of this universal order. Either scenario embedded a deep particularism into Laurel's universalism, while naturalizing that particularism.

As it did for most Pan-Asianists since the late nineteenth century, the theory of natural selection crucially informed Laurel's racialized understanding of the world order and supported his Pan-Asianism. In a 1959 pamphlet, "Opportunism and the Darwinian Aspect of Current Political Struggles," he wrote: "Natural selection, and the law of the survival of the fittest, as elaborated by Darwin, have no ethical principles, but merely concern themselves with the preservation of the species; and one may add, perhaps that it does not matter one way or the other whether the species to be preserved are opportunistic politicians, habitual grafters."[96] However, he perceived a "higher suggestive lesson": "Since [the Philippines is] still a young and weak state why not continue propping ourselves up for a while longer with supports from stronger friends?"[97] He asked: "Why cannot the survival of the Filipino nation, amid so many adverse conditions, and formidable risks, be assured by unsentimental and realistic bargains and relationships with all nations, far and near, which could give help or benefits to us for the time being?"[98] Yet, in this position he still did not seem to condone an alliance with the West, which he did not believe shared the Philippines's interests, thus making Pan-Asian solidarity the only natural conclusion left for Laurel.

Laurel believed that Asiatic solidarity was a repudiation of imperialism itself, which he defined as Western. He asserted in his December 1927 speech that "the fundamental problem for the Orientals" was the need to "acquire political and economic freedom so that they and their posterity will be able to emerge from the present form of political and economic bondage imposed upon them by the so-called superior people." He declared, "We can do this task by de-hypnotizing ourselves and casting away self-distrust"—with 'self' here referring to other 'Orientals.'" Hence, he imagined Pan-Asian solidarity to be a triumph over Western imperialism, which guarded against a "united and compact Orient."[99] In his speech to the Assembly of the Greater East Asia Conference in November 1943, he detailed this imperial program: "America and England have always intended to divide the peoples of Greater

East Asia in accordance with the principle of 'dive et impera' in order to weaken the morale, the vigor and the vitality of the peoples of Greater East Asia. America and England have divided these peoples by establishing divisions in their religion, in their classes and by encouraging political differences among them."[100]

Laurel defined Western imperialism through its materialism and intention to dominate weaker peoples, particularly those of the Orient who were neither of their race nor culture. This definition allowed Laurel, once president, to rationalize Japanese empire as something distinct from Western imperialism. The retreat from Western imperialism figured for Laurel as a retreat from the infection of Western immorality. "We can combat the virtue of excessive materialism which we inherited from the West," Laurel stated in his inaugural address, "only by a return to the spiritual ways of the East where we rightfully belong."[101] He similarly warned against the tendency to accumulate wealth, a temptation that the West introduced.[102] To Laurel, the Japanese were of the Orient and limited their empire to its putative cultural-territorial space, seeking to unite Asians and give them freedom to develop and maintain their own cultures. His championing of explicit political (rather than vaguer intellectual) Pan-Asianism through Japan's Greater East Asia Co-Prosperity Sphere rested publicly on an ideological commitment to the "co-existence, cooperation and co-prosperity" with "recognition of, and respect for, the autonomy and independence of every integral unit" within the sphere.[103] Laurel asserted that the Co-Prosperity Sphere was designed such that "each nation may develop in accordance with its own institutions" but "without any particular member monopolizing the resulting prosperity to [sic] the other integral units," while acknowledging that "the prosperity of all is the prosperity of the integral parts, but that the prosperity of the integral parts is not necessarily the prosperity of the whole."[104]

This imperial vision represented, for Laurel, a potentially new form of empire based on solidarity and autonomy that aimed at a more inclusive universal understanding of prosperity. "Just as the East was the cradle of civilization," Laurel contended, "so the East may again be the foundation of a new code of international relations based on moral justice and aimed at the common happiness and prosperity of all the members."[105] Moral codes and older notions of a moral universe and moral government infused this new imagined diplomacy with a rhetoric that recalled classical Confucian discourse. "Diplomacy is wisdom, diplomacy is trenchant, diplomacy is cooperation, diplomacy is mutual understanding," Laurel intoned at a dinner given in honor of Kenkiti Yoshizawa, Japanese Ambassador to Indochina, on January 13, 1944.[106] Crucial in this vision for diplomacy, however, was a notion of belonging and commonality that would make possible such mutuality. "In the case of the Philippines which is returning to her Oriental fold to which she, by nature, by traditions, by culture and by geographical propinquity, belongs," Laurel asserted, "these synonyms of diplomacy should be developed and followed."[107] Here one sees the particular political vision that Pan-Asianism sincerely held for Laurel and that animated his geopolitical position both as a Filipino political thinker since the 1920s and as president.

What emerges in Laurel's thought are cultures of nation and universe tied deeply to the legacies of empire both in the Philippines and in the imagination of those in Asia who felt themselves to have been the objects of, rather than subjects in, a Western world order. The theoretical moves found within the development of Pan-Asianism mirrored those within Laurel's intellectual development: the premise of an anti-Western, anti-imperial critique formed the basis for building a conception of a shared identity that sought to enact a broader understanding of universal world order. Laurel saw the Orient and Occident as real, historical entities through their dialectical relationship with each other and with "civilization." The circularity of this process—historical entities produced as historical products only through their dialectic—reflected the similarly circular relationship between universalism and particularism in Laurel's thought. Laurel's universalism existed always in tension with his particularism, and his movements between the two revealed the ways in which particularist, historical contingency was deeply embedded in and constitutive of his "universalist" vision. This tension resulted from what I argue was his understanding of natural law, which was at once divinely homogenous and necessarily differentiated. Although universal, his natural law also took for granted as natural the particular historical innovation of the nation and its political agenda. This innovation, too, bore the legacy of Western imperialism, the experience of which pushed Laurel to defend and protect the sanctity of the nation-state as a guard against imperialism while also engendering fantasies of universalism and Pan-Asian solidarity to secure such particularist national freedoms. In what seemed to be a mounting race war, both the weapons of the nation-state and of a reconceived Pan-Asian Oriental empire seemed necessary in the unfinished struggle against Western imperialism.

The Telescoped Đông Du Project Under Japanese Occupation

The history of peripheral Pan-Asianism transitioned from late-nineteenth-century Southeast Asian Pan-Asianists seeking to obtain material revolutionary aid from the Japanese to early twentieth-century Southeast Asian nationalists seeking to emulate the Japanese model, until finally nearly all of Southeast Asia experienced direct Japanese occupation during World War II. So what was direct Pan-Asianist schooling under the Greater East Asia Co-Prosperity Sphere like? Long after the Katipunan's exhortations for its members to study in Japan, a kind of telescoped version of the Vietnamese Đông Du project would eventually come to the Philippines when the Japanese Empire brought Southeast Asian youth to study in Japan, including Filipino *pensionados*—government-sponsored student boarders abroad. This idea had not died with Rizal, the Katipunan, or Phan Bội Châu. Pio Duran had lamented that the private and public education system in the Philippines under the United States had not given Asian history the importance it deserved and that Filipinos lacked an understanding of Japanese, Chinese, and Malayan civilizations.[108] "On the other hand," he wrote, "the American controlled newspapers in the Philippines take advantage of every opportunity to malign the good name of the Japanese, and to picture that country as a warlike nation awaiting the first opportunity to seize the Philippine Islands."[109] Ricarte had also discussed the great potential of Japanese learning in his *Nippon at Busido*. "In the near future, there will be a lot of brilliant students brought from the Philippines to Japan," he wrote, and "those who will study there will learn the ways of the Japanese education . . . after that, they could bring the Japanese methods of teaching back here to the Philippines."[110] Not merely an educational opportunity, Ricarte depicted this as a distinct privilege and access to the source of Japanese power. "There, they will breathe the same air, walk the same land, and be taught by the same teachers in Japan" as the Japanese are.[111] It was an opportunity to inhabit the environment and *place* of Japan, which was imbued with an aspect of symbolic power. How did the Filipinos regard this opportunity, however? The diary of one the pensionados, Leocadio de Asis, provides an intimate record.

After the fall of Bataan during World War II and Leocadio de Asis's capture as part of the Second Regular Division, U.S. Army Forces in the Far East, de Asis was one of the Filipinos selected by the Japanese on account of his health and his academic and professional records to attend a training program, amid the ongoing war, as part of the reconstituted, Japanese-established Philippine Constabulary Academy. The Japanese intended the group to be the vanguard of the new future national police force in the Philippines—familiar with Japanese culture, society, and values (particularly those of the imperial Japanese police), and able to bring a Japanese-style order to the supposedly "anarchic" Americanized Philippine society.[112] Despite the difficulties of the state of war, de Asis went to Japan with a deep curiosity. He was of the later generation of Filipinos who had come of age completely convinced of the Americans' invincibility; and the speed, efficiency, and totality with which the Japanese overthrew the United States in the Philippines was a numbing shock. His diary shows that prior to 1941 de Asis had almost no knowledge of Japan, and like his twenty-six fellow pensionados, the opportunity to come to know Japan firsthand was, despite their personal reservations and service to the United States, an alluring, exciting prospect. He wrote on August 10, 1943: "Today is the first anniversary of my release from the war prisoners' camp at Del Pilar, Pampanga. I thanked the Lord sincerely for His Infinite Goodness and all His favors." He further recorded, "In the short span of one year, so many things have happened. I trained at the Constabulary Academy No. 3, was appointed later as instructor there, then transferred to Constabulary Academy No. 4 and, now, just one year after my last day as prisoner, I am a pensionado right in the 'very center of the Greater East Asia Co-Prosperity Sphere' in Tokyo."[113] His reflections on the grim, disturbing time he spent in the concentration camps did not seem to stop him from forming connections with the Japanese people he met. That same day he wrote, unbothered, "This p.m. showed some of my Japanese neighbors my family and Malacañan pictures. Tonight during study period had very nice talk with Mr. Murakami, the university student who stays with us. I told him about things Philippine and talked to him specifically about Bataan, the concentration camps and my experiences in connection with the anniversary of my release today. Felt the second earthquake tonight at 10:05. Quite slight."[114]

Leocadio de Asis remarked on the many Japanese Christians he encountered, the Japanese fluency with multiple languages, the deep learning of the Japanese people, and the refined demeanor of the Japanese he met. Additionally, he wrote on July 27, 1943: "Reading the *Nippon Times* every day, we get candid news and editorial comments which our [Manila] *Tribune* never publishes. The reason is the difference in the temperament and psychology of the people." To elucidate this, he provided the following example, "This morning's *Times*, for instance, played on the imminence of enemy raids over Japan proper in view of the increasing force of the enemy on the China continent. I enjoy reading the *Nippon Times* and its candid views and news analysis."[115] Rather than a reading of the Japanese temperament or of its comparison with that of any other peoples, this seems to reflect de Asis's own prior belief in the invincibility of the American colonial power that had dominated and controlled the Philippine press. To read stories of the threats to and weaknesses of the Japanese power must have been refreshing to colonial subjects used to an aggrandizing press.

One of the most interesting aspects of the diary is the way it shows de Asis's prior parochialism disappearing, not merely through incorporation of firsthand understanding of the Japanese, but through the training program's realization of an embodied greater East Asia community. In this microcosmic community, the constituents collaborated and fraternized, and in doing so formed a sense of the oft-referenced "greater," but always as representatives of distinct national units. De Asis described meeting with Burmese students, with whom he talked about Burmese independence on August 4, 1943; he saw an exhibition on Thailand and its people a few days later, on August 8. Also on August 8, de Asis wrote of his visit to José Abad Santos Jr.'s dormitory in the International Students' Society: "In this dormitory are quartered Indonesians, Annamese, Siamese and J. Abad Santos. . . . I was impressed by Santos's room. He has a Filipino flag on the wall, several religious pictures and images and quite a lot of English and Japanese books."[116] This dormitory may have seemed like a picture of a new kind of modernity, at once regionalist, global, and Asian.

De Asis often pointedly referred to the failing morale, poor attitude, and lack of discipline characterizing the Filipino group, which he believed reflected badly in the eyes of the Japanese administration. This was an innately *relational* realization that emerged precisely through comparison, facilitated by this greater East Asia community of which he was now part. It reflected his understanding of the total community and the community's idealized vision for its members, as well as the Philippines's standing by those measures. "I hope we all behave properly for the sake of our country and race," reads a typical diary entry.[117] Besides their direct viewing of Japanese propaganda materials, such as the film *World of Love* and the Daitoa (Greater East Asia) News, for students the Pan-Asian community took on a corporal shape through their physical, lived experience, in which intermixing only heightened awareness of what they perceived to be national distinctions.

De Asis regarded José P. Laurel very highly, calling him "one of the greatest living Filipinos."[118] To the pensionados in Tokyo, Laurel was a pillar in the Greater East Asia Co-Prosperity Sphere, reportedly inspiring even those who were not Filipino through his intelligence and sensitivity—at least that was the perception in which de Asis took pride. On November 8, 1943, de Asis wrote: "President Laurel's speeches have received a great ovation from all quarters in Japan. At school, too, the Annamese students, whose national consciousness is being awakened (during the athletic meet yesterday they refused to carry the banner which labeled them as 'French Indo-China' and not 'Annam'), have been greatly impressed by Dr. Laurel's speech, especially the part where he mentions the sad plight of the still oppressed peoples of India, Indo-China, Java, Sumatra, and Malaya." He noted, "Talking to us, they told us how they admire the Filipino president, who was the only one of the Great East Asia representatives who did not forget the other nations who do not as yet enjoy a free existence."[119] Indeed the presumably Japanese-supplied banner reading "French Indo-China" is significant for its insensitivity and the continued Western imperial cartography it imposed on this embodied Greater East Asia.

Representatives from all over Asia were invited to the Greater East Asia Conference in Tokyo on November 6, 1943. It was of the highest importance for the Japanese imperial project, both for the Greater Asia it was seeking to effect as well as for Western observers. Hatano Sumio notes that in a discussion on the drafting of the Greater East Asia Joint Declaration, which was the communiqué for the conference, Japanese diplomats expressly stated that "if we are to give Britain and America the impression that we are doing good in Greater East Asia and induce their cooperation," they would have "no choice but to refer to the Atlantic Charter, which specified the Allies' *raison d'être* for going to war."[120] Their counterstatement to the 1941 Atlantic Charter, which had been issued by President Franklin D. Roosevelt and Prime Minister Winston Churchill, declared, "The United States of America and the British Empire have in seeking their own prosperity oppressed other nations and peoples. Especially in East Asia, they indulged in insatiable aggression and exploitation, and sought to satisfy their inordinate ambitions of enslaving the entire region, and finally they came to menace seriously the stability of East Asia," which led to World War II. Greater East Asia nations were declared to be fighting to "liberate their region," ensure their "self existence and self-defense," and to build a Greater East Asia in accordance with the principles of "mutual cooperation" for "common prosperity . . . based upon justice"; "fraternity of nations" by respect of "sovereignty and independence" and practice of "mutual assistance and amity"; "respecting one another's traditions and developing the creative faculties of each race" to enhance their common Greater East Asian culture and civilization; "economic development through close cooperation upon a basis of reciprocity"; and work to achieve "friendly relations with all the countries of the world," "abolition of racial discrimination," "promotion of cultural intercourse and the opening of resources throughout the world" toward the "progress of mankind."[121] De Asis described the conference as a "historic parley calculated . . . to bolster the morale of the 1,000,000,000 people of East Asia." He proudly reported that the students there (not merely Filipinos but all the represented nationalities of the Greater East Asia Co-Prosperity Sphere) "were all so proud of *our* leaders. . . . The way they carry themselves with such dignity and self-mastery has impressed us a lot." He went on to report that "the speeches of President Laurel, with his typical eloquence and forcefulness, have impressed the Japanese public, and even our instructors at school are commenting on President Laurel's scholarly statements."[122]

The Japanese facilitated such heightened national identification and let the pensionados feel Filipino. On National Heroes' Day on November 30, 1943, the Filipinos raised the Filipino flag in front of their dormitory.[123] They also often performed Filipino folk dances for an audience. But the Filipinos often found Japanese representations of Filipino identity to be lacking. This crucially delegitimized the Japanese attempts to cohere and construct a Greater East Asian culture that could sublimate such heightened national distinctions while simultaneously nurturing them. The Japanese-produced opera *Madame Rosaria* was "highly advertised as a musical masterpiece which is another contribution to Filipino-Japanese cultural relations," but to the Filipino pensionados, it was "a flop," de Asis wrote on December 5, 1943. "We were utterly disgusted when the character, Joaquin Navarro, supposed to be a typical Filipino *padre de familia* appeared dressed in *sarong* (*tapi* [a piece of cloth usually wrapped around the body from the waist down]) looking more like a Burmese or Indonesian or anything else but a Filipino."[124] The depiction of Filipino womanhood was also judged lacking and unrepresentative.

The message of a "common culture" in the East Asia Co-Prosperity Sphere (and in late-nineteenth-century and early twentieth-century Pan-Asian thought) had set a very high bar. Under this imperial framework, the constituents of this common culture would immediately be able to judge when imperial rule felt inauthentic. This is a significant change from the traditional framework of imperial rule, which is impersonal, federal, and differentiated for the ruling and the ruled. There were also other ways by which the Filipinos did not merely accede to the imperial power's judgment. For example, the Filipino pensionados had less respect for "Víbora," the nickname of General Artemio Ricarte, than did the Japanese, who greatly esteemed him. De Asis wrote on January 28, 1944, on the occasion of Ricarte's visit to the pensionados, "During our intimate chat with this grand old man, we were not much impressed, especially by certain points we talked about."[125] This may reflect, on de Asis's part, his position between two imperial powers. Having believed in the invincibility of the United States until their defeat by the Japanese, he could not now behold the Japanese or their opinions with the same lack of criticality.

So what did de Asis make of his experience in Japan in the end? How did he square his former service to the Americans with his tutelage under the Japanese, which itself was undertaken while his fellow Filipinos were experiencing Japanese occupation? On October 3, 1943, Laurel visited the pensionados at a party in Tokyo. De Asis wrote: "We gathered around President Laurel in a very cordial conversation, cameras clicked and flashed as newspapermen got busy. The President was very approachable, and we did not hesitate to talk to him about the Philippines and her independence." More specifically, he recounted, "President Laurel literally gave us a discourse on his views about our coming independence, emphasizing the fact that freedom from any source, whether from America or from Japan, does not make any difference provided it is real freedom. We could notice how sincerely he spoke, tears dimming his eyes."[126] Of his own allegiance and purpose there, de Asis later wrote from Tokyo, "Now that we see the sincerity in the actions of Japan and the high ideals for which she is fighting, we cannot help but feel grateful for the opportunity granted to us to work for our country in particular and for Great East Asia in general."[127]

While one diary is not enough to draw wide conclusions, it would seem that de Asis (if not his larger pensionado cohort in Japan) was different from the ilustrado and Katipunan Asianists in two key ways. First, the Asianists of the Propaganda Movement and the Philippine Revolution did not always fully trust Japan's intentions, and were quite pragmatic in their appeals to and admiration of Japan. The same was true of a few Filipino Asianists during the period of American colonization—particularly Pio Duran, who tempered his Asianism with calls for a return to its "pure" form, disavowing the expansive, aggressive form then being exhibited by Japan in China and elsewhere. Second, the turn-of-the-twentieth-century Asianists were not dependent upon Japan's good intentions. Meanwhile, these young pensionados living abroad under Japanese sponsorship and undergoing training for a Japanese-dominated future were. The pensionados were not the direct legacy of the long Philippine Revolution's Asianists, then, but rather they were its telescoped inverse.

The Reinvigorated Pan-Malay Vision in the New Third Worldist Landscape

The Japanese occupation of Southeast Asia came to an end in 1945. The Japanese defeat and revelations of their brutal prewar and wartime abuses in China and Southeast Asia, as well as their particularly bloody exits from certain countries, such as the Philippines, irreparably damaged the "high ideals" once associated with Japan-centered Pan-Asianism. Further, following massive destruction and decolonization, the prior world systems that had caused such suffering, whether under global war or oppressive colonialism, were deeply delegitimized. It was this global landscape that formed the context for nonalignment, Third Worldism, and Pan-Malayism to grow in the Philippines, and it was these political positions and geographies of political affinity that carried certain strands of the former Philippine Pan-Asianism into the second half of the twentieth century. The logic of such internationalisms and cosmopolitanism was not a given, however, and indeed, as Tim Harper has chronicled, was badly damaged in the immediate aftermath of the war: "Many post-war journeys from Southeast Asia, South Asia and China were passages into banishment or exile. Dying empires and new nations guarded their frontiers jealously. Much was lost in the process."[128] He judged this to be the passing of a great era of globalization in Asia. "The dream of a greater Malay nation floundered against the Dutch blockade of the Indonesian Republic. Once prosperous ports—Rangoon, Penang, Surabaya—became backwaters, and their cosmopolitan-minded minorities: Baghdadi Jews, Hadrami Arabs, Peranakan Indians and Straits Chinese went into decline. More enclosed state structures were being erected that placed more importance on internal identity politics, the local defence of status and nationality, than the pursuit of global sympathies."[129]

In the Philippines, the postwar Pan-Malay vision was related to both the ilustrados' discourse on the Malay race and that discourse's development under American colonialism. In the 1930s the Pan-Malay vision found its most passionate expression in the person of Wenceslao Vinzons, a University of the Philippines law student.[130] In 1932 he established a "Malay Association" with a Dutch-influenced Bahasa name, Perhempoenan Orang Melayoe, to be "a miniature league of Malayan brotherhood."[131] Indonesian, Malay, Polynesian as well as Filipino students living in Manila joined the organization that "promoted the study of the history, civilizations, and culture of the Malay race."[132] By 1934 this organization grew to a national scale and was called Young Philippines. It saw itself as a self-conscious advance in the "development of the Malay race," working toward the eventual "establishment of a confederation of free Malayan Republics" in Southeast Asia.[133] In this project, Young Philippines drew to its membership such prominent Filipino nationalists as those who would go on to become President Manuel Roxas, Speaker of the House of Representatives José P. Laurel Jr., President Diosdado Macapagal, and President of the United Nations General Assembly and Minister of Foreign Affairs Carlos P. Romulo.[134] Though this organization eventually died out in importance, particularly after Vinzons's execution in 1942 by the Japanese occupiers, mainstream Filipino politics and discourse continued to identify the Filipinos as part of the wider Malay race. Postwar politicians would also very conveniently dress their attempts at forging better relations with Indonesia and Malaysia in overtures of Malay solidarity.[135]

The Filipino Muslim Ahmed Ibn Parfahn published a wild, fanciful Pan-Malayan treatise, *Malayan Grandeur: A Narrative of History by a Hundred Seers and Our Intellectual Revolution* in 1967. It included a section called "Jesus Had a Malayan Birth" that detailed the Malayan custom of labor and delivery that Jesus experienced. It also featured a section titled "The Malay Nation Can Be Great Again" with the subsection "Racial consciousness must be taught to the Filipino." His "Intellectual Revolution Manifesto," included in the book, also angrily declared that "the Europeans at their beginning had nothing to show in the way of culture and civilized living until they had borrowed from 'the parent stock of the human species'—the Malays—their letters, their arts and sciences, their mathematics, the entire paraphernalia of religion and even Gods."[136] This declaration summarizes his book's overall historical interpretation. After its wide-ranging narrative of Malay history and unfounded claims on behalf of the Malay civilization, *Malayan Grandeur* included in its appendix "The Intellectual Revolution Credo" that Ahmed Ibn Parfahn espoused. He advocated for "the rule of Truth," which he presented as directly related to the "nascent Third World Force."[137] He concluded his credo with an appeal for Pan-Malay and Third Worldist solidarity. He enjoined Filipinos to think of their Malayan brothers in Vietnam, which he described as "the embattled Malayan citadel." He described the Vietnamese victory at Dien Bien Phu and subsequent plight under American attack as "but the repetition of the Philippine experience: Defeating Spain in 1898, the little Malolos Republic befriended heretofore, was snuffed out by these same Americans. MAY GOD SAVE VIETNAM!"[138] While representing the very edge of the political fringe in the Philippines, certain points of Ahmed Ibn Parfahn's thought find echoes elsewhere. The Pan-Africanist Marxist Frantz Fanon in his *The Wretched of the Earth* (1961) united all the colonized into what he saw as a single struggle and consciousness. Also referring to Vietnamese history, he wrote: "The great victory of the Vietnamese people at Dien Bien Phu is no longer strictly speaking a Vietnamese victory. From July 1954 onward the colonial peoples have been asking themselves: 'What must we do to achieve a Dien Bien Phu? How should we go about it?'" He concluded, "A Dien Bien Phu was now within reach of every colonized subject."[139] Meanwhile, Ahmed Ibn Parfahn's Pan-Malayism was the extreme reflection of a more mainstream, longstanding sentiment. Not only did his inventive history recall Pedro Paterno's fanciful (though, of course, less radical) history of ancient Tagalog civilization, but its politics also related to that of President Macapagal.

If José P. Laurel could be considered the Philippine Pan-Asianist president, which I have argued elsewhere,[140] then Diosdado Macapagal (1961–65) could be thought of as the Philippine Pan-Malayan president. In August 1963 he facilitated an accord with Indonesia and Malaya to take initial steps to establish the pact known as Maphilindo—a "reunion of brothers"—proposing a nonpolitical confederation of the three countries.[141] Macapagal designed Maphilindo to erase the artificial, imperially imposed divisions among the peoples of the Malay race and directly related his vision to that of his 1930s activism alongside Vinzons—"under our rallying cry Malaysia Irredenta."[142] The Maphilindo confederation was Macapagal's brainchild, but it reflected the shared sentiment of all three leaders who wished to bring about regional cooperation without interference from the great powers and to establish a neutral zone in Southeast Asia.[143] At the closing ceremony of the Manila Conference that inaugurated Maphilindo on August 5, 1963, Sukarno retold Asia's history of falling behind the West—that is, until the beginning of the twentieth century at the time of the Philippine Revolution when, he declared, "History awakened. We Asians awakened."[144]

Though solidarity with a Greater Malaya periodically recurred in Malaysia, Anthony Reid contends that this expansive vision of the Malay race—a "more Europe-derived racial sense of a vast family of peoples of diverse languages and religions"—was sustained primarily in the Philippines.[145] However, solidarity seems to have flown in the reverse direction as well. Even today one frequently meets Malaysians named "Rizal" or "Reezal" after the Filipino hero José, who is often referred to as the "Greatest Malay." In Indonesia the most famous Rizal is General Tengku Rizal Nurdin, who became governor of North Sumatra in 1998 and is noted for re-establishing Malay culture there for the first time following the Indonesian Revolution.[146]

For the Philippines, a resurgent Pan-Malay vision, the short-lived Maphilindo experiment, and Third Worldist solidarity were the intellectual outgrowths of the Philippines's earlier Asianism. They updated Asianism's emancipatory spirit of transnational solidarity among the oppressed peoples to a world vastly changed by Japanese occupation, World War II destruction, and global decolonization. As with Asianism before it, Third Worldism and nonalignment connected Filipino political thinkers and actors to their Southeast Asian neighbors, who were again undertaking similar intellectual, national, and political work. Whereas the Southeast Asian transnational moment of the turn of the twentieth century saw imperial subjugation hardening empires and firing local resistance across the region, the transnational moment of the wake of World War II saw mass decolonization and national revolutions lighting up Southeast Asia, again connecting these polities through shared problems and existential conditions.

Though the world was deeply changed by these two global moments, in the Philippines certain Asianist rhetorical tactics, intellectual moves, and geographies of political affinity have persisted through both eras. Indeed, even the contemporary Philippine president Rodrigo Duterte, elected in 2016, recalls them. *Fengyu Taipingyang*, a novel by overseas Chinese Du Ai, written at the end of his life from 1980 to 1993, features the Chinese guerrilla resistance movement Wha Chi that operated during World War II. It blends histories and references between China and the Philippines to render a shared, or at least mutually recognizable, experience of political suffering and struggle, as Caroline S. Hau's article "Du Ai, Lin Bin, and Revolutionary Flows" explores. At one point, the character Li Jinfu leads her art class through a history lesson, expounding: "Children, Bonifacio's assassination is similar to what happened in China. When so-called Generalissimo Jiang Jieshi saw the revolution was being won in Shanghai and Nanjing, he embarked on counter-revolution and massacred many revolutionaries in order to steal the fruit of revolution. Classmates, isn't it hateful?" After Li Jinfu recounted the intervention of the Americans, who merely replaced the Spaniards, the novel tells how, "When the children heard this, they felt that the Philippines was indeed weighed down by calamity and, with China, formed a pair of suffering brothers."[147]

After World War I, the Bolshevik Revolution and Wilsonian principles undercut the international appeal of Pan-Asianism. After World War II, the suffering and disillusionment caused by Japanese occupation and the new exigencies of decolonization and strident domestic nationalisms disenchanted Southeast Asia with the idea of Japanese-led Pan-Asianism. Nevertheless, the distinct mode of critique and the alternative visions of cosmopolitanism, modernity, and world order that Pan-Asianism represented were neither unimportant nor short-lived in Southeast Asia. Not only did they live on in the postwar Third Worldism and Pan-Malayism of the region, they are embedded in the very foundations of the nationalism and nation of the Philippines.

We have too often viewed the global moment of the turn of the twentieth century in Asia through a Western-orientated bilateral framework to the exclusion of all other relations and frameworks, particularly at crucial moments such as the French imperial incursion in Vietnam. So too limited is our understanding of the Philippine Revolution and the Philippine nation that came of age in this period, whose regional Asian and cosmopolitan moorings demand their due place in this rich, regional history. This rich history, in turn, attests to the more complex, dualistic internationalist formal experimentation that obtained in the Southeast Asian periphery within the twentieth-century history of the rise of the nation-state as *the* legitimate political form. The particular logic, priorities, and conditions of power in the Southeast Asian periphery at the turn of the twentieth century, meanwhile, make clear Social Darwinism's role in this Asian internationalist moment, where and when the world appeared to be arrayed into two camps, making forms of global federalism seem necessary and natural to constituent Asian nation-states' existence and survival. Many Filipino thinkers and revolutionaries grounded anticolonial political legitimacy in supposedly inalienable understandings of place and nation, but like their Vietnamese neighbors, among others, they fortified such national groundings within wider racial camps, which were assumed to share various interests—if not outright civilizational destinies. This history of transnational anti-colonial Pan-Asianism in the Southeast Asian "periphery" was not only distinct from that which emanated from the Sinic East Asian "center" of Pan-Asianism, but would also help form the basis for a more coherent political region of "Southeast Asia" later in the twentieth century. While turning to East-East relations and to contact *between* peripheries, among others, this book has not occasioned a simple reorientation of historical attention away from the West in order to recover something "internal" within and to Asian history. It is, rather, an attempt to recover a wider range of the structures of thought— Eastern, Western, imperial, anti-colonial, peripheral, core—involved in Filipino conceptualizations of a universal human history of civilization, and how Filipinos carved and grounded their constructed national places within it.

Notes

All English translations from Spanish are the author's unless otherwise noted.

1. A Transnational Turn of the Century in Southeast Asia

1. Robert Bruce Cruikshank, "A History of Samar Island, The Philippines, 1768–1898" (PhD diss., University of Wisconsin-Madison, 1975), 181.
2. Sophia Marco, "Dios-Dios in the Visayas," *Philippine Studies* 49, no. 1 (2001): 50.
3. Filomeno V. Aguilar Jr., *Clash of Spirits: The History of Power and Sugar Planter Hegemony on a Visayan Island* (Quezon City: University of the Philippines Press, 1998), 167.
4. Though the prior Creole liberal revolts of the 1820s, under "Conde Filipino" Luis Rodriguez Varela, among others, were similarly international in consciousness and were contemporaneous with important Latin American wars of independence, they were ultimately only Manila-based, though they had styled themselves as *hijos del país* (sons of the nation).
5. See Alfred W. McCoy and Ed. C. de Jesus, eds., *Philippine Social History: Global Trade and Local Transformations* (Quezon City: Ateneo de Manila University Press, 1982).
6. The regulation of *libre comercio* in 1778 had introduced additional Spanish ports and challenged the monopolistic framework of the Manila-Acapulco galleon trade, which itself ended in 1815. The decades from 1820 to 1870 saw increased foreign trade in the Philippines, due to Spanish government shipping subsidies and an overall increase in trade and navigation in Asia that the opening of the Suez Canal in 1869 only compounded. Benito J. Legarda, *After the Galleons: Foreign Trade, Economic Change and Entrepreneurship in the Nineteenth-Century Philippines* (Madison: University of Wisconsin Center for Southeast Asian Studies,

1999), 179. The trading houses in the Spanish colony during the nineteenth century were predominantly Anglo-American, and their introduction of agricultural machinery, advanced money on crops, and other innovations helped to transform the Philippines from a subsistence economy into an export economy. Legarda, *After the Galleons*, 186. Of course, as Filomeno V. Aguilar Jr. reminds us in *Clash of Spirits*, such an economically "international" colony had emerged only after the cessation of the Manila Galleon, before which Philippine commercial trade under the Spanish was more traditionally bilateral, with exclusive privileges for the mother colony. Indeed, after 1898, the Philippines would re-acquire traditional, privileged, bilateral metropole-colony relations under the United States, thereby ending almost a century of economic "internationality."

7. By convention the years 1896–1902 mark the period of the Philippine Revolution, but I am dating the end of the Philippine Revolution at 1906 because I consider the surrender of Mariano Sakay y de León to mark the real end of the revolution.

8. D. G. E. Hall, *A History of Southeast Asia*, 4th ed. (London: Macmillan, 1981).

9. Elleke Boehmer, *Empire, the National, and the Postcolonial, 1890–1920: Resistance in Interaction* (Oxford: Oxford University Press, 2002), 2. See also Michael Goebel, *Anti-Imperial Metropolis: Interwar Paris and the Seeds of Third-World Nationalism* (New York: Cambridge University Press, 2015); Noor-Aiman I Khan, *Egyptian-Indian Nationalist Collaboration and the British Empire* (New York: Palgrave Macmillan, 2015).

10. Goebel, *Anti-Imperial Metropolis*, 15. See Partha Chatterjee's *Nationalist Thought and the Colonial World: A Derivative Discourse?* (London: Zed Books for the United Nations University, 1986) and *The Nation and Its Fragments: Colonial and Postcolonial Histories* (Princeton, NJ: Princeton University Press, 1993); Cemil Aydin's *Politics of Anti-Westernism in Asia: Visions of World Order in Pan-Islamic and Pan-Asian Thought* (New York: Columbia University Press, 2007); and Erez Manela's *The Wilsonian Moment: Self-Determination and the International Origins of Anticolonial Nationalism* (Oxford: Oxford University Press, 2007).

11. Matsuda Koichiro, "The Concept of 'Asia' before Pan-Asianism," in *Pan-Asianism, A Documentary History*, vol. 1, *1850–1920*, ed. Sven Saaler and Christopher W. A. Szpilman (Lanham, MD: Rowman & Littlefield, 2011), 45.

12. Victor Lieberman, *Strange Parallels: Southeast Asia in Global Context c. 800–1830*, vol. 1, *Integration in the Mainland* (Cambridge: Cambridge University Press, 2003), 14–15.

13. Once the pressing impetus of anticolonialism was removed and Southeast Asian nation-states were exploring various arrangements of alliances and regional blocs to little effect, scholars asked: "Can the spirit of regional cooperation that developed in the first flush of anti-colonial awakening ever be recovered now that the South East Asian countries are all free of Western dominance?" Ben Kiernan, "Asian Drama Unfolds," *Inside Asia* (September–October 1985): 19.

14. The ilustrado newspaper and central mouthpiece of the Filipino Propaganda Movement, *La Solidaridad*, for example, compared the lot of the British colonies in Asia as a whole to those of the French.

15. I use the then contemporary name of the Spanish colony (Filipinas) when discussing the archipelago prior to the idea of the Filipino nation and when discussing the colony as distinct from the imagination of that nation.

16. *Ilustrado* is the term for the educated elite of Philippine society, which through its slippery usage in Philippine historiography requires more exact definition in relation to the various strata of the elite and educated Filipinos. For a discussion of the terminology of elites, *ilustrados*, *caciques*, and so on, see John N. Schumacher, S. J., "Recent Perspectives on the Revolution," *Philippine Studies* 30, no. 4 (1982): 446, 449–50. I use it here to refer to the educated elite whose ideas shaped the national Philippine Revolution and the First Philippine Republic's government.

17. These works include Teodoro M. Kalaw, *La Masonería Filipina: su origen, desarollo y vicisitudes, hasta la época presente* (Manila: Bureau of Printing, 1920); Juan Causing, *Freemasonry in the Philippines* (Cebu City: G. T. Printers, 1969); Cesar Adib Majul, "Principales, Ilustrados, Intellectuals and the Original Concept of a Filipino National Community," *Asian Studies* 15 (1977): 1–20; Cesar Adib Majul, *Apolinario Mabini: Revolutionary* (Manila: National Historical Institute, 1993); Cesar Adib Majul, *The Political and Constitutional Ideas of the Philippine Revolution* (Quezon City: University of the Philippines Press, 1996); John N. Schumacher S. J., *The Propaganda Movement, 1880–1895: The Creation of a Filipino Consciousness, the Making of the Revolution* (Quezon City: Ateneo University Press, 1997); and John N. Schumacher S. J., *Revolutionary Clergy: The Filipino Clergy and the Nationalist Movement, 1850–1903* (Quezon City: Ateneo University Press, 1998).

18. Reynaldo Clemeña Ileto, *Pasyon and Revolution* (Quezon City: Ateneo de Manila University Press, 1979).

19. David R. Sturtevant, *Popular Uprisings in the Philippines, 1840–1940* (Ithaca, NY: Cornell University Press, 1976); Reynaldo Clemeña Ileto, *Filipinos and their Revolution: Event, Discourse, and Historiography.* Quezon City: Ateneo de Manila University Press, 1998.

20. Christopher L. Hill, *National History and the World of Nations: Capital, State, and the Rhetoric of History in Japan, France, and the United States* (Durham, NC: Duke University Press, 2008), 34.

21. Julian Go and Anne L. Foster, eds., *The American Colonial State in the Philippines: Global Perspectives* (Durham, NC: Duke University Press, 2003); Julian Go, *American Empire and the Politics of Meaning: Elite Political Cultures in the Philippines and Puerto Rico* (Durham, NC: Duke University Press, 2008); Alfred W. McCoy, Josep M. Fradera, and Stephen Jacobson, eds., *Endless Empire: Spain's Retreat, Europe's Eclipse, America's Decline* (Madison: University of Wisconsin Press, 2012).

22. Resil B. Mojares, *Brains of the Nation: Pedro Paterno, T. H. Pardo de Tavera, Isabelo de Los Reyes, and the Production of Modern Knowledge* (Quezon City: Ateneo de Manila University Press, 2006).

23. Megan C. Thomas, *Orientalists, Propagandists, and Ilustrados: Filipino Scholarship and the end of Spanish Colonialism* (Minneapolis: University of Minnesota Press, 2012), 15.

24. Benedict Anderson, *Under Three Flags: Anarchism and the Anti-Colonial Imagination* (London: Verso, 2005), 230.

25. D. B. Miller, ed., *Peasants and Politics: Grass Roots Reactions to Change in Asia* (New York: St. Martin's Press, 1979) examines the relationship in Asia between peasants and political process, in which Dennis Shoesmith's study of the Rizalista Philippine folk religion sits alongside studies as disparate as those of land reform in Communist Vietnam and the Burmese peasant response to nineteenth-century British rule. Stewart Lone, ed., *Daily Lives of Civilians in Wartime Asia: From the Taiping Rebellion to the Vietnam War* (Westport, CT: Greenwood Press, 2007) places the civilian experience of the Philippine Revolution alongside the civilian wartime experiences of the Taiping and Nian Rebellions, the Pacific War in Japan, Indonesia from 1939 to 1949, and the Korean War, among others. Researcher and journalist John Nery, in *Revolutionary Spirit: Jose Rizal in Southeast Asia* (Quezon City: Ateneo de Manila University Press, 2011), traces the influence of the Filipino national hero on later Indonesian nationalism and Malaysian scholarship.

26. See Caroline S. Hau and Kasian Tejapira, eds., *Traveling Nation-Makers: Transnational Flows and Movements in the Making of Modern Southeast Asia* (Singapore: NUS Press, 2011); Resil B. Mojares, "Los itineraries de Mariano Ponce y el imaginario político filipino," in *Filipinas, un país entre dos imperios*, ed. María Dolores Elizalde and Josep M. Delgado (Barcelona: Ediciones Bellaterra, 2011); Resil B. Mojares, *Isabelo's Archive* (Mandaluyong City: Anvil Publishing, 2013); and Francis A. Gealogo, "Mariano Ponce and Pan Asianism," in *Naning: Mariano Ponce 150th Birth Anniversary Commemorative Lectures & Selected Articles in La Solidaridad*, ed. National Historical Commission of the Philippines (Manila: National Historical Commission of the Philippines, 2013).

27. Mojares, Brains of the Nation; "Los itineraries de Mariano Ponce"; Isabelo's Archive; "Rizal Reading Pigafetta," in *Waiting for Mariang Makiling: Essays in Philippine Cultural History* (Quezon City: Ateneo de Manila University Press, 2002); "Early 'Asianism' in the Philippines," *IDEYA: Journal of the Humanities* 11, no. 1 (2009): 1–8; and "The Emergence of Asian Intellectuals," *Asian Studies: Journal of Critical Perspectives on Asia* 49, no. 2 (2013): 1–13.

28. See Josefa M. Saniel, *Japan and the Philippines, 1868–1898* (Quezon City: University of the Philippines Press, 1969); Grant K. Goodman, "General Artemio Ricarte and Japan," *Journal of Southeast Asian History* No. 2 (September 1966): 48–60; Goodman, "Japanese Pan-Asianism in the Philippines: The Hirippin Dai Ajia Kyōkai," *Studies on Asia* (1966); Goodman, "The Philippine Society of Japan," *Monumenta Nipponica* 22, no. 1/2 (1967): 131–46; Goodman, "Pio Duran and Philippine Japanohilism," *The Historian* 32, no. 2 (February 1970): 228–42; Goodman, "The Problem of Philippine Independence and Japan: The First Three Decades of American Colonial Rule," *Southeast Asia* 1, no. 3 (Summer 1971): 165–92; Goodman, "A Sense of Kinship: Japan's Cultural Offensive in the Philippines during the 1930s," *Crossroads: An Interdisciplinary Journal of Southeast Asian Studies* 1, no. 2 (June 1983): 31–44; Goodman, "Consistency Is the Hobgoblin: Manuel L. Quezon and Japan, 1899–1934," *Journal of Southeast Asian Studies* 14, no. 1 (March 1983): 79–94; Goodman, "An Interview With Benigno Ramos: Translated from the Japanese," *Philippine Studies* 37, no. 2 (1989): 215–20; Goodman, "Filipino Secret Agents, 1896–1910," *Philippine Studies* 46, no. 3 (1998): 376–87; Goodman,

"Japan and Philippine Commonwealth Politics," *Philippine Studies* 52, no. 2 (2004): 208–23; Motoe Terami-Wada, "Benigno Ramos and the Sakdal Movement," *Philippine Studies* 36, no. 4 (1988): 427–42; Terami-Wada, "The Sakdal Movement, 1930–34," *Philippine Studies* 36, no. 2 (1988): 131–50; Terami-Wada, "Japanese Propaganda Corps in the Philippines," *Philippine Studies* 38 (1990): 279–300; Terami-Wada, *Sakdalistas' Struggle for Philippine independence, 1930-1945* (Manila: Ateneo de Manila University Press, 2014); Terami-Wada, *The Japanese in the Philippines 1880s-1990s* (Manila: National Historical Commission of the Philippines, 2015); Caroline S. Hau and Takashi Shiraishi, "Daydreaming About Rizal and Tetchō: On Asianism as Network and Fantasy," *Philippine Studies* 57, no. 3 (2009): 329–88; Lydia N. Yu-Jose, *Japan Views the Philippines, 1900-1944* (Quezon City: Ateneo de Manila University Press, 1992); Takamichi Serizawa, "A Genealogy of Japanese Solidarity Discourse on Philippine History: War with America and Area Studies in the Cold War" (PhD diss., National University of Singapore, 2013); Rebecca E. Karl, *Staging the World: Chinese Nationalism at the Turn of the Twentieth Century* (Durham, NC: Duke University Press, 2002); Lorraine Marion Paterson, "Tenacious Texts: Vietnam, China, and Radical Cultural Intersections, 1890–1930" (PhD diss., Yale University, 2006); Christopher E. Goscha, *Vietnam or Indochina?: Contesting Concepts of Space in Vietnamese Nationalism, 1887-1954* (Copenhagen: NIAS Press, 1995).

29. Ranging from "fellow"/"fraternity" (*nakama*) to "business company" (*kaisha*). Alexander B. Woodside, *Community and Revolution in Modern Vietnam* (Boston: Houghton Mifflin Company, 1976), 54.

30. Woodside additionally notes that "no sooner had East Asian revolutionaries domesticated the idea of society than they were forced to begin breaking it down. Which elements of society would promote or cooperate with change, and which elements of society would resist change, according to Western theorists?" *Community and Revolution in Modern Vietnam*, 54.

31. See Lydia He Liu, *Translingual Practice: Literature, National Culture, and Translated Modernity—China, 1900-1937* (Stanford, CA: Stanford University Press, 1995).

32. Woodside, *Community and Revolution in Modern Vietnam*, 54.

33. Mark Philip Bradley, "Becoming 'Van Minh:' Civilizational Discourse and Visions of the Self in Twentieth-century Vietnam," *Journal of World History* 15, no. 1 (2004): 66.

34. Paterson, "Tenacious Texts," 2.

35. See Karl's *Staging the World*.

36. Phan Bội Châu, *Phan Bội Châu niên biểu : tức Tự phê phán* (1929; Ithaca, NY: Cornell University Photo Science, 1973).

37. Though the members of the different East Asian countries did not share a spoken language, they could communicate with one another through brush script Chinese, which had traditionally been the official written language of their states and courts.

38. Paterson, "Tenacious Texts," 80.

39. Sven Matthiessen, *Japanese Pan-Asianism and the Philippines from the Late Nineteenth Century to the End of World War II: Going to the Philippines Is Like Coming Home?* (Leiden: Brill, 2016), 225.

40. See Hill, *National History and the World of Nations*.
41. See John A. Hobson, *Imperialism: A Study* (1902; Nottingham, UK: Spokesman Books, 2011); Hannah Arendt, *The Origins of Totalitarianism The Origins of Totalitarianism*. (New York: Harcourt, 1973); Vladimir I. Lenin, *Imperialism, the Highest Stage of Capitalism* (1917), accessed September 13, 2016, https://www.marxists .org/archive/lenin/works/1916/imp-hsc/.
42. Aydin, *Politics of Anti-Westernism*, 8.
43. Karl, *Staging the World*, 84.
44. Karl, *Staging the World*, 84.
45. Sven Saaler and J. Victor Koschmann, eds., *Pan-Asianism in Modern Japanese History: Colonialism, Regionalism and Borders* (London: Routledge, 2007), 3.
46. Aydin, *Politics of Anti-Westernism in Asia*, 3.
47. Aydin, *Politics of Anti-Westernism in Asia*, 8.
48. Aydin, *Politics of Anti-Westernism in Asia*, 8.
49. Saaler and Koschmann, *Pan-Asianism in Modern Japanese History*, 10.
50. See Sven Saaler and Christopher W. A. Szpilman, eds., *Pan-Asianism: A Documentary History*, vol. 1, *1850–1920* (Lanham, MD: Rowman & Littlefield, 2011).
51. Saaler and Koschmann, *Pan-Asianism in Modern Japanese History*, 10.
52. Eri Hotta, *Pan-Asianism and Japan's War 1931–1945* (New York: Palgrave Macmillan, 2007); Hau and Shiraishi, "Daydreaming About Rizal and Tetchō," 332.
53. Hau and Shiraishi, "Daydreaming About Rizal and Tetchō," 332.
54. Hotta, *Pan-Asianism and Japan's War*, 44.
55. Hotta, *Pan-Asianism and Japan's War*, 44.
56. Hotta, *Pan-Asianism and Japan's War*, 44.
57. Aydin, *Politics of Anti-Westernism in Asia*, 2.
58. Aydin, *Politics of Anti-Westernism in Asia*, 6.
59. See Peter Kropotkin's *Mutual Aid: A Factor of Evolution* (1902), which studied mutually beneficial cooperation within species and its role in the creation of social institutions. Available at Anarchy Archives, https://www.marxists.org/reference /archive/kropotkin-peter/1902/mutual-aid/.
60. Saaler and Koschmann, *Pan-Asianism in Modern Japanese History*, 15.
61. Li Narangoa, "Universal Values and Pan-Asianism: The Vision of Ōmotokyō," in Saaler and Koschmann, *Pan-Asianism in Modern Japanese History*, 52.
62. Narangoa, "Universal Values and Pan-Asianism," 52.
63. Narangoa, "Universal Values and Pan-Asianism," 54.
64. Narangoa, "Universal Values and Pan-Asianism," 55.
65. Narangoa, "Universal Values and Pan-Asianism," 66.
66. As articulated in Kant's 1795–96 essay "Toward Perpetual Peace," published in *Toward Perpetual Peace and Other Writings on Politics, Peace, and History (Rethinking the Western Tradition)*, ed. and intro., Pauline Kleingeld, trans. David L. Colclasure (New Haven, CT: Yale University Press, 2006).
67. John Namjun Kim, "The Temporality of Empire: The Imperial Cosmopolitanism of Miki Kiyoshi and Tanabe Hajime," in Saaler and Koschmann, *Pan-Asianism in Modern Japanese History*, 152.
68. See William Miles Fletcher III, *The Search for a New Order: Intellectuals and Fascism in Prewar Japan* (Chapel Hill: University of North Carolina Press, 1982).

69. Kim, "Temporality of Empire," 154.

70. Kim, "Temporality of Empire," 156.

71. Kim, "Temporality of Empire," 157.

72. See Nicole CuUnjieng, "Cultures of Empire, Nation, and Universe in Pres. José P. Laurel's Political Thought, 1927–1949," *Philippine Studies: Historical and Ethnographic Viewpoints* 65, no. 1 (March 2017): 3–30.

73. Kevin M. Doak, "The Concept of Ethnic Nationality and its Role in Pan-Asianism in Imperial Japan," in Saaler and Koschmann, *Pan-Asianism in Modern Japanese History*, 170.

74. Doak, "Concept of Ethnic Nationality," 170. For further discussion of other bases for regionalisms, see Marc Frey and Nicola Spakowski, eds., *Asianisms: Regionalist Interactions and Asian Integration* (Singapore: NUS Press, 2016).

75. For supplemental literature on Pan-Asianism beyond those considered in this chapter and from a wider range of historical perspectives, see Yumiko Iida, "Fleeing the West, Making Asia Home: Transpositions of Otherness in Japanese Pan-Asianism, 1905–1930," *Alternatives: Global, Local, Political* 22, no. 3 (July–Sept. 1997): 409–32; Eri Hotta, "Rash Behari Bose and his Japanese Supporters," *Interventions* 8, no. 1 (2006): 116–32; Brian Tsui, "The Plea for Asia—Tan Yunshan, Pan-Asianism and Sino-Indian Relations," *China Report* 46, no. 4 (2010): 353–70; Rustin B. Gates, "Pan-Asianism in Prewar Japanese Foreign Affairs: The Curious Case of Uchida Yasuya," *Journal of Japanese Studies* 37, no. 1 (Winter 2011): 1–27; Mikiya Koyagi, "The Hajj by Japanese Muslims in the Interwar Period: Japan's Pan-Asianism and Economic Interests in the Islamic World," *Journal of World History* 24, no. 4 (December 2013): 849–76; Sven Saaler, "The Kokuryūkai (Black Dragon Society) and the Rise of Nationalism, Pan-Asianism, and Militarism in Japan, 1901–1925," *International Journal of Asian Studies* 11, no. 2 (2014): 125–60. For recent studies of Pan-Asianism from outside the historical discipline, see Otto F. von Feigenblatt, "Pan-Asianism, Socio-Cultural Integration, and Regionalism in Greater East Asia: Comparing Emic and Etic Interpretations of Elite Discourse Through the Application of Structural Dynamics and Grounded Theory" (PhD diss., Nova Southeastern University, 2013); and Philip S. Cho, Nathan Bullock, and Dionna Ali, "The Bioinformatic Basis of Pan-Asianism," *East Asian Science, Technology and Society: An International Journal* 7, no. 2 (2013): 283–309.

76. See Akira Iriye, "Japan's Drive to Great Power Status," in *The Cambridge History of Japan,* vol. 5, edited by Peter Duus (Cambridge: Cambridge University Press, 1989), 721–82.

77. See Iida, "Fleeing the West," 409–32.

78. Saaler and Koschmann, *Pan-Asianism in Modern Japanese History.*

79. Aydin, *Politics of Anti-Westernism in Asia,* 9–10.

80. Tal Tovy and Sharon Halevi, "The Emergence of a New Rivalry: The War and the United States," in *The Impact of the Russo-Japanese War,* ed. Rotem Kowner, 137–52 (London: Routledge, 2007); Harold Z. Schiffrin, "The Impact of the War on China," in Kowner, *Impact of the Russo-Japanese War,* 169–82.

81. Barbara Watson Andaya, "From Rūm to Tokyo: The Search for Anticolonial Allies by the Rulers of Riau, 1899–1914" *Indonesia* no. 24 (October 1977): 123–56.

82. Michael Laffan, "Tokyo As a Shared Mecca of Modernity: War Echoes in the Colonial Malay World," in Kowner, *Impact of the Russo-Japanese War*, 220.
83. Laffan, "Tokyo As a Shared Mecca of Modernity," 222.
84. T. R. Sareen, "India and the War," in Kowner, *Impact of the Russo-Japanese War*, 248.
85. Sareen, "India and the War," 248.
86. Sareen, "India and the War," 248.
87. Sareen, "India and the War," 248.
88. Paul A. Rodell, "Southeast Asian Nationalism and the Russo-Japanese War: Reexamining Assumptions," *Southeast Review of Asian Studies* 29 (2007): 20.
89. Aydin, *Politics of Anti-Westernism in Asia*, 11–12.
90. See David G. Marr, *Vietnamese Anticolonialism, 1885–1925* (Berkeley: University of California Press, 1971); Woodside *Community and Revolution in Modern Vietnam*.
91. See William J. Duiker, "Phan Boi Chau: Asian Revolutionary in a Changing World," *Journal of Asian Studies* 31, no. 1 (1971): 77–88; Marr, *Vietnamese Anticolonialism*; Woodside, *Community and Revolution in Modern Vietnam*; and Vinh Sinh, ed., *Phan Boi Chau and the Dong-Du Movement* (New Haven, CT: Yale Southeast Asia Studies, 1988).
92. Phan Chau Trinh, *Phan Châu Trinh and His Political Writings*, trans. and ed. Vinh Sinh (Ithaca, NY: Cornell Southeast Asia Program Publications, 2009), 81.
93. Trinh, *Phan Châu Trinh and His Political Writings*, 139.
94. Vu Duc Bang, "The Viet Nam Independent Education Movement (1900–1908)," (PhD diss., University of California, Los Angeles, 1971), 251.
95. Woodside, *Community and Revolution in Modern Vietnam*, 39.
96. Bradley, "Becoming 'Van Minh,'" 72.
97. Woodside, *Community and Revolution in Modern Vietnam*, 40.
98. Woodside, *Community and Revolution in Modern Vietnam*, 40.
99. Though the correspondence in the National Archives at Kew did not specify the full name of the acting consul, I assume that this refers to Deputy Consul Machida Sanekazu. See Benjamin Wai-ming Ng, "Making of a Japanese Community in Prewar Period (1841–1941) in *Foreign Communities in Hong Kong, 1840s–1950s*, ed. Cindy Yik-yi Chu (New York: Palgrave Macmillan, 2005), 118. Quoted in Despatch, "Caricature on Japanese Soldiers," December 30, 1883, C.O. 2596, No. 2596, War and Colonial Department and Colonial Office: Hong Kong, Original Correspondence, Records of the Colonial Office, Commonwealth and Foreign and Commonwealth Offices, Empire Marketing Board, and related bodies, in the National Archives, Kew, United Kingdom, 361.
100. Despatch, "Caricature on Japanese Soldiers," December 30, 1883, 361.
101. Despatch, "Caricature on Japanese Soldiers," December 30, 1883, 360.
102. See Elizabeth J. Perry, "Moving the Masses: Emotion Work in the Chinese Revolution," *Mobilization: An International Journal* 7, no. 2 (2002): 111–28.
103. For the paradigmatic historical scholarship bearing out this argument, see especially Frederick Cooper's *Citizenship Between Empire and Nation: Remaking France and French Africa, 1945–1960* (Princeton, NJ: Princeton University Press, 2014).

104. See Samuel Moyn, "Fantasies of Federalism," *Dissent* (Winter 2015), https://www
.dissentmagazine.org/article/fantasies-of-federalism.

2. Constructing Asia and the Malay Race, 1887–1895

1. Cesar Adib Majul, "Principales, Ilustrados, Intellectuals and the Original Concept of a Filipino National Community," *Asian Studies* 15 (1977): 13.

2. Josefa M. Saniel, *Japan and the Philippines, 1868-1898* (Quezon City: University of
the Philippines Press, 1969), 8–9.

3. Majul, "Principales, Ilustrados, Intellectuals," 13.

4. Remigio E. Agpalo, *Jose P. Laurel: National Leader and Political Philosopher* (Quezon
City: Jose P. Laurel Memorial Corporation, 1992), 61.

5. Saniel, *Japan and the Philippines*, 10.

6. For further study of Pedro Paterno's scholarship, see John N. Schumacher, "The
Propagandists' Reconstruction of the Philippine Past," in *Perceptions of the Past
in Southeast Asia*, ed. Anthony Reid and David Marr, 264–80 (Singapore: Heine-
mann Educational Books, 1979); Resil B. Mojares, *Brains of the Nation: Pedro Paterno,
T. H. Pardo de Tavera, Isabelo de los Reyes, and the Production of Modern Knowledge*
(Quezon City: Ateneo de Manila University Press, 2006); and Eugenio Matibag,
"The Spirit of Nínay: Pedro Paterno and the First Philippine Novel," *Humanities
Diliman* 7, no. 2 (2010): 34–59.

7. Saniel, *Japan and the Philippines*, 63.

8. Saniel, *Japan and the Philippines*, 66.

9. For further study of Rizal, see Cesar Adib Majul, *Rizal's Concept of a Filipino Nation*
(Quezon City: University of the Philippines Press, 1959); Miguel Bernad, *Rizal and
Spain: An Essay in Biographical Context* (Manila: Navotas Press, 1986); Ambeth
Ocampo, *Rizal Without the Overcoat* (Manila: Anvil Publishing, 1990); Austin
Coates, *Rizal: Filipino Nationalist and Martyr* (Manila: Solidaridad Publishing
House, 1992); Raul J. Bonoan, "José Rizal: Revolution of the Mind," in *The World
of 1896*, ed. Lorna Kalaw-Tirol (Manila: Ateneo de Manila University Press, 1998),
213–35.

10. "For Burke the link between place and identity is a psychological one in which
feelings (such as love) and cognitive associations and not merely preferences . . .
are galvanized," as Uday Singh Mehta writes. Uday Singh Mehta, *Liberalism and
Empire* (Chicago: University of Chicago Press, 1999), 133.

11. Mehta, *Liberalism and Empire*, 123.

12. See Edmund Burke, "Speech on Opening of Impeachment 15, 16, 18, 19 February 1788" (1788–1827), in *The Writings and Speeches of Edmund Burke*, vol. 6, *India: The
Launching of the Hastings Impeachment: 1786-1788*, ed. P. J. Marshall and William B.
Todd (Oxford Scholarly Editions Online 2014), https://www.oxfordscholarlyedi
tions.com/view/instance.00040471?milestones=265; Edmund Burke, "Speech
on Fox's India Bill 1 December 1783" (1783–1827), in *The Writings and Speeches of
Edmund Burke*, vol. 5, *India: Madras and Bengal: 1774-1785*, ed. P. J. Marshall and

William B. Todd (Oxford Scholarly Editions Online 2014), https://www.oxford scholarlyeditions.com/view/instance.00040450?milestones=379.

13. For a deep theorization of "place" in the Philippine discursive and political landscape, see also Ramon Guillermo, *Translation and Revolution: A Study of Jose Rizal's Guillermo Tell* (Honolulu: University of Hawai'i Press, 2009).

14. "Conclusión de lo pronunciado en honor del Señor Becerra 23 de Diciembre," *La Solidaridad* 3, no. 51, March 15, 1891, in *La Solidaridad*, trans. Guadalupe Fores-Ganzon (Pasig City: Fundacion Santiago, 1996), 113.

15. "Conclusión de lo pronunciado en honor del Señor Becerra."

16. "Crónica," *La Solidaridad* 2, no. 33, June 15, 1890.

17. See Victor Lieberman, *Strange Parallels: Southeast Asia in Global Context c. 800–1830*, vol. 2, *Mainland Mirrors* (Cambridge: Cambridge University Press, 2009).

18. John Leddy Phelan, *The Hispanization of the Philippines: Spanish Aims and Filipino Responses, 1565–1700* (Madison: University of Wisconsin Press, 1967); and Vicente L. Rafael, *Contracting Colonialism: Translation and Christian Conversion in Tagalog Society Under Early Spanish Rule* (Durham, NC: Duke University Press, 1988) explore more deeply the sweeping Spanish social program and the political, religious, and economic dislocations it wrought in the Philippines.

19. Benedict Anderson, "Cacique Democracy in the Philippines: Origins and Dreams," *New Left Review* 169 (May/June 1988): 6.

20. Vicente L. Rafael argues that Christian conversion was a process less of internalizing colonial-Christian conventions than of evading their totalizing power by marking the differences between the Tagalog and Castilian languages and between the Tagalog and Spanish interests within this new, colonial, Christian framework. See Rafael, *Contracting Colonialism*.

21. See James Francis Warren, *The Sulu Zone 1768–1898: The Dynamics of External trade, Slavery and Ethnicity in the Transformation of a Southeast Asian Maritime State* (1981).

22. Anthony Milner, *The Invention of Politics in Colonial Malaya: Contesting Nationalism and the Expansion of the Public Sphere* (New York: Cambridge University Press, 1995), 51.

23. Anthony Reid, *Imperial Alchemy: Nationalism and Political Identity in Southeast Asia* (New York: Cambridge University Press, 2012), 97–98.

24. For a deeper examination of the evolutions and historical meanings of "Melayu" and the category of "Malays," see Reid, *Imperial Alchemy*, chapter 4, "Malay (*Melayu*) and Its Descendants."

25. Milner, *Invention of Politics in Colonial Malaya*, 51.

26. Joel S. Kahn, *Other Malays: Nationalism and Cosmopolitanism in the Modern Malay World* (Singapore: Singapore University Press, ASAA Southeast Asia Publication Series, 2006), 104.

27. Kahn, *Other Malays*, 106. On the historiography of the Malay race, Kahn records that, "there have been the various arguments about how Malay-ness was constructed out of an imperial discourse characterized by the myth of Malay laziness and/or a so-called Social Darwinist ideology of race," such as Syed Hussein Alatas, *The Myth of the Lazy Native: A Study of the Image of the Malays, Filipinos and Javanese from the 16th to the 20th Century and Its Function in the Ideology of Colonial Capitalism* (London: Frank Cass, 1977) and Edward W. Said, *Culture and*

Imperialism (New York: Vintage Books, 1993). Kahn, *Other Malays*, 2. There has also been important work on the writings of leading Malay secular-nationalist intellectuals regarding how modern European discourses of nationhood shaped emerging understandings of Malay identity and of nation. See, for example, Charles Hirschman, *Ethnic and Social Stratification in Peninsular Malaysia* (Washington, DC: American Sociological Association, 1975) and A. B. Shamsul, *From British to Bumiputera Rule: Local Politics and Rural Development in Peninsular Malaya* (Singapore: Institute of Southeast Asian Studies, 1986).

28. Resil B. Mojares, *Isabelo's Archive* (Mandaluyong City: Anvil Publishing, 2013), 127.

29. Mojares, *Isabelo's Archive*, 126.

30. Mojares, *Isabelo's Archive*, 126. Mojares elaborates: "He speculates that Tagalogs, Pampangos, and other groups in Luzon must have come by way of *Borney* and *Samatra* while 'the nations of the Bisayas and Pintados' (including Bicolanos) probably came from the districts *of Macasar* although there are among them ('lighter-complexioned, braver, and of better proportions than the pure Visayans') who may be Borneans or Ternatans" (126–27).

31. Raquel A. G. Reyes, *Love, Passion and Patriotism: Sexuality and the Philippine Propaganda Movement, 1882-1892* (Singapore: NUS Press, 2008), 200.

32. Besides declaring himself so in *La Solidaridad*, in a letter on January 14, 1899, to Blumentritt he referred to himself as "Malayo-Tagalog," but to Antonio Ma. Regidor as "mestizo Filipino." John Nery, *Revolutionary Spirit: Jose Rizal in Southeast Asia* (Quezon City: Ateneo de Manila University Press, 2011), 107.

33. See José Rizal, *Sucesos de las Islas Filipinas por el Doctor Antonio de Morga: Obra publicada en Méjico el año de 1609. Nuevamente sacada a luz y anotada por José Rizal y precedida de un prólogo del Fernando Blumentritt* (1890; Manila: Comisión Nacional del Centenario de José Rizal, 1961).

34. Max Bernard, *Columnas Volantes de la Federación Malaya (Contribución a la Historia del Periodismo Filipino)* (n.p., 1928), 2.

35. José Rizal, *Rizal's Correspondence with Fellow Reformists* (Manila: National Historical Institute, 1992), 158.

36. Rizal, *Rizal's Correspondence*, 159.

37. Rizal reportedly traveled over this trip to Tokyo, Utsunomiya, Nikko, Kouzu, Odawara, Yoshihama, Hakone, Miyanoshita, Yumoto, Enoshima, Kamakura, Nara, Kyoto, Tozuka, Odawara, among other places. Caesar Z. Lanuza and Gregorio F. Zaide, *Rizal in Japan* (Tokyo: Philippine Reparations Mission, 1961), 25.

38. José Rizal, "Appendix C: Letter to Prof. Blumentritt," in Lanuza and Zaide, *Rizal in Japan*, 75.

39. Resil B. Mojares, "Rizal Reading Pigafetta," in *Waiting for Mariang Makiling: Essays in Philippine Cultural History* (Quezon City: Ateneo de Manila University Press, 2002), 73.

40. Rizal, "Appendix C: Letter to Prof. Blumentritt," 77.

41. Lanuza and Zaide, *Rizal in Japan*, 41.

42. Rizal, "Appendix C: Letter to Prof. Blumentritt," 77.

43. "We find ourselves still much worse off than before," the staff wrote in "Se Vende Cuba?" *La Solidaridad* 1, no. 4, March 28, 1889.

44. "Movimiento Político: Política a vista de pajaro," *La Solidaridad* 1, no. 3, March 15, 1889.

45. "In the Philippines: The Chinese Pharmacists and Doctors" [in Spanish], *La Solidaridad* 2, no. 44, November 30, 1890.

46. Ferdinand Blumentritt, "Filipinas. Problema Fundamental," *La Solidaridad* 3, no. 53, April 15, 1891, 171.

47. The anti-Filipino writer was a Spanish writer who used the pseudonym Quioquiap.

48. See José Rizal, "Sobre la indolencia de los Filipinos," published serially from July–September 1890 in *La Solidaridad*.

49. Segismundo Moret y Prendergast, "Japan and the Philippines" [in Spanish], *La Solidaridad* 7, no. 156, July 31, 1895.

50. Rizal, *Rizal's Correspondence*, 187.

51. Rizal, *Rizal's Correspondence*, 197.

52. Mojares, *Isabelo's Archive*, 8.

53. See Pedro A. Paterno, *La Antigua Civilización Tagalog* (1887; Manila: Colegio de Sto. Tomás, 1915).

54. Mojares, *Isabelo's Archive*, 8.

55. Masaya Shiraishi, "Phan Boi Chau in Japan," in *Phan Boi Chau and the Dong-Du Movement*, ed. Vinh Sinh (New Haven, CT: Yale Southeast Asia Studies, 1988), 63.

56. Shiraishi, "Phan Boi Chau in Japan," 63.

57. Del Pilar writes: "On one side its future, and on the other the attitude of China, Japan, and other nations that from Europe and Asia fix their sights on the map of Oceania, offer the thinker serious considerations that perhaps in time we should take advantage of to prevent and cast out future difficulties. . . . We have proof that, in Spain's colonial distresses, the Filipino people join in the glories and misfortunes of its mother country." Marcelo H. del Pilar, *La Soberanía Monacal en Filipinas: Apuntes Sobre la Funesta Preponderancia del Fraile en Las Islas, así en lo Político como en lo Económico y Religioso* (n.p., 1888), 6.

58. For further discussion, see Vladimir Tikhonov, "Korea's First Encounters with Pan-Asianism Ideology in the Early 1880s," *Review of Korean Studies* 5, no. 2, 2002: 212–14.

59. Laon Laan, "Los Viajes," *La Solidaridad* 1, no. 7, May 15, 1889. Laon Laan was one of Rizal's pen names when writing for *La Solidaridad*.

60. See Nicole CuUnjieng, "Cultures of Empire, Nation, and Universe in Pres. José P. Laurel's Political Thought, 1927–1949," *Philippine Studies: Historical and Ethnographic Viewpoints* 65, no. 1 (March 2017): 3–30.

61. Rafael Ginard de la Rosa, "Las mujeres de Oriente," *La Solidaridad* 5, no. 109, August 1, 1893.

62. José Rizal, "Your Excellency, Mr. Vicente Barrantes (Titles and honors, etc., follow.) (Conclusion)" [in Spanish], *La Solidaridad* 1, no. 10, June 30, 1889.

63. "Hauling Water" [in Spanish], *La Solidaridad* 3, no. 62, August 31, 1891.

64. "Hauling Water."

65. "Hauling Water."

66. Rafael Ginard de la Rosa, "Los cantos del Pasig," *La Solidaridad*, October 15, 1893.

67. De la Rosa, "Los cantos del Pasig."

68. Christopher L. Hill, *National History and the World of Nations: Capital, State, and the Rhetoric of History in Japan, France, and the United States* (Durham, NC: Duke University Press, 2008), 27.

69. Isabelo de los Reyes, *El Folk-lore Filipino: Colección Comentada y Publicada bajo la dirección de D. Isabelo de los Reyes*, vol. 2 (Manila: Imprenta de Santa Cruz, 1890). Available at https://archive.org/details/elfolklorefilip00florgoog. For further study of Isabelo de los Reyes, see Megan Thomas, "Isabelo de los Reyes and the Philippine Contemporaries of La Solidaridad," *Philippine Studies* 54, no. 3 (2006): 381–411; and Mojares, *Isabelo's Archive.*

70. Mellie Leandicho Lopez, *A Handbook of Philippine Folklore* (Quezon City: University of the Philippines Press, 2006), 5.

71. De los Reyes's other works include *Las islas Visayas en la época de la conquista* (Manila: Tipo-litografía de Chofre y Cia, 1889); *Artículos varios sobre etnografía, historia y costumbres de Filipinas*, 2nd ed. (Manila: J.A. Ramos, 1888); *Historia de Ilocos, vol. 1* (Manila: Establecimiento tipográfico La Opinión, 1890).

72. Majul, "Principales, Ilustrados, Intellectuals," 17.

73. Of Morga's work, John N. Schumacher writes: "Written only a few decades after the conquest by a learned member of the *Real Audiencia*, Morga's chronicle gave much attention to ancient Filipino customs. For Rizal, already committed to the destruction of the prestige and power of the friars in the Philippines, it had the added attraction of being the only major chronicle not written by a Spanish missionary." Schumacher, "The Propagandists' Reconstruction," 271.

74. Quoted in Ambeth R. Ocampo, "Rizal's Morga and Views of Philippine History," *Philippine Studies: Historical and Ethnographical Viewpoints* 46, no. 2 (1998): 204.

75. José Rizal, *Sucesos de las Islas Filipinas por el Doctor Antonio de Morga: Obra publicada en Méjico el año de 1609. Nuevamente sacada a luz y anotada por José Rizal y precedida de un prólogo del Fernando Blumentritt* (1890; Manila: Comisión Nacional del Centenario de José Rizal, 1961), 23.

76. Ocampo, "Rizal's Morga and Views of Philippine History," 196–97.

77. This assertion appears too in Rizal's article "Filipinas dentro de cien años" in *La Solidaridad*, published serially from September 1889 to January 1890, available at https://www.free-ebooks.net/ebook/Filipinas-Dentro-de-Cien-A-os -Estudio-Pol-tico-Social.

78. Schumacher, "The Propagandists' Reconstruction," 270.

79. Mojares, "Rizal Reading Pigafetta," 60.

80. Rizal, *Sucesos de las Islas Filipinas*, 28.

81. See Sankar Muthu, *Enlightenment Against Empire* (Princeton, NJ: Princeton University Press, 2003).

82. Marcelo H. del Pilar, "Cultura?," *La Solidaridad* 3, no. 66, October 31, 1891.

83. Del Pilar, "Cultura?"

84. Del Pilar, "Cultura?"

85. Del Pilar, "Cultura?"

86. Del Pilar, "Cultura?"

87. Del Pilar, "Cultura?"

88. While in the 1860s Gregor Johann Mendel, a scientist and Augustinian friar, was already mathematically studying the inheritance patterns of traits in plants,

it wasn't until the 1890s that the importance of his work gained wider understanding. In 1905 William Bateson, following Mendel's work, coined the word "genetics."

89. "Tattooing and the Superior Race" [in Spanish], *La Solidaridad* 3, no. 60, July 31, 1891.
90. "Tattooing and the Superior Race."
91. Blumentritt, "Filipinas. Problema Fundamental."
92. Marcelo H. del Pilar, "The Assimilation of the Philippines" [in Spanish], *La Solidaridad* 1, no. 16, September 30, 1889.
93. Del Pilar, "Assimilation of the Philippines."
94. See Rizal, "Filipinas dentro de cien años."
95. José Rizal, "Seamos Justos," *La Solidaridad* 2, no. 29, April 15, 1890.
96. Ferdinand Blumentritt, "Notes on the Meaning of the Word 'Malay'" [in Spanish], *La Solidaridad* 2, no. 35, June 15, 1890.
97. Blumentritt, "Notes on the Meaning of the Word 'Malay.'"
98. Blumentritt, "Notes on the Meaning of the Word 'Malay.'"
99. "G. A. Wilken," *La Solidaridad* 3, no. 64, September 30, 1890.
100. Mariano Ponce, "Pag-diwata Barrantes," *La Solidaridad* 2, no. 31, May 15, 1890.
101. Ponce, "Pag-diwata Barrantes."
102. "Recuerdos de España," Box 33, Folder 3, in T. H. Pardo de Tavera Archives, Ateneo de Manila University.
103. Reid, *Imperial Alchemy*, 99.
104. Rizal, "Filipinas dentro de cien años."
105. Rizal, "Filipinas dentro de cien años."
106. Rizal, "Filipinas dentro de cien años."
107. Rizal, "Sobre la indolencia de los Filipinos."
108. Rizal, "Sobre la indolencia de los Filipinos."
109. Del Pilar, for example, consulted the scholarly works and European commentaries of Dr. Hans Meyer, Antonio de Morga, Pedro Chirino, Francisco Colin, Bartholomé Leonardo de Argensola, Gaspar de San Agustin, and Antonio Pigafetta.
110. De los Reyes, *El Folk-Lore Filipino*.
111. See Ernest Gellner, *Nations and Nationalism* (Ithaca, NY: Cornell University Press, 1983).
112. See Victor Lieberman, *Strange Parallels: Southeast Asia in Global Context c. 800–1830*, vol. 1, *Integration in the Mainland* (Cambridge: Cambridge University Press, 2003).
113. "Hispano-Japanese Treaty," *La Solidaridad* 6, no. 138, October 31, 1894.
114. "Hispano-Japanese Treaty."
115. "Relación entre Las Cortes y el archipielago Filipino," *La Solidaridad* 7, no. 145, February 15, 1895.
116. See Mariano Ponce, "What Is Important to Us" [in Spanish], *La Solidaridad* 5, no. 111, September 15, 1893; Marcelo H. del Pilar, "Dangerous Alliances" [in Spanish], *La Solidaridad* 6, no. 136, September 30, 1894; and "The Sino-Japanese Question: The Japanese Empire" [in Spanish], *La Solidaridad* 6, no. 137, October 15, 1894.

117. Marcelo H. del Pilar, "Human Interest and Patriotic Interest" [in Spanish], *La Solidaridad* 6, no. 142, December 31, 1894.

118. Del Pilar, "Human Interest and Patriotic Interest."

119. Saniel, *Japan and the Philippines*, 172.

120. Saniel, *Japan and the Philippines*, 172.

121. For further study, see Grant K. Goodman, "Filipino Secret Agents, 1896–1910," *Philippine Studies* 46, no. 3 (1998): 376–87.

122. Saniel, *Japan and the Philippines*, 174.

123. Saniel, *Japan and the Philippines*, 174–75.

124. Saniel, *Japan and the Philippines*, 175.

125. Marcelo H. del Pilar, "Conferencia del Sr. Moret," *La Solidaridad* 7, no. 143, January 15, 1895, 3–5.

126. Del Pilar, "Conferencia del Sr. Moret," 5.

127. See "Peligros y Temores," *La Solidaridad* 7, no. 151, May 15, 1895.

128. Del Pilar, "Conferencia del Sr. Moret," 7

129. Del Pilar, "Conferencia del Sr. Moret," 7.

130. "España y Japón en Filipinas," *La Solidaridad* 7, no. 144, January 31, 1895, 31.

131. "España y Japón en Filipinas," 31.

132. An article in *La Solidaridad* reported the tentative state of Philippines-Japan trade—"in the Philippines, the idea of opening commercial relations with the Japanese Empire is gaining ground"—and recommended encouraging Philippine commerce by establishing "direct commercial relations with Japan through the creation of regular shipping lines between Manila and the ports of Yokohama, Nagasaki, and Kobe." "Filipinas en el Mercado del Japón," *La Solidaridad* 1, no. 5, April 15, 1889.

133. Saniel, *Japan and the Philippines*, 138–37.

134. Saniel, *Japan and the Philippines*, 139.

135. Saniel, *Japan and the Philippines*, 6.

136. In July 1891 a consular agent notified the government in Madrid that an imperial ordinance was set to annex the Volcano Islands to Japan. As Saniel records, three months later the colonial government in the Philippines became responsible for verifying whether the islands were within the "jurisdictional waters of the Marianas." *Japan and the Philippines*,153. Though the annexation went through, there was shortly thereafter, in February 1892, another transient moment of diplomatic anxiety due to "the suspicious circumstances surrounding the arrival of Japanese warships in Manila" (157). See the chapter "On Apprehensions and Intentions," in Saniel, *Japan and the Philippines*,) for more on this diplomatic history.

137. Saniel, *Japan and the Philippines*, 145.

138. Saniel, *Japan and the Philippines*, 17.

139. Saniel, *Japan and the Philippines*, 146.

140. See Izumi Yanagida, "Nihon bungaku ni okeru Jose Rizal" [Jose Rizal in Japanese literature], in *Jose Rizal to Nihon* [Jose Rizal and Japan], ed. Kimura Ki (Tokyo: Appolon-sha, 1961), 50–72; Suguru Hatano, "Firipin dokuritsu undō to Nihon no taiō" [The Philippine independence movement and Japanese responses] *Ajia*

Kenkyu [Asian studies] 34, no. 4 (1988): 69–95; Setsuho Ikehata, "Japan and the Philippines, 1885–1905: Mutual Images and Interests," in *Philippines-Japan Relations*, ed. Setsuho Ikehata and Lydia N. Yu Jose (Quezon City: Ateneo de Manila University Press, 2003), 19–46; Lydia N. Yu-Jose, *Japan Views the Philippines 1900-1944* (Quezon City: Ateneo de Manila University Press, 1992); Michiko Yamashita, "Nanshin no manazashi" [Views on southward advance], *Sōgō Bunka Kenkyū* [Transcultural studies] 3 (1999): 77–99; Hiromu Shimizu, "Imagining the Filipino Revolution 100 Years Ago," in *Junctions Between Filipinos and Japanese: Transborder Insights and Reminiscences*, ed. Arnold Azurin and Sylvano Mahiwo (Quezon City: Kultura't Wika, 2007), 49–67; Carol Hau and Takashi Shiraishi, "Daydreaming About Rizal and Tetchō: On Asianism as Network and Fantasy," *Philippine Studies* 57, no. 3 (2009): 329–88; Takamichi Serizawa, "A Genealogy of Japanese Solidarity Discourse on Philippine History: War with America and Area Studies in the Cold War" (PhD diss., National University of Singapore, 2013); and Takamichi Serizawa, "Japanese Solidarity Discourse on the Philippines During the Second World War," *Philippine Studies: Historical and Ethnographic Viewpoints* 63, no. 1 (March 2015): 71–100.

141. Hau and Shiraishi, "Daydreaming About Rizal and Tetchō," 341. See Ikehata, "Japan and the Philippines Shimizu, "Imagining the Filipino Revolution 100 Years Ago" for studies of fantasy/imagination in Japanese writings on the Philippines, and see Shin'ichi Yamamuro, *Kimera: Manshūkoku no shōzo* [Kimera: A portrait of Manzhouguo] (Tokyo: Chūokōronsha, 1993); Shin'ichi Yamamuro, *Shiso kadai to shite no Ajia: Kijiku, rensa, toki* [Asia as a question of thought: Axes, series, and projects] (Tokyo: Iwanami Shoten, 2001); Louise Young, *Japan's Total Empire: Manchuria and the Culture of Wartime Imperialism* (Berkeley: University of California Press, 1998); and Prasenjit Duara, *Sovereignty and Authenticity: Manchukuo and the East Asian Modern* (Lanham, MD: Rowman & Littlefield, 2003) for examples of the role of ideology in Japanese empire building.

142. These include a comic travelogue, *Oshi no ryokō* (Mutes' travels) from 1889; a compilation of notes on his trip to France, *Kōsetsu-roku* (Stork prints on snow) from 1889; and the political novel *Arashi no nagori* (Remains of the storm) from 1891.

143. Serizawa, "Japanese Solidarity Discourse on the Philippines," 76.

144. Shimizu, "Imagining the Filipino Revolution 100 Years Ago," 65.

145. Miyazaki Tōten (1871–1922) was a Japanese political thinker and activist who believed that all the men in the world were "one single family." He famously aided and supported Sun Yat-sen in his political work in China. Tōten's autobiography, *My Thirty-Three Years' Dream*, details not only his assistance to Sun Yat-sen and Kang Yu-wei and lifetime devotion to China's revolutionary movement, but also his attempts alongside Sun Yat-sen to procure arms for the First Philippine Republic's Revolutionary Government, as chapter 4 of this book details. For this account, see Miyazaki Tōten, *My Thirty-Three Year's Dream: The Autobiography of Miyazaki Tōten*, ed. and trans. Marius B. Jansen and Eto Shinkichi (1902; Princeton, NJ: Princeton University Press, 2014), chap. 17. For

further information on Miyazaki's Pan-Asianism, see Christopher W. A. Szpil-man, "Miyazaki Tōten's Pan-Asianism, 1915–1919," in *Pan-Asianism: A Documentary History*, vol. 1, *1850–1920*, ed. Sven Saaler and Christopher W. A. Szpilman, (Lanham, MD: Rowman & Littlefield, 2011), 133–39.

146. Miyazaki Tōten, *My Thirty-Three Year's Dream*, 73–74.
147. Miyazaki Tōten, *My Thirty-Three Year's Dream*, 74.
148. Saniel, *Japan and the Philippines*, 178.
149. Saniel, *Japan and the Philippines*, 179.
150. Marius B. Jansen, *China in the Tokugawa World* (Cambridge, MA: Harvard University Press, 1992), 106.
151. Jansen, *China in the Tokugawa World*, 103.
152. Jansen, *China in the Tokugawa World*, 104.
153. For more information on Pan-Asianism in Korea, see Tikhonov, "Korea's First Encounters with Pan-Asianism Ideology."
154. Tikhonov, "Korea's First Encounters with Pan-Asianism Ideology," 226.
155. Tikhonov, "Korea's First Encounters with Pan-Asianism Ideology," 197.
156. For further information, see the chapter "Personalities and Precedents" in Marius B. Jansen, *The Japanese and Sun Yat-sen* (Cambridge, MA: Harvard University Press, 1967).
157. Jansen, *The Japanese and Sun Yat-sen*, 32–33.
158. Jansen, *The Japanese and Sun Yat-sen*, 33.
159. Jansen, *The Japanese and Sun Yat-sen*, 34.
160. Jansen, *The Japanese and Sun Yat-sen*, 41.
161. Jansen, *The Japanese and Sun Yat-sen*, 42.
162. Jansen, *The Japanese and Sun Yat-sen*, 43
163. Jansen, *The Japanese and Sun Yat-sen*, 42.
164. Jansen, *China in the Tokugawa World*, 105.
165. Jansen, *China in the Tokugawa World*, 106.
166. Jansen, *The Japanese and Sun Yat-sen*, 44.
167. Sven Saaler and Christopher W. A. Szpilman, "Part II: The Era of Imperialism and Pan-Asianism in Japan, 1900–1914," in *Pan-Asianism: A Documentary History*, vol. 1, *1850–1920*, eds. Sven Saaler and Christopher W. A. Szpilman (Lanham, MD: Rowman & Littlefield, 2011), 113–14.
168. Rebecca E. Karl, *Staging the World: Chinese Nationalism at the Turn of the Twentieth Century* (Durham, NC: Duke University Press, 2002), 169.
169. Lorraine Marion Paterson, "Tenacious Texts: Vietnam, China, and Radical Cultural Intersections, 1890–1930" (PhD diss., Yale University, 2006), 91.
170. Paterson, "Tenacious Texts," 91.
171. Hau and Shiraishi, "Daydreaming About Rizal and Tetchō," 362.
172. Hau and Shiraishi, "Daydreaming About Rizal and Tetchō," 362.
173. Brij Tankha, ed., *Okakura Tenshin and Pan-Asianism: Shadows of the Past* (Kent, UK: Global Oriental, 2009), 43n21.
174. Hau and Shiraishi, "Daydreaming About Rizal and Tetchō," 333.
175. Hau and Shiraishi, "Daydreaming About Rizal and Tetchō," 333.
176. See Miyazaki Tōten, *My Thirty-Three Year's Dream*, 203.

177. Jansen, *China in the Tokugawa World*, 107.
178. Jansen, *China in the Tokugawa World*, 107.

3. The Philippine Revolution Mobilizes Asia, 1892–1898

1. "Colonies of Foreign Countries" [in Spanish], *La Solidaridad* 4, no. 81, June 15, 1892.
2. For example, there appeared in the paper a long history of Cochinchina, beginning in the May 31, 1892, issue.
3. Marcelo H. del Pilar, "Hong Kong y Filipinas," *La Solidaridad*, June 30, 1894.
4. Del Pilar, "Hong Kong y Filipinas."
5. José Rizal, *Rizal's Correspondence with Fellow Reformists* (Manila: National Historical Institute, 1992), 521.
6. On April 4, 1891, Rizal wrote to Basa: "My very dear friend Basa, In reply to your letter, I wish to tell you that I would very much like to join you there [in Hong Kong] as soon as possible. Only the lack of traveling expenses keeps me here. If you could kindly advance me the amount through an order to the Messageries Maritimes for one first class ticket [to] Hong Kong, I could realize my idea." *Rizal's Correspondence*, 546.
7. "At Hong Kong I plan to practice ophthalmology and earn my living through it." Rizal, *Rizal's Correspondence*, 547. In his letter on April 19 to Basa, he wrote again of the request for passage money to Hong Kong, "Now I again insist on it; I am decided to leave as soon as I receive your letter, for nothing now detains me in Europe." He continued, "I will board the first boat; if I had the money now, I would embark at once" (555).
8. Rizal, *Rizal's Correspondence*, 558.
9. Rizal, *Rizal's Correspondence*, 559. He explained that he would be leaving Europe so that he could take up his profession and "start earning a small fortune," for, he wrote, "if at last, after the end of a few years, I become financially independent, I shall be able to undertake a more vigorous and effective campaign than I have been doing until now" (560).
10. Rizal, *Rizal's Correspondence*, 624.
11. Rizal, *Rizal's Correspondence*, 624–25.
12. For further study of Bonifacio, see Teodoro A. Agoncillo, *The Revolt of the Masses: The Story of Bonifacio and the Katipunan* (Quezon City: University of the Philippines, 1956) and *The Writings and Trial of Andres Bonifacio* (Manila: Manila Bonifacio Centennial Commission, 1963); Epifanio de los Santos, *The Revolutionists: Aguinaldo, Bonifacio, Jacinto*, trans. and ed. Teodoro A. Agoncillo (Manila: National Historical Commission, 1973); Reynaldo C. Ileto, *Pasyon and Revolution* (Quezon City: Ateneo de Manila University Press, 1979); Alejo Villanueva, *Bonifacio's Unfinished Revolution* (Quezon City: New Day Publishers, 1989); and Glenn May, *Inventing a Hero: The Posthumous Re-Creation of Andres Bonifacio* (Madison: University of Wisconsin Press, 1996).

13. For further study of Mabini, see Cesar Adib Majul, *Apolinario Mabini: Revolutionary* (Manila: National Historical Institute, 1993); and Ambeth R. Ocampo, *Mabini's Ghost* (Pasig City: Anvil, 1995).

14. Alfredo S. Veloso, *Discursos y Debates de Malolos* (Quezon City: Asvel, 1960), 10.

15. Manila, Bulacan, Pampanga, Tarlac, Nueva Ecija, Laguna, Batangas, and Cavite.

16. For further study of Aguinaldo, see Pedro S. De Achutegui and Miguel A. Bernad, *Aguinaldo and the Revolution of 1896: A Documentary History* (Quezon City: Ateneo de Manila University Press, 1972); and De los Santos, *The Revolutionists*.

17. Apolinario Mabini, "Letter to Del Pilar: August 19, 1895," in *The Letters of Apolinario Mabini* (Manila: National Heroes Commission, 1965), 34.

18. Mabini, "Letter to Del Pilar: August 19, 1895," 34.

19. Mabini, "Letter to Del Pilar: August 19, 1895," 34.

20. "Think of how our brother Rizal could escape Dapitan and go to Japan, accompanied by two or three maids, so that there he could be our representative." "Carta de un firmante como Primer Relámpago en la que explica un plan para la escapatoria de Rizal y medio de atacar Manila," Caja 5677, Legajo 1.88, Archivo General Militar de Madrid.

21. "Carta de un firmante como Primer Relámpago."

22. "Carta de un firmante como Primer Relámpago."

23. "Carta de un firmante como Primer Relámpago."

24. Albert Camus, *The Rebel*, trans. A. Bower (New York, 1961), 13, 106, quoted in Huỳnh Kim Khánh, *Vietnamese Communism, 1925-1945* (Ithaca, NY: Cornell University Press, 1982), 82.

25. Khánh, *Vietnamese Communism*, 81–82.

26. Nguyen Ai Quoc in Nguyen Thuong Huyen, *Cach menh*, AOM, SLOTFOM, vol. 5, carton 45, quoted in Khánh, *Vietnamese Communism*, 83.

27. See Ileto, *Pasyon and Revolution*.

28. See "Ritual for the initiation of a Bayani, c. 1894," Caja 5677, Legajo 1.40, Archivo General Militar de Madrid.

29. Jim Richardson, *The Light of Liberty: Documents and Studies on the Katipunan, 1892–1897* (Quezon City: Ateneo de Manila University Press, 2013), 88.

30. Richardson, *The Light of Liberty*, 170–71.

31. Richardson, *The Light of Liberty*, 20. See "Kasaysayan; Pinag-kasundoan; Manga dakuilang kautusan," August 1892, Caja 5677, Legajo 1.34, Archivo General Militar de Madrid.

32. Richardson, *The Light of Liberty*, xvi.

33. Richardson, *The Light of Liberty*, 210. See Emilio Jacinto, "Sa Bayang tinubuan," Caja 5677, Legajo 1.96, Archivo General Militar de Madrid.

34. Richardson, *The Light of Liberty*, 173.

35. Richardson, *The Light of Liberty*, 131.

36. The literature and memoirs of various revolutionaries contest the date and place of the official beginning of the Philippine Revolution. General Artemio Ricarte dates it to August 23 with the Cry of Balintawak, General Santiago Alvarez dates it to August 29 with the "First Cry of the Katipunan." Santiago V. Alvarez, *The Katipunan and the Revolution: Memoirs of a General with the Original*

Tagalog Text, trans. Paula Carolina S. Malay (Manila: Ateneo de Manila University Press, 1992), 262. Scholar Teodoro Agoncillo in *The Revolt of the Masses* dates it to August 23 but in Pugadlawin, not Balintawak, based on the testimony of revolutionary Pío Valenzuela. Teodoro A. Agoncillo, *The Revolt of the Masses: The Story of Bonifacio and the Katipunan* (Quezon City: University of the Philippines, 2002), 346. Taking all this into account, John Nery judges the first skirmish to have taken place in Balintawak, but that "after that clash, the Katipunan spread the word that the uprising would officially begin on 29 August; in Cavite, the rebellion broke out the following day." John Nery, *Revolutionary Spirit: Jose Rizal in Southeast Asia* (Quezon City: Ateneo de Manila University Press, 2011), 101n1.

37. De Achutegui and Bernad, *Aguinaldo and the Revolution of 1896*, 9.

38. José Alejandrino met the government in exile in Hong Kong at the end of December in 1897, after they had signed the Pact of Biak-na-Bato with Spain and left the Philippines. Alejandrino noted that Aguinaldo was not thirty years old at the time, and that neither were any of his co-revolutionaries who had then arrived in Hong Kong. José Alejandrino, *La Senda del Sacrificio: Episodios y Anecdotas de Nuestras Luchas Por La Libertad* (Manila: n.p., 1933), University of the Philippines, Special Collections, 68. They lived frugally in Hong Kong, careful not to spend the money they had planned to dedicate to continuing the war. Alejandrino, *La Senda del Sacrificio*, 69. While in exile in Hong Kong, the junta continued its plans for revolution and debated seeking a formal alliance with Japan, but they ultimately rejected that plan, remembering the Katipunan's unsuccessful attempt to gain formal alliance with and recognition by Japan. Teodoro A. Agoncillo, *Malolos: The Crisis of the Republic* (1960; Quezon City: University of the Philippines, 1997), 97. Aguinaldo organized for a diplomatic offensive in August 1898. He instructed Agoncillo to publish the "Act of Proclamation" and "Manifesto to Foreign Governments" in the Hong Kong newspapers on August 7, in order to show the foreign governments that the Filipinos had already formed their own government and had organized for a forthcoming meeting of the Congress of Representatives, and that civil society organizations were already active in the provinces. While organizing this offensive, however, Aguinaldo suspected that Japan and the British Empire had come to a private understanding regarding the Philippine question, which favored leaving the United States to retain possession of the islands and thus not disturb the existing balance of power. Agoncillo, *Malolos: The Crisis of the Republic*, 256. For that reason he was doubtful of official Japanese aid. Of Aguinaldo's conduct while in exile, Alejandrino attested that he had never until then seen any example in Philippine history of a man, abroad, in possession of 400,000 pesos in his name in a bank, display such "disinterested self-negation"—instead wishing to return to his country to exhibit through his own life an ideal, "which was the ideal of his people and his race." Alejandrino, *La Senda del Sacrificio*, 178.

39. Remigio E. Agpalo, *Jose P. Laurel: National Leader and Political Philosopher* (Quezon City: Jose P. Laurel Memorial Corporation, 1992), 61.

40. Emilio Jacinto (attributed), "Sa mga kababayan," in Richardson *The Light of Liberty*, 178. See "Sa mga kababayan," Caja 5395, Legajo 4.25, Archivo General Militar de Madrid.

41. Emilio Jacinto (attributed), "Sa mga kababayan," in Richardson, *The Light of Liberty*, 178. See "Sa mga kababayan," Caja 5395, Legajo 4.25, Archivo General Militar de Madrid.
42. Richardson, *The Light of Liberty*, 102.
43. Emilio Jacinto (attributed) "Pahayag," in Richardson, *The Light of Liberty*, 181.
44. Christopher L. Hill, *National History and the World of Nations: Capital, State, and the Rhetoric of History in Japan, France, and the United States* (Durham, NC: Duke University Press, 2008), xii.
45. Andres Bonifacio (attributed), "Ang dapat mabatid ng mga tagalog," in Richardson, *The Light of Liberty*, 191.
46. Richardson, *The Light of Liberty*, 88. See Andres Bonifacio (attributed), "Ritual for the initiation of a Bayani, c. 1894," Caja 5677, Legajo 1.40, Archivo General Militar de Madrid.
47. Andres Bonifacio (attributed), "Ritual for the initiation of a Bayani, c. 1894," in Richardson, *The Light of Liberty*, 96. See Andres Bonifacio (attributed), "Ritual for the initiation of a Bayani, c. 1894," Caja 5677, Legajo 1.40, Archivo General Militar de Madrid.
48. "Pagbubukas ng Karurukan ng K.K.K.N.M.A.N.B.," in Richardson, *The Light of Liberty*, 114.
49. Andres Bonifacio (attributed), "Pagibig sa tinubuang Bayan," in Richardson, *The Light of Liberty*, 201–2. See Caja 5677, Legajo 1.94, Archivo General Militar de Madrid.
50. Andres Bonifacio (attributed), "Pagibig sa tinubuang Bayan," in Richardson, *The Light of Liberty*, 203. See Caja 5677, Legajo 1.94, Archivo General Militar de Madrid.
51. Andres Bonifacio (attributed), "Pagibig sa tinubuang Bayan," in Richardson, *The Light of Liberty*, 203. See Caja 5677, Legajo 1.94, Archivo General Militar de Madrid.
52. *Pangulo* means "president"—the term used to refer to the executive.
53. Agpalo, *Jose P. Laurel*, 82.
54. "Maitim man at maputi ang kulay ng balat, lahat ng tao'y magkakapantay; mangyayaring ang isa'y higtan sa dunong, sa yaman, sa ganda . . .; ngunit di mahihigtan sa pagkatao." Emilio Jacinto, "Kartilya ng Katipunan" (1896), Philippine Center for Masonic Studies, 2006, http://www.philippinemasonry.org/kartilya-ng-katipunan.html.
55. "Ang kamahalan ng tao'y wala sa pagkahari, wala sa tangus ng ilong at puti ng mukha, wala sa pagkaparing kahalili ng Dios wala sa mataas na kalagayan sa balat ng lupa." Jacinto, "Kartilya ng Katipunan."
56. Richardson, *The Light of Liberty*, 103.
57. "Paglaganap ng mga aral na ito at maningning na sumikat ang araw ng mahal na Kalayaan dito sa kaabaabang Sangkalupuan, at sabugan ng matamis niyang liwanag ang nangagkaisang magkalahi't magkakapatid ng ligaya ng walang katapusan, ang mga ginugol na buhay, pagud, at mga tiniis na kahirapa'y labis nang natumbasan." Jacinto, "Kartilya ng Katipunan."
58. "Document 98," in de Achutegui and Bernad, *Aguinaldo and the Revolution of 1896*, 331.
59. "Document 98," in de Achutegui and Bernad, *Aguinaldo and the Revolution of 1896*, 332.

60. "Document 98," in de Achutegui and Bernad, *Aguinaldo and the Revolution of 1896*, 332.
61. "Akoy si___, nanumpa sa ngalan ng Dios na aking gugulin ang aking buhay, ang aking lakas, ang kaonting mga maasahan ay aking idinadamay na lahat ang pagmamahal ko sa aking asaua, anak magulang at kapatid ay aking iguinugugol na lahat alang alang sa pagtatangol sa ating Inang bayan at sapagka api n gating lahi sa sankatagalugan at sa K.K.K. N. M.A.N.B." "Document 1," in de Achutegui and Bernad, *Aguinaldo and the Revolution of 1896*, 10.
62. "Katipunan nang mga A.N.B. sa may nasang makisanib sa katipunang ito," in Richardson, *The Light of Liberty*, 134. "Sa salitang *tagalog* katutura'y ang lahat nang tumubo sa Sangkapuluang ito; sa makatuid, *bisaya* man, *iloko* man, kapangpangan man, etc., ay tagalog din" (131).
63. Onofre D. Corpuz, *Saga and Triumph: The Filipino Revolution Against Spain* (Manila: Philippine Centennial Commission, 1999), 78.
64. "Document 4," in Achutegui and Bernad, *Aguinaldo and the Revolution of 1896*, 20.
65. "Desde Estas Montañas," in de Achutegui and Bernad, *Aguinaldo and the Revolution of 1896*, 434.
66. "Document 124," in de Achutegui and Bernad, *Aguinaldo and the Revolution of 1896*, 438.
67. "Document 124," in de Achutegui and Bernad, *Aguinaldo and the Revolution of 1896*, 438.
68. Corpuz, *Saga and Triumph*, 78.
69. Corpuz, *Saga and Triumph*, 78.
70. Corpuz, *Saga and Triumph*, 78.
71. "Filipinas-Cuestión Palpitante: Lo Urgentísimo," *El Imparcial*, October 2, 1896, Hemeroteca Digital, Biblioteca Nacional de España, accessed April 18, 2016, http://hemerotecadigital.bne.es/issue.vm?id=0000768146&search=&lang=en.
72. Josefa M. Saniel, *Japan and the Philippines, 1868-1898* (Quezon City: University of the Philippines Press, 1969), 137.
73. Saniel, *Japan and the Philippines*, 137.
74. Saniel, *Japan and the Philippines*, 137.
75. Three Japanese shops were established in 1889 following the opening of the Japanese Consulate. Prior to that, Japanese wares were reportedly sold through and handled by Indian shops in Manila. The direct presence of Japan in Manila was rather limited. Saniel, *Japan and the Philippines*, 138.
76. Camilo Garcia de Polavieja de Castillo, "Apuntos oficiales sobre los sucesos de la Insurrección Filipina facilitados por las ordenes Religiosas al ser nombrado Gobernador General del Archipielago," July 24, 1896, Archivo de Camilo Garcia de Polavieja de Castillo, Diversos, 27, Archivo General de Indias, Seville, Spain.
77. De Castillo, "Apuntos oficiales sobre los sucesos de la Insurrección Filipina," July 24, 1896.
78. Camilo Garcia de Polavieja de Castillo, "Antecedentes de la Insurreción y su estado en 1st Dibre 1896. Recibidos en Singapur," October 28, 1896, Archivo de Camilo Garcia de Polavieja de Castillo, Diversos, 27, Archivo General de Indias, Seville, Spain.

79. De Castillo, "Antecedentes de la Insurreción."
80. De Castillo, "Antecedentes de la Insurreción."
81. Quoted in David Joel Steinberg, *The Philippines: A Singular and a Plural Place*, 4th ed. (1982; Boulder, CO: Westview Press, 2000), 61.
82. Filomeno V. Aguilar Jr., *Clash of Spirits: The History of Power and Sugar Planter Hegemony on a Visayan Island* (Quezon City: University of the Philippines Press, 1998), 156.
83. Saniel, *Japan and the Philippines*, 3.
84. Aguilar, *Clash of Spirits*, 156.
85. De Castillo, "Antecedentes de la Insurreción."
86. Camilo Garcia de Polavieja de Castillo, "Apuntos oficiales sobre los sucesos de la Insurrección Filipina facilitados por las ordenes Religiosas al ser nombrado Gobernador General del Archipielago," May 7, 1896, Archivo de Camilo Garcia de Polavieja de Castillo, Diversos, 27, Archivo General de Indias, Seville, Spain.
87. Camilo Garcia de Polavieja de Castillo, "Apuntos oficiales sobre los sucesos de la Insurrección Filipina facilitados por las ordenes Religiosas al ser nombrado Gobernador General del Archipielago," April 17, 1896, Archivo de Camilo Garcia de Polavieja de Castillo, Diversos, 27, Archivo General de Indias, Seville, Spain.
88. De Castillo, "Antecedentes de la Insurreción."
89. Ministerio de Ultramar, 1897, Ultramar, Legajo 5361, Exp. 9, No. 29, Archivo Histórico Nacional, Madrid, Spain.
90. Al Ministerio de Ultramar, January 3, 1898, Ultramar, Legajo 5361, Exp. 10, No. 2, Archivo Histórico Nacional, Madrid, Spain.
91. Camilo Garcia de Polavieja de Castillo, "Apuntos oficiales sobre los sucesos de la Insurrección Filipina facilitados por las ordenes Religiosas al ser nombrado Gobernador General del Archipielago," July 12, 1896, Archivo de Camilo Garcia de Polavieja de Castillo, Diversos, 27, Archivo General de Indias, Seville, Spain.
92. De Castillo, "Antecedentes de la Insurreción."
93. Camilo Garcia de Polavieja de Castillo, "Apuntos oficiales sobre los sucesos de la Insurrección Filipina facilitados por las ordenes Religiosas al ser nombrado Gobernador General del Archipielago," May 2, 1896, Archivo de Camilo Garcia de Polavieja de Castillo, Diversos, 27, Archivo General de Indias, Seville, Spain.
94. Camilo Garcia de Polavieja de Castillo, "Apuntos oficiales sobre los sucesos de la Insurrección Filipina facilitados por las ordenes Religiosas al ser nombrado Gobernador General del Archipielago," July 6, 1896, Archivo de Camilo Garcia de Polavieja de Castillo, Diversos, 27, Archivo General de Indias, Seville, Spain.
95. De Castillo, "Apuntos oficiales," July 6, 1896.
96. De Castillo, "Apuntos oficiales," May 2, 1896.
97. Camilo Garcia de Polavieja de Castillo, "Apuntos oficiales sobre los sucesos de la Insurrección Filipina facilitados por las ordenes Religiosas al ser nombrado

Gobernador General del Archipielago," June 1, 1896, Archivo de Camilo Garcia de Polavieja de Castillo, Diversos, 27, Archivo General de Indias, Seville, Spain.

98. De Castillo, "Apuntos oficiales," June 1, 1896.

99. Subsecretario del Ministerio de Ultramar, "Ataque de la prensa de Hong Kong contra el Gobernador General de Filipinas," November 21, 1892, Ultramar, Legajo 5329, Exp. 8, Archivo Histórico Nacional, Madrid, Spain.

100. Subsecretario del Ministerio de Ultramar, "Ataque de la prensa de Hong Kong."

101. Camilo Garcia de Polavieja de Castillo, "Apuntos oficiales sobre los sucesos de la Insurrección Filipina facilitados por las ordenes Religiosas al ser nombrado Gobernador General del Archipielago," June 30, 1896, Archivo de Camilo Garcia de Polavieja de Castillo, Diversos, 27, Archivo General de Indias, Seville, Spain.

102. Camilo Garcia de Polavieja de Castillo, "Apuntos oficiales sobre los sucesos de la Insurrección Filipina facilitados por las ordenes Religiosas al ser nombrado Gobernador General del Archipielago," April 30, 1896, Archivo de Camilo Garcia de Polavieja de Castillo, Diversos, 27, Archivo General de Indias, Seville, Spain.

103. Rizal, *Rizal's Correspondence*, 312.

104. De Castillo, "Antecedentes de la Insurreción."

105. De Castillo, "Antecedentes de la Insurreción."

106. Pierre Brocheux, *The Mekong Delta: Ecology, Economy, and Revolution, 1860–1960* (Madison: University of Wisconsin-Madison Center for Southeast Asian Studies, 1995), 140.

107. See Huang Fuqing, *Chinese Students in Japan in the Late Ch'ing Period* (Tokyo: Centre for East Asian Cultural Studies, 1983).

108. Lorraine Marion Paterson, "Tenacious Texts: Vietnam, China, and Radical Cultural Intersections, 1890–1930" (PhD diss., Yale University, 2006), 77.

109. Paterson, "Tenacious Texts," 77.

110. Paterson, "Tenacious Texts," 77.

111. Paterson, "Tenacious Texts," 77.

112. Prince Cường Để was a royal relative of the Nguyễn dynasty and its heir. He was also a Vietnamese revolutionary who worked with Phan Bội Châu in Japan to liberate Vietnam from French colonial occupation. He died in exile in Japan. See My-Van Tran, *A Vietnamese Royal Exile in Japan: Prince Cuong De (1882-1951)* (London: Routledge, 2005) for further study.

113. Phan Boi Chau, *Overturned Chariot: The Autobiography of Phan-Boi-Chau*, trans. Vinh Sinh and Nicholas Wickenden (Honolulu: University of Hawai'i Press, 1999), 106.

114. Phan Boi Chau, *Overturned Chariot*, 108.

115. Phan Boi Chau, *Overturned Chariot*, 108.

116. Phan Boi Chau, *Overturned Chariot*, 111.

117. Phan Boi Chau, *Overturned Chariot*, 137.

118. Phan Boi Chau, *Overturned Chariot*, 137.

119. Phan Boi Chau, *Overturned Chariot*, 136.

120. Paterson, "Tenacious Texts," 86.

121. Paterson, "Tenacious Texts," 80.

122. Paterson, "Tenacious Texts," 81.

123. Phan Boi Chau, *Overturned Chariot*, 144.

124. Quoted in Paterson, "Tenacious Texts," 82.

125. Quoted in Paterson, "Tenacious Texts," 83.

126. Paterson, "Tenacious Texts," 83.

127. Furuta Motoo, "Vietnamese Political Movements in Thailand: Legacy of the Dong-Du Movement," in *Phan Boi Chau and the Dong-Du Movement*, ed. Vinh Sinh (New Haven, CT: Yale Southeast Asia Studies, 1988), 150.

128. Nguyen Van Khanh and Nguyen Van Suu, "Eastern-Country-Study-Tour (Dong Du) Movement in the Revolutionary Process of Vietnam National Liberation and in Cultural, Educational Relations Between Vietnam and Japan," *Vietnam National University, Journal of Science, Social Sciences & Humanities* no. 4E (2005), 18. Later, after learning of the Chinese revolution of 1911, in 1912 an inspired Châu would go to Canton to launch the Việt Nam Quang Phục Hội (Vietnam restoration society) there, while also establishing a branch in Thailand, which was the first political organization amongst Vietnamese in Thailand. Though transnational in operation, however, this still represents a marshaling of Vietnamese toward a national Vietnamese cause. Furuta, "Vietnamese Political Movements in Thailand," 152.

129. Rizal, *Rizal's Correspondence*, 730.

130. Rizal, *Rizal's Correspondence*, 730.

131. Rizal, *Rizal's Correspondence*, 730.

132. Rizal, *Rizal's Correspondence*, 730.

133. Rizal, *Rizal's Correspondence*, 731.

134. Rizal, *Rizal's Correspondence*, 731.

135. See Sven Matthiessen, *Japanese Pan-Asianism and the Philippines from the Late Nineteenth Century to the End of World War II: Going to the Philippines Is Like Coming Home?* (Leiden: Brill, 2016).

136. Phan Boi Chau, "The History of the Loss of the Country," in *Sources of Vietnamese Tradition*, ed. George E. Dutton, Jayne S. Werner, and John K. Whitmore (1905; New York: Columbia University Press, 2012), 342.

137. William J. Duiker, "Phan Boi Chau: Asian Revolutionary in a Changing World," *Journal of Asian Studies* 31, no. 1 (1971): 78.

138. Phan Châu Trinh supposedly wrote this poem while in Japan.

139. Paterson, "Tenacious Texts," 92.

140. Prasenjit Duara, "The Discourse of Civilization and Pan-Asianism," *Journal of World History* 12, no. 1 (2001): 101.

141. Paterson, "Tenacious Texts," 6.

142. Masaya Shiraishi, "Phan Boi Chau in Japan," in *Phan Boi Chau and the Dong-Du Movement*, ed. Vinh Sinh (New Haven, CT: Yale Southeast Asia Studies, 1988), 58.

143. Shiraishi, "Phan Boi Chau in Japan," 58–59.

144. Shiraishi, "Phan Boi Chau in Japan," 59.

145. Phan Boi Chau, "A Letter from Abroad Written in Blood," in *Sources of Vietnamese Tradition*, edited by George E. Dutton, Jayne S. Werner, and John K. Whitmore (New York: Columbia University Press, 2012), 358.

146. Shiraishi, "Phan Boi Chau in Japan," 79.

147. Shiraishi, "Phan Boi Chau in Japan," 62.

148. See Joël Joos, "The Genyōsha (1881) and Premodern Roots of Japanese Expansionism" (61–68) and Sven Saaler, "The Kokuryūkai, 1901–1920" (121–32) in Sven Saaler and Christopher W. A. Szpilman, eds., *Pan-Asianism: A Documentary History*, vol. 1, *1850–1920* (Lanham, MD: Rowman & Littlefield, 2011).

149. Akira Iriye, *Japan and the Wider World: From the Mid-Nineteenth Century to the Present* (New York: Longman, 1997), 18–19.

150. Iriye, *Japan and the Wider World*, 19.

151. See Kakuzo Okakura, *The Book of Tea* (1906; London: Penguin Classics, 2016).

152. Iriye, *Japan and the Wider World*, 19.

153. Marius B. Jansen, *The Japanese and Sun Yat-sen* (Cambridge, MA: Harvard University Press, 1967), 69.

154. Supreme Council, "Kataastaasang Sangunian Sa mga Pinakakatawan sa K.K.," in Richardson, *The Light of Liberty*, 248. See "Kataastaasang Sangunian Sa mga Pinakakatawan sa K.K.," Caja 5677, Legajo 1.27, Archivo General Militar de Madrid.

155. Sb. Mahiganti, "Record of meeting held on May 30, 1896," in Richardson, *The Light of Liberty*, 250. See "Record of meeting held on May 30, 1896," Caja 5677, Legajo 1.58, Archivo General Militar de Madrid.

156. "Memoirs of Dr. Pio Valenzuela," in Katipunan, *Minutes of the Katipunan* (Manila: National Heroes Commission, 1964), 93.

157. "Memoirs of Dr. Pio Valenzuela," 94.

158. "Memoirs of Dr. Pio Valenzuela," 94.

159. "Memoirs of Dr. Pio Valenzuela," 97.

160. "Memoirs of Dr. Pio Valenzuela," 98.

161. Supreme Council, "Letter to Mariano Alvarez and Santiago Alvarez, October 29–30, 1896," in Richardson, *The Light of Liberty*, 265.

162. Supreme Council, "Letter to Mariano Alvarez and Santiago Alvarez, October 29–30, 1896," in Richardson, *The Light of Liberty*, 265.

163. Supreme Council, "Letter to Mariano Alvarez and Santiago Alvarez, October 29–30, 1896," in Richardson, *The Light of Liberty*, 265. Bonifacio wrote: "We wanted to send a letter to our compatriots in Japan about the lack of guns and other weapons we need, and also to persuade our brother soldiers to take the field, but our Japanese friend Moritaro seems to be frightened" (267).

164. Reprinted in Alejandrino, *La Senda del Sacrificio*, 49–59.

165. Agoncillo, *Malolos*, 254.

166. See Alejandrino's letter dated February 26, 1897, reprinted in Alejandrino, *La Senda del Sacrificio*, 50–53.

167. Alejandrino, *La Senda del Sacrificio*, 55.

168. Alejandrino, *La Senda del Sacrificio*, 56. See Alejandrino's letter dated March 6, 1897, reprinted in Alejandrino, *La Senda del Sacrificio*, 54–56.

169. See Saniel, *Japan and the Philippines*, 226–34, for further study.

170. Saniel, *Japan and the Philippines*, 227.

171. Saniel, *Japan and the Philippines*, 229.

172. Saniel, *Japan and the Philippines*, 231.

173. Saniel, *Japan and the Philippines*, 231.

174. Saniel, *Japan and the Philippines*, 237.

175. Saniel, *Japan and the Philippines*, 238.

176. Saniel, *Japan and the Philippines*, 238.

177. Saniel, *Japan and the Philippines*, 239.

178. Saniel, *Japan and the Philippines*, 242.

179. Saniel, *Japan and the Philippines*, 243.

180. "Letter of Manuel Luengo, Civil Governor of Manila, to the Minister of the Colonies," in Katipunan, *Minutes of the Katipunan* (Manila: National Heroes Commission, 1964), 213. The Japanese were thrown into this race war too. "The information supplied by the *Cuerpo de Vigilancia* has made it possible for the authorities to know clearly all that is going on in Japan, to such a degree that in the S.S. Sungkiang which arrived three days ago from Japan there came two Japanese . . . who went to stay at the Hotel Oriente," Manuel Luengo reported on October 1, 1896 (216). These Japanese "are being carefully shadowed so that everything they do, the visits they make and receive, and all their movements may be known, that such steps as may be necessary may be taken" (216).

181. "Letter of Manuel Luengo," 214.

182. "Letter of Manuel Luengo," 214.

183. Apolinario Mabini, *The Philippine Revolution: With Other Documents of the Epoch* (1901; Manila: National Historical Institute, 2007), 104.

184. Mabini, *The Philippine Revolution*, 104.

185. Mabini, *The Philippine Revolution*, 105.

186. Mabini, *The Philippine Revolution*, 105.

187. "El Mensaje de Aguinaldo," in Veloso, *Discursos y Debates de Malolos*, 15.

188. "Sesión del 23 de Noviembre," in Veloso, *Discursos y Debates de Malolos*, 72.

189. "Sesión del 29 de Noviembre," Veloso, 96.

190. Clemente Zulueta, Epifanio de los Santos, and Benito Lopez published *La Malasia*, which only ran two issues.

191. Nery, *Revolutionary Spirit*, 57.

192. Nery, *Revolutionary Spirit*, 57–58.

193. Record Group 350, Records of the Bureau of Insular Affairs, Personal Name Information File, 1914–45, Box 376, Personal Name File: Mabini, Apolinario, the National Archives and Records Administration at College Park, Maryland.

194. Mabini, "Letter to Remontado: November 3, 1899," in *The Letters of Apolinario Mabini*, 231.

195. Mabini, "Letter to Remontado," 231.

196. Mabini, "Letter to Remontado," 232.

197. Mabini, "Letter to Remontado," 232.

198. Mabini, "Letter to Remontado," 232.

199. Mabini, "Letter to Remontado," 232.

200. Mabini, "Letter to Remontado," 232.

201. "When this young nation, full of strength and abundant in love, inherits the experience of another which is already old and worn out, the sciences will advance greatly and will humanize, so to say, the sentiments to the extent

required by the aspired universal equilibrium." Mabini, "Letter to Remontado," 232.

4. The First Philippine Republic's Pan-Asian Emissary, 1898–1912

1. Mariano Ponce, "Recuerdos de España," n.d., Box 33, Folder 3, T. H. Pardo de Tavera Archives, Ateneo de Manila University, Quezon City, Philippines.
2. Ponce, "Recuerdos de España."
3. For more about Mariano Ponce, see Ma. Luisa T. Camagay, "Mariano Ponce: Emissary to Japan," *Asian and Pacific Migration Journal* 8, nos. 1–2 (1999): 101–15; Jean Paul Zialcita, "Mariano Ponce and the Philippine-American War: A View of the Man and His Deeds Through His Letters from Japan," *Social Science Diliman* 7, no. 2 (December 2011): 30–48; Resil B. Mojares, "Los itineraries de Mariano Ponce y el imaginario político Filipino," in *Filipinas, un país entre dos imperios*, ed. María Dolores Elizalde and Josep M. Delgado (Barcelona: Ediciones Bellaterra, 2011); and the National Historical Commission of the Philippines, ed., *Naning: Mariano Ponce 150th Birth Anniversary Commemorative Lectures & Selected Articles in La Solidaridad* (Manila: National Historical Commission of the Philippines, 2013).
4. See "Hispano-Japanese Treaty," *La Solidaridad* 6, no. 138, October 31, 1894; and "Relación entre Las Cortes y el archipielago Filipino," *La Solidaridad* 7, no. 145, February 15, 1895.
5. See Mariano Ponce, "El Folk-lore Bulaqueño," in Isabelo de los Reyes, *El Folk-lore Filipino: Colección Comentada y Publicada bajo la dirección de D. Isabelo de los Reyes* (Manila: Imprenta de Santa Cruz, 1890), 2:41–80, available at https://archive.org/details/elfolklorefilip00florgoog.
6. "Otras que parecen extrañas," de los Reyes, *El Folk-lore Filipino*, 2:6.
7. Lino L. Dizon, "Ponce, the Folklorist," in National Historical Commission of the Philippines, *Naning*, 21.
8. Resil B. Mojares, "Los itineraries de Mariano Ponce y el imaginario político filipino," in *Filipinas, un país entre dos imperios*, ed. María Dolores Elizalde and Josep M. Delgado (Barcelona: Ediciones Bellaterra, 2011), 87.
9. "Regimes of the Colonial Government," *La Solidaridad*, April 30, 1894.
10. Mojares, "Los itineraries de Mariano Ponce," 85–86.
11. Mariano Ponce, "Carta a Blumentritt" (1897), in *Cartas sobre la revolución 1897–1900* (Manila: Bureau of Printing, 1932), 68, in Multimedia Collection, MMC R383a I3951a, National Library of the Philippines.
12. Motoe Terami-Wada, *The Japanese in the Philippines 1880s-1990s* (Manila: National Historical Commission of the Philippines, 2015), 22.
13. Mojares, "Los itineraries de Mariano Ponce," 93–94.
14. Mojares, "Los itineraries de Mariano Ponce," 94.
15. Mojares, "Los itineraries de Mariano Ponce," 94.
16. Felipe Agoncillo was a prominent lawyer originally from Batangas, minister plenipotentiary of the revolutionary government, and the temporary president

of the Hong Kong junta in 1898; he fled Spanish arrest and deportation from the Philippines in December 1896, which is when he arrived in Hong Kong and helped organize the committee there.

17. Mariano Ponce, "Carta a William Jones, Esq." (1898), in *Cartas sobre la revolución 1897-1900*, 121.

18. Miyazaki Tōten, *My Thirty-Three Year's Dream: The Autobiography of* Miyazaki Tōten, ed. and trans. Marius B. Jansen and Eto Shinkichi (1902; Princeton, NJ: Princeton University Press, 2014), 141.

19. Quoted in Kaiyuan Zhang, "Ideals and Reality: Sun Yat-sen's Dream for Asia," *Journal of Cultural Interactions in East Asia* 3 (2012): 60.

20. Miyazaki Tōten, *My Thirty-Three Year's Dream*, 46.

21. Miyazaki Tōten, *My Thirty-Three Year's Dream*, 47.

22. My-Van Tran, *A Vietnamese Royal Exile in Japan: Prince Cuong De (1882-1951)* (London: Routledge, 2005), 129.

23. Tran, *A Vietnamese Royal Exile in Japan*, 129.

24. Tran, *A Vietnamese Royal Exile in Japan*, 88.

25. Tran, *A Vietnamese Royal Exile in Japan*, 88.

26. Tran, *A Vietnamese Royal Exile in Japan*, 88.

27. Tran, *A Vietnamese Royal Exile in Japan*, 129.

28. Alexander B. Woodside, *Community and Revolution in Modern Vietnam* (Boston: Houghton Mifflin Company, 1976), 48.

29. Masaya Shiraishi, "Phan Boi Chau in Japan," in *Phan Boi Chau and the Dong-Du Movement*, ed. Vinh Sinh (New Haven, CT: Yale Southeast Asia Studies, 1988), 70.

30. Phan Chau Trinh, *Phan Châu Trinh and His Political Writings*, trans. and ed. Vinh Sinh (Ithaca, NY: Cornell Southeast Asia Program Publications, 2009), 61.

31. Don Faustino Lichauco, "Appendix XII: Questions and Answers Sent by Don Faustino Lichauco to Col. Fukushima, July 17, 1898," trans. Jose Ramos, in *Japan and the Philippines, 1868-1898*, by Josefa M. Saniel (Quezon City: University of the Philippines Press, 1969), 374.

32. Lichauco, "Appendix XII: Questions and Answers," 374.

33. Lichauco, "Appendix XII: Questions and Answers," 375.

34. Lichauco, "Appendix XII: Questions and Answers," 375.

35. Lichauco, "Appendix XII: Questions and Answers," 375.

36. Mariano Ponce, "Carta a F. Agoncillo" (1898), in *Cartas sobre la revolución 1897-1900*, 129.

37. Ponce, "Carta a F. Agoncillo" (1898), 152.

38. I am reporting the financial amounts exactly as stated in the letter, as I do subsequently in this chapter. Though the exact currency is not named, is only denoted in currency symbols, and does not feature annotation from the collection editor, I assume that all of the dollar currency figures I quote in this chapter from Mariano Ponce's letters refer to Hong Kong dollars. I assume this because the letters are sent from Japan to Hong Kong and elsewhere Ponce refers specifically to Japanese yen and Philippine pesos, through currency symbol and/or currency name, also without annotation by the collection editor.

39. Mariano Ponce, "Carta a D. W. Jones" (1898), in *Cartas sobre la revolución 1897-1900*, 155. "William Jones, Esq.," is identified in the *Cartas sobre la revolución* annotation

to the July 7, 1898, letter from Mariano Ponce as referring to Felipe Agoncillo. Elsewhere, Augusto V. de Viana has identified "William Jones" as one of the aliases of Felipe Agoncillo (1859–1941). Augusto V. de Viana, "The Development of the Philippine Foreign Service During the Revolutionary Period and the Filipino-American War (1896–1906): A Story of Struggle from the Formation of Diplomatic Contacts to the Philippine Republic," *Antoninus Journal* 2 (February 2016): 34. Letters from Ponce also appear in the collection during the same year written on the same topic to "Don William Jones," "D. W. Jones," and "Don W. Jones," without the same clarifying annotation; I, however, am assuming that all these aliases belong to Felipe Agoncillo.

40. This may refer to a Kondo Katsu more probably.

41. Mariano Ponce, "Carta a G. Apacible" (1898), in *Cartas sobre la revolución 1897-1900*, 223.

42. Galicano Apacible was one of the founders of *La Solidaridad* and a cousin of José Rizal. From 1885 to 1889 he lived in Spain and contributed to the Propaganda Movement from Barcelona alongside Marcelo H. del Pilar and Graciano López Jaena. He returned to Manila in 1892, but left again to Hong Kong to escape the reprisals and suppression then occurring under Gobernador General Polavieja. In Hong Kong he served as chairman of the Central Committee, and, before Ponce's posting to Japan, made trips there to procure arms for the Philippine Revolution.

43. Mariano Ponce, "Carta a Apacible" (1898), in *Cartas sobre la revolución 1897-1900* (Manila: Bureau of Printing, 1932), 241.

44. Ponce, "Carta a Apacible" (1898), 241. "Tokishawa" likely refers to Captain Tokizawa, who is discussed in chapter 3.

45. Ponce, "Carta a Apacible" (1898), 241.

46. Mariano Ponce, "Carta a Mabini" (1898), in *Cartas sobre la revolución 1897-1900*, 246–247.

47. Mariano Ponce, "Carta a Apacible" (1899), in *Cartas sobre la revolución 1897-1900*, 256.

48. Though the minister of war is not explicitly named, the date of the letter, January 2, 1899, suggests that it was most likely Baldomero Aguinaldo.

49. Ponce, "Carta a Apacible" (1899), 258.

50. Ponce, "Carta a Apacible" (1899), 268.

51. Ponce, "Carta a Apacible" (1899), 268.

52. Ponce, "Carta a Apacible" (1899), 269.

53. Ponce, "Carta a Apacible" (1899), 353.

54. Ponce, "Carta a Apacible" (1899), 353.

55. According to the collected letters from Aguinaldo to Ponce on December 16, 1898, from Ponce to Apacible on January 27, 1899, and from Apacible to Aguinaldo on February 20, 1899, in the James A. Robertson Papers. Cited in Luis Camara Dery, *The Army of the First Philippine Republic and Other Historical Essays* (Manila: De La Salle University Press, 1995), 93.

56. Dery, *Army of the First Philippine Republic*, 93.

57. Mariano Ponce, *Sun Yat-sen: The Founder of the Republic of China* (1912; Manila: Filipino-Chinese Cultural Foundation, 1965), 3.

58. Miyazaki, *My Thirty-Three Year's Dream*, 174.

59. Miyazaki, *My Thirty-Three Year's Dream*, 141–42.

60. Miyazaki, *My Thirty-Three Year's Dream*, 142.

61. Miyazaki, *My Thirty-Three Year's Dream*, 143.

62. Miyazaki, *My Thirty-Three Year's Dream*, 174.

63. Lorraine Marion Paterson, "Tenacious Texts: Vietnam, China, and Radical Cultural Intersections, 1890–1930" (PhD diss., Yale University, 2006), 97.

64. See Caroline S. Hau and Takashi Shiraishi, "Daydreaming About Rizal and Tetchō: On Asianism as Network and Fantasy," *Philippine Studies* 57, no. 3 (2009): 329–88.

65. Hau and Shiraishi also argue for this point regarding the role of fantasy in Pan-Asianism in "Daydreaming about Rizal and Tetchō."

66. Miyazaki, *My Thirty-Three Year's Dream*, 133.

67. Miyazaki, *My Thirty-Three Year's Dream*, 133–34.

68. Miyazaki, *My Thirty-Three Year's Dream*, 137.

69. Miyazaki, *My Thirty-Three Year's Dream*, 137.

70. Miyazaki, *My Thirty-Three Year's Dream*, 138.

71. Miyazaki, *My Thirty-Three Year's Dream*, 174.

72. Mojares, "Los itineraries de Mariano Ponce," 96.

73. Miyazaki, *My Thirty-Three Year's Dream*, 175.

74. Miyazaki, *My Thirty-Three Year's Dream*, 175.

75. Mojares, "Los itineraries de Mariano Ponce," 96

76. Mojares, "Los itineraries de Mariano Ponce," 96.

77. Quoted in Marius B. Jansen, *The Japanese and Sun Yat-sen* (Cambridge, MA: Harvard University Press, 1967), 72.

78. Hirayama Shu's account appears in his "Shina kakumeitō oyobi himitsu kessha" (The Chinese revolutionary party and the secret societies) and *Nihon oyobi Nihonjin* (Japan and the Japanese; Tokyo, November 1911). Jansen, *The Japanese and Sun Yat-sen*, 72.

79. Jansen, *The Japanese and Sun Yat-sen*, 72.

80. Jansen, *The Japanese and Sun Yat-sen*, 72.

81. Jansen, *The Japanese and Sun Yat-sen*, 73; and Miyazaki, *My Thirty-Three Year's Dream*, 44.

82. Jansen, *The Japanese and Sun Yat-sen*, 73.

83. Miyazaki, *My Thirty-Three Year's Dream*, 244.

84. Jansen, *The Japanese and Sun Yat-sen*, 73.

85. Miyazaki, *My Thirty-Three Year's Dream*, 181–82.

86. Mariano Ponce, "Appendix III: Mariano Ponce's Letters to Dr. Sun Yat-Sen, Letter 1," in Ponce, *Sun Yat-sen*, 58.

87. Mariano Ponce, "Carta a Foujita" (1899), in *Cartas sobre la revolución 1897-1900*, 416.

88. Ponce, "Carta a Foujita" (1899), 417.

89. See Records of Foreign Service Posts, Consular Posts, Hong Kong, China, Record Group 84, Volume 44, National Archives at College Park, Maryland.

90. "U.S. Consul General Hong Kong, China to General E.S Otis 20th July 1899," Records of Foreign Service Posts, Consular Posts, Hong Kong, China, Record Group 84, Volume 044, National Archives at College Park, Maryland.

91. Mojares, "Los itineraries de Mariano Ponce," 97.
92. Miyazaki, *My Thirty-Three Year's Dream*, 44–45.
93. Miyazaki, *My Thirty-Three Year's Dream*, 45.
94. Teodoro A. Agoncillo, *Malolos: The Crisis of the Republic* (1960; Quezon City: University of the Philippines, 1997), 260.
95. "U.S. Consul Hong Kong, China to General W. Merritt, 13th August 1898," Records of Foreign Service Posts, Consular Posts, Hong Kong, China, Record Group 84, Volume 045, National Archives at College Park, Maryland.
96. Mojares, "Los itineraries de Mariano Ponce," 98.
97. Rebecca E. Karl, *Staging the World: Chinese Nationalism at the Turn of the Twentieth Century* (Durham, NC: Duke University Press, 2002), 103.
98. Karl, *Staging the World*, 103.
99. Karl, *Staging the World*, 103–4.
100. Quoted in Karl, *Staging the World*, 105.
101. Motoo Furuta, "Vietnamese Political Movements in Thailand: Legacy of the Dong-Du Movement," in *Phan Boi Chau and the Dong-Du Movement*, ed. Vinh Sinh (New Haven, CT: Yale Southeast Asia Studies, 1988), 150.
102. Phan Boi Chau, *Overturned Chariot: The Autobiography of Phan-Boi-Chau*, trans. Vinh Sinh and Nicholas Wickenden (Honolulu: University of Hawai'i Press, 1999), 164.
103. Furuta, "Vietnamese Political Movements in Thailand," 151.
104. William J. Duiker, "Phan Boi Chau: Asian Revolutionary in a Changing World," *Journal of Asian Studies* 31, no. 1 (1971): 82.
105. Duiker, "Phan Boi Chau," 82.
106. Tonkin Free School, "A Civilization of New Learning" (1904), in *Sources of Vietnamese Tradition*, ed. George E. Dutton, Jayne S. Werner, and John K. Whitmore (New York: Columbia University Press, 2012), 370.
107. My-Van Tran, "Japan Through Vietnamese Eyes (1905–1945)," *Journal of Southeast Asian Studies* 30, no. 1 (1999): 132.
108. Paterson, "Tenacious Texts," 126.
109. Tran, "Japan Through Vietnamese Eyes (1905–1945)," 132.
110. Tran, "Japan Through Vietnamese Eyes (1905–1945)," 132.
111. Tran, "Japan Through Vietnamese Eyes (1905–1945)," 132.
112. Tonkin Free School, "A Civilization of New Learning," 375.
113. Tonkin Free School, "A Civilization of New Learning," 370–71.
114. Phan Boi Chau, "A Letter from Abroad Written in Blood" (1907), in *Sources of Vietnamese Tradition*, ed. George E. Dutton, Jayne S. Werner, and John K. Whitmore (New York: Columbia University Press, 2012), 369.
115. David G. Marr, *Vietnamese Anticolonialism, 1885–1925* (Berkeley: University of California Press, 1971), 97.
116. Marr, *Vietnamese Anticolonialism*, 97.
117. Mariano Ponce, "Carta a Sugimura" (1899), in *Cartas sobre la revolución 1897–1900*, 285.
118. Francis A. Gealogo, "Mariano Ponce and Pan Asianism," in National Historical Commission of the Philippines, *Naning*, 42.

119. Mariano Ponce, "Carta a Hirata" (1899), in *Cartas sobre la revolución 1897–1900*, 259.

120. He noted in particular the works "Hopiki," "Nikongi," "Dainihonsiki," "Nihon Guaiehi," "Genpei Seisuiki"; the poets "Manyoshiu" and "Haukuninshin," which may refer to "Kojiki," "Nihon Shoki," "Nihon Gaishi," "Genpei Seisuiki" and the poetry collections "Man'yōshū" and "Ogura Hyakunin Isshu." Mariano Ponce, "Carta a Miura" (1898), in *Cartas sobre la revolución 1897–1900*, 208–9.

121. Ponce, "Carta a Miura" (1898), 208–9.

122. "By especial command of my Government," Ponce wrote Y. Yamagata on February 14, 1899, "I am making a thorough study of Japanese institutions." Mariano Ponce, "Carta a Yamagata" (1899), in *Cartas sobre la revolución 1897–1900*, 276.

123. See Mariano Ponce, "Carta a Apacible" (1898) and "Carta a Mabini" (1898), in *Cartas sobre la revolución 1897–1900*, 241, 248.

124. Ponce, "Carta a Miura" (1898), 208.

125. Ponce, "Carta a Apacible" (1898), 240.

126. Sven Matthiessen, *Japanese Pan-Asianism and the Philippines from the Late Nineteenth Century to the End of World War II: Going to the Philippines Is Like Coming Home?* (Leiden: Brill, 2016), 185.

127. Ponce, "Carta a Apacible" (1898), 224.

128. Ponce, "Carta a Apacible" (1898), 224.

129. Ponce, "Carta a Apacible" (1898), 224–25.

130. Ponce, "Carta a Apacible" (1898), 225.

131. Ponce, "Appendix III: Mariano Ponce's Letters to Dr. Sun Yat-Sen, Letter 2," in Ponce, *Sun Yat-sen*, 59.

132. Gealogo, "Mariano Ponce and Pan Asianism," 42.

133. Gealogo, "Mariano Ponce and Pan Asianism," 44.

134. Ponce, "Carta a Mabini" (1898), 247–48.

135. Ponce, "Carta a Sugimura" (1899), 285.

136. Ponce, "Carta a Sugimura" (1899), 285.

137. Ponce, "Carta a Sugimura" (1899), 285.

138. Ponce, "Carta a Apacible" (1899), 317.

139. See Roger H. Brown, "Sun Yat-sen: 'Pan-Asianism,' 1924," in *Pan-Asianism: A Documentary History,* vol. 2, *1920–Present*, ed. Sven Saaler and Christopher W. A. Szpilman (Lanham, MD: Rowman & Littlefield, 2011), 75–85.

140. Ponce, *Sun Yat-sen*, 40.

141. Ponce, *Sun Yat-sen*, 40.

142. Ponce, *Sun Yat-sen*, 40.

143. Ponce, *Sun Yat-sen*, 40.

144. Gealogo, "Mariano Ponce and Pan Asianism," 41.

145. Gealogo, "Mariano Ponce and Pan Asianism," 41.

146. Ponce, *Sun Yat-sen*, 42.

147. Ponce, *Sun Yat-sen*, 42.

148. Ponce, *Sun Yat-sen*, 42.

149. Ponce, *Sun Yat-sen*, 41.

150. Ponce, *Sun Yat-sen*, 41.

151. Ponce, *Sun Yat-sen*, 41.

152. Quoted in Takamichi Serizawa, "Japanese Solidarity Discourse on the Philippines During the Second World War," *Philippine Studies: Historical and Ethnographic Viewpoints* 63, no. 1 (March 2015): 83–84.
153. Apolinario Mabini, "Letter to Remontado: November 3, 1899," in *The Letters of Apolinario Mabini* (Manila: National Heroes Commission, 1965), 231.
154. Mabini, "Letter to Remontado: November 3, 1899," 231.
155. Mabini, "Letter to Remontado: November 3, 1899," 231.
156. Mabini, "Letter to Remontado: November 3, 1899," 231.
157. Chao Phraya Surasakmontri (1851–1933) married into the Bunnag family, served the modernizing Thai king Rama V in his security forces, was denounced in 1883, and subsequently resigned from the Royal Guard before being appointed commander of expeditions against rebellions in northern Thailand, ultimately reaching the rank of major general and receiving the title Chao Phraya, which is equivalent to the Japanese Kōshaku (Prince), for which reason Miyazaki refers to him as "Prince." He later served as minister of agriculture until 1896, was a member of Rama VI's privy council, received the surname Saeng-Xuto, and was later named field marshal by Rama VII. Miyazaki, *My Thirty-Three Year's Dream*, 69n27.
158. Miyazaki, *My Thirty-Three Year's Dream*, 105–6.
159. Suenaga Setsu (1869–1965) was a Fukuoka adventurer who accompanied Japanese armies in the Sino-Japanese War, was affiliated with the expansionist Kokuryūkai Society, and dreamed of a great "East Asian Free Empire." Miyazaki, *My Thirty-Three Year's Dream*, 84n36.
160. Miyazaki, *My Thirty-Three Year's Dream*, 106.
161. "The 'Revue Diplomatique' on the Philippine Question," *Japan Times*, August 16, 1898.
162. Charles H. Cramp, "The Coming Sea Power," *Japan Times*, December 4, 1897.
163. Cramp, "The Coming Sea Power."
164. Cramp, "The Coming Sea Power."
165. "The 'Revue Diplomatique.'"
166. Paula Harrell, *Asia for the Asians: China in the Lives of Five Meiji Japanese* (Honolulu: University of Hawai'i Press, 2012), 256.
167. Ricardo T. Jose, "The Russo-Japanese War and the Philippines," in *Pilipinas Muna! The Philippines Is a Priority!*, ed. Maria V. Stanyukovich (St. Petersburg, Russia: Maclay Publications, Issue 4, 2011), 60.
168. Jose, "The Russo-Japanese War and the Philippines," 63.
169. Jose, "The Russo-Japanese War and the Philippines," 63.
170. Jose, "The Russo-Japanese War and the Philippines," 64.
171. Jose, "The Russo-Japanese War and the Philippines," 62.
172. Jose, "The Russo-Japanese War and the Philippines," 62.
173. Jose, "The Russo-Japanese War and the Philippines," 65.
174. Jose, "The Russo-Japanese War and the Philippines," 65.
175. Niall Ferguson, *Colossus: The Rise and Fall of the American Empire* (New York: Penguin Books, 2005); Tomiyama Ichirō, "Colonialism and the Sciences of the Tropical Zone: The Academic Analysis of Difference in 'the Island Peoples,'" in *Formations of Colonial Modernity in East Asia*, ed. Tani E. Barlow (Durham, NC: Duke University Press, 2007), 216.

176. See also Anne L. Foster, *Projections of Power: The United States and Europe in Colonial Southeast Asia, 1919-1941* (Durham, NC: Duke University Press, 2010); and Anders Stephanson, *Manifest Destiny: American Expansion and the Empire of Right* (New York: Hill and Wang, 1995).
177. Quoted in Akira Iriye, *Japan and the Wider World: From the Mid-Nineteenth Century to the Present* (New York: Longman, 1997), 44–45.
178. The Chinese Exclusion Act of 1882 was followed by the Pacific Coast race riots in 1907 in San Francisco against the Japanese, in order to win segregation of schools. Later that year, Japan and the United States concluded a gentleman's agreement by which the Japanese government agreed to prohibit emigration to the United States and the United States agreed in turn to impose fewer restrictions on Japanese immigrants already present. The Asiatic Barred Zone of 1917 prohibited immigration to the United States from Southeast Asia, South Asia, and the Middle East, while the Immigration Act of 1924 introduced national origin quotas for the whole Eastern Hemisphere and barred the immigration of "aliens ineligible for citizenship." In great part, these early twentieth-century measures were a response to the inclusion of the Philippines as a colony, and the racial fears of migration and competition that that sparked in the United States.
179. Iriye, *Japan and the Wider World*, 45.
180. Iriye, *Japan and the Wider World*, 45.
181. For a full study of this proposal and its history, see Naoko Shimazu, *Japan, Race and Equality: The Racial Equality Proposal of 1919* (London: Routledge, 1998).
182. Ponce, *Sun Yat-sen*, 6.
183. Ponce, *Sun Yat-sen*, 6.
184. Ponce, *Sun Yat-sen*, 20.
185. Ponce, *Sun Yat-sen*, 22.
186. See Ponce, "Indo-China: Conference da-da en el Centro Escolar de Señoritas, el 3 de Octubre de 1914," Boletín No. 1, Multimedia Collection, Banas Collection, National Library of the Philippines. This and all subsequent translations from this text are my own.
187. Ponce, "Indo-China," 21.
188. Ponce, "Indo-China," 21.
189. The assassination of two Spanish Dominican bishops, Father José María Díaz y Sanjurjo and Father Melchor San Pedro, in 1857 and 1858, respectively, was the pretext for Spanish participation in the French conquest.
190. Ponce, "Indo-China," 7.
191. Ponce, "Indo-China," 12.
192. Mojares, "Los itineraries de Mariano Ponce y el imaginario político Filipino," 104.
193. Ponce, "Indo-China," 13.
194. Ponce, "Indo-China," 13.
195. Ponce, "Indo-China," 13.
196. Ponce, "Indo-China," 15.
197. Ponce, "Indo-China," 15.
198. Shawn Frederick McHale, *Print and Power: Confucianism, Communism and Buddhism in the Making of Modern Vietnam* (Honolulu: University of Hawai'i Press, 2004), 182.

199. See Christopher Goscha, *Thailand and the Southeast Asian Networks of the Vietnamese Revolution, 1885–1954* (Richmond, VA: Curzon Press, 1999); and Goscha, *Vietnam or Indochina?: Contesting Concepts of Space in Vietnamese Nationalism, 1887–1954* (Copenhagen: NIAS Press, 1995).

200. Ponce, *Sun Yat-sen*, xi.

201. Ponce, *Sun Yat-sen*, xi.

202. Ponce, *Sun Yat-sen*, xi.

203. Ponce, *Sun Yat-sen*, xiv.

204. Ponce, *Sun Yat-sen*, xiv.

205. José Alejandrino, "The Emancipation of the Far East," *Boletín de la Sociedad Orientalista de Filipinas* 1, no. 9 (September 1918).

206. Alejandrino, "Emancipation of the Far East."

207. See the confidential reports from August 15, 17, 20, and 23, 1917, of the Philippine Constabulary, Records of the Bureau of Insular Affairs, Special Records Relating to the Philippine Islands, Record Group 350, Entry 50: Reports of the Philippine Constabulary, 1917, Box 1, National Archives at College Park, Maryland.

208. Philippine Constabulary, "Confidential Report August 11, 1917," Records of the Bureau of Insular Affairs, Special Records Relating to the Philippine Islands, Record Group 350, Entry 50: Reports of the Philippine Constabulary, 1917, Box 1, National Archives at College Park, Maryland.

209. Philippine Constabulary, "Confidential Report August 11, 1917."

210. Philippine Constabulary, "Confidential Report August 11, 1917."

211. Philippine Constabulary, "'La Vanguardia,' Tuesday, August 14, 1917," Records of the Bureau of Insular Affairs, Special Records Relating to the Philippine Islands, Record Group 350, Entry 50: Reports of the Philippine Constabulary, 1917, Box 1, National Archives at College Park, Maryland.

212. Philippine Constabulary, "'La Nacion,' Friday, September 7, 1917," Records of the Bureau of Insular Affairs, Special Records Relating to the Philippine Islands, Record Group 350, Entry 50: Reports of the Philippine Constabulary, 1917, Box 1, National Archives at College Park, Maryland.

213. Philippine Constabulary, "'La Nacion,' Friday, September 7, 1917."

214. Philippine Constabulary, "'La Nacion,' Tuesday, September 4, 1917," Records of the Bureau of Insular Affairs, Special Records Relating to the Philippine Islands, Record Group 350, Entry 50: Reports of the Philippine Constabulary, 1917, Box 1, National Archives at College Park, Maryland.

215. Philippine Constabulary, "'La Nacion,' Tuesday, September 4, 1917."

5. The Afterlife of the Philippine Revolution

1. Both Junko Koizumi, "The 'Last' Friendship Exchanges Between Siam and Vietnam, 1879–1882: Siam Between Vietnam and France—and Beyond," *TRaNS: Trans-Regional and -National Studies of Southeast Asia* 4, no. 1 (January

2016): 131–64; and John Crawfurd, *Journal of an Embassy to the Courts of Siam and Cochin China* (Kuala Lumpur: Oxford University Press, 1967) illustrate this fact.

2. Rebecca E. Karl, *Staging the World: Chinese Nationalism at the Turn of the Twentieth Century* (Durham, NC: Duke University Press, 2002).

3. Christopher L. Hill, *National History and the World of Nations: Capital, State, and the Rhetoric of History in Japan, France, and the United States* (Durham, NC: Duke University Press, 2008), 38. See also Partha Chatterjee, *Nationalist Thought and the Colonial World: A Derivative Discourse?* (London: Zed Books for the United Nations University, 1986); Chatterjee, *The Nation and Its Fragments: Colonial and Postcolonial Histories* (Princeton, NJ: Princeton University Press, 1993); and Michael Goebel, *Anti-Imperial Metropolis: Interwar Paris and the Seeds of Third-World Nationalism* (New York: Cambridge University Press, 2015).

4. See Megan C. Thomas, *Orientalists, Propagandists, and Ilustrados: Filipino Scholarship and the End of Spanish Colonialism* (Minneapolis: University of Minnesota Press, 2012).

5. See Hill, *National History and the World of Nations*; Benedict Anderson, *Imagined Communities: Reflections on the Origin and Spread of Nationalism* (London: Verso Books, 1983); and Ernest Gellner, *Nations and Nationalism* (Ithaca, NY: Cornell University Press, 1983).

6. Karl, *Staging the World*, 16.

7. Karl, *Staging the World*, 84.

8. Quoted in Karl, *Staging the World*, 86.

9. Lorraine Marion Paterson, "Tenacious Texts: Vietnam, China, and Radical Cultural Intersections, 1890–1930" (PhD diss., Yale University, 2006), 97.

10. Paterson, "Tenacious Texts," 97.

11. Karl, *Staging the World*, 88.

12. Karl, *Staging the World*, 110–11.

13. Karl, *Staging the World*, 93.

14. Paul W. Van der Veur, *The Lion and the Gadfly: Dutch Colonialism and the Spirit of E. F. E. Douwes Dekker* (Leiden: KiTLV Press, 2006), 247.

15. John Nery, *Revolutionary Spirit: Jose Rizal in Southeast Asia* (Quezon City: Ateneo de Manila University Press, 2011), 111.

16. Nery, *Revolutionary Spirit*, 114.

17. Nery, *Revolutionary Spirit*, 130.

18. Tan Malaka, *From Jail to Jail*, vol. 1, trans. Helen Jarvis (Athens: Ohio University Press, 1991), 117.

19. Malaka, *From Jail to Jail*, 118.

20. Nery, *Revolutionary Spirit*, 164.

21. Sukarno, *An Autobiography*, trans. Cindy Adams (Indianapolis, IN: Bobbs-Merrill, 1965), 34.

22. Ganis Harsono, *Recollections of an Indonesian Diplomat in the Sukarno Era*, ed. C. L. M. Penders and B. B. Hering (St. Lucia: University of Queensland Press, 1977), 259.

23. Nery, *Revolutionary Spirit*, 45.

24. Maitrii Aung-Thwin, "Structuring Revolt: Communities of Interpretation in the Historiography of the Saya San Rebellion," *Journal of Southeast Asian Studies* 39, no. 2 (June 2008): 297.

25. Aung-Thwin, "Structuring Revolt," 297.

26. For studies of the relationship between Japan and Indochina, see Masaya Shiraishi, *Vietnamese Phuc Quoc League and the 1940 Insurrection* (Tokyo: Center of Excellence, Contemporary Asian Studies, Waseda University, 2004); Masaya Shiraishi, "The Nan'you Gakuin: A Japanese Institute in Saigon from 1942–1945" (working paper, vol. 13, Contemporary Asian Studies, Waseda University, 2005); Masaya Shiraishi, "Japan Toward the Indochina Sub-Region," *Journal of Asia-Pacific Studies* (Waseda University) 13 (October 2009): 13–36; and Masaya Shiraishi, "Japan and the Reconstruction of Indochina," in *New Dynamics Between China and Japan in Asia: How to Build the Future from the Past?*, ed. Guy Faure (Singapore: World Scientific, 2010), 125–61.

27. Christopher E. Goscha, *Thailand and the Southeast Asian Networks of the Vietnamese Revolution, 1885–1954* (Richmond, VA: Curzon Press, 1999), 7. For further discussions of such parallel journeys, see Masaya Shiraishi, *Vietnamese Nationalism and Its Relations with Japan and Asia: Phan Boi Chau's Ideas of Revolution and the World* (Tokyo: Gannando Shoten, 1993); Denys Lombard, "Le voyage de Parada Harahap au 'Pays du Soleil levant' (1933–34)," in *Recits de voyage des Asiatiques: Genres mentalités conception de l'espace,* ed. Claudine Salmon (Paris: Ecole Francaise D'extreme-Orient, 2005), 281–96; and Grant K. Goodman, "Consistency Is the Hobgoblin: Manuel L. Quezon and Japan, 1899–1934," *Journal of Southeast Asian Studies* 14, no. 1 (March 1983): 79–94.

28. Phan Boi Chau, *Overturned Chariot: The Autobiography of Phan-Boi-Chau,* trans. Vinh Sinh and Nicholas Wickenden (Honolulu: University of Hawai'i Press, 1999), 88.

29. Bunchan Mul, "The Umbrella War of 1942," in *Peasants and Politics in Kampuchea, 1942–1981,* ed. Ben Kiernan and Chanthou Boua (London: Zed, 1982), 114–26; Marie Alexandrine Martin, *Cambodia: A Shattered Society,* trans. Mark W. McLeod (Berkeley: University of California Press, 1989), 45–46.

30. Ben Kiernan, *How Pol Pot Came to Power: Colonialism, Nationalism, and Communism in Cambodia, 1930–1975* (1985; New Haven, CT: Yale University Press, 2004), 45.

31. Kiernan, *How Pol Pot Came to Power,* 45–46.

32. Francois Guillemot, "Vietnamese Nationalist Revolutionaries and the Japanese Occupation: The Case of the Dai Viet Parties (1936–1946)," in *Imperial Japan and National Identities in Asia, 1895–1945,* ed. Li Narangoa and Robert Cribb (London: RoutledgeCurzon, 2003), 222.

33. Guillemot, "Vietnamese Nationalist Revolutionaries," 223.

34. Guillemot, "Vietnamese Nationalist Revolutionaries," 237.

35. Harsono, *Recollections of an Indonesian Diplomat,* 30.

36. Harsono, *Recollections of an Indonesian Diplomat,* 37–38.

37. Harsono, *Recollections of an Indonesian Diplomat,* 38

38. Harsono, *Recollections of an Indonesian Diplomat,* 45.

39. Harsono, *Recollections of an Indonesian Diplomat,* 45.

40. Harsono, *Recollections of an Indonesian Diplomat in the Sukarno Era,* 45.

41. Bernhard Dahm, *Sukarno and the Struggle for Indonesian Independence*, trans. Mary F. Somers Heidhues (Ithaca, NY: Cornell University Press, 1969), 68.

42. Sukarno, "Indonesianisme dan Panasiatisme" (July 1928), in Dahm, *Sukarno and the Struggle for Indonesian Independence*, 69.

43. Dahm, *Sukarno and the Struggle for Indonesian Independence*, 115.

44. Dahm, *Sukarno and the Struggle for Indonesian Independence*, 115n192.

45. J. D. Legge, *Sukarno: A Political Biography* (London: Allen Lane/Penguin, 1972), 163.

46. Dahm, *Sukarno and the Struggle for Indonesian Independence*, 121.

47. Josef Silverstein, "Introduction," in *The Political Legacy of Aung San, Revised Edition with an Introductory Essay*, ed. Josef Silverstein (Ithaca, NY: Cornell Southeast Asia Program, 1993), 3.

48. Silverstein, "Introduction," 4.

49. Silverstein, "Introduction," 16.

50. Aung San, "The Resistance Movement. Address delivered at the meeting of the East and West Association held on 29th August 1945, at the city hall of Rangoon," in Silverstein, *The Political Legacy of Aung San*, 103.

51. For studies on Japanese-Philippine relations during American colonization, see Grant K. Goodman's "The Philippine Society of Japan," *Monumenta Nipponica* 22, no. 1/2 (1967): 131–46; "The Problem of Philippine Independence and Japan: The First Three Decades of American Colonial Rule," *Southeast Asia* 1, no. 3 (Summer 1971): 165–92; "A Sense of Kinship: Japan's Cultural Offensive in the Philippines During the 1930s," *Crossroads: An Interdisciplinary Journal of Southeast Asian Studies* 1, no. 2 (June 1983): 31–44; and "Japan and Philippine Commonwealth Politics," *Philippine Studies* 52, no. 2 (2004): 208–23. For studies on Philippine Pan-Asianism during the American colonial period, see Grant K. Goodman, "Japanese Pan-Asianism in the Philippines: The Hirippin Dai Ajia Kyōkai," *Studies on Asia* (1966): 133–43.

52. Guerrero's *Rizal: The First Filipino* was published in 1962 and won first prize in the Rizal Biography Contest, sponsored by the José Rizal National Centennial Commission.

53. For an in-depth interrogation of President Laurel's political thought as it related to empire, universe, Asia, and Pan-Asianism, as well as his intellectual debt to the Philippine Revolution's history, see Nicole CuUnjieng's "Cultures of Empire, Nation, and Universe in Pres. José P. Laurel's Political Thought, 1927–1949," *Philippine Studies: Historical and Ethnographic Viewpoints* 65, no. 1 (March 2017): 3–30.

54. For further background, see General Artemio Ricarte, *Himagsikan nang manga Pilipino laban sa Kastila* (Yokohama: n.p., 1927) and *Memoirs of General Artemio Ricarte with a Preface by Alejandro R. Roces and an Introduction by Armando J. Malay; Selected and Edited from Manuscripts in the Watson Collection* (Manila: National Heroes Commission,1963); Grant K. Goodman, "General Artemio Ricarte and Japan," *Journal of Southeast Asian History* 2 (September 1966): 48–60; Maria Pilar S. Luna, "General Artemio Ricarte y Garcia: A Filipino Nationalist," *Asian Studies* 9 (August 1971): 229–41; Mercedes Amistoso, "General Artemio Ricarte 1896–1915" (PhD diss., Ateneo de Manila University, 1974); Ara Satoshi, "Si General Artemio Ricarte at Ang Kasarinlan ng Pilipinas, 1915–1945" (PhD diss., University of

the Philippines, 1997); Ma. Luisa D. Fleetwood, *General Artemio Ricarte (Víbora)* (Manila: National Historical Institute, 1997); and Ricardo T. Jose, "Exile as Protest: Artemio Ricarte," *Asian and Pacific Migration Journal* 8, no. 1–2 (1999): 131–56.

55. Ricarte, *Memoirs of General Artemio Ricarte*, 138.
56. For further information on the Japanese propaganda efforts in the Philippines under occupation, see Motoe Terami-Wada, "Japanese Propaganda Corps in the Philippines," *Philippine Studies* 38 (1990): 279–300.
57. Artemio Ricarte, *Nippon at Busido* (n.p., 1943), 17. Translation by Gian Francisco Bermudez.
58. Ricarte, *Nippon at Busido*, 17.
59. Ricarte, *Nippon at Busido*, 37.
60. Though Ricarte cites one servant, in the story Momotaro brought three.
61. Ricarte, *Nippon at Busido*, 37.
62. Ricarte, *Nippon at Busido*, 37.
63. Ricarte, *Nippon at Busido*, 37.
64. For further detail, see Grant K. Goodman, "Pio Duran and Philippine Japanophilism," *The Historian* 32, no. 2 (February 1970): 228–42; and Pio Duran and F. B. Icasiano, *Wartime Japan as Viewed by Filipinos* (n.p.: Nippon Bunka Kaikan, 1944).
65. Pio Duran, *Philippine Independence and the Far Eastern Question* (Manila: Community Publishers, 1935), 151.
66. For discussions of potential regionalisms in Asia, see Peter J. Katzenstein and Takashi Shiraishi, eds., *Network Power: Japan and Asia* (Ithaca, NY: Cornell University Press, 1997) and *Beyond Japan: The Dynamics of East Asian Regionalism* (Ithaca, NY: Cornell University Press, 2006); Prasenjit Duara, ed., *Asia Redux: Conceptualising a Region for Our Times* (Singapore: ISEAS-Yusof Ishak Institute, 2013); Li Narangoa and Robert Cribb, eds., *Imperial Japan and National Identities in Asia, 1895–1945* (London: RoutledgeCurzon, 2003); and Joseph Francois, Pradumma B. Rana, and Ganeshan Wignaraja, eds., *Pan-Asian Integration: Linking East and South Asia* (London: Palgrave Macmillan, 2009).
67. See Motoe Terami-Wada, "Benigno Ramos and the Sakdal Movement," *Philippine Studies* 36, no. 4 (1988): 427–42; "The Sakdal Movement, 1930–34," *Philippine Studies* 36, no. 2 (1988): 131–50; and *Sakdalistas' Struggle for Philippine Independence, 1930–1945* (Manila: Ateneo de Manila University Press, 2014); and Grant K. Goodman, "An Interview with Benigno Ramos: Translated from the Japanese," *Philippine Studies* 37, no. 2 (1989): 215–20.
68. Terami-Wada, "Benigno Ramos and the Sakdal Movement," 435.
69. Terami-Wada, "Benigno Ramos and the Sakdal Movement," 438.
70. Goodman, "An Interview with Benigno Ramos," 215.
71. Goodman, "An Interview with Benigno Ramos," 216.
72. Terami-Wada, "Benigno Ramos and the Sakdal Movement," 442.
73. José Laurel's family had been embroiled in the Philippine Revolution against both Spain and the United States. José was the son of Sotero Laurel Sr., an official in President Emilio Aguinaldo's revolutionary government and a signatory to the 1899 Malolos Constitution. Before World War II, José received a doctor of civil laws degree from Yale University and served in the Philippine Commonwealth

as a senator and associate justice of the Philippine Supreme Court. Yet, José sent one of his sons to study at the Imperial Military Academy in Tokyo from 1934 to 1937; José also received an honorary doctorate from Tokyo University, publicly praised certain Japanese institutions, and maintained close relationships with Japanese officials, even serving as a prewar lobbyist for Japanese business interests. He was a strong critic of U.S. rule in the Philippines even as he served in the Commonwealth government. David Joel Steinberg, *Philippine Collaboration in World War II* (Manila: Solidaridad Publishing, 1967), 74.

74. Terami-Wada, "Benigno Ramos and the Sakdal Movement," 442.

75. Remigio E. Agpalo, *Jose P. Laurel: National Leader and Political Philosopher* (Quezon City: Jose P. Laurel Memorial Corporation, 1992), 184–85.

76. José P. Laurel, *Forces that Make a Nation Great* (Manila: Bureau of Printing, 1944), 3.

77. José P. Laurel, *War Memoirs of Dr. Jose P. Laurel: Written in Yokohama Prison, Sept. 15–Nov. 16 1945 and Resumed in Sugamo Prison Outside Tokyo; Completed Dec. 25, 1945* (Manila: Jose P. Laurel Memorial Foundation, 1962), 21.

78. José P. Laurel, *His Excellency Jose P. Laurel, President of the Second Philippine Republic: Speeches, Messages & Statements October 14, 1943 to December 19, 1944* (Manila: Lyceum of the Philippines, 1997), 49.

79. José P. Laurel, *Assertive Nationalism: A Collection of Articles and Addresses on Local Problems* (Manila: National Teachers College, 1931), 2–3.

80. Laurel, *Speeches, Messages & Statements*, 250.

81. Hannah Arendt, *The Origins of Totalitarianism* (New York: Harcourt, 1973), 226.

82. Laurel, *Assertive Nationalism*, 8.

83. Laurel, *Speeches, Messages & Statements*, 44.

84. Laurel, *Assertive Nationalism*, 8.

85. José P. Laurel, *Moral and Political Orientation* (Manila: n.p.,1949), vi.

86. Laurel, *Speeches, Messages & Statements*, 26.

87. Laurel, *Speeches, Messages & Statements*, 31.

88. Theodore Friend, *The Blue-Eyed Enemy: Japan Against the West in Java and Luzon, 1942-1945* (Princeton, NJ: Princeton University Press, 1988), 3.

89. Laurel, *Moral and Political Orientation*, vi.

90. Laurel, *Moral and Political Orientation*, vi.

91. Laurel, *Moral and Political Orientation*, 56.

92. Laurel, *Assertive Nationalism*, 6.

93. Laurel, *Assertive Nationalism*, 6.

94. Laurel, *Speeches, Messages & Statements*, 26.

95. Laurel, *Assertive Nationalism*, 3.

96. Jose P. Laurel, *Jose P. Laurel: On Polity, Economy & Education*, ed. Clemen C. Aquino (Manila: Lyceum of the Philippines, 1997), 90.

97. Laurel, *Jose P. Laurel: On Polity, Economy & Education*, 90.

98. Laurel, *Jose P. Laurel: On Polity, Economy & Education*, 91.

99. Laurel, *Assertive Nationalism*, 8.

100. Laurel, *Speeches, Messages & Statements*, 24.

101. Jose P. Laurel, *Inaugural Address of His Excellency Jose P. Laurel, President of the Republic of the Philippines* (Manila: n.p., 1943), 10–11.

102. Laurel, *Assertive Nationalism*, 7.

103. Laurel, *Speeches, Messages & Statements*, 24.

104. Laurel, *Speeches, Messages & Statements*, 24.

105. Laurel, *Speeches, Messages & Statements*, 29.

106. Laurel, *Speeches, Messages & Statements*, 94.

107. Laurel, *Speeches, Messages & Statements*, 94.

108. Duran, *Philippine Independence and the Far Eastern Question*, 119.

109. Duran, *Philippine Independence and the Far Eastern Question*, 120.

110. Ricarte, *Nippon at Busido*, 17.

111. Ricarte, *Nippon at Busido*, 17.

112. Leocadio de Asis, *From Bataan to Tokyo: Diary of a Filipino Student in Wartime Japan 1943-1944*, ed. Grant K. Goodman (Lawrence: Center for East Asian Studies, University of Kansas, 1979), xvi.

113. De Asis, *From Bataan to Tokyo*, 21.

114. De Asis, *From Bataan to Tokyo*, 22.

115. De Asis, *From Bataan to Tokyo*, 15.

116. De Asis, *From Bataan to Tokyo*, 20–21.

117. De Asis, *From Bataan to Tokyo*, 19.

118. De Asis, *From Bataan to Tokyo*, 23.

119. De Asis, *From Bataan to Tokyo*, 77.

120. Quoted in Shogo Suzuki, "Imagining 'Asia:' Japan and 'Asian' International Society in Modern History," in *Contesting International Society in East Asia*, ed. Barry Buzan and Yongjin Zhang (Cambridge: Cambridge University Press, 2014), 65.

121. "Speech by Prime Minister Speech by Prime Minister General Hideki Tojo to the Assembly of Greater East-Asiatic Nations, Tokyo, Japan, November 5, 1943," World Future Fund, accessed September 29, 2018, http://www.worldfuturefund.org/wffmaster/Reading/Japan/tojo%20summit.htm.

122. Emphasis mine. De Asis, *From Bataan to Tokyo*, 74–75.

123. De Asis, *From Bataan to Tokyo*, 89.

124. De Asis, *From Bataan to Tokyo*, 91.

125. De Asis, *From Bataan to Tokyo*, 112.

126. De Asis, *From Bataan to Tokyo*, 55.

127. De Asis, *From Bataan to Tokyo*, 145.

128. Tim Harper, "Chapter Two: A Long View on the Great Asian War," in *Legacies of World War II in South and East Asia*, ed. David Koh Wee Hock (ISEAS: Singapore, 2007), 10.

129. Harper, "Chapter Two," 10–11.

130. Anthony Reid, *Imperial Alchemy: Nationalism and Political Identity in Southeast Asia* (New York: Cambridge University Press, 2012), 99.

131. Reid, *Imperial Alchemy*, 99.

132. Reid, *Imperial Alchemy*, 99.

133. Reid, *Imperial Alchemy*, 100.

134. Reid, *Imperial Alchemy*, 100.

135. Reid, *Imperial Alchemy*, 100.

136. Ahmed Ibn Parfahn, *Malayan Grandeur: A Narrative of History by a Hundred Seers and Our Intellectual Revolution* (Davao City: San Pedro Press, 1967), 252.

137. Parfahn, *Malayan Grandeur*, 245.

138. Parfahn, *Malayan Grandeur*, unpaginated.
139. Frantz Fanon, *The Wretched of the Earth* (1961; New York: Grove Press, 2004), 30–31.
140. For a full defense of this argument, see CuUnjieng, "Cultures of Empire, Nation, and Universe in Pres. José P. Laurel's Political Thought."
141. Reid, *Imperial Alchemy*, 100. See also Gerald Sussman, "Macapagal, the Sabah Claim and Maphilindo: The Politics of Penetration," *Journal of Contemporary Asia* 13, no. 2 (January 1983): 210–28.
142. Quoted in Reid, *Imperial Alchemy*, 100.
143. Harsono, *Recollections of an Indonesian Diplomat in the Sukarno Era*, 251.
144. Angus McIntyre, "In Sukarno's Time: An Exploration of His View of History," in *Sukarno*, Annual Indonesia Lecture Series No. 24, ed. John Legge (Clayton, Victoria, Australia: Monash University Press, 2002), 27.
145. Reid, *Imperial Alchemy*, 102.
146. Reid, *Imperial Alchemy*, 111.
147. Caroline S. Hau, "Du Ai, Lin Bin, and Revolutionary Flows," in *Traveling Nation-Makers: Transnational Flows and Movements in the Making of Modern Southeast Asia*, ed. Caroline S. Hau and Kasian Tejapira (Singapore: NUS Press, 2011), 167.

Bibliography

Archives

Cuba

Archivo Nacional de la República de Cuba (Havana)
Centro de Estudios Martianos (Havana)
Fundación Antonio Núñez Jiménez (Havana)

Philippines

Ateneo de Manila University Archives (Quezon City)
American Historical Collection, Ateneo de Manila University (Quezon City)
José P. Laurel Memorial Foundation (Manila)
National Archives of the Philippines (Manila)
National Library of the Philippines (Manila)
T. H. Pardo de Tavera Archives, Ateneo de Manila University (Quezon City)
University of the Philippines Manuscripts and Archives (Quezon City)
University of the Philippines Special Collections (Quezon City)

Spain

Archivo General de Indias (Seville)
Archivo General Militar de Madrid (Madrid)

Archivo Histórico Nacional (Madrid)
Hemeroteca Municipal de Madrid (Madrid)

United Kingdom

The British Library (London)
Cambridge University Library, University Archives (Cambridge)
The National Archives at Kew (London)

United States

The National Archives at College Park (Maryland)
National Archives and Records Administration (Washington, DC)
Yale University Manuscripts and Archives (New Haven, CT)

Other Locations

Macau Historical Archives (Macau)
National University of Singapore Archives (Singapore)
The Public Records Office of Hong Kong (Hong Kong)

Publications

Achutegui, Pedro S. de, and Miguel A. Bernad. *Aguinaldo and the Revolution of 1896: A Documentary History*. Quezon City: Ateneo de Manila University Press, 1972.
Agoncillo, Teodoro A. *Malolos: The Crisis of the Republic*. Quezon City: University of the Philippines, 1997. Originally published 1960.
———. *The Revolt of the Masses: The Story of Bonifacio and the Katipunan*. Quezon City: University of the Philippines, 2002. Originally published 1956.
———. *The Writings and Trial of Andres Bonifacio*. Manila: Manila Bonifacio Centennial Commission, 1963.
Agpalo, Remigio E. *Liwanag at Dilim: The Political Philosophy of Emilio Jacinto*. Quezon City: University of the Philippines Press, 1976.
———. *Jose P. Laurel: National Leader and Political Philosopher*. Quezon City: Jose P. Laurel Memorial Corporation, 1992.
"Agreement between Dewey and Aguinaldo." *San Francisco Call* 8, no. 18, June 18, 1898. Accessed April 18, 2016. http://cdnc.ucr.edu/cgi-bin/cdnc?a=d&d=SFC18980618.2.3.
Aguilar, Filomeno V., Jr. *Clash of Spirits: The History of Power and Sugar Planter Hegemony on a Visayan Island*. Quezon City: University of the Philippines Press, 1998.

Alatas, Syed Hussein. *The Myth of the Lazy Native: A Study of the Image of the Malays, Filipinos and Javanese from the 16th to the 20th Century and Its Function in the Ideology of Colonial Capitalism.* London: Frank Cass, 1977.

Alejandrino, José. "The Emancipation of the Far East." *Boletín de la Sociedad Orientalista de Filipinas* 1, no. 9 (1918).

Alvarez, Santiago V. *The Katipunan and the Revolution: Memoirs of a General with the Original Tagalog Text.* Translated by Paula Carolina S. Malay. Manila: Ateneo de Manila University Press, 1992.

Amistoso, Mercedes. "General Artemio Ricarte 1896–1915." PhD diss., Ateneo de Manila University, 1974.

Andaya, Barbara Watson. "From Rūm to Tokyo: The Search for Anticolonial Allies by the Rulers of Riau, 1899–1914." *Indonesia* no. 24 (October 1977): 123–56.

Anderson, Benedict. "Cacique Democracy in the Philippines: Origins and Dreams." *New Left Review* 169 (May/June 1988): 3–31.

———. *Imagined Communities: Reflections on the Origin and Spread of Nationalism.* London: Verso Books, 1983.

———. *The Spectre of Comparisons: Nationalism, Southeast Asia and the World.* London: Verso Books, 1998.

———. *Under Three Flags: Anarchism and the Anti-Colonial Imagination.* London: Verso Books, 2005.

Ara, Satoshi. "Si General Artemio Ricarte at Ang Kasarinlan ng Pilipinas, 1915–1945." PhD diss., University of the Philippines, 1997.

Arendt, Hannah. *The Origins of Totalitarianism.* New York: Harcourt, 1973.

Asis, Leocadio de. *From Bataan to Tokyo: Diary of a Filipino Student in Wartime Japan 1943–1944.* Edited with an introduction by Grant K. Goodman. Lawrence: Center for East Asian Studies, University of Kansas, 1979.

Aung San. "The Resistance Movement. Address Delivered at the Meeting of the East and West Association Held on 29th August 1945, at the City Hall of Rangoon." In *The Political Legacy of Aung San, Revised Edition with an Introductory Essay,* edited by Josef Silverstein. Ithaca, NY: Cornell Southeast Asia Program, 1993.

Aydin, Cemil. *Politics of Anti-Westernism in Asia: Visions of World Order in Pan-Islamic and Pan-Asian Thought.* New York: Columbia University Press, 2007.

Bang, Vu Duc. "The Viet Nam Independent Education Movement (1900–1908)." PhD diss., University of California, Los Angeles, 1971.

Beasley, W. G. "Japan and Pan-Asianism: Problems of Definition." In *The Collected Writings of W.G. Beasley, The Collected Writings of Modern Western Scholars on Japan.* Vol. 5., 210–22. Tokyo: Edition Synapse, 2001.

Bernad, Miguel, S. J. *Rizal and Spain: An Essay in Biographical Context.* Manila: Navotas Press, 1986.

Bernard, Max. *Columnas Volantes de la Federación Malaya (Contribución a la Historia del Periodismo Filipino).* N.p., 1928.

Boehmer, Elleke. *Empire, the National, and the Postcolonial, 1890–1920: Resistance in Interaction.* Oxford: Oxford University Press, 2002.

Bonoan, Raul J., S. J. "José Rizal: Revolution of the Mind." In *The World of 1896,* edited by Lorna Kalaw-Tirol, 213–35. Manila: Ateneo de Manila University Press, 1998.

Bradley, Mark Philip. "Becoming 'Van Minh:' Civilizational Discourse and Visions of the Self in Twentieth-century Vietnam." *Journal of World History* 15, no. 1 (2004): 65–83.

Brocheux, Pierre. *The Mekong Delta: Ecology, Economy, and Revolution, 1860-1960.* Madison: University of Wisconsin-Madison Center for Southeast Asian Studies, 1995.

Brown, Roger H. "Sun Yat-sen: 'Pan-Asianism,' 1924." In Saaler and Szpilman, *Pan-Asianism: A Documentary History,* vol. 2, *1920-Present,* 75–85.

Bunchan Mul. "The Umbrella War of 1942." In *Peasants and Politics in Kampuchea, 1942-1981,* edited by Ben Kiernan and Chanthou Boua, 114–26. London: Zed, 1982.

Burke, Edmund. "Speech on Fox's India Bill 1 December 1783" (1783–1827). In *The Writings and Speeches of Edmund Burke.* Vol. 5, *India: Madras and Bengal: 1774-1785,* edited by P. J. Marshall and William B. Todd. Oxford Scholarly Editions, 2014. https://www.oxfordscholarlyeditions.com/view/instance.00040450?milestones=379.

———. "Speech on Opening of Impeachment 15, 16, 18, 19 February 1788" (1788–1827). In *The Writings and Speeches of Edmund Burke.* Vol. 6, *India: The Launching of the Hastings Impeachment: 1786-1788,* edited by P. J. Marshall and William B. Todd. Oxford Scholarly Editions, 2014. https://www.oxfordscholarlyeditions.com/view/instance.00040471?milestones=265.

Calderon, Felipe G. *Mis memorias sobre la Revolución Filipina: Segunda etapa (1898 a 1901).* Manila: Imprenta de "El Renacimiento," 1907.

Camagay, Ma. Luisa T. "Mariano Ponce: Emissary to Japan." *Asian and Pacific Migration Journal* 8, nos. 1–2 (1999): 101–15.

Causing, Juan. *Freemasonry in the Philippines.* Cebu City: G. T. Printers, 1969.

Chatterjee, Partha. *The Nation and Its Fragments: Colonial and Postcolonial Histories.* Princeton, NJ: Princeton University Press, 1993.

———. *Nationalist Thought and the Colonial World: A Derivative Discourse?* London: Zed Books for the United Nations University, 1986.Cho, Philip S., Nathan Bullock, and Dionna Ali. "The Bioinformatic Basis of Pan-Asianism." *East Asian Science, Technology and Society: An International Journal* 7, no. 2 (2013): 283–309.

Chu, Cindy Yik-yi, ed. *Foreign Communities in Hong Kong, 1840s-1950s.* New York: Palgrave Macmillan, 2005.

Coates, Austin. *Rizal: Filipino Nationalist and Martyr.* Manila: Solidaridad Publishing House, 1992.

Cooper, Frederick. *Citizenship Between Empire and Nation: Remaking France and French Africa, 1945-1960.* Princeton, NJ: Princeton University Press, 2014.

Corpuz, Onofre D. *Saga and Triumph: The Filipino Revolution Against Spain.* Manila: Philippine Centennial Commission, 1999.

Crawfurd, John. *Journal of an Embassy to the Courts of Siam and Cochin China.* Kuala Lumpur: Oxford University Press, 1967.

Cruikshank, Robert Bruce. "A History of Samar Island, The Philippines, 1768–1898." PhD diss., University of Wisconsin-Madison, 1975.

CuUnjieng, Nicole. "Cultures of Empire, Nation, and Universe in Pres. José P. Laurel's Political Thought, 1927–1949." *Philippine Studies: Historical and Ethnographic Viewpoints* 65, no. 1 (March 2017): 3–30.

Dahm, Bernhard. *Sukarno and the Struggle for Indonesian Independence.* Translated by Mary F. Somers Heidhues. Ithaca, NY: Cornell University Press, 1969.

Dery, Luis Camara. *The Army of the First Philippine Republic and Other Historical Essays.* Manila: De La Salle University Press, 1995.

Dizon, Lino L. "Ponce, the Folklorist." In National Historical Commission of the Philippines, *Naning*, 15–32.

Doak, Kevin M. "The Concept of Ethnic Nationality and its Role in Pan-Asianism in Imperial Japan." In Saaler and Koschmann, *Pan-Asianism in Modern Japanese History*, 168–82.

Duara, Prasenjit, ed. *Asia Redux: Conceptualizing a Region for Our Times.* Singapore: ISEAS-Yusof Ishak Institute, 2013.

———. "The Discourse of Civilization and Pan-Asianism." *Journal of World History* 12, no. 1 (2001): 99–130.

———. *Sovereignty and Authenticity: Manchukuo and the East Asian Modern.* Lanham, MD: Rowman & Littlefield, 2003.

Duiker, William J. "Phan Boi Chau: Asian Revolutionary in a Changing World." *Journal of Asian Studies* 31, no. 1 (1971): 77–88.

Duran, Pio. *Philippine Independence and the Far Eastern Question.* Manila: Community Publishers, 1935.

Duran, Pio, and F. B. Icasiano. *Wartime Japan as Viewed by Filipinos.* N.p.: Nippon Bunka Kaikan, 1944.

Elizalde, María Dolores, and Josep M. Delgado, eds. *Filipinas, un país entre dos imperios.* Barcelona: Ediciones Bellaterra, 2011.

Fanon, Frantz. *The Wretched of the Earth.* New York: Grove Press, 2004. Originally published 1961.

Ferguson, Niall. *Colossus: The Rise and Fall of the American Empire.* New York: Penguin Books, 2005.

"Filipinas-Cuestión Palpitante: Lo Urgentísimo." *El Imparcial*, October 2, 1896. Hemeroteca Digital, Biblioteca Nacional de España. Accessed April 18, 2016. http://hemerotecadigital.bne.es/issue.vm?id=0000768146&search=&lang=en.

Fleetwood, Ma. Luisa D. *General Artemio Ricarte (Víbora).* Manila: National Historical Institute, 1997.

Fletcher, William Miles, III. *The Search for a New Order: Intellectuals and Fascism in Prewar Japan.* Chapel Hill: University of North Carolina Press, 1982.

Foster, Anne L. *Projections of Power: The United States and Europe in Colonial Southeast Asia, 1919–1941.* Durham, NC: Duke University Press, 2010.

Francois, Joseph, Pradumma B. Rana, and Ganeshan Wignaraja, eds. *Pan-Asian Integration: Linking East and South Asia.* London: Palgrave Macmillan, 2009.

Frey, Marc, and Nicole Spakowski, eds. *Asianisms: Regionalist Interactions and Asian Integration.* Singapore: NUS Press, 2016.

Friend, Theodore. *The Blue-Eyed Enemy: Japan Against the West in Java and Luzon, 1942–1945.* Princeton, NJ: Princeton University Press, 1988.

Furuta, Motoo. "Vietnamese Political Movements in Thailand: Legacy of the Dong-Du Movement." In *Phan Boi Chau and the Dong-Du Movement*, edited by Vinh Sinh, 150–81. New Haven, CT: Yale Southeast Asia Studies, 1988.

Gates, Rustin B. "Pan-Asianism in Prewar Japanese Foreign Affairs: The Curious Case of Uchida Yasuya." *Journal of Japanese Studies* 37, no. 1 (Winter 2011): 1–27.

Gealogo, Francis A. "Mariano Ponce and Pan Asianism." In National Historical Commission of the Philippines, *Naning*, 33–50.

Gellner, Ernest. *Nations and Nationalism.* Ithaca, NY: Cornell University Press, 1983.

Go, Julian. *American Empire and the Politics of Meaning: Elite Political Cultures in the Philippines and Puerto Rico.* Durham, NC: Duke University Press, 2008.

Go, Julian, and Anne L. Foster, eds. *The American Colonial State in the Philippines: Global Perspectives.* Durham, NC: Duke University Press, 2003.

Goebel, Michael. *Anti-Imperial Metropolis: Interwar Paris and the Seeds of Third-World Nationalism.* New York: Cambridge University Press, 2015.

Goodman, Grant K. "Consistency Is the Hobgoblin: Manuel L. Quezon and Japan, 1899–1934." *Journal of Southeast Asian Studies* 14, no. 1 (March 1983): 79–94.

——. "Filipino Secret Agents, 1896–1910." *Philippine Studies* 46, no. 3 (1998): 376–87.

——. "General Artemio Ricarte and Japan." *Journal of Southeast Asian History* 2 (September 1966): 48–60.

——. "An Interview with Benigno Ramos: Translated from the Japanese." *Philippine Studies* 37, no. 2 (1989): 215–20.

——. "Japan and Philippine Commonwealth Politics." *Philippine Studies* 52, no. 2 (2004): 208–23.

——. "Japanese Pan-Asianism in the Philippines: The Hirippin Dai Ajia Kyōkai." *Studies on Asia* (1966): 133–43.

——. "The Philippine Society of Japan." *Monumenta Nipponica* 22, no. 1/2 (1967): 131–46.

——. "Pio Duran and Philippine Japanohilism." *The Historian* 32, no. 2 (February 1970): 228–42.

——. "The Problem of Philippine Independence and Japan: The First Three Decades of American Colonial Rule." *Southeast Asia* 1, no. 3 (Summer 1971): 165–92.

——. "A Sense of Kinship: Japan's Cultural Offensive in the Philippines during the 1930s." *Crossroads: An Interdisciplinary Journal of Southeast Asian Studies* 1, no. 2 (June 1983): 31–44.

Goscha, Christopher E. *Thailand and the Southeast Asian Networks of the Vietnamese Revolution, 1885–1954.* Richmond, VA: Curzon Press, 1999.

——. *Vietnam or Indochina?: Contesting Concepts of Space in Vietnamese Nationalism, 1887–1954.* Copenhagen: NIAS Press, 1995.

Gripaldo, Ronaldo M. *Liberty and Love: The Political and Ethical Philosophy of Emilio Jacinto.* Manila: De La Salle University Press, 2001.

Guillemot, Francois. "Vietnamese Nationalist Revolutionaries and the Japanese Occupation: The Case of the Dai Viet Parties (1936–1946)." In *Imperial Japan and National Identities in Asia, 1895–1945*, edited by Li Narangoa and Robert Cribb, 221–48. London: RoutledgeCurzon, 2003.

Guillermo, Ramon. *Translation and Revolution: A Study of Jose Rizal's Guillermo Tell.* Honolulu: University of Hawai'i Press, 2009.

Hall, D. G. E. *A History of Southeast Asia.* 4th ed. London: Macmillan, 1981.

Harper, Tim. "Chapter Two: A Long View on the Great Asian War." In *Legacies of World War II in South and East Asia*, edited by David Koh Wee Hock. Singapore: ISEAS, 2007.

Harrell, Paula. *Asia for the Asians: China in the Lives of Five Meiji Japanese.* Honolulu: University of Hawai'i Press, 2012.

Harsono, Ganis. *Recollections of an Indonesian Diplomat in the Sukarno Era*, edited by C. L. M. Penders and B. B. Hering. St. Lucia: University of Queensland Press, 1977.

Hatano, Suguru. "Firipin dokuritsu undō to Nihon no taiō" [The Philippine independence movement and Japanese responses]. *Ajia Kenkyu* [Asian studies] 34, no. 4 (1988): 69–95.

Hau, Caroline S. "Du Ai, Lin Bin, and Revolutionary Flows." In *Traveling Nation-Makers: Transnational Flows and Movements in the Making of Modern Southeast Asia*, edited by Caroline S. Hau and Kasian Tejapira, 153–87. Singapore: NUS Press, 2011.

Hau, Caroline S., and Kasian Tejapira, eds. *Traveling Nation-Makers: Transnational Flows and Movements in the Making of Modern Southeast Asia*. Singapore: NUS Press, 2011.

Hau, Caroline S., and Takashi Shiraishi. "Daydreaming About Rizal and Tetchō: On Asianism as Network and Fantasy." *Philippine Studies* 57, no. 3 (2009): 329–88.

Hill, Christopher L. *National History and the World of Nations: Capital, State, and the Rhetoric of History in Japan, France, and the United States*. Durham, NC: Duke University Press, 2008.

Hirschman, Charles. *Ethnic and Social Stratification in Peninsular Malaysia*. Washington, DC: American Sociological Association, 1975.

Hobson, John A. *Imperialism: A Study*. Nottingham, UK: Spokesman Books, 2011. Originally published 1902.

Hotta, Eri. *Pan-Asianism and Japan's War 1931–1945*. New York: Palgrave Macmillan, 2007.

——. "Rash Behari Bose and his Japanese Supporters." *Interventions* 8, no. 1 (2006): 116–132.

Huang Fuqing. *Chinese Students in Japan in the Late Ch'ing Period*. Tokyo: Centre for East Asian Cultural Studies, 1983.

Iida, Yumiko. "Fleeing the West, Making Asia Home: Transpositions of Otherness in Japanese Pan-Asianism, 1905–1930." *Alternatives: Global, Local, Political* 22, no. 3 (July–Sept. 1997): 409–32.

Ikehata, Setsuho. "Japan and the Philippines, 1885–1905: Mutual Images and Interests." In *Philippines-Japan Relations*, edited by Setsuho Ikehata and Lydia N. Yu Jose, 19–46. Quezon City: Ateneo de Manila University Press, 2003.

Ileto, Reynaldo Clemeña. *Filipinos and Their Revolution: Event, Discourse, and Historiography*. Quezon City: Ateneo de Manila University Press, 1998.

——. *Pasyon and Revolution*. Quezon City: Ateneo de Manila University Press, 1979.

Iriye, Akira. *After Imperialism: The Search for a New Order in the Far East, 1921–1931*. Harvard East Asian Series, 22. Cambridge, MA: Harvard University Press, 1965.

——. *Japan and the Wider World: From the Mid-Nineteenth Century to the Present*. New York: Longman, 1997.

——. "Japan's Drive to Great Power Status." In *The Cambridge History of Japan*. Vol. 5, edited by Peter Duus, 721–82. Cambridge: Cambridge University Press, 1989.

Jacinto, Emilio. "Kartilya ng Katipunan." Philippine Center for Masonic Studies, 2006. Originally published 1896. Accessed June 14, 2016. http://www.philippinemasonry .org/kartilya-ng-katipunan.html.

Jansen, Marius B. *China in the Tokugawa World*. Cambridge, MA: Harvard University Press, 1992.

——. *The Japanese and Sun Yat-sen*. Cambridge, MA: Harvard University Press, 1967.

Joos, Joël. "The Genyōsha (1881) and Premodern Roots of Japanese Expansionism." In Saaler and Szpilman, *Pan-Asianism: A Documentary History,* vol. 1, *1850–1920,* 61–68.

Jose, Ricardo T. "Exile as Protest: Artemio Ricarte." *Asian and Pacific Migration Journal* 8, no. 1–2 (1999): 131–56.

———. "The Russo-Japanese War and the Philippines." In *Pilipinas Muna! The Philippines is a Priority!,* edited and compiled by Maria V. Stanyukovich. St. Petersburg, Russia: Maclay Publications, Issue 4, 2011.

Kahn, Joel S. *Other Malays: Nationalism and Cosmopolitanism in the Modern Malay World.* Singapore: Singapore University Press, ASAA Southeast Asia Publication Series, 2006.

Kalaw, Teodoro M. *La Masonería Filipina: Su origen, desarollo y vicisitudes, hasta la época presente.* Manila: Bureau of Printing, 1920.

———. *The Philippine Revolution.* Manila: Manila Book, 1925.

Kant, Immanuel. *Toward Perpetual Peace and Other Writings on Politics, Peace, and History (Rethinking the Western Tradition).* Edited and with an introduction by Pauline Kleingeld. Translated by David L. Colclasure. New Haven, CT: Yale University Press, 2006.

Karl, Rebecca E. *Staging the World: Chinese Nationalism at the Turn of the Twentieth Century.* Durham, NC: Duke University Press, 2002.

Katipunan. *Minutes of the Katipunan.* Manila: National Heroes Commission, 1964.

Katzenstein, Peter J., and Takashi Shiraishi, eds. *Beyond Japan: The Dynamics of East Asian Regionalism.* Ithaca, NY: Cornell University Press, 2006.

———. *Network Power: Japan and Asia.* Ithaca, NY: Cornell University Press, 1997.

Khan, Noor-Aiman I. *Egyptian-Indian Nationalist Collaboration and the British Empire.* New York: Palgrave Macmillan, 2015.

Khánh, Huỳnh Kim. *Vietnamese Communism, 1925–1945.* Ithaca, NY: Cornell University Press, 1982.

Kiernan, Ben. "Asian Drama Unfolds." *Inside Asia* (September–October 1985): 17–19.

———. *How Pol Pot Came to Power: Colonialism, Nationalism, and Communism in Cambodia, 1930–1975.* New Haven, CT: Yale University Press, 2004.

Kim, John Namjun. "The Temporality of Empire: The Imperial Cosmopolitanism of Miki Kiyoshi and Tanabe Hajime." In Saaler and Koschmann, *Pan-Asianism in Modern Japanese History,* 151–67.

Koizumi, Junko. "The 'Last' Friendship Exchanges Between Siam and Vietnam, 1879–1882: Siam Between Vietnam and France—and Beyond." *TRaNS: Trans-Regional and -National Studies of Southeast Asia* 4, no. 1 (January 2016): 131–64.

Koyagi, Mikiya. "The Hajj by Japanese Muslims in the Interwar Period: Japan's Pan-Asianism and Economic Interests in the Islamic World." *Journal of World History* 24, no. 4 (December 2013): 849–76.

Kropotkin, Peter. *Mutual Aid: A Factor of Evolution* (1902). Anarchy Archives. https://www.marxists.org/reference/archive/kropotkin-peter/1902/mutual-aid/.

La Solidaridad. Vols. 1–7. Translated by Guadalupe Fores-Ganzon. Pasig City: Fundacion Santiago, 1996.

Laffan, Michael. "Tokyo as a Shared Mecca of Modernity: War Echoes in the Colonial Malay World." In *The Impact of the Russo-Japanese War,* edited by Rotem Kowner, 219–38. London: Routledge, 2007.

Lanuza, Caesar Z., and Gregorio F. Zaide. *Rizal in Japan.* Tokyo: Philippine Reparations Mission, 1961.

Laurel, José P. *Assertive Nationalism: A Collection of Articles and Addresses on Local Problems.* Manila: National Teachers College, 1931.

——. *Forces That Make a Nation Great.* Manila: Bureau of Printing, 1944. Originally published 1943.

——. *His Excellency Jose P. Laurel, President of the Second Philippine Republic: Speeches, Messages & Statements October 14, 1943, to December 19, 1944.* Manila: Lyceum of the Philippines, 1997.

——. *Inaugural Address of His Excellency José P. Laurel, President of the Republic of the Philippines.* Manila: n.p., 1943.

——. *Jose P. Laurel: On Polity, Economy & Education,* edited by Clemen C. Aquino. Manila: Lyceum of the Philippines, 1997.

——. *Moral and Political Orientation.* Manila: n.p., 1949.

——. *War Memoirs of Dr. Jose P. Laurel: Written in Yokohama Prison, Sept. 15–Nov. 16 1945 and Resumed in Sugamo Prison Outside Tokyo; Completed Dec. 25, 1945.* Manila: Jose P. Laurel Memorial Foundation, 1962.

Legarda, Benito J. *After the Galleons: Foreign Trade, Economic Change and Entrepreneurship in the Nineteenth-Century Philippines.* Madison: University of Wisconsin Center for Southeast Asian Studies, 1999.

Legge, J. D. *Sukarno: A Political Biography.* London: Allen Lane/Penguin, 1972.

Lenin, Vladimir I. *Imperialism, the Highest Stage of Capitalism* (1917). Accessed September 13, 2016. https://www.marxists.org/archive/lenin/works/1916/imp-hsc/.

Lichauco, Don Faustino. "Appendix XII: Questions and Answers Sent by Don Faustino Lichauco to Col. Fukushima, July 17, 1898." Translated by Jose Ramos. In *Japan and the Philippines, 1868–1898,* by Josefa M. Saniel, 373–376. Quezon City: University of the Philippines Press, 1969.

Lieberman, Victor. *Strange Parallels: Southeast Asia in Global Context c. 800–1830.* Vol. 1, *Integration in the Mainland.* Cambridge: Cambridge University Press, 2003.

——. *Strange Parallels: Southeast Asia in Global Context c. 800–1830.* Vol. 2, *Mainland Mirrors.* Cambridge: Cambridge University Press, 2009.

Liu, Lydia He. *Translingual Practice: Literature, National Culture, and Translated Modernity—China, 1900–1937.* Stanford, CA: Stanford University Press, 1995.

Lombard, Denys. "Le voyage de Parada Harahap au 'Pays du Soleil levant' (1933–34)." In *Recits de voyage des Asiatiques: Genres mentalités conception de l'espace,* edited by Claudine Salmon, 281–96. Paris: Ecole Francaise D'extreme-Orient, 2005.

Lone, Stewart, ed. *Daily Lives of Civilians in Wartime Asia: From the Taiping Rebellion to the Vietnam War.* Westport, CT: Greenwood Press, 2007.

Lopez, Mellie Leandicho. *A Handbook of Philippine Folklore.* Quezon City: University of the Philippines Press, 2006.

Los Reyes, Isabelo de. *Artículos varios sobre etnografía, historia y costumbres de Filipinas.* Segunda edición. Manila: J.A. Ramos, 1888. Available at https://archive.org/details/artculosvarioss00siergoog/page/n12.

——. *El Folk-lore Filipino: Colección Comentada y Publicada bajo la dirección de D. Isabelo de los Reyes.* Vol. 2. Manila: Imprenta de Santa Cruz, 1890. Originally written 1889. Available at https://archive.org/details/elfolklorefilip00florgoog.

——. *Historia de Ilocos.* Vol. 1. Manila: Establecimiento tipográfico La Opinión, 1890.

——. *Las islas Visayas en la época de la conquista*. Manila: Tipo-litografía de Chofre y Cia, 1889. Available at https://archive.org/details/lasislasvisayase00reye/page/n6.

Los Santos, Epifanio de. *The Revolutionists: Aguinaldo, Bonifacio, Jacinto*. Translated and edited by Teodoro A. Agoncillo. Manila: National Historical Commission, 1973.

Luna, Maria Pilar S. "General Artemio Ricarte y Garcia: A Filipino Nationalist." *Asian Studies* 9 (August 1971): 229–41.

Maaruf, Shaharuddin bin. *Concept of a Hero in Malay Society*. Singapore: Eastern Universities Press, 1984.

Mabini, Apolinario. *The Letters of Apolinario Mabini*. Manila: National Heroes Commission, 1965.

——. *The Philippine Revolution: With Other Documents of the Epoch*. Manila: National Historical Institute, 2007. First published 1901.

Maitrii Aung-Thwin. "Structuring Revolt: Communities of Interpretation in the Historiography of the Saya San Rebellion." *Journal of Southeast Asian Studies* 39, no. 2 (June 2008): 297–317.

Majul, Cesar Adib. *Apolinario Mabini: Revolutionary*. Manila: National Historical Institute, 1993.

——. *The Political and Constitutional Ideas of the Philippine Revolution*. Quezon City: University of the Philippines Press, 1996.

——. "Principales, Ilustrados, Intellectuals and the Original Concept of a Filipino National Community," *Asian Studies* 15 (1977): 1–20.

——. *Rizal's Concept of a Filipino Nation*. Quezon City: University of the Philippines Press, 1959.

Manela, Erez. *The Wilsonian Moment: Self-Determination and the International Origins of Anticolonial Nationalism*. Oxford: Oxford University Press, 2007.

Marco, Sophia. "Dios-Dios in the Visayas." *Philippine Studies* 49, no. 1 (2001): 42–77.

Marr, David G. *Vietnamese Anticolonialism, 1885–1925*. Berkeley: University of California Press, 1971.

Martin, Marie Alexandrine. *Cambodia: A Shattered Society*. Translated by Mark W. McLeod. Berkeley: University of California Press, 1989.

Matsuda, Koichiro. "The Concept of 'Asia' Before Pan-Asianism." In Saaler and Szpilman, Pan-Asianism, A Documentary History. Vol. 1, 1850–1920, 45–52.

Matthiessen, Sven. *Japanese Pan-Asianism and the Philippines from the Late Nineteenth Century to the End of World War II: Going to the Philippines Is Like Coming Home?* Leiden: Brill, 2016.

Matibag, Eugenio. "The Spirit of Nínay: Pedro Paterno and the First Philippine Novel." *Humanities Diliman* 7, no. 2 (2010): 34–59.

May, Glenn A. *Inventing a Hero: The Posthumous Re-Creation of Andres Bonifacio*. Madison: University of Wisconsin Press, 1996.

McCoy, Alfred W., and Ed. C. de Jesus, eds. *Philippine Social History: Global Trade and Local Transformations*. Quezon City: Ateneo de Manila University Press, 1982.

McCoy, Alfred W., Josep M. Fradera, and Stephen Jacobson, eds. *Endless Empire: Spain's Retreat, Europe's Eclipse, America's Decline*. Madison: University of Wisconsin Press, 2012.

McHale, Shawn Frederick. *Print and Power: Confucianism, Communism and Buddhism in the Making of Modern Vietnam.* Honolulu: University of Hawai'i Press, 2004.

McIntyre, Angus. "In Sukarno's Time: An Exploration of His View of History." In *Sukarno,* Annual Indonesia Lecture Series No. 24, edited by John Legge. Clayton, Victoria, Australia: Monash University Press, 2002.

Mehta, Uday Singh. *Liberalism and Empire.* Chicago: University of Chicago Press, 1999.

Miller, D. B., ed. *Peasants and Politics: Grass Roots Reactions to Change in Asia.* New York: St. Martin's Press, 1979.

Milner, Anthony. *The Invention of Politics in Colonial Malaya: Contesting Nationalism and the Expansion of the Public Sphere.* New York: Cambridge University Press, 1995.

Miyazaki, Tōten. *My Thirty-Three Year's Dream: The Autobiography of Miyazaki Tōten,* edited and translated by Marius B. Jansen and Eto Shinkichi. Princeton, NJ: Princeton University Press, 2014. Originally published 1902.

Mojares, Resil B. *Brains of the Nation: Pedro Paterno, T.H. Pardo de Tavera, Isabelo de los Reyes, and the Production of Modern Knowledge.* Quezon City: Ateneo de Manila University Press, 2006.

——. "Early 'Asianism' in the Philippines." *IDEYA: Journal of the Humanities* 11, no. 1 (2009): 1–8.

——. "The Emergence of Asian Intellectuals." *Asian Studies: Journal of Critical Perspectives on Asia* 49, no. 2 (2013): 1–13.

——. *Isabelo's Archive.* Mandaluyong City: Anvil Publishing, 2013.

——. "Los itineraries de Mariano Ponce y el imaginario político filipino." In *Filipinas, un país entre dos imperios,* edited by María Dolores Elizalde and Josep M. Delgado, 79–121. Barcelona: Ediciones Bellaterra, 2011.

——. "Rizal Reading Pigafetta." In *Waiting for Mariang Makiling: Essays in Philippine Cultural History,* 52–86. Quezon City: Ateneo de Manila University Press, 2002.

Morga, Antonio de. *Sucesos de las Islas Filipinas: Obra publicada en Mejico el año de 1609. Nuevamente sacada a luz y anotada por José Rizal y precedida de un prólogo del Fernando Blumentritt.* Paris: Librería de Garnier Hermanos, 1890.

Moyn, Samuel. "Fantasies of Federalism." *Dissent* (Winter 2015). https://www.dissentmagazine.org/article/fantasies-of-federalism.

Muthu, Sankar. *Enlightenment Against Empire.* Princeton, NJ: Princeton University Press, 2003.

Narangoa, Li. "Universal Values and Pan-Asianism: The Vision of Ōmotokyō." In Saaler and Koschmann, *Pan-Asianism in Modern Japanese History,* 52–66.

Narangoa, Li, and Robert Cribb, eds. *Imperial Japan and National Identities in Asia, 1895–1945.* London: RoutledgeCurzon, 2003.

National Historical Commission of the Philippines, ed. *Naning: Mariano Ponce 150th Birth Anniversary Commemorative Lectures & Selected Articles in La Solidaridad.* Manila: National Historical Commission of the Philippines, 2013.

Nery, John. *Revolutionary Spirit: Jose Rizal in Southeast Asia.* Quezon City: Ateneo de Manila University Press, 2011.

Ng, Benjamin Wai-ming. "Making of a Japanese Community in Prewar Period (1841–1941)." In *Foreign Communities in Hong Kong, 1840s–1950s,* edited by Cindy Yik-yi Chu, 111–32, New York: Palgrave Macmillan, 2005.

Nguyen, Van Khanh and Nguyen Van Suu. "Eastern-Country-Study-Tour (Dong Du) Movement in the Revolutionary Process of Vietnam National Liberation and in Cultural, Educational Relations Between Vietnam and Japan." *Vietnam National University, Journal of Science, Social Sciences & Humanities*, no. 4E (2005): 17–25.

Norie, Captain E. W. M. 1896. *Note on the Philippine Islands*. Simla: Government Central Printing Office.

Ocampo, Ambeth R. *Mabini's Ghost*. Pasig City: Anvil, 1995.

——. *Rizal Without the Overcoat*. Manila: Anvil Publishing, 1990.

——. "Rizal's Morga and Views of Philippine History." *Philippine Studies: Historical and Ethnographical Viewpoints* 46, no. 2 (1998): 184–214.

——. *Mabini's Ghost*. Pasig City: Anvil, 1995.

Okakura, Kakuzo. *The Book of Tea*. London: Penguin Classics, 2016. Originally published 1906.

Parfahn, Ahmed Ibn. *Malayan Grandeur: A Narrative of History by a Hundred Seers and Our Intellectual Revolution*. Davao City: San Pedro Press, 1967.

Paterno, Pedro A. *La Antigua Civilización Tagalog*. Manila: Colegio de Sto. Tomás, 1915. Originally published 1887.

Paterson, Lorraine Marion. "Tenacious Texts: Vietnam, China, and Radical Cultural Intersections, 1890–1930." PhD diss., Yale University, 2006.

Perry, Elizabeth J. "Moving the Masses: Emotion Work in the Chinese Revolution" *Mobilization: An International Journal* 7, no. 2 (2002): 111–28.

Phan Boi Chau. "The History of the Loss of the Country" (1905). In *Sources of Vietnamese Tradition*, edited by George E. Dutton, Jayne S. Werner, and John K. Whitmore. New York: Columbia University Press, 2012.

——. "A Letter from Abroad Written in Blood" (1907). In *Sources of Vietnamese Tradition*, edited by George E. Dutton, Jayne S. Werner, and John K. Whitmore. New York: Columbia University Press, 2012.

——. *Overturned Chariot: The Autobiography of Phan-Boi-Chau*. Translated by Vinh Sinh and Nicholas Wickenden. Honolulu: University of Hawai'i Press, 1999.

——. *Phan Bội Châu niên biểu : tức Tự phê phán*. Ithaca, NY: Cornell University Photo Science, 1973. Originally published 1929.

Phan Chau Trinh. *Phan Châu Trinh and His Political Writings*. Translated and edited by Vinh Sinh. Ithaca, NY: Cornell Southeast Asia Program Publications, 2009.

Phelan, John Leddy. *The Hispanization of the Philippines: Spanish Aims and Filipino Responses, 1565–1700*. Madison: University of Wisconsin Press, 1967.

Pilar, Marcelo H. del. *La Soberanía Monacal en Filipinas: Apuntes Sobre la Funesta Preponderancia del Fraile en Las Islas, así en lo Político como en lo Económico y Religioso*. N.p., 1888.

Ponce, Mariano. *Cartas sobre la revolución 1897-1900*. Manila: Bureau of Printing, 1932. In Multimedia Collection, MMC R383a I3951a, National Library of the Philippines.

——. *Cuestión Filipina: Una exposición histórico-crítica de hechos relativos a la guerra de la independencia*. N.p., n.d.

——. "El folk-lore Bulaqueño." In *El Folk-lore Filipino: Colección Comentada y Publicada bajo la dirección de D. Isabelo de los Reyes*, 41–80. Manila: Imprenta de Santa Cruz, 1890. Available at https://archive.org/details/elfolklorefilip00florgoog.

——. *Sun Yat-sen: The Founder of the Republic of China*. Manila: Filipino-Chinese Cultural Foundation, 1965. Originally published 1912.

Rafael, Vicente L. *Contracting Colonialism: Translation and Christian Conversion in Taga-log Society Under Early Spanish Rule*. Durham, NC: Duke University Press, 1993.

Reid, Anthony. *Imperial Alchemy: Nationalism and Political Identity in Southeast Asia*. New York: Cambridge University Press, 2012.

Reyes, Raquel A. G. *Love, Passion and Patriotism: Sexuality and the Philippine Propaganda Movement, 1882-1892*. Singapore: NUS Press, 2008.

Ricarte, Artemio. *Himagsikan nang manga Pilipino laban sa Kastila*. Yokohama: n.p., 1927.

———. *Memoirs of General Artemio Ricarte with a Preface by Alejandro R. Roces and an Intro-duction by Armando J. Malay; Selected and Edited from Manuscripts in the Watson Col-lection*. Manila: National Heroes Commission, 1963.

———. *Nippon at Busido*. N.p., 1943.

Richardson, Jim. *The Light of Liberty: Documents and Studies on the Katipunan, 1892-1897*. Quezon City: Ateneo de Manila University Press, 2013.

Rizal, José. *Rizal's Correspondence with Fellow Reformists*. Manila: National Historical Institute, 1992.

———. "Sobre la indolencia de los Filipinos." Originally published serially in *La Soli-daridad* July 15, 31, August 15, 31, September 15, 1890. Cervantes Virtual. http://www.cervantesvirtual.com/obra-visor/sobre-la-indolencia-de-los-filipinos/html/4870d544-19c1-4319-a240-e4269802e6b3_11.html.

———. *Sucesos de las Islas Filipina por el Doctor Antonio de Morga: Obra publicada en Méjico el año de 1609. Nuevamente sacada a luz y anotada por José Rizal y precedida de un prólogo del Fernando Blumentritt*. Manila: Comisión Nacional del Centenario de José Rizal, 1961. Originally published 1890.

Rodell, Paul A. "Southeast Asian Nationalism and the Russo-Japanese War: Reexam-ining Assumptions." *Southeast Review of Asian Studies* 29 (2007): 20–40.

Saaler, Sven. "The Kokuryūkai, 1901–1920." In Saaler and Szpilman, *Pan-Asianism: A Documentary History,* vol. 1, *1850–1920,* 121–32.

———. "The Kokuryūkai (Black Dragon Society) and the Rise of Nationalism, Pan-Asianism, and Militarism in Japan, 1901–1925." *International Journal of Asian Stud-ies* 11, no. 2 (2014): 125–60.

Saaler, Sven, and J. Victor Koschmann, eds. *Pan-Asianism in Modern Japanese History: Colonialism, Regionalism and Borders*. London: Routledge, 2007.

Saaler, Sven, and Christopher W. A. Szpilman, eds. *Pan-Asianism: A Documentary His-tory*. Vol. 1, *1850–1920*. Lanham, MD: Rowman & Littlefield, 2011.

———. *Pan-Asianism: A Documentary History*. Vol. 2, *1920–Present*. Lanham, MD: Rowman & Littlefield, 2011.

Said, Edward W. *Culture and Imperialism*. New York: Vintage Books, 1993.

Salmon, Claudine, ed. *Recits de voyage des Asiatiques: Genres mentalités conception de l'espace*. Paris: Ecole Francaise D'extreme-Orient, 2005.

Saniel, Josefa M. *Japan and the Philippines, 1868-1898*. Quezon City: University of the Philippines Press, 1969.

Sareen, T. R. "India and the War." In *The Impact of the Russo-Japanese War*, edited by Rotem Kowner, 239–50. London: Routledge, 2007.

Schiffrin, Harold Z. "The Impact of the War on China." In *The Impact of the Russo-Japanese War*, edited by Rotem Kowner, 169–82. London: Routledge, 2007.

Schumacher, John N., S. J. *The Propaganda Movement, 1880–1895: The Creation of a Filipino Consciousness, the Making of the Revolution.* Quezon City: Ateneo University Press, 1997.

——. "The Propagandists' Reconstruction of the Philippine Past." In *Perceptions of the Past in Southeast Asia*, edited by Anthony Reid and David Marr, 264–80. Singapore: Heinemann Educational Books, 1979.

——. "Recent Perspectives on the Revolution." *Philippine Studies* 30, no. 4 (1982): 445–92.

——. *Revolutionary Clergy: The Filipino Clergy and the Nationalist Movement, 1850–1903.* Quezon City: Ateneo University Press, 1998.

Serizawa, Takamichi. "A Genealogy of Japanese Solidarity Discourse on Philippine History: War with America and Area Studies in the Cold War." PhD diss., National University of Singapore, 2013.

——. "Japanese Solidarity Discourse on the Philippines During the Second World War." *Philippine Studies: Historical and Ethnographic Viewpoints* 63, no. 1 (March 2015): 71–100.

Shamsul, A. B. *From British to Bumiputera Rule: Local Politics and Rural Development in Peninsular Malaya.* Singapore: Institute of Southeast Asian Studies, 1986.

Shimazu, Naoko. *Japan, Race and Equality: The Racial Equality Proposal of 1919.* London: Routledge, 1998.

Shimizu, Hiromu. "Imagining the Filipino Revolution 100 Years Ago." In *Junctions Between Filipinos and Japanese: Transborder Insights and Reminiscences*, edited by Arnold Azurin and Sylvano Mahiwo, 49–67. Quezon City: Kultura't Wika, 2007.

Shiraishi, Masaya. "Japan and the Reconstruction of Indochina." In *New Dynamics Between China and Japan in Asia: How to Build the Future from the Past?*, edited by Guy Faure, 125–61. Singapore: World Scientific, 2010.

——. "Japan Toward the Indochina Sub-Region." *Journal of Asia-Pacific Studies* (Waseda University) 13 (October 2009): 13–36.

——. "The Nan'you Gakuin: A Japanese Institute in Saigon from 1942–1945." Working Paper, Vol. 13, Contemporary Asian Studies, Waseda University, 2005.

——. "Phan Boi Chau in Japan." In *Phan Boi Chau and the Dong-Du Movement*, edited by Vinh Sinh, 52–100. New Haven, CT: Yale Southeast Asia Studies, 1988.

——. *Vietnamese Nationalism and its Relations with Japan and Asia: Phan Boi Chau's Ideas of Revolution and the World.* Tokyo: Gannando Shoten, 1993.

——. *Vietnamese Phuc Quoc League and the 1940 Insurrection.* Tokyo: Center of Excellence, Contemporary Asian Studies, Waseda University, 2004.

Silverstein, Josef. "Introduction." In *The Political Legacy of Aung San, Revised Edition with an Introductory Essay*, edited by Josef Silverstein. Ithaca, NY: Cornell Southeast Asia Program, 1993.

Sinh, Vinh, ed. *Phan Boi Chau and the Dong-Du Movement.* New Haven, CT: Yale Southeast Asia Studies, 1998.

"Speech by Prime Minister Speech by Prime Minister General Hideki Tojo to the Assembly of Greater East-Asiatic Nations, Tokyo, Japan, November 5, 1943." World Future Fund. Accessed September 29, 2018. http://www.worldfuturefund.org/wffmaster/Reading/Japan/tojo%20summit.htm.

Szpilman, Christopher W. A. "Miyazaki Tōten's Pan-Asianism, 1915–1919." In Saaler and Szpilman, *Pan-Asianism: A Documentary History*, vol. 1, *1850–1920*, 133–39.

Steinberg, David Joel. *Philippine Collaboration in World War II*. Manila: Solidaridad Publishing, 1967.

——. *The Philippines: A Singular and a Plural Place*. 4th Ed. Boulder, CO: Westview Press, 2000. First published 1982.

Stephanson, Anders. *Manifest Destiny: American Expansion and the Empire of Right*. New York: Hill and Wang, 1995.

Sturtevant, David R. *Popular Uprisings in the Philippines, 1840-1940*. Ithaca, NY: Cornell University Press, 1976.

Sukarno. *An Autobiography*. Translated by Cindy Adams. Indianapolis, IN: Bobbs-Merrill, 1965.

Sussman, Gerald. "Macapagal, the Sabah Claim and Maphilindo: The Politics of Penetration." *Journal of Contemporary Asia* 13, no. 2 (January 1983): 210–28.

Suzuki, Shogo. "Imagining 'Asia:' Japan and 'Asian' International Society in Modern History." In *Contesting International Society in East Asia*, edited by Barry Buzan and Yongjin Zhang. Cambridge: Cambridge University Press, 2014.

Tagore, Rabindranath, and Noguchi Yonejirō. *Poet to Poet: Full Text of Correspondence Between Yone Noguchi and Rabindranath Tagore on the Sino-Japanese Conflict*. Reprinted from *Visva Bharati Quarterly* 4, no. 3. Nanking and Santiniketan: The Sino-Indian Cultural Society, 1940.

Tan Malaka. *From Jail to Jail*. Vol. 1. Translated by Helen Jarvis. Athens: Ohio University Press, 1991.

Tankha, Brij, ed. *Okakura Tenshin and Pan-Asianism: Shadows of the Past*. Kent, UK: Global Oriental, 2009.

Terami-Wada, Motoe. "Benigno Ramos and the Sakdal Movement." *Philippine Studies* 36, no. 4 (1988): 427–42.

——. *The Japanese in the Philippines 1880s-1990s*. Manila: National Historical Commission of the Philippines, 2015.

——. "Japanese Propaganda Corps in the Philippines." *Philippine Studies* 38 (1990): 279–300.

——. "The Sakdal Movement, 1930-34," *Philippine Studies* 36, no. 2 (1988): 131–50.

——. *Sakdalistas' Struggle for Philippine Independence, 1930-1945*. Manila: Ateneo de Manila University Press, 2014.

Thomas, Megan C. "Isabelo de los Reyes and the Philippine Contemporaries of La Solidaridad." *Philippine Studies* 54, no. 3 (2006): 381–411.

——. *Orientalists, Propagandists, and Ilustrados: Filipino Scholarship and the End of Spanish Colonialism*. Minneapolis: University of Minnesota Press, 2012.

Tikhonov, Vladimir. "Korea's First Encounters with Pan-Asianism Ideology in the Early 1880s." *Review of Korean Studies* 5, no. 2 (2002): 195–232.

Tomiyama, Ichirō. "Colonialism and the Sciences of the Tropical Zone: The Academic Analysis of Difference in 'the Island Peoples.'" In *Formations of Colonial Modernity in East Asia*, edited by Tani E. Barlow, 199–221. Durham, NC: Duke University Press, 1997.

Tonkin Free School. "A Civilization of New Learning" (1904). In *Sources of Vietnamese Tradition*, edited by George E. Dutton, Jayne S. Werner, and John K. Whitmore, 369–74. New York: Columbia University Press, 2012.

Tovy, Tal, and and Sharon Halevi. "The Emergence of a New Rivalry: The War and the United States." In *The Impact of the Russo-Japanese War*, edited by Rotem Kowner, 137–52. London: Routledge, 2007.

Tran, My-Van. "Japan Through Vietnamese Eyes (1905–1945)." *Journal of Southeast Asian Studies* 30, no. 1 (1999): 126–46.

——. *A Vietnamese Royal Exile in Japan: Prince Cuong De (1882–1951)*. London: Routledge, 2005.

Tsui, Brian. "The Plea for Asia—Tan Yunshan, Pan-Asianism and Sino-Indian Relations." *China Report* 46, no. 4 (2010): 353–70.

Van der Veur, Paul W. *The Lion and the Gadfly: Dutch Colonialism and the Spirit of E. F. E. Douwes Dekker*. Leiden: KiTLV Press, 2006.

Veloso, Alfredo S., trans. *Discursos y Debates de Malolos*. Quezon City: Asvel, 1960.

Viana, Augusto V. de. "The Development of the Philippine Foreign Service During the Revolutionary Period and the Filipino-American War (1896–1906): A Story of Struggle from the Formation of Diplomatic Contacts to the Philippine Republic." *Antoninus Journal* 2 (February 2016): 19–52.

Villanueva, Alejo. *Bonifacio's Unfinished Revolution*. Quezon City: New Day Publishers, 1989.

Von Feigenblatt, Otto F. "Pan-Asianism, Socio-Cultural Integration, and Regionalism in Greater East Asia: Comparing Emic and Etic Interpretations of Elite Discourse Through the Application of Structural Dynamics and Grounded Theory." PhD diss., Nova Southeastern University, 2013.

Warren, James F. 1981. *The Sulu Zone, 1768–1898*. Singapore: Singapore University Press.

Woodside, Alexander B. *Community and Revolution in Modern Vietnam*. Boston: Houghton Mifflin Company, 1976.

Yamamuro, Shin'ichi. *Kimera: Manshūkoku no shōzo* [Kimera: A portrait of Manzhou-guo]. Tokyo: Chūokōronsha, 1993.

——. *Shiso kadai to shite no Ajia: Kijiku, rensa, toki* [Asia as a question of thought: Axes, series, and projects]. Tokyo: Iwanami Shoten, 2001.

Yamashita, Michiko. "Nanshin no manazashi" [Views on southward advance]. *Sōgō Bunka Kenkyū* [Transcultural studies] 3 (1999): 77–99.

Yanagida, Izumi. "Nihon bungaku ni okeru Jose Rizal" [Jose Rizal in Japanese literature]. In *Jose Rizal to Nihon* [Jose Rizal and Japan], edited by Kimura Ki, 50–72. Tokyo: Appolon-sha, 1961.

Young, Louise. *Japan's Total Empire: Manchuria and the Culture of Wartime Imperialism*. Berkeley: University of California Press, 1998.

Yu-Jose, Lydia N. *Japan Views the Philippines, 1900–1944*. Quezon City: Ateneo de Manila University Press, 1992.

Zialcita, Jean Paul. "Mariano Ponce and the Philippine-American War: A View of the Man and His Deeds Through His Letters from Japan." *Social Science Diliman* 7, no. 2 (December 2011): 30–48.

Zhang, Kaiyuan. "Ideals and Reality: Sun Yat-sen's Dream for Asia." *Journal of Cultural Interaction in East Asia* 3 (2012): 57–67.

Index

Solidaridad, La (association), 34
Solidaridad, La (newspaper): Apacible
    and, 212n42; on British colonies,
    184n14; on British Malaya, 74; on
    Japan, 42–43, 61–62, 64, 112–13; Liga
    Filipina and, 76–77; on Malay
    language, 143; on Malay race, 64;
    Malay race and, 55–61; Pan-
    Asianism and, 45–48; on place,
    36–37; place and, 49; Ponce and,
    112–13; Propaganda Movement and,
    34–35; Reyes and, 50; Rizal and, 59,
    75; Spanish government and, 61–62
Son Ngoc Thanh, 155
Southeast Asia: as biotic zone, 5; as
    coherent region and episteme, 4–5;
    Japanese occupation of, 155–56,
    171–77. See also Pan-Asianism
Spain: Japan and, 65–66, 67–68;
    Philippine Revolution and, 1–2, 89–94,
    97, 104; Philippines as colony of, 38
Spanish Constitution (1876), 32
Spanish language, 32, 38, 85, 87–88
Spanish liberalism, 32, 33
Spanish West Indies, 104
Spencer, Herbert, 98
Spetz, Lieutenant, 89
Staging the World (Karl), 14, 149,
    150–51
Stoddard, Lothrop, 141–42
Straits Times (newspaper), 93
Strange Parallels (Lieberman), 60–61
Sturtevant, David, 8
Sucesos de las Islas Filipinas por el Doctor
    Antonio de Morga (Rizal), 40–41,
    51–52, 54, 143
Suehiro Tetchō, 66, 71
Suenaga Setsu, 137–38
Suez Canal, 32, 183n6
Sugimura, K., 130, 134
Sukarno, 153, 157–58, 180
Sulu Sultanate, 38, 90
Sun, The (newspaper), 131
Sun Yat-sen: Japanese Pan-Asianism
    and, 67, 72–73, 115; Ponce and, 114,
    120–26, 130, 133, 134–35, 142–43

Sun Yat-sen (Ponce), 135–36, 142–43,
    145
Surasakmontri, Thai Chao Phraya, 137

Taft, William Howard, 140
Tagalogs: Katipunan and, 82–88;
    language and orthography, 41,
    44–46, 79–80, 85–87, 109; Propaganda
    Movement and, 60; Rizal and, 42, 52;
    use of term, 87
Tagawa, José Moritaro, 103
Taiwan (Formosa), 2, 66, 130–31
Tang Tiaoding, 127
Tarui Tôkichi, 68, 69
Tawalisi (Ibn Battuta), 52
Tax Protest Movement (1907), 78
Tejapira, Kasian, 9
Terami-Wada, Motoe, 9–10
Thailand, 155, 207n128
Thanh Niên (weekly paper), 78
Third Anglo-Burmese War (1885), 2
Third Worldism, 149, 162–63, 177–78,
    180–81
Thomas, Megan, 9, 149–50
Tijdschrift, Het (journal), 152
Tingues, 40
Tōa Dōbun Shoin, 16
Tōa Dōbun-kai (Society for Asian
    Solidarity), 16, 100
Tōa Dōmei Kai (Society for East Asian
    Alliance), 127
Toho Kyōkai (Oriental Cooperation
    Society), 114
Tōkai Sanshi, 99
Tokizawa, Captain, 105–6, 119, 131
Tokugawa Iemitsu, 64
Tokyo, 28
Tokyo shimpō (newspaper), 105
Tomiyama Ichiro, 141
Tóngménghuì, 116
Torre, Carlos María de la, 32, 33
Tovy, Tal, 21
Toyo Jiyu-to (East Asian Liberal
    Party), 68
Trần Huy Liệu, 11–12
Tran My-Van, 128, 129

COLUMBIA STUDIES IN INTERNATIONAL AND GLOBAL HISTORY
Cemil Aydin, Timothy Nunan, and Dominic Sachsenmaier, Series Editors

Cemil Aydin, *The Politics of Anti-Westernism in Asia: Visions of World Order
in Pan-Islamic and Pan-Asian Thought*

Adam M. McKeown, *Melancholy Order: Asian Migration and the Globalization of Borders*

Patrick Manning, *The African Diaspora: A History Through Culture*

James Rodger Fleming, *Fixing the Sky: The Checkered History
of Weather and Climate Control*

Steven Bryan, *The Gold Standard at the Turn of the Twentieth Century:
Rising Powers, Global Money, and the Age of Empire*

Heonik Kwon, *The Other Cold War*

Samuel Moyn and Andrew Sartori, eds., *Global Intellectual History*

Alison Bashford, *Global Population: History, Geopolitics, and Life on Earth*

Adam Clulow, *The Company and the Shogun: The Dutch Encounter with Tokugawa Japan*

Richard W. Bulliet, *The Wheel: Inventions and Reinventions*

Simone M. Müller, *Wiring the World: The Social and Cultural Creation
of Global Telegraph Networks*

Will Hanley, *Identifying with Nationality: Europeans, Ottomans,
and Egyptians in Alexandria*

Perin E. Gürel, *The Limits of Westernization: A Cultural History of America in Turkey*

Dominic Sachsenmaier, *Global Entanglements of a Man Who Never Traveled:
A Seventeenth-Century Chinese Christian and His Conflicted Worlds*

Perrin Selcer, *The UN and the Postwar Origins of the Global Environment:
From World Community to Spaceship Earth*

Ulbe Bosma, *The Making of a Periphery: How Island Southeast Asia
Became a Mass Exporter of Labor*

Raja Adal, *Beauty in the Age of Empire: Japan, Egypt,
and the Global History of Aesthetic Education*

Mona L. Siegel, *Peace on Our Terms: The Global Battle for Women's Rights
After the First World War*